Frontiers in Quantitative Finance

Founded in 1807, John Wiley & Sons is the oldest independent publishing company in the United States. With offices in North America, Europe, Australia and Asia, Wiley is globally committed to developing and marketing print and electronic products and services for our customers' professional and personal knowledge and understanding.

The Wiley Finance series contains books written specifically for finance and investment professionals as well as sophisticated individual investors and their financial advisors. Book topics range from portfolio management to e-commerce, risk management, financial engineering, valuation and financial instrument analysis, as well as much more.

For a list of available titles, visit our Web site at www.WileyFinance.com.

Frontiers in Quantitative Finance

*Volatility and
Credit Risk Modeling*

RAMA CONT, Editor

WILEY

John Wiley & Sons, Inc.

Library of Congress Cataloging-in-Publication Data:

Frontiers in quantitative finance : volatility and credit risk modeling
/ [edited by] Rama Cont.
    p. cm. – (Wiley finance series)
ISBN 978-0-470-29292-1 (cloth)
 1. Finance–Mathematical models. 2. Derivative securities–
Mathematical models. I. Cont, Rama.
  HG106.F76 2009
  332.01'5195–dc22

                                        2008026309

Printed in the United States of America

10 9 8 7 6 5 4 3 2 1

Contents

Preface

When I started my research career in mathematical modeling in finance in the 1990s, I was struck by the huge gap between, on one hand, academic seminars in Paris on mathematical finance, which tended to be rather technical and inaccessible to quants and risk managers and, on the other hand, practitioner seminars that discussed many interesting problems but often failed to link them with the vibrant research community in quantitative finance. A few discussions with Stéphane Denise, a friend who was at the time a fixed-income quant, led to the idea of creating a monthly seminar on quantitative finance, which would be an interface between the academic and practitioner community in quantitative finance: the *Petit Déjeuner de la Finance*. This seminar, which I have been co-organizing since 1998, first with Stéphane Denise and, for the last few years, with Yann Braouezec, has progressively become a platform for exchange of ideas in quantitative finance and risk management between quants, risk managers, and academics, with a long list of speakers, among which are many of the major contributors to the recent developments in quantitative finance. Our recognition goes to those speakers who have made the *Petit Déjeuner de la Finance* a successful seminar and to the sponsoring institutions that have made this seminar possible through their support.

This volume is a selection of recent contributions from the *Petit Déjeuner de la Finance*, dealing with topics of current interest in financial engineering, which arrives in time to celebrate the tenth anniversary of the seminar! The contributing authors, leading quants and academic researchers who have contributed to the recent developments in quantitative finance, discuss emerging issues in quantitative finance, with a focus on portfolio credit risk and volatility modeling.

The volume is divided into two parts. The first part (Chapters 1 through 5) deals with advances in option pricing and volatility modeling in the context of equity and index derivatives. The second part (Chapters 6 through 11) covers recent advances in pricing models for portfolio credit derivatives.

OPTION PRICING

Chapter 1 deals with the simplest setting for option pricing, a static one-period model. As shown by Alexandre d'Aspremont, this framework, albeit simple, turns out to be quite rich in mathematical structure, with links to harmonic analysis and semidefinite programming. Aspremont derives necessary and sufficient conditions for the absence of static or buy-and-hold arbitrage opportunities in a one period market by mapping the problem to a generalized moment problem: he shows that this no-arbitrage condition is equivalent to the positive semidefiniteness of matrices formed by the market prices of tradeable securities and their products and applies this result to a market with multiple assets and basket call options.

In Chapter 2, Shalom Benaim, Peter Friz, and Roger Lee survey their recent results on the behavior of the Black-Scholes implied volatility at extreme strikes. These results lead to simple and universal formulae that give quantitative links between tail behavior and moment explosions of the underlying on one hand, and growth of the implied volatility smile on the other hand. In addition to surveying former results of the authors, this chapter also includes original, previously unpublished results on this topic.

The emergence of new volatility instruments—variance swaps—has inspired a renewed interest in volatility modeling. Variance swap markets give direct, observable, quotes on future realized variance as opposed to indirect ones via option prices. In Chapter 3, Lorenzo Bergomi proposes a new class of volatility models, which are based on using the forward variances as state variables and calibrating them to the observable variance swap term structure. This approach, known by now as the Bergomi model, has opened new directions in volatility modeling and enables a meaningful analysis of the volatility exposure of cliquet options and other exotic equity derivatives.

Implied volatility asymptotics is also the focus of Pierre Henry-Labordère's contribution, in Chapter 4. Henry-Labordère's results, published here for the first time, enable us to obtain first-order asymptotics for implied volatility for any stochastic volatility model using a geometric approach based on the heat kernel expansion on a Riemannian manifold. This formula is useful for the calibration of such models. Examples that are treated include a *SABR model with a mean-reversion term*, corresponding in this geometric framework to the Poincaré hyperbolic plane.

Chapter 5 discusses jump-diffusion models, which form another large class of models generalizing the Black-Scholes option pricing model to take into account sudden market moves or "jumps" in prices. Peter Tankov and Ekaterina Voltchkova review important properties of jump-diffusion models and show that these models can be used as a practical tool for option pricing and hedging, without dwelling on technical details. After introducing several widely used jump-diffusion models, Tankov and Voltchkova discuss Fourier transform–based methods for European option pricing, partial differential equations for barrier and American options, and the existing approaches to calibration and hedging.

CREDIT RISK MODELING

The second part of the book deals with credit risk modeling, a topic which has increasingly occupied the forefront of mathematical modeling in finance in the recent years. Credit risk modeling has witnessed the emergence of a wide variety of approaches that seem to have little in common, both at the single name level—where structural models compete with reduced-form models—and at the level of portfolio credit risk modeling, where "bottom-up" models coexist with "top-down" approaches. This diversity of approaches has created the need for comparative studies of various modeling approaches.

Chris Rogers opens this part with a discussion of the methodology for modeling credit risk in Chapter 6: note that this text, first prepared in 1999, is still relevant in many respects after 10 years and several credit crises! In particular, structural approaches are compared with reduced-form approaches and the choice of state variables is discussed.

The main focus of credit risk modeling in the late decade has been the modeling and pricing of collateralized debt obligations (CDOs), for which static default-time copula models have been frequently used. In Chapter 7, Jean-Paul Laurent and Areski Cousin present a review of factor models for CDO pricing and the link between factor representations and copula representations.

Index CDO markets have led to observable quotes for "default correlation": practitioners speak of implied correlation "smiles" and "skews." In Chapter 8, Erik and Lütz Schlögl explore how this analogy can be taken a step further to extract implied factor distributions from the market quotes for synthetic CDO tranches.

In Chapter 9, Julien Turc and Philippe Very also focus on the implied correlation skew: they introduce a local correlation function that makes default correlation dependent on the state of the economy and argue that this allows one to fit the model to the correlation smile and price exotic CDO products consistently with implied correlations.

The dramatic failure of copula-based models in the 2007 market turmoil has led to a renewed interest in dynamic models of credit risk. The last two chapters present material related to dynamic reduced-form models of portfolio credit risk that are, arguably, more amenable to pricing and simulation.

Dynamic reduced-form models of portfolio credit risk can be divided into two categories: in a *bottom-up* model, the portfolio intensity is an aggregate of the constituent intensities, while in a *top-down* model, the portfolio intensity is specified as the intensity of the aggregate loss process. In Chapter 10, Kay Giesecke, who has been among the active contributors to the literature on top-down pricing models, compares these approaches, emphasizing the role of the information (filtration) in the modeling process.

One of the issues in the pricing of portfolio credit derivatives has been the numerical obstacles that arise in the computation of quantities of interest such as CDO tranche spreads and sensitivities, for which the main approach has been quadrature methods and Monte Carlo simulation. In Chapter 11, Cont and Savescu introduce an alternative approach for computing the values of CDO tranche spreads, based on the solution of a system of ordinary differential equations. This approach, which is the analog for portfolio credit derivatives of Dupire's famous equation for call option prices, allows one to efficiently price CDOs and other portfolio credit derivatives without Monte Carlo simulation. This equation can also be used as a first ingredient in efficient calibration of top-down pricing models.

Special thanks go to Stéphane Denise and Yann Braouezec, with whom I have had the pleasure of organizing the *Petit Déjeuner de la Finance* for the past 10 years. I also thank Jennifer McDonald and Caitlin Cornish from Wiley for encouraging this project and for their patience and support.

We hope that this timely volume will be useful to readers eager to know about current developments in quantitative finance. Enjoy!

RAMA CONT
New York, March 2008

About the Editor

Rama Cont is associate professor in the School of Engineering and Applied Science and director of the Center for Financial Engineering at Columbia University (New York), Senior Research Scientist in Mathematics at the Centre National de Recherche Scientifique (CNRS, France), and founding partner of *Finance Concepts*, a risk management advisory based in Paris and New York. He is a coauthor of *Financial Modelling with Jump Processes* (CRC Press, 2003) and *Credit Derivatives and Structured Credit* (John Wiley and Sons, Inc., 2005).

He has been co-organizing since 1998 the *Petit Déjeuner de la Finance* seminar in Paris, from which this volume originated.

About the Contributors

Alexandre d'Aspremont is an assistant professor in the Department of Operations Research and Financial Engineering at Princeton University. His research concerns convex optimization, semidefinite programming and application to interest rate models and multivariate problems in finance.

Shalom Benaim holds a master's degree from Imperial College, London, and a PhD degree from Cambridge University. He currently works for RBOS.

Lorenzo Bergomi is head of equity derivatives research at Société Générale. After receiving his PhD in theoretical physics in the theory group at CEA, Saclay, Lorenzo spent two years in the physics department at MIT before joining SG in 1997 as a quantitative analyst on the exotics desk. He now heads a research team on equity derivatives at Société Generale, which currently focuses on models and algorithms for exotics, proprietary trading strategies, and credit/equity models.

Areski Cousin is a PhD candidate at Institut de Sciences Financieres et Actuarielles (ISFA) actuarial school, University of Lyon. He holds an engineer's degree from Ecole Nationale Superieure d'Informatique et Mathematiques Appliquees de Grenoble (ENSIMAG), France, and a master's degree in actuarial sciences from ISFA, France. His research focuses on dependence modeling of credit portfolios, risk management of CDOs within factor models, and hedging issues for CDOs.

Peter Friz is a reader at the Statistical Laboratory, Cambridge University. Before joining Cambridge, he worked in Jim Gatheral's group at Merrill Lynch, New York, for a year. He holds a PhD from the Courant Institute of Mathematical Sciences (New York University) and continues to work in quantitative finance and stochastic analysis. His recent research in finance includes applications of diffusion short-time asymptotics to basket options, pricing of volatility derivatives as inverse problem, Malliavin calculus for jump diffusions, and smile asymptotics.

Kay Giesecke is an assistant professor of management science and engineering at Stanford University. Kay's research and teaching address the quantitative modeling of financial risk, in particular credit risk. Kay has served as a consultant to financial institutions and the European Commission. Prior to joining Stanford in 2005, he taught financial engineering at Cornell University's School of Operations Research and Information Engineering. He holds an MSc in electrical engineering and economics and a PhD in economics.

Pierre Henry-Labordère works with the equity derivatives quantitative research team at Société Générale as a quantitative analyst. After receiving an engineering degree from Ecole Centrale de Paris and a PhD at Ecole Normale Supérieure (Paris) in superstring theory, he worked in the Theoretical Physics Department at Imperial College (London) and subsequently at Barclays Capital before joining SocGen.

Jean-Paul Laurent is professor of finance at Institut des Sciences Financières et Actuarielles (ISFA), Université Claude Bernard (Lyon, France). He is also a consultant with BNP Paribas.

Roger Lee is an assistant professor of mathematics at the University of Chicago, and was previously a member of the mathematics faculty at Stanford University and a visiting member of the Courant Institute at NYU. His research topics include asymptotics of implied volatility; analytic and computational aspects of Fourier methods for option pricing; and robust hedging of path-dependent derivatives, including derivatives on realized volatility.

Chris Rogers holds the chair of statistical science at Cambridge University and leads the quantitative finance group in the Statistical Laboratory. Chris works in the theory of probability and its applications, particularly in quantitative finance. His work in finance includes the potential approach to the term structure of interest rates, complete models of stochastic volatility, portfolio turnpike theorems, improved binomial pricing, robust hedging, liquidity modeling, axiomatics of valuation operators, the equity premium puzzle, duality in optimal investment/consumption, and Monte Carlo valuation of American options. He is coauthor, with Professor David Williams, of the two-volume classic work *Diffusions, Markov Processes, and Martingales*.

Ioana Savescu is a quantitative analyst at Merrill Lynch, London. She holds and engineering degree and a master's degree in probability and finance from Ecole Polytechnique (France).

Erik Schlögl is the director of the Quantitative Finance Research Centre at the University of Technology, Sydney (UTS). He received his PhD in economics from the University of Bonn in 1997 and has held positions at the University of New South Wales (Australia) and the University of Bonn. He has consulted for financial institutions and software developers in Europe, Australia, and the United States. He has also conducted a variety of professional development seminars at UTS, at the conferences organized by *Risk* magazine, and in-house at major banks. His current research interests focus on credit risk modeling as well as integrating foreign exchange and interest rate risk.

Lutz Schlögl is an executive director at Lehman Brothers in London and responsible for quantitative credit research, ABS modeling, and credit strategy in Europe, as well as global synthetic CDO modeling. Having joined Lehman as an associate in 2000, his research has been focused on the development of models for the pricing and risk management of exotic credit derivatives, in particular correlation products such as default baskets, synthetic CDO tranches, and CDO^2. He holds a PhD in financial economics from the University of Bonn.

Peter Tankov is assistant professor at Paris VII University, where he teaches mathematical finance. He holds a doctoral degree in applied mathematics from Ecole Polytechnique (France) and a bachelor's degree from the University of St. Petersburg. His research focuses on copulas and dependency modeling, applications of Lévy processes in finance, computational finance, and quantitative risk management. He is a coauthor of the book *Financial Modelling with Jump Processes* (CRC Press, 2003).

Julien Turc is head of quantitative strategy at Société Générale Corporate & Investment Banking. His team is active on the credit, fixed income, and foreign exchange markets and provides research to hedge funds and institutional investors worldwide. Over the past 10 years, Julien's research has covered topics ranging from exotic credit derivatives pricing to statistical relative value trading, equity-credit modeling and cross-asset strategies. Julien is a graduate of the Ecole Polytechnique and ENSAE and teaches credit derivatives at Paris VI University.

Philippe Very is a correlation trader on the credit derivatives proprietary trading and arbitrage desk at Natixis. Formerly, Philippe was a quantitative strategist at Societe Generale Corporate & Investment Banking in the Credit & Fixed Income Research Group, where he focused on credit structured products strategies and equity-credit modeling. Philippe graduated from Ecole Nationale de Statistique et Administration Economique (EN-SAE) and Paris-Dauphine University.

Ekaterina Voltchkova is assistant professor in applied mathematics at Université de Toulouse I (France). She holds a doctoral degree in applied mathematics from Ecole Polytechnique (France) and a BS in mathematics from the University of Novoibirsk (Russia). Her research has focused on computational finance, in particular numerical methods for models with jumps and the numerical solution of partial integro-differential equations (PIDEs).

Option Pricing and Volatility Modeling

CHAPTER 1

A Moment Approach to Static Arbitrage

Alexandre d'Aspremont

1.1 INTRODUCTION

The fundamental theorem of asset pricing establishes the equivalence between absence of arbitrage and existence of a martingale pricing measure, and is the foundation of the Black and Scholes [5] and Merton [24] option pricing methodology. Option prices are computed by an arbitrage argument, as the value today of a dynamic, self-financing hedging portfolio that replicates the option payoff at maturity. This pricing technique relies on at least two fundamental assumptions: it posits a model for the asset dynamics and assumes that markets are frictionless, that is, that continuous trading in securities is possible at no cost. Here we take the complementary approach: we do not make any assumption on the asset dynamics and we only allow trading today and at maturity. In that sense, we revisit a classic result on the equivalence between positivity of state prices and absence of arbitrage in a one-period market. In this simple market, we seek computationally *tractable* conditions for the absence of arbitrage, directly formulated in terms of *tradeable* securities.

Of course, these results are not intended to be used as a pricing framework in liquid markets. Our objective here instead is twofold. First, market data on derivative prices, aggregated from a very diverse set of sources, is very often plagued by liquidity and synchronicity issues. Because these price data sets are used by derivatives dealers to calibrate their models, we seek a set of arbitrarily refined tests to detect unviable prices in the one-period market or, in other words, detect prices that would be incompatible with *any* arbitrage free dynamic model for asset dynamics. Second, in some very illiquid markets, these conditions form simple upper or lower hedging portfolios and diversification strategies that are, by construction, immune to model misspecification and illiquidity issues.

Work on this topic starts with the [1] result on equilibrium, followed by a stream of works on multiperiod and continuous time models stating the equivalence between existence of a martingale measure and absence of dynamic arbitrage, starting with [15] and [16], with the final word probably belonging to [8] and [12]. Efforts to express these conditions directly in terms of asset prices can be traced back to [7] and [14], who derive equivalent conditions on a continuum of (possibly nontradeable) call options. [7], [19] and [20] use similar results to infer information on the asset distribution from the market price of calls using a minimum entropy approach. Another stream of works by [21] and more recently [28] derives explicit bounds on European call prices given moment information on the pricing measure. Results on the existence of martingales with given marginals can be traced back to Blackwell, Stein, Sherman, Cartier, Meyer, and Strassen and found financial applications in [13] and [22], among others. A recent paper by [11] uses this set of results to provide explicit no arbitrage conditions and option price bounds in the case where only a few single-asset call prices are quoted in a multiperiod market. Finally, contrary to our intuition on static arbitrage bounds, recent works by [18] and [10] show that these price bounds are often *very close* to the price bounds obtained using a Black-Scholes model, especially so for options that are outside of the money.

Given the market price of tradeable securities in a one-period market, we interpret the question of testing for the existence of a state price measure as a generalized moment problem. In that sense, the conditions we obtain can be seen as a direct generalization of Bochner-Bernstein-type theorems on the Fourier transform of positive measures. Market completeness is then naturally formulated in terms of moment determinacy. This allows us to derive equivalent conditions for the absence of arbitrage between *general payoffs* (not limited to single-asset call options). We also focus on the particular case of basket calls or European call options on a basket of assets. Basket calls appear in equity markets as index options and in interest rate derivatives market as spread options or swaptions, and are key recipients of market information on correlation.

The paper is organized as follows. We begin by describing the one period market and illustrate our approach on a simple example, introducing the payoff semigroup formed by the market securities and their products. Section 2 starts with a brief primer on harmonic analysis on semigroups after which we describe the general no-arbitrage conditions on the payoff semigroup. We also show how the products in this semigroup complete the market. We finish in Section 3 with a case study on spread options.

1.1.1 One-Period Model

We work in a one-period model where the market is composed of n assets with payoffs at maturity equal to x_i and price today given by p_i for $i = 1, \ldots, n$. There are also m derivative securities with payoffs $s_j(x) = s_j(x_1, \ldots, x_n)$ and price today equal to p_{n+j} for $j = 1, \ldots, m$. Finally, there is a riskless asset with payoff 1 at maturity and price 1 today and we assume, without loss of generality here, that interest rates are equal to zero (we work in the forward market). We look for conditions on p precluding arbitrage in this market, that is, buy and hold portfolios formed at no cost today which guarantee a strictly positive payoff at maturity.

We want to answer the following simple question: Given the market price vector p, is there an arbitrage opportunity (a buy-and-hold arbitrage in the continuous market terminology) between the assets x_i and the securities $s_j(x)$? Naturally, we know that this is equivalent to the existence of a state price (or probability) measure μ with support in $\mathbb{R}^n_+$ such that:

$$\mathbf{E}_\mu[x_i] = p_i, \quad i = 1, \ldots, n,$$
$$\mathbf{E}_\mu[s_j(x)] = p_{n+j}, \quad j = 1, \ldots, m \quad (1.1.1)$$

Bertsimas and Popescu [4] show that this simple, fundamental problem is computationally hard (in fact NP-Hard). In fact, if we simply discretize the problem on a uniform grid with L steps along each axis, this problem is still equivalent to an exponentially large linear program of size $O(L^n)$. Here, we look for a discretization that does not involve the state price measure but instead formulates the no arbitrage conditions directly on the market price vector p. Of course, NP-Hardness means that we cannot reasonably hope to provide an efficient, exact solution to all instances of problem (1.1.1). Here instead, we seek an arbitrarily refined, computationally efficient relaxation for this problem and NP-Hardness means that we will have to trade off precision for complexity.

1.1.2 The Payoff Semigroup

To illustrate our approach, let us begin here with a simplified case where $n = 1$; that is, there is only one forward contract with price p_1, and the derivative payoffs $s_j(x)$ are monomials with $s_j(x) = x^j$ for $j = 2, \ldots, m$. In this case, conditions (1.1.1) on the state price measure μ are written:

$$\mathbf{E}_\mu[x^j] = p_j, \quad j = 2, \ldots, m,$$
$$\mathbf{E}_\mu[x] = p_1 \quad (1.1.2)$$

with the implicit constraint that the support of μ be included in $\mathbb{R}_+$. We recognize (1.1.2) as a Stieltjes moment problem. For $x \in \mathbb{R}_+$, let us form the column vector $v_m(x) \in \mathbb{R}^{m+1}$ as follows:

$$v_m(x) \triangleq (1, x, x^2, \ldots, x^m)^T$$

For each value of x, the matrix $P_m(x)$ formed by the outer product of the vector $v_m(x)$ with itself is given by:

$$P_m(x) \triangleq v_m(x)v_m(x)^T = \begin{pmatrix} 1 & x & \cdots & x^m \\ x & x^2 & & x^{m+1} \\ \vdots & & \ddots & \vdots \\ x^m & x^{m+1} & \cdots & x^{2m} \end{pmatrix}$$

$P_m(x)$ is a *positive semidefinite* matrix (it has only one nonzero eigenvalue equal to $\|v_m(x)\|^2$). If there is no arbitrage and there exists a state price measure μ satisfying the price constraints (1.1.2), then there must be a symmetric moment matrix $M_m \in \mathbb{R}^{(m+1)\times(m+1)}$ such that:

$$M_m \triangleq \mathbf{E}_\mu[P_m(x)] = \begin{pmatrix} 1 & p_1 & \cdots & p_m \\ p_1 & p_2 & & \mathbf{E}_\mu[x^{m+1}] \\ \vdots & & \ddots & \vdots \\ p_m & \mathbf{E}_\mu[x^{m+1}] & \cdots & \mathbf{E}_\mu[x^{2m}] \end{pmatrix}$$

and, as an average of positive semidefinite matrices, M_m must be positive semidefinite. In other words, the existence of a positive semidefinite matrix M_m whose first row and columns are given by the vector p is a necessary condition for the absence of arbitrage in the one period market. In fact, positivity conditions of this type are also *sufficient* (see [27] among others). Testing for the absence of arbitrage is then equivalent to solving a *linear matrix inequality*, that is finding matrix coefficients corresponding to $\mathbf{E}_\mu[x^j]$ for $j = m+1, \ldots, 2m$ that make the matrix $M_m(x)$ positive semidefinite.

This chapter's central result is to show that this type of reasoning is not limited to the unidimensional case where the payoffs $s_j(x)$ are monomials but extends to arbitrary payoffs. Instead of looking only at monomials, we will consider the *payoff semigroup* $\mathbb{S}$ generated by the payoffs 1, x_i and $s_j(x)$ for $i = 1, \ldots, n$ and $j = 1, \ldots, m$ and their products (in graded lexicographic order):

$$\mathbb{S} \triangleq \{1, x_1, \ldots, x_n, s_1(x), \ldots, s_m(x), x_1^2, \ldots, x_i s_j(x), \ldots, s_m(x)^2, \ldots\} \quad (1.1.3)$$

In the next section, we will show that the no-arbitrage conditions (1.1.1) are equivalent to positivity conditions on matrices formed by the prices of the assets in $\mathbb{S}$. We also detail under which technical conditions the securities in $\mathbb{S}$ make the one-period market complete. In all the results that follow, we will assume that the asset distribution has *compact support*. As this can be made arbitrarily large, we do not lose much generality from a numerical point of view and this compactness assumption greatly simplifies the analysis while capturing the key link between moment conditions and arbitrage. Very similar but much more technical results hold in the noncompact case, as detailed in the preprint [9].

1.1.3 Semidefinite Programming

The key incentive for writing the no-arbitrage conditions in terms of linear matrix inequalities is that the latter are *tractable*. The problem of finding coefficients that make a particular matrix positive semidefinite can be written as:

$$
\begin{aligned}
&\text{find} \quad && y \\
&\text{such that} \quad && C + \sum_{k=1}^{m} y_k A_k \succeq 0
\end{aligned}
\tag{1.1.4}
$$

in the variable $y \in \mathbb{R}^m$, with parameters C, $A_k \in \mathbb{R}^{n \times n}$, for $k = 1, \ldots, m$, where $X \succeq 0$ means X positive semidefinite. This problem is convex and is also known as a semidefinite feasibility problem. Reasonably large instances can be solved efficiently using the algorithms detailed in [25] or [6] for example.

1.2 NO-ARBITRAGE CONDITIONS

In this section, we begin with an introduction on harmonic analysis on semigroups, which generalizes the moment conditions of the previous section to arbitrary payoffs. We then state our main result on the equivalence between no arbitrage in the one-period market and positivity of the price matrices for the products in the payoff semigroup $\mathbb{S}$ defined in (1.1.3):

$$
\mathbb{S} = \left\{ 1, x_1, \ldots, x_n, s_1(x), \ldots, s_m(x), x_1^2, \ldots, x_i s_j(x), \ldots, s_m(x)^2, \ldots \right\}
$$

1.2.1 Harmonic analysis on semigroups

We start with a brief primer on harmonic analysis on semigroups (based on [2] and the references therein). Unless otherwise specified, all measures are supposed to be positive.

A function $\rho(s) : \mathbb{S} \to \mathbb{R}$ on a semigroup $(\mathbb{S}, \cdot)$ is called a *semicharacter* if and only if it satisfies $\rho(st) = \rho(s)\rho(t)$ for all s, $t \in \mathbb{S}$ and $\rho(1) = 1$. The dual of a semigroup $\mathbb{S}$, that is, the set of semicharacters on $\mathbb{S}$, is written $\mathbb{S}^*$.

Definition 1.1. A function $f(s) : \mathbb{S} \to \mathbb{R}$ is a *moment function* on $\mathbb{S}$ if and only if $f(1) = 1$ and $f(s)$ can be represented as:

$$f(s) = \int_{\mathbb{S}^*} \rho(s) d\mu(\rho), \quad \text{for all } s \in \mathbb{S} \tag{1.2.5}$$

where μ is a Radon measure on $\mathbb{S}^*$.

When $\mathbb{S}$ is the semigroup defined in (1.1.3) as an enlargement of the semigroup of monomials on $\mathbb{R}^n$, its dual $\mathbb{S}^*$ is the set of applications $\rho_x(s) :$ $\mathbb{S} \to \mathbb{R}$ such that $\rho_x(s) = s(x)$ for all $s \in \mathbb{S}$ and all $x \in \mathbb{R}^n$. Hence, when $\mathbb{S}$ is the payoff semigroup, to each point $x \in \mathbb{R}^n$ corresponds a semicharacter that evaluates a payoff at that point. In this case, the condition $f(1) = 1$ on the price of the cash means that the measure μ is a *probability measure* on $\mathbb{R}^n$ and the representation (1.2.5) becomes:

$$f(s) = \int_{\mathbb{R}^n} s(x) d\mu(x) = \mathbf{E}_\mu [s(x)], \quad \text{for all payoffs } s \in \mathbb{S} \tag{1.2.6}$$

This means that when $\mathbb{S}$ is the semigroup defined in (1.1.3) and there is no arbitrage, a moment function is a function that for each payoff $s \in \mathbb{S}$ returns its *price* $f(s) = \mathbf{E}_\mu[s(x)]$. Testing for no arbitrage is then equivalent to testing for the existence of a moment function f on $\mathbb{S}$ that matches the market prices in (1.1.1).

Definition 1.2. *A function* $f(s) : \mathbb{S} \to \mathbb{R}$ *is called* positive semidefinite *if and only if for all finite families* $\{s_i\}$ *of elements of* $\mathbb{S}$, *the matrix with coefficients* $f(s_i s_j)$ *is positive semidefinite.*

We remark that moment functions are necessarily positive semidefinite. Here, based on results by [2], we exploit this property to derive necessary and sufficient conditions for representation (1.2.6) to hold.

The central result in [2, Th. 2.6] states that the set of exponentially bounded positive semidefinite functions $f(s) : \mathbb{S} \to \mathbb{R}$ such that $f(1) = 1$ is a Bauer simplex whose extreme points are given by the semicharacters in $\mathbb{S}^*$. Hence a function f is positive semidefinite and exponentially bounded if and only if it can be represented as $f(s) = \int_{\mathbb{S}^*} \rho d\mu(\rho)$ with the support of μ included in some compact subset of $\mathbb{S}^*$. Bochner's theorem on the Fourier transform of positive measures and Bernstein's corresponding theorem for the Laplace transform are particular cases of this representation result. In what follows, we use it to derive tractable necessary and sufficient conditions for the function $f(s)$ to be represented as in (1.2.6).

1.2.2 Main Result: No Arbitrage Conditions

We assume that the asset payoffs are bounded and that $\mathbb{S}$ is the payoff semigroup defined in (1.1.3), this means that without loss of generality, we can assume that the payoffs $s_j(x)$ are positive. To simplify notations here, we define the functions $e_i(x)$ for $i = 1, \ldots, m+n$ and $x \in \mathbb{R}_+^n$ such that $e_i(x) = x_i$ for $i = 1, \ldots, n$ and $e_{n+j}(x) = s_j(x)$ for $j = 1, \ldots, m$.

Theorem 1.3. *There is no arbitrage in the one period market and there exists a state price measure μ such that:*

$$\mathbf{E}_\mu[x_i] = p_i, \quad i = 1, \ldots, n,$$
$$\mathbf{E}_\mu[s_j(x)] = p_{n+j}, \quad j = 1, \ldots, m$$

if and only if there exists a function $f(s) : \mathbb{S} \to \mathbb{R}$ satisfying:

(i) $f(s)$ is a positive semidefinite function of $s \in \mathbb{S}$
(ii) $f(e_i s)$ is a positive semidefinite function of $s \in \mathbb{S}$ for $i = 1, \ldots, n+m$
(iii) $(\beta f(s) - \sum_{i=1}^{n+m} f(e_i s))$ is a positive semidefinite function of $s \in \mathbb{S}$
(iv) $f(1) = 1$ and $f(e_i) = p_i$ for $i = 1, \ldots, n+m$

for some (large) constant $\beta > 0$, in which case we have $f(s) = \mathbf{E}_\mu[s(x)]$ and f is linear in s.

Proof. By scaling $e_i(x)$ we can assume without loss of generality that $\beta = 1$. For s, u in $\mathbb{S}$, we note E_s the shift operator such that for $f(s) : \mathbb{S} \to \mathbb{R}$, we have $E_u(f(s)) \stackrel{\Delta}{=} f(su)$ and we let ε be the commutative algebra generated by the shift operators on $\mathbb{S}$. The family of shift operators

$$\tau = \{\{E_{e_i}\}_{i=1,\ldots,n+m}, \left(I - \sum_{i=1}^{n+m} E_{e_i}\right)\} \subset \mathcal{E}$$

is such that $I - T \in \text{span}^+\tau$ for each $T \in \tau$ and $\text{span}\tau = \varepsilon$, hence τ is linearly admissible in the sense of [3] or [23], which states that (ii) and (iii) are equivalent to f being τ-positive. Then, [23, Th. 2.1] means that f is τ-positive if and only if there is a measure μ such that $f(s) = \int_{\mathbb{S}_*} \rho(s) d\mu(\rho)$, whose support is a compact subset of the τ-positive semicharacters. This means in particular that for a semicharacter $\rho_x \in \text{supp}(\mu)$ we must have $\rho_x(e_i) \geq 0$, for $i = 1, \ldots, n$ hence $x \geq 0$. If ρ_x is a τ-positive semicharacter then we must have $\{x \geq 0 : \|x\|_1 \leq 1\}$, hence f being τ-positive is equivalent to f admitting a representation of the form $f(s) = \mathbf{E}_\mu[s(x)]$, for all $s \in \mathbb{S}$ with μ having a compact support in a subset of the unit simplex. Linearity of f simply follows from the linearity of semicharacters on the market semigroup in (1.1.3).

Let us remark that, at first sight, the payoff structures do not appear explicitly in the above result so nothing apparently distinguishes the no arbitrage problem from a generic moment problem. However, payoffs do play a role through the semigroup structure. Suppose, for example, that s_1 is a straddle, with $s_1(x) = |x_1 - K|$, then $s_1(x)^2 = x_1^2 - 2Kx_1 + K^2$ and by linearity of the semicharacters $\rho_x(s)$, the function f satisfies the following linear constraint:

$$f(s_1(x)^2) = f(x_1^2) - 2Kf(x_1) + K^2$$

This means in practice that algebraic relationships between payoffs translate into linear constraints on the function f and further restrict the arbitrage constraints. When no such relationships exist however, the conditions in Theorem 1.3 produce only trivial numerical bounds. We illustrate this point further in Section 1.3.

1.2.3 Market Completeness

As we will see below, under technical conditions on the asset prices, the moment problem is determinate and there is a one-to-one correspondence between the price $f(s)$ of the assets in $s \in \mathbb{S}$ and the state price measures μ, in other words, the payoffs in $\mathbb{S}$ make the market *complete*.

Here, we suppose that there is no arbitrage in the one period market. Theorem 1.3 shows that there is at least one measure μ such that $f(s) = \mathbf{E}_\mu[s(x)]$, for all payoffs $s \in \mathbb{S}$. In fact, we show below that when asset payoffs have compact support, this pricing measure is unique.

Theorem 1.4. *Suppose that the asset prices x_i for $i = 1, \ldots, n$ have compact support, then for each set of arbitrage free prices $f(s)$ there is a unique state price measure μ with compact support satisfying:*

$$f(s) = \mathbf{E}_\mu [s(x)], \quad \text{for all payoffs } s \in \mathbb{S}$$

Proof. If there is no arbitrage and asset prices x_i for $i = 1, \ldots, n$ have compact support, then the prices $f(s) = \mathbf{E}_\mu[s(x)]$, for $s \in \mathbb{S}$ are exponentially bounded in the sense of [2, §4.1.11] and [2, Th. 6.1.5] shows that the measure μ associated to the market prices $f(s)$ is unique.

This result shows that the securities in $\mathbb{S}$ make the market complete in the compact case.

1.2.4 Implementation

The conditions in Theorem 1.3 involve testing the positivity of infinitely large matrices and are of course not directly implementable. In practice, we can get a reduced set of conditions by only considering elements of $\mathbb{S}$ up to a certain (even) degree $2d$:

$$\mathbb{S}_d \triangleq \{1, x_1, \ldots, x_n, s_1(x), \ldots, s_m(x), x_1^2, \ldots, x_i s_j(x), \ldots,$$

$$s_m(x)^2, \ldots, s_m(x)^{2d}\} \tag{1.2.7}$$

We look for a moment function f satisfying conditions (i) through (iv) in Theorem 1.3 for all elements s in the reduced semigroup $\mathbb{S}_d$. Conditions (i) through (iii) now amount to testing the positivity of matrices of size $N_d = \binom{n+m+2d}{n+m}$ or less. Condition (i) for example is written:

$$
\begin{pmatrix}
1 & p_1 & \cdots & p_{m+n} & f(x_1^2) & \cdots & f\left(s_m(x)^{\frac{N_d}{2}}\right) \\
p_1 & f(x_1^2) & \cdots & f(x_1 s_m(x)) & f(x_1^3) & \cdots & f\left(x_1 s_m(x)^{\frac{N_d}{2}}\right) \\
\vdots & \vdots & \ddots & & \vdots & & \\
p_{m+n} & f(x_1 s_m(x)) & & & \vdots & & \\
f(x_1^2) & f(x_1^3) & & \cdots & f(x_1^4) & & \\
\vdots & \vdots & & & & & \vdots \\
f\left(s_m(x)^{\frac{N_d}{2}}\right) & f\left(x_1 s_m(x)^{\frac{N_d}{2}}\right) & & & \cdots & & f\left(s_m(x)^{N_d}\right)
\end{pmatrix} \geq 0
$$

because the market price conditions in (1.1.1) impose $f(x_i) = p_i$ for $i = 1, \ldots, n$ and $f(s_j(x)) = p_{n+j}$ for $j = 1, \ldots, m$. Condition (ii) stating that $f(x_1 s)$ be a positive semidefinite function of s is then written as:

$$
\begin{pmatrix}
p_1 & f\left(x_1^2\right) & f(x_1 x_2) & \cdots & f\left(x_1 s_m(x)^{\frac{N_d}{2}-1}\right) \\
f\left(x_1^2\right) & f\left(x_1^4\right) & f\left(x_1^3 x_2\right) & & \\
f(x_1 x_2) & f\left(x_1^3 x_2\right) & f\left(x_1^2 x_2^2\right) & & \\
\vdots & & & \ddots & \vdots \\
f\left(x_1 s_m(x)^{\frac{N_d}{2}-1}\right) & & & \cdots & f\left(x_1^2 s_m(x)^{N_d-2}\right)
\end{pmatrix} \succeq 0
$$

and the remaining linear matrix inequalities in conditions (ii) and (iii) are handled in a similar way. These conditions are a finite subset of the full conditions in Theorem 1.3 and form a set of linear matrix inequalities in the values of $f(s)$ (see Section 1.1.3). The exponential growth of N_d with n and m means that only small problem instances can be solved using current numerical software. This is partly because most interior point–based semidefinite programming solvers are designed for small or medium scale problems with high precision requirements. Here instead, we need to solve large problems which don't require many digits of precision. Finally, as we will see in Section 1.3 on spread options, for common derivative payoffs the semigroup structure in (1.2.7) can considerably reduce the size of these problems.

1.2.5 Hedging Portfolios and Sums of Squares

We write $\mathcal{A}(\mathbb{S})$ the algebra of polynomials on the payoff semigroup $\mathbb{S}$ defined in (1.1.3). We let here $\Sigma \subset \mathcal{A}(\mathbb{S})$ be the set of polynomials that are sums of squares of polynomials in $\mathcal{A}(\mathbb{S})$, and $\mathcal{P}$ the set of positive semidefinite functions on $\mathbb{S}$. In this section, we will see that the relaxations detailed in the previous section essentially substitute to the conic duality between probability measures and positive portfolios:

$$
p(x) \geq 0 \Leftrightarrow \int p(x) dv \geq 0, \quad \text{for all probability measures } v,
$$

the conic duality between positive semidefinite functions and sums of squares polynomials:

$$
\langle f, p \rangle \geq 0 \text{ for all } p \in \Sigma \iff f \in \mathcal{P}. \tag{1.2.8}
$$

having defined $\langle f, p \rangle = \sum_i q_i f(s_i)$ for $p = \sum_i q_i \chi_{s_i} \in \mathcal{A}(\mathbb{S})$ and $f : \mathbb{S} \to \mathbb{R}$

(see [2]). While the set of nonnegative portfolios is intractable, the set of portfolios that are sums of squares of payoffs in $\mathbb{S}$ (hence nonnegative) can be represented using linear matrix inequalities. The previous section used positive semidefinite functions to characterize viable price sets, here we use sums of squares polynomials to characterize super/subreplicating portfolios. Let us start from the following subreplication problem:

$$
\begin{aligned}
\text{minimize} \quad & \mathbf{E}_\mu[s_1(x)] \\
\text{subject to} \quad & \mathbf{E}_\mu[x_i] = p_i, \quad i = 1, \ldots, n, \\
& \mathbf{E}_\mu[s_j(x)] = p_{n+j}, \quad j = 2, \ldots, m
\end{aligned} \tag{1.2.9}
$$

in the variable μ. Theorem 1.3 shows that this is equivalent to the following problem:

$$
\begin{aligned}
\text{minimize} \quad & f(s_1(x)) \\
\text{subject to} \quad & f(s) \in \mathcal{P} \\
& f(x_i s) \in \mathcal{P}, \quad i = 1, \ldots, n, \\
& f(s_i s) \in \mathcal{P}, \quad i = 2, \ldots, m, \\
& \left(\beta f(s) - \sum_{i=1}^{n} f(x_i s) - \sum_{i=2}^{m} f(s_i s) \right) \in \mathcal{P} \\
& f(1) = 1, \; f(x_i) = p_i, \quad i = 1, \ldots, n, \\
& f(s_i) = p_{n+i}, \quad i = 2, \ldots, m
\end{aligned} \tag{1.2.10}
$$

which is a semidefinite program in the variables $f(s) : \mathbb{S} \to \mathbb{R}$. Using the conic duality in (1.2.8) and the fact that:

$$
\langle f(sq), p \rangle = \langle f(s), qp \rangle,
$$

for any $p, q \in \mathcal{A}(\mathbb{S})$. We can form the Lagrangian:

$$
\begin{aligned}
L(f(s), \lambda, q) = {} & f(s_1(x)) - \langle f(s), q_0 \rangle - \sum_{i=1}^{n} \langle f(s), x_i q_i \rangle \\
& - \sum_{i=2}^{m} \langle f(s), s_i q_{n+i} \rangle - \sum_{i=1}^{n} \lambda_i (f(x_i) - p_i) \\
& - \sum_{i=2}^{m} \lambda_i (f(s_i) - p_i) - \lambda_0 (f(1) - 1) - \langle \beta f(s), q_{n+m+1} \rangle \\
& + \sum_{i=1}^{n} \langle f(s), x_i q_{n+m+1} \rangle + \sum_{i=2}^{m} \langle f(s), s_i q_{n+m+1} \rangle
\end{aligned}
$$

where the polynomials $q_i \in \Sigma$ are sums of squares. We then get the dual as:

$$\text{maximize} \quad \lambda_0 + \sum_{i=1}^{n} \lambda_i p_i + \sum_{i=2}^{m} \lambda_i p_{n+i}$$

$$\text{subject to} \quad s_1(x) - \lambda_0 - \sum_{i=1}^{n} \lambda_i x_i - \sum_{i=2}^{m} \lambda_i s_i(x) = q_0 + \sum_{i=1}^{n} x_i q_i + \sum_{i=2}^{m} s_i(x) q_{n+i}$$

$$+ \left(\beta - \sum_{i=1}^{n} x_i - \sum_{i=2}^{m} s_i(x) \right) q_{m+n+1} \qquad (1.2.11)$$

in the variables $\lambda \in \mathbb{R}^{n+m}$ and $q_i \in \Sigma, i = 0, \ldots, n+m+1$. We can compare this last program to the classic portfolio subreplication problem:

$$\text{maximize} \quad \lambda_0 + \sum_{i=1}^{n} \lambda_i p_i + \sum_{i=2}^{m} \lambda_i p_{n+i}$$

$$\text{subject to} \quad s_1(x) - \lambda_0 - \sum_{i=1}^{n} \lambda_i x_i - \sum_{i=2}^{m} \lambda_i s_i(x) \geq 0, \quad \text{for all } x \in \mathbb{R}_+^n$$

in the variable $\lambda \in \mathbb{R}^{n+m}$, which is numerically intractable except in certain particular cases (see [4], [10] or [11]). The key difference between this program and (1.2.11) is that the (intractable) portfolio positivity constraint is replaced by the tractable condition that this portfolio be written as a combination of sums of squares of polynomials in $\mathcal{A}(\mathbb{S})$, which can be constructed directly as the dual solution of the semidefinite program in (1.2.10).

1.2.6 Multi-Period Models

Suppose now that the products have multiple maturities $T_1, \ldots, T_q$. We know from [15] and [16] that the absence of arbitrage in this dynamic market is equivalent to the existence of a martingale measure on the assets $x_1, \ldots, x_n$. Theorem 1.3 gives conditions for the existence of *marginal* state price measures μ_i at each maturity T_i and we need conditions guaranteeing the existence of a martingale measure whose marginals match these distributions μ_i at each maturity date T_i. A partial answer is given by the following majorization result, which can be traced to Blackwell, Stein, Sherman, Cartier, Meyer, and Strassen.

Theorem 1.5. *If μ and ν are any two probability measures on a finite set $A = \{a_1, \ldots, a_N\}$ in $\mathbb{R}^N$ such that $\mathbf{E}_\mu[\phi] \geq \mathbf{E}_\nu[\phi]$ for every continuous concave function ϕ defined on the convex hull of A, then there is a martingale transition matrix Q such that $\mu Q = \nu$.*

Finding *tractable* conditions for the existence of a martingale measure with given marginals, outside of the particular case of vanilla European call options considered in [11] or for the density families discussed in [22], remains however an open problem.

1.3 EXAMPLE

To illustrate the results of section 1.2, we explicitly treat the case of a one period market with two assets x_1, x_2 with positive, bounded payoff at maturity and price p_1, p_2 today. European call options with payoff $(x - K_i)^+$ for $i = 1, 2$, are also traded on each asset with prices p_3 and p_4. We are interested in computing bounds on the price of a spread option with payoff $(x_1 - x_2 - K)^+$ given the prices of the forwards and calls.

We first notice that the complexity of the problem can be reduced by considering straddle options with payoffs $|x_i - K_i|$ instead of calls. Because a straddle can be expressed as a combination of calls, forwards, and cash:

$$|x_i - K_i| = (K_i - x_i) + 2(x_i - K_i)^+$$

The advantage of using straddles is that the square of a straddle is a polynomial in the payoffs x_i, $i = 1, 2$, so using straddles instead of calls very significantly reduces the number of elements in the semigroup $\mathbb{S}_d$ because various payoff powers are linearly dependent: when k option prices are given on 2 assets, this number is $(k+1)\binom{2+2d}{2}$, instead of $\binom{2+k+2d}{n+k}$. The payoff semigroup $\mathbb{S}_d$ is now:

$$\mathbb{S}_d = \left\{ 1, x_1, x_2, |x_1 - K_1|, |x_2 - K_2|, |x_1 - x_2 - K|, \ldots, x_1|x_1 - K_1|, \ldots, x_2^{2d} \right\}$$

By sampling the conditions in Theorem 1.3 on $\mathbb{S}_d$ as in section 1.2.4, we can compute a lower bound on the minimum (respectively, an upper bound on the maximum) price for the spread option compatible with the absence of arbitrage. This means that we get an upper bound on the solution of:

$$\begin{aligned}
\text{maximize} \quad & \mathbf{E}_\mu[|x_1 - x_2 - K|] \\
\text{subject to} \quad & \mathbf{E}_\mu[|x_i - K_i|] = p_{i+2} \\
& \mathbf{E}_\mu[x_i] = p_i, \quad i = 1, 2
\end{aligned}$$

by solving the following program:

maximize $f(|x_1 - x_2 - K|)$

subject to

$$
\begin{pmatrix}
1 & p_1 & \cdots & f\left(x_2^d\right) \\
p_1 & f\left(x_1^2\right) & & \\
\vdots & & \ddots & \vdots \\
f\left(x_2^d\right) & & \cdots & f\left(x_2^{2d}\right)
\end{pmatrix} \succeq 0
$$

$$\vdots$$

$$
\begin{pmatrix}
f(b(x)) & f(b(x)x_1) & \cdots & f\left(b(x)x_2^{d-1}\right) \\
f(b(x)x_1) & f\left(b(x)^2 x_1^2\right) & & \\
\vdots & & \ddots & \vdots \\
f\left(b(x)x_2^{d-1}\right) & & \cdots & f\left(b(x)^2 x_2^{2(d-1)}\right)
\end{pmatrix} \succeq 0
$$

$$(1.3.12)$$

where

$$b(x) = \beta - x_1 - x_2 - |x_1 - K_1| - |x_2 - K_2| - |x_1 - x_2 - K|$$

is coming from condition (iii) in Theorem 1.3. This is a semidefinite program (see Section 1.1.3) in the values of $f(s)$ for $s \in \mathbb{S}_d$. This is a large-scale, structured semidefinite program which could, in theory, be solved efficiently using numerical packages for semialgebraic optimization such as SOSTOOLS by [26] or GLOPTIPOLY by [17]. In practice however, problem size and conditioning issues still make problems such as (1.3.12) numerically hard. This is partly due to the fact that these packages do not explicitly exploit the group structure of the problems derived here to reduce numerical complexity. Overall, solving the large-scale semidefinite programs arising in semialgebraic optimization remains an open issue.

1.4   CONCLUSION

We have derived tractable necessary and sufficient conditions for the absence of static or buy-and-hold arbitrage opportunities in a perfectly liquid, one-period market and formulated the positivity of Arrow-Debreu prices as a generalized moment problem to show that this no-arbitrage condition is equivalent to the positive semidefiniteness of matrices formed by the market prices of tradeable securities and their products. By interpreting the no-arbitrage conditions as a moment problem, we have derived equivalent conditions directly written on the price of tradeable assets instead of state prices. This also shows how allowing trading in the products of market payoffs completes the static market.

REFERENCES

1. Arrow, K. J., and G. Debreu. (1954). The existence of an equilibrium for a competitive economy. *Econometrica* 22: 265–269.
2. Berg, C., J. P. R. Christensen, and P. Ressel. (1984). *Harmonic Analysis on Semigroups: Theory of Positive Definite and Related Functions.* Volume 100 of *Graduate Texts in Mathematics.* New York: Springer-Verlag.
3. Berg, C., and P. H. Maserick. (1984). Exponentially bounded positive definite functions. *Illinois Journal of Mathematics* 28(1): 162–179.
4. Bertsimas, D., and I. Popescu. (2002). On tahe relation between option and stock prices: A convex optimization approach. *Operations Research* 50(2): 358–374.
5. Black, F., and M. Scholes. (1973). The pricing of options and corporate liabilities. *Journal of Political Economy* 81: 637–659.
6. Boyd, S., and L. Vandenberghe. (2004). *Convex Optimization.* Cambridge: Cambridge University Press.
7. Breeden, D. T., and R. H. Litzenberger. (1978). Price of state-contingent claims implicit in option prices. *Journal of Business* 51(4): 621–651.
8. Dalang, R. C., A. Morton, and W. Willinger. (1990). Equivalent martingale measures and no-arbitrage in stochastic securities market models. *Stochastics and Stochastics Reports* 29(2): 185–201.
9. d'Aspremont, A. (2003). A harmonic analysis solution to the static basket arbitrage problem. Available at http://arxiv.org/pdf/math/0309048.
10. d'Aspremont, A., and L. El Ghaoui. (2006). Static arbitrage bounds on basket option prices. *Mathematical Programming* 106(3): 467–489.
11. Davis, M. H., and D. G. Hobson. (2007). The range of traded option prices. *Mathematical Finance* 17(1): 1–14.
12. Delbaen, F., and W. Schachermayer. (2005). *The Mathematics of Arbitrage.* New York: Springer Finance.
13. Dupire, B. (1994). Pricing with a smile. *Risk* 7(1): 18–20.
14. Friesen, P. H. (1979). The Arrow-Debreu model extended to financial markets. *Econometrica* 47(3): 689–707.
15. Harrison, J. M., and S. M. Kreps. (1979). Martingales and arbitrage in multi-period securities markets. *Journal of Economic Theory* 20: 381–408.
16. Harrison, J. M., and S. R. Pliska. (1981). Martingales and stochastic integrals in the theory of continuous trading. *Stochastic Processes and Their Applications* 11: 215–260.
17. Henrion, D., and J. B. Lasserre. (2003). GloptiPoly: Global optimization over polynomials with Matlab and SeDuMi. *ACM Transactions on Mathematical Software (TOMS)* 29(2): 165–194.

18. Hobson, D., P. Laurence, and T. H. Wang. (2005). Static arbitrage upper bounds for the prices of basket options. *Quantitative Finance* 5(4): 329–342.
19. Jackwerth, J., and M. Rubinstein. (1996). Recovering probability distributions from option prices. *Journal of Finance* 51/bl !bl(5): 1611–1631.
20. Laurent, J. P., and D. Leisen. (2000). Building a consistent pricing model from observed option prices. In M. Avellaneda, ed., *Quantitative Analysis in Financial Markets*. River Edge, NJ: World Scientific Publishing.
21. Lo, A. (1987). Semi-parametric bounds for option prices and expected payoffs. *Journal of Financial Economics* 19: 372–387.
22. Madan, D. B., and M. Yor. (2002). Making Markov martingales meet marginals: with explicit constructions. *Bernoulli* 8(4): 509–536.
23. Maserick, P. H. (1977). Moments of measures on convex bodies. *Pacific Journal of Mathematics* 68(1): 135–152.
24. Merton, R. C. (1973). Theory of rational option pricing. *Bell Journal of Economics and Management Science* 4: 141–183.
25. Nesterov, Y., and A. Nemirovskii. (1994): *Interior-Point Polynomial Algorithms in Convex Programming*. Philadelphia: Society for Industrial and Applied Mathematics.
26. Prajna, S., A. Papachristodoulou, and P. A. Parrilo. (2002). Introducing SOS-TOOLS: A general purpose sum of squares programming solver. *Proceedings of the 41st IEEE Conference on Decision and Control* 1.
27. Vasilescu, F.-H. (2002). Hamburger and Stieltjes moment problems in several variables. *Transactions of the American Mathematical Society* 354: 1265–1278.
28. Zuluaga, L. F., J. Pena, and D. Du. (2006). Extensions of Lo's semiparametric bound for European call options. Working paper.

CHAPTER 2

On Black-Scholes Implied Volatility at Extreme Strikes

Shalom Benaim, Peter Friz, and Roger Lee

We survey recent results on the behavior of the Black-Scholes implied volatility at extreme strikes. There are simple and universal formulae that give quantitative links between tail behavior and moment explosions of the underlying on one hand, and growth of the famous volatility smile on the other hand. Some original results are included as well.

2.1 INTRODUCTION

Let S be a nonnegative $\mathbb{P}$-martingale, and let $S_0 > 0$. Think of S as a forward price and $\mathbb{P}$ as forward risk-neutral measure. Write $\mathbb{E}$ for expectation with respect to $\mathbb{P}$.

For a fixed maturity T, let $C(k) := \mathbb{E}(S_T - S_0 e^k)^+$ be the forward price of a call as a function of moneyness k, the log of the strike-to-S_0 ratio.

Let $c(k) := C(k)/S_0$ be the S_0-normalized forward call price.

With

$$d_{1,2}(k, \sigma) := -k/\sigma \pm \sigma/2$$

let

$$c_{BS}(k, \sigma) := \Phi(d_1) - e^k \Phi(d_2)$$

be the S_0-normalized forward Black-Scholes formula as a function of moneyness k and unannualized volatility σ.

For each k define the unannualized implied volatility $V(k)$ uniquely by

$$c(k) = c_{BS}(k, V(k))$$

Our project is to study the $k \to \infty$ behavior of $V(k)$ and $V(-k)$. Two examples of applications are the choice of a functional form for the extrapolation of an implied volatility skew into the tails, and the inference of parameters of underlying dynamics, given observations of tail slopes of the volatility skew.

Unless otherwise stated, each limit, lim sup, lim inf, and asymptotic relation is taken as $k \to \infty$. In particular, $g(k) \sim h(k)$ means that $g(k)/h(k) \to 1$ as $k \to \infty$.

2.2 THE MOMENT FORMULA

The *moment formula* [30] explicitly relates the $k \to \infty$ behavior of $V(k)$ to the right-hand critical exponent

$$\tilde{p} := \sup\{p : \mathbb{E}S_T^{1+p} < \infty\}$$

via the strictly decreasing function $\psi : [0, \infty] \to [0, 2]$ defined by

$$\psi(x) := 2 - 4(\sqrt{x^2 + x} - x)$$

Theorem 2.1. *(Right-hand moment formula).*

$$\limsup \frac{V^2(k)}{k} = \psi(\tilde{p})$$

Some consequences are as follows:

The implied volatility tail cannot grow *faster* than $\sqrt{k}$, by which we mean that for k large enough, $V(k) \le \sqrt{\beta k}$. The moment formula makes precise how small the constant coefficient β in that bound can be chosen.

Moreover, unless S_T has finite moments of all orders, the implied volatility tail cannot grow *slower* than $\sqrt{k}$, by which we mean that $V(k)$ cannot be $o(\sqrt{k})$.

These conclusions are fully model independent, requiring *no distributional assumptions* on S_T.

2.2.1 Intuition of Proof

Define $f_1 := f_-$ and $f_2 := f_+$ where

$$f_\pm(y) := \left(\frac{1}{\sqrt{y}} \pm \frac{\sqrt{y}}{2}\right)^2 = \frac{1}{y} \pm 1 + \frac{y}{4} \qquad (2.2.1)$$

Note that ψ is the inverse of $\frac{1}{2} f_1$ and that

$$f_j(\sigma^2/k) = d_j^2(k, \sigma)/k, \quad j = 1, 2 \qquad (2.2.2)$$

Using the normal cumulative distribution function (CDF) asymptotics

$$\Phi(-z) \sim \frac{e^{-z^2/2}}{\sqrt{2\pi} z}, \qquad z \to \infty \qquad (2.2.3)$$

we have, for constant $\beta \geq 0$,

$$c_{BS}(k, \sqrt{\beta k}) = \Phi(-\sqrt{f_1(\beta)k}) - e^k \Phi(-\sqrt{f_2(\beta)k}) \qquad (2.2.4)$$

$$\sim \frac{1}{\sqrt{2\pi}} \left(\frac{e^{-f_1(\beta)k/2}}{\sqrt{f_1(\beta)k}} - \frac{e^k e^{-f_2(\beta)k/2}}{\sqrt{f_2(\beta)k}}\right) = \frac{e^{-f_1(\beta)k/2}}{B\sqrt{k}} \qquad (2.2.5)$$

where B depends only on β, not k.

On the other hand, $c(k) = O(e^{-kp})$ holds for all p with $\mathbb{E}S_T^{1+p} < \infty$. So

$$c(k) \approx e^{-k\tilde{p}} \qquad (2.2.6)$$

where we will not define "$\approx$", as our purpose here is just to give intuition.

The decay rates in (2.2.5) and (2.2.6) match only if $\tilde{p} = f_1(\beta)/2$ or equivalently,

$$\beta = \psi(\tilde{p}) \qquad (2.2.7)$$

Because βk was the square of the volatility argument in (2.2.4), this makes plausible the moment formula

$$\limsup V^2(k)/k = \psi(\tilde{p}) \qquad (2.2.8)$$

Of course, we have not *proved* the moment formula here; see Lee [30] for the rigorous proof.

2.2.2 Left-Hand Moment Formula

The left-hand moment formula explicitly relates the $k \to \infty$ behavior of $V(-k)$ to the left-hand moment index

$$\tilde{q} := \sup\{q : \mathbb{E}\, S_T^{-q} < \infty\}$$

Theorem 2.2. (left-hand moment formula).

$$\limsup \frac{V^2(-k)}{k} = \psi(\tilde{q})$$

This follows from measure-change of the right-hand moment formula, as shown in [30]. Start by writing $V(-k) \equiv V(-k; S, \mathbb{P})$ to emphasize the dependence on the underlier and the measure. Then verify the symmetries

$$V(-k; S, \mathbb{P}) = V(k; 1/S, \mathbb{Q}) \tag{2.2.9}$$

$$\mathbb{E}\, S_T^{-p} = S_0 \mathbb{E}^{\mathbb{Q}}\left[(1/S_T)^{1+p}\right] \tag{2.2.10}$$

where the "foreign" risk-neutral measure $\mathbb{Q}$ is defined by $d\mathbb{Q}/d\mathbb{P} = S_T/S_0$ (provided that $\mathbb{P}(S_T > 0) = 1$, else a separate case is needed). Now apply Theorem 2.1 to obtain

$$\limsup \frac{V^2(-k)}{k} = \limsup \frac{V^2(k; 1/S, \mathbb{Q})}{k}$$

$$= \psi(\sup\{p : \mathbb{E}^{\mathbb{Q}}(1/S_T)^{1+p} < \infty\}) = \psi(\tilde{q})$$

as claimed.

2.2.3 Conjectures

It is natural to conjecture the following two extensions of the moment formula.

First, can we replace the lim sup with a limit? In other words,

Conjecture 1.

$$V^2(k)/k \to \psi(\tilde{p}). \tag{2.2.11}$$

Second, consider the complementary cumulative distribution function (CCDF) $\bar{F}$ of the log return:

$$\bar{F}(k) := 1 - F(k) \qquad (2.2.12)$$

$$F(k) := \mathbb{P}(\log(S_T/S_0) \le k) \qquad (2.2.13)$$

where $\log 0 := -\infty$.

In the special case that $\bar{F} \sim e^{-ak}$, one could hope to argue that

$$\tilde{p} = a - 1 \sim -\log \bar{F}(k)/k - 1 \qquad (2.2.14)$$

implies that (2.2.11) can be rewritten with $-\log \bar{F}/k - 1$ in place of $\tilde{p}$. One could conjecture more generally:

Conjecture 2. *For arbitrary* $\bar{F}$,

$$V^2(k)/k \sim \psi(-\log \bar{F}(k)/k - 1) \qquad (2.2.15)$$

We construct an example of an S_T distribution for which neither conjectural generalization holds. Actually, instead of directly specifying a distribution, we can specify the distribution's call prices, as function h of strike, provided that h satisfies condition (b) in:

Proposition 2.3. *Let* $h : [0, \infty) \to [0, \infty)$. *The following are equivalent:*

(a) *There exists (on some probability space) a nonnegative integrable random variable* S_T *such that* $(S_T - K)^+$ *has expectation* $h(K)$ *for all* K.
(b) *The function* $H(K) := h(K)\mathbb{I}_{K \ge 0} + (h(0) - K)\mathbb{I}_{K < 0}$ *is convex on* $\mathbb{R}$, *and* $\lim_{K \to \infty} h(K) = 0$.

To show that $(b) \Rightarrow (a)$, let S_T have distribution H'', which exists as a measure; we omit the details.

Proceeding with our example, let $S_0 = 1$ and choose $\beta \in (\psi(2), \psi(1))$. We will construct h such that

$$\mathbb{E}S_T^2 = \infty, \quad \text{hence} \limsup V^2(k)/k \ge \psi(1) > \beta \qquad (2.2.16)$$

but such that there exists $k_n \equiv \log K_n \to \infty$ with

$$h(K_n) = c_{BS}(k_n, \sqrt{\beta k_n}), \quad \text{hence} \liminf V^2(k)/k \le \beta \qquad (2.2.17)$$

and with

$$-h'(K_n+) \le K_n^{-3}, \text{ so } \psi(-\log \bar{F}(k_n)/k_n - 1) \le \psi(2) < \beta = \frac{V^2(k_n)}{k_n} \quad (2.2.18)$$

Indeed, let $K_0 := 0$, and $h(K_0) := S_0$. Given K_n and $h(K_n)$, define

$$K_{n+1} := K_n + \max(1/h(K_n), K_n^3 h(K_n))$$

$$h(K_{n+1}) := c_{BS}(k_{n+1}, \sqrt{\beta k_{n+1}})$$

For all $K \ne K_n$, define $h(K)$ by linear interpolation.

The (b) condition holds, so h induces a legitimate distribution. Conjecture 1 fails by 2.2.16 and 2.2.17. Conjecture 2 fails by 2.2.18.

Therefore, without additional assumptions, the moment formula *cannot be sharpened* in the sense of 2.2.11 or 2.2.15. The next section will impose the additional assumption of *regular variation* to obtain results of the form 2.2.11 or 2.2.15.

2.3 REGULAR VARIATION AND THE TAIL-WING FORMULA

The example of section 2.2.3 shows that if the distribution of S_T is allowed to concentrate its mass arbitrarily, then it disconnects the asymptotics of $\bar{F}$ from the asymptotics of c (and hence of V), and moreover it allows implied volatility to oscillate, separating lim sup from lim inf.

So in order to extend the moment formula in the sense of 2.2.11 or 2.2.15, we need to impose some additional regularity assumption on $\bar{F}$. A natural condition is that of *regular variation*.

Definition 2.4. *A positive measurable function g satisfying*

$$g(\lambda x)/g(x) \to 1, \quad x \to \infty$$

for all $\lambda > 0$ is said to be slowly varying.

In the following examples, let $p \in \mathbb{R}$ be a constant.

The following functions are slowly varying: any positive constant; the logarithm function; sums, products, and pth powers of slowly varying functions; any function asymptotically equivalent to a slowly varying function.

The following functions are not slowly varying: $2 + \sin x$ and x^p for $p \neq 0$.

Definition 2.5. *If* $g(x) = x^\alpha g_0(x)$ *where* g_0 *is slowly varying and* $\alpha \in \mathbb{R}$, *then we say that* g *is* regularly varying with index α *and we write* $g \in R_\alpha$.

With regular variation and a mild moment condition, Conjecture 2's conclusion holds, as shown by [11]:

Theorem 2.6. (Right-tail-wing formula). *Assume that* $\mathbb{E}S_T^{1+\varepsilon} < \infty$ *for some* $\varepsilon > 0$. *Let* φ *denote either the CCDF* $\bar{F}$ *in 2.2.12 or, if it exists, the density* f *of* $\log(S_T/S_0)$.
If $-\log\varphi \in R_\alpha$ *for some* $\alpha > 0$, *then*

$$V^2(k)/k \sim \psi(-\log c(k)/k) \sim \psi(-\log\varphi(k)/k - 1). \tag{2.3.1}$$

The tail-wing formula links tail-asymptotics of φ *on a logarithmic scale* (similar to the logarithmic scale of large deviations) and the implied volatility at extreme strikes.

2.3.1 Outline of Proof

Using Bingham's Lemma ([14], Theorem 4.2.10), it can be shown that, in the case $\varphi = f$,

$$-\log f(k) \sim -\log\bar{F}(k) \in R_\alpha, \tag{2.3.2}$$

and that hence it suffices to consider the case $\varphi = \bar{F}$.
The $\mathbb{E}S_T^{1+\varepsilon} < \infty$ assumption implies $-d_{1,2} \to \infty$. So

$$c(k) = \Phi(d_1) - e^k\Phi(d_2) \sim -\frac{1}{\sqrt{2\pi}\,d_1}e^{-d_1^2/2} + \frac{1}{\sqrt{2\pi}\,d_2}e^k e^{-d_2^2/2}$$

$$\sim \frac{1}{\sqrt{2\pi}}\left(-\frac{1}{d_1} + \frac{1}{d_2}\right)e^{-d_1^2/2}$$

Therefore,

$$\log c(k) \sim \log(1/d_2 - 1/d_1) - d_1^2/2 = \log(V/(k^2/V^2 - V^2/4)) - d_1^2/2$$
$$\sim -d_1^2/2 \tag{2.3.3}$$

where the last step is justified by $-\log \bar{F} \in R_\alpha$, or the weaker condition that $-\log c \in R_\alpha$, or the still weaker condition that $\liminf \log V / \log k > -\infty$. Now divide by $-k$ and apply ψ, to obtain the first relation in 2.3.1:

$$V^2(k)/k \sim \psi(-\log c(k)/k)$$

For the second relation in 2.3.1, write

$$c(k) = \mathbb{E}(S_T/S_0 - e^k)^+ = \int_{e^k}^\infty \bar{F}(\log y)\mathrm{d}y = \int_k^\infty e^{x+\log \bar{F}(x)}\mathrm{d}x \qquad (2.3.4)$$

Bingham's lemma states that, if $g \in R_\alpha$ with $\alpha > 0$, then

$$\log \int_k^\infty e^{-g(x)}\mathrm{d}x \sim -g(k) \qquad (2.3.5)$$

So verify that $-x - \log \bar{F}(x) \in R_\alpha$ and apply 2.3.5 to obtain

$$\log c(k) \sim \log \bar{F}(k) + k \qquad (2.3.6)$$

Divide by $-k$ and apply ψ to conclude. For a complete proof see [11].

2.3.2 Tail-Wing Formula for the Left Wing

To formulate the small-strike counterpart of Theorem 2.6, denote the S_0-normalized forward put price by $p(k) := \mathbb{E}(e^k - S_T/S_0)^+$.

Theorem 2.7. (Left-tail-wing formula). *Assume $\mathbb{E}S_T^{-\varepsilon} < \infty$ for some $\varepsilon > 0$. Let ϕ denote either the CDF F in 2.2.13 or, if it exists, the density f of $\log(S_T/S_0)$.*
If $-\log \phi(-k) \in R_\alpha$ for some $\alpha > 0$, then

$$V^2(-k)/k \sim \psi(-1 - \log p(-k)/k) \sim \psi(-\log \phi(-k)/k).$$

This follows from Theorem 2.6 and the measure-change argument of Section 2.2.2, using the symmetries: (2.2.9–2.2.10), and $\log c(k; 1/S, \mathbb{Q}) = \log p(-k; S; \mathbb{P}) + k$, and $\log f(k; 1/S, \mathbb{Q}) = \log f(-k; S, \mathbb{P}) - k$, and $\log \bar{F}(k; 1/S, \mathbb{Q}) \sim \log F(-k; S, \mathbb{P}) - k$. The extra arguments on c, p, f, F, $\bar{F}$ emphasize dependence on the underlier (S or $1/S$) and the measure ($\mathbb{P}$ or $\mathbb{Q}$).

2.4 RELATED RESULTS

This section extends the results of the previous two sections.

Let us write, as earlier, φ for the CCDF or the density of $X := \log(S_T/S_0)$. The tail-wing formula has the following consequences.

First, if $-\log\varphi(k)/k$ has limit $L \in [1, \infty)$, then the moment formula's lim sup is a genuine limit; this gives a sufficient condition for Conjecture 1's conclusion that

$$V^2(k)/k \to \psi(\bar{p}) = \psi(L-1) \qquad (2.4.1)$$

(For $L > 1$ the proof is by direct application of the tail-wing formula; for $L = 1$, the $\mathbb{E}S_t^{1+\varepsilon} < \infty$ assumption may fail, but the conclusion holds by dominating the tails of distributions having tail CCDF e^{-pk} for $p > 1$, for which the tail-wing formula *does* hold.) In turn, the question arises, of how to guarantee the convergence of $-\log\varphi(k)/k$. We answer this in section 4.1 by finding sufficient conditions on the moment generating function of X.

Second, if $-\log\varphi(k)/k \to \infty$ and Theorem 2.6's assumptions hold, then the $x \to \infty$ relation $\psi(x) \sim 1/(2x)$ implies

$$V^2(k)/k \sim 1/(-2\log\varphi(k)/k) \qquad (2.4.2)$$

which gives more precise information than the moment formula's conclusion that $V^2(k)/k \to 0$. Those assumptions entail that the log-return distribution decays faster than exponentially, but not *so* quickly that the R_α assumption fails. This excludes, for example, the case of exponential decay of the *underlying* S_T (hence *iterated* exponential decay of log-return), which requires a separate analysis, in section 4.2.

We may state left-hand versions of these results in terms of ϕ, the CDF or density of X. If $-\log\phi(-k)/k$ has limit $L \in [0, \infty)$ then $V^2(-k)/k \to \psi(L)$; if instead $-\log\phi(-k)/k \to \infty$, then $V^2(-k)/k \sim 1/(-2\log\phi(-k)/k)$, provided that Theorem 2.7's assumptions hold. With the change-of-measure argument seen earlier, we can and henceforth will restrict our discussion to the right tail.

2.4.1 MGFs and the Moment Formula

We first note that $\mathbb{E}S_T^r$ is a constant multiple of $M(r) := \mathbb{E}\left(e^{rX_T}\right)$, the moment generating function of X. For many models, such a moment-generating function (MGF) is available in closed form so that option pricing (and calibration in particular) can be based on fast Fourier methods [15, 31]. For our purposes, explicit knowledge of M allows one to read off the critical exponent

$$\tilde{r} := \sup\{r : M(r) < \infty\}$$

simply by spotting the first singularity in M for positive r. Assuming that $\tilde{r} \in (1, \infty)$, we see that $\tilde{p} = \tilde{r} - 1$ is exactly what is needed for the (right-hand) moment formula and so

$$\limsup_{k \to \infty} \frac{V^2(k)}{k} = \psi(\tilde{p}). \tag{2.4.3}$$

We are now looking for practical conditions which will guarantee that

$$\lim_{k \to \infty} \frac{V^2(k)}{k} = \psi(\tilde{p}). \tag{2.4.4}$$

If $-\log \varphi(k)/k$ converges to a limit in $(1, \infty)$, then $\varphi \in R_1$ and $\mathbb{E}S_T^{1+\varepsilon} < \infty$ for some $\varepsilon > 0$. All conditions of the tail-wing formula are satisfied, so 2.4.4 indeed follows. The problem with this criterion is that it requires knowledge of the tail asymptotics of φ which may be unknown. The good news is that the required tail asymptotics, at least on the logarithmic scale of interest to us, can be obtained from the MGF via Tauberian theory, in which conditions on a distribution's transform imply properties of the distribution. The following regularity criteria on the MGF will cover most, if not all, examples with known MGF of log-price, provided $\tilde{r} \in (1, \infty)$. In essence, Criterion I below says that M, or one of its derivatives, blows up in a regularly varying way as the argument approaches the critical value $\tilde{r}$. Criterion II deals with exponential blow up near $\tilde{r}$.

Criterion I. *For some integer $n \geq 0$ and some real $\rho > 0$,*

$$M^{(n)}(\tilde{r} - 1/s) \in R_\rho, \quad s \to \infty.$$

Criterion II. *For some real $\rho > 0$*

$$\log M(\tilde{r} - 1/s) \in R_\rho, \quad s \to \infty.$$

Theorem 2.8. *Let X be a real-valued random variable with moment generating function* $M(r) := \mathbb{E}\left(e^{r X_T}\right)$, *critical exponent* $\tilde{r} := \sup\{r : M(r) < \infty\} \in$

$(0, \infty)$ *and CCDF* $\bar{F}(k) := \mathbb{P}(X > k)$. *If M satisfies Criterion I or II then*

$$\lim_{k \to \infty} \frac{\log \bar{F}(k)}{k} = -\tilde{r}. \tag{2.4.5}$$

The main idea of the proof is an Esscher-type change of measure which reduces the problem to the application of a more standard Tauberian theorem (e.g., Karamata's Tauberian theorem for Criterion I). Theorem 2.8 really belongs to Tauberian theory and we refer to [12] for the proof, see also [9] for full asymptotics under further assumptions.

It must be emphasized that conclusion (2.4.5) fails if one omits the regularity criteria on M. (For a counterexample, consider the distribution specified by $\mathbb{P}(X \leq k) = 1 - \exp\{-e^{[\log k]}\}$, where $[\cdot]$ denotes the integer part of a real number). What remains true without regularity assumptions is a lim sup statement: by Chebyshev we have $\mathbb{P}(X > k) \leq e^{-rk}\mathbb{E}\left(e^{r X_T}\right)$ so that $\log \bar{F}(k) \leq -rk + \log M(r) \sim -rk$ for all $r \in (0, \tilde{r})$; it easily follows that

$$\limsup_{k \to \infty} \frac{\log \bar{F}(k)}{k} \leq -r$$

and, using the very definition of $\tilde{r}$, one sees that equality holds with $\tilde{r}$. A formal insertion in the tail-wing formula would bring us back to the moment formula in its lim sup form. More interestingly, we see that (2.4.5) leads in full rigor to 2.4.4. Omitting a similar "left-hand" formula we summarize our findings in

Theorem 2.9. (Right-hand moment formula, for regular MGFs). *Assume that* $X = \log (S_T/S_0)$ *has MGF M with critical exponent* $\tilde{r} \equiv \tilde{p} + 1 \in (1, \infty)$ *such that M satisfies Criterion I or II. Then*

$$V^2(k)/k \to \psi(\tilde{p}) \text{ as } k \to \infty.$$

2.4.2 Tail-Wing Formula for Exponential Decay

In Section 3 we discussed the limiting behavior of the implied volatility when the log of the distribution function of the returns is regularly varying. This condition is sometimes violated, for example if the log of the distribution function of the underlying is regularly varying, and therefore the distribution function of the returns will decay more quickly; we will discuss such an example below. Nonetheless, if one views the tail-wing formula as a meta-theorem in which the regular variation condition is replaced by the (undefined) "reasonable tail-behavior" one can hope that the tail-wing formula still gives the correct result. We will now prove this for another type of "reasonable tail behavior."

We will make the following assumption on the distribution of the underlying:

Assumption 1. *The log of the distribution function of the underlying is regularly varying with positive exponent. That is:*

$$-\log \bar{F}_{S_T} \in R_\alpha \quad for \quad \alpha > 0.$$

To compare with the assumption we made originally, note that this implies that the distribution function of the returns satisfies:

$$\log\{-\log \bar{F}_{\log S_T/S_0}(x)\} \sim \alpha x. \tag{2.4.6}$$

If we assume this, a straightforward application of Bingham's lemma allows us to obtain an expression for the call price in the large strike limit:

Lemma 2.10. *Under Assumption 1, the call price $C(K)$ as a function of strike satisfies:*

$$\log C(K) \sim \log \bar{F}_{S_T}(K) \, as \, K \to \infty$$

Proof. Using Fubini,

$$C(K) = \mathbb{E}(S_T - K)^+ = \mathbb{E}\int_K^\infty \mathbb{I}(S_T > u)\mathrm{d}u = \int_K^\infty \bar{F}_{S_T}(u)\mathrm{d}u.$$

The result follows from Bingham's lemma.

To use this to analyse the implied volatility, we need to approximate the Black-Scholes formula in the range of interest to us. The calculations in the proof of the tail-wing formula do not apply directly to our case because the assumptions behind (2.3.3) are violated here. We note that the implied volatility for a model satisfying Assumption 1 is bounded as the strike goes to infinity because the density must ultimately be dominated by any Gaussian density. We can therefore use the following approximation.

Lemma 2.11. *Given any $\varepsilon > 0$ and $\bar{\sigma} > 0$, there exists a real number k_1 such that for all $k > k_1$ and for all $0 < \sigma < \bar{\sigma}$,*

$$-(1+\varepsilon)\frac{k^2}{2\sigma^2} \leq \log c_{BS}(k,\sigma) \leq -(1-\varepsilon)\frac{k^2}{2\sigma^2}.$$

Proof. The Black-Scholes formula satisfies

$$c_{BS}(k,\sigma) > c_{BS}(k(1+\varepsilon),\sigma)$$

$$= \Phi\left(-\frac{k(1+\varepsilon)}{\sigma} + \frac{\sigma}{2}\right) - e^{k(1+\varepsilon)}\Phi\left(-\frac{k(1+\varepsilon)}{\sigma} - \frac{\sigma}{2}\right)$$

and the normal distribution function Φ has the following well-known bounds, obtainable by integration by parts (or other methods):

$$\frac{e^{-x^2/2}}{\sqrt{2\pi}x}\left(1 - \frac{1}{x^2}\right) \leq \Phi(-x) \leq \frac{e^{-x^2/2}}{\sqrt{2\pi}x}, \quad x > 0 \qquad (2.4.7)$$

Therefore, for $k > \bar{\sigma}^2$ and $0 < \sigma < \bar{\sigma}$,

$$c_{BS}(k,\sigma) > \frac{e^{-(k(1+\varepsilon)/\sigma-\sigma/2)^2/2}}{\sqrt{2\pi}} Err(k,\sigma)$$

where

$$Err(k,\sigma) := \frac{1}{k(1+\varepsilon)/\sigma - \sigma/2} - \frac{1}{k(1+\varepsilon)/\sigma + \sigma/2} - \frac{1}{(k(1+\varepsilon)/\sigma - \sigma/2)^3}$$

$$= \frac{\sigma^3}{k^2(1+\varepsilon)^2 - \sigma^4/4} - \frac{\sigma^3}{(k(1+\varepsilon) - \sigma^2/2)^3}$$

satisfies

$$|Err(k,\sigma)| \leq \frac{\bar{\sigma}^3}{k^2(1+\varepsilon)^2 - \bar{\sigma}^4/4} + \frac{\bar{\sigma}^3}{(k(1+\varepsilon) - \bar{\sigma}^2/2)^3} = O\left(\frac{1}{k^2}\right)$$

as $k \to \infty$, uniformly in σ. Taking logs, we have

$$\log c_{BS}(k, \sigma) > -\frac{1}{2}\left(\frac{k(1+\varepsilon)}{\sigma} - \frac{\sigma}{2}\right)^2 + O(\log k)$$

$$> -\frac{k^2(1+\varepsilon)^2}{2\sigma^2} + \frac{k}{2} - \frac{\bar{\sigma}^2}{8} + O(\log k)$$

$$= -\frac{k^2(1+\varepsilon)^2}{2\sigma^2} + O(k)$$

as required.

For the upper bound, observe that for $k > \bar{\sigma}^2$ and $0 < \sigma < \bar{\sigma}$,

$$c_{BS}(k, \sigma) < \Phi\left(-\frac{k}{\sigma} + \frac{\sigma}{2}\right) \leq \frac{1}{\sqrt{2\pi}}e^{-(k/\sigma - \sigma/2)^2/2}\frac{\sigma}{k - \sigma^2/2}$$

where the last inequality follows again from 2.4.7. So

$$\frac{\sigma}{k - \sigma^2/2} \leq \frac{\bar{\sigma}}{k - \bar{\sigma}^2/2} = O\left(\frac{1}{k}\right)$$

as $k \to \infty$. Taking logs, we have

$$\log c_{BS}(k, \sigma) < -\frac{1}{2}\left(\frac{k}{\sigma} - \frac{\sigma}{2}\right)^2 + O(\log k)$$

$$= -\frac{k^2}{2\sigma^2} + O(k)$$

as required.

Combining the lemmas yields

Theorem 2.12. ([10]). *Under Assumption 1,*

$$V^2(k) \sim \frac{k^2}{-2\log \bar{F}_{S_T}(e^k)} = \frac{k^2}{-2\log \bar{F}_{\log S_T}(k)} \text{ as } k \to \infty$$

Proof. Because V is bounded for k large enough, Lemma 2.11 implies that, for any $\varepsilon > 0$, for k large enough,

$$-(1 - \varepsilon)\frac{k^2}{2\log c_{BS}(k, V(k))} \leq V^2(k) \leq -(1 + \varepsilon)\frac{k^2}{2\log c_{BS}(k, V(k))}$$

hence

$$V^2(k) \sim \frac{k^2}{-2\log c_{BS}(k, V(k))} \sim \frac{k^2}{-2\log \bar{F}_{S_T}(e^k)}$$

by Lemma 2.10.

2.5 APPLICATIONS

2.5.1 Exponential Lévy Models

We first note that the recent Lévy-tail estimates from Albin-Bengtsson [1, 2], in conjunction with the tail-wing formula, allow to compute the implied volatility asymptotics of virtually *all* exponential Lévy models, regardless of whether the underlying has finite moments of all orders. Only in the latter case do moment formulae (in the regular MGF form or not) give quantitative information. A nice example where all methods discussed work is *Barndorff-Nielsen's Normal Inverse Gaussian model* in which $X = \log(S_T/S_0) \sim NIG(\alpha, \beta, \mu T, \delta T)$. The moment-generating function is given by

$$M(r) = \exp\left[T\left(\delta\left\{\sqrt{\alpha^2 - \beta^2} - \sqrt{\alpha^2 - (\beta + r)^2}\right\} + \mu r\right)\right]$$

When r approaches $\tilde{r} = \alpha - \beta$ the argument of the second square-root approaches the branching point singularity 0. It then follows from the moment formula that

$$\limsup_{k \to \infty} V^2(k)/k = \psi(\tilde{p}) \quad \text{with } \tilde{p} = \tilde{r} - 1$$

Observe that $M(r)$ does not blow up as $r \uparrow \tilde{r}$ but its first derivative does. Indeed, $M'(\tilde{r} - 1/s) \sim 2\delta\alpha\sqrt{2\alpha}s^{1/2}M(\tilde{r})$ as $s \to \infty$ and we see that Criterion I holds with $n = 1$ and the regular MGF moment formula implies $\lim_{k \to \infty} V^2(k)/k = \psi(\tilde{p})$. Alternatively, one can take a direct route as follows. It is known, from [8] and the references therein, that X has density f with asymptotics

$$f(k) \sim C |k|^{-3/2} e^{-\alpha|k|+\beta k} \text{ as } k \to \pm\infty$$

These are more than enough to see that $-\log f$ is regularly varying (with index 1) and $-\log f(k)/k \to \alpha - \beta$ as $k \to +\infty$. The right-tail-wing formula now leads to $V^2(k)/k \to \psi(\alpha - \beta - 1)$ which is, of course, in agreement with our findings above.

Among the Lévy examples to which one can apply the regular MGF moment formula (with Criterion I, $n = 0$), we mention *Carr-Madan's Variance Gamma model*. An example to which Criterion II applies is given by *Kou's Double Exponential model*. See [12] for details.

As remarked earlier, in models in which the underlying has finite moments of all orders moment formulae only give sublinear behavior of implied variance, namely $V^2(k)/k \to 0$; whereas the tail-wing formula still provides a complete asymptotic answer. Among the exponential Lévy examples with sublinear behavior of implied variance, we mention the *Black-Scholes model* as a sanity check example, *Merton's jump diffusion* as a borderline example in which the sublinear behavior comes from a subtle logarithmic correction term, and *Carr-Wu's Finite Moment Logstable model* for which tail asymptotics can be derived by Kasahara's Tauberian theorem. All these examples are discussed in detail in [11].

2.5.2 Time-Changed Lévy Models

Consider a Lévy process $L = L(t)$ described through its cumulant generating function (CGF) at time 1, denoted by K_L where

$$K_L(v) = \log \mathbb{E}\left[\exp\left(vL_1\right)\right]$$

and an independent random clock $\tau = \tau(\omega) \geq 0$ with CGF K_τ.

It follows that the MGF of $X \equiv L \circ \tau$ is given by

$$M(v) = \mathbb{E}\left[\mathbb{E}\left(e^{vL_\tau}|\tau\right)\right] = \mathbb{E}\left[e^{K_L(v)\tau}\right] = \exp\left[K_\tau(K_L(v))\right]$$

Frequently used random clocks [36, 12] are the *Gamma-Ornstein-Uhlenbeck* clock and the *Cox-Ingersoll-Ross* clock. More information on time-changed Lévy processes can be found in the textbooks [35, 16].

What matters for our purposes is that the MGF is explicitly known (provided K_τ and K_L are explicitly known) so that one can hope to apply the moment formula (for regular MGFs) in order to understand the implied volatility at extreme strikes for such models. The following result translates the regularity conditions (i.e., Criteria I and II) on M into "manageable" conditions in terms of K_τ, K_L. (The algebraic expression for M may be explicit but can be complicated!)

Define $M_\tau \equiv \exp(K_\tau)$ and $M_L \equiv \exp(K_L)$ and set

$$\tilde{r}_L = \sup\{r : M_L(r) < \infty\}, \tilde{r}_\tau = \sup\{r : M_\tau(r) < \infty\}.$$

We then have the following result (a similar "left-hand" result is omitted).

Theorem 2.13. *Let* $\bar{F}$ *denote the CCDF of* $X = L \circ \tau$. *Assume* $\tilde{r}_L, \tilde{r}_\tau \in (0, \infty)$. *If both* M_τ, M_L *satisfy Criterion I or II, then* M *does.*

Moreover, if $K_L(r) = \tilde{r}_\tau$ *for some* $r \in [0, \tilde{r}_L]$ *then* $r = \tilde{r}$, *the critical exponent of* M. *Otherwise, if* $K_L(r) < \tilde{r}_\tau$ *for all* $r \in [0, \tilde{r}_L]$, *then* $\tilde{r}_L = \tilde{r}$. *Either way, we have*

$$V^2(k)/k \sim \psi(\tilde{p}) \text{ with } \tilde{p} = \tilde{r} - 1.$$

The proof is little more than a careful analysis of $\exp[K_\tau(K_L(v))]$ with regard to our MGF regularity criteria, and is found in [12]. In the same paper, as illustration and straightforward application of the last theorem, the *Variance Gamma with Gamma-OU time change* and *Normal Inverse Gaussian with Cox Ingersoll-Ros (CIR) time* models are discussed. Applied with parameters obtained from real-world market calibrations, the asymptotic regime for the implied volatility becomes visible at a remarkably low level of moneyness k and several plots are given in [12].

2.5.3 Heston Model

Heston's stochastic volatility model seems to require no introduction these days! It suffices to say that its MGF M is known (see [25] for instance), and a direct analysis shows that the moment formula (for regular MGFs) is applicable. (For zero correlation, the Heston model becomes a Brownian motion run with an independent CIR clock, which falls into the previous section of time-changed Lévy models, simplifying the discussion a bit.) The critical exponent of M is computed by Andersen-Piterbarg [3]; the authors then apply the original moment formula with lim sup statements. Tail asymptotics for the Heston models are also known [20].

2.6 CEV AND SABR

We now discuss the constant elasticity of variance (CEV) model, followed by its extension to stochastic volatility, the SABR model [26]. Both are of interest to practitioners, and both have an interesting behavior of implied volatility at extreme strikes.

2.6.1 CEV Model

This model generates a skew via the stochastic differential equation

$$dS_t = \sigma S_t^{1-\beta} dW_t$$

where σ and $\beta \in (0, 1)$ are constants. (When $\beta > 1/2$, boundary conditions at zero have to be specified.) The density in this model can be written explicitly in terms of the modified Bessel function [18], but the following heuristic argument using large deviation theory (which has in common with the tail-wing formula the same crude, logarithmic scale) may be more enlightening. Large deviations for stochastic differential equations (also known as Freidlin-Wentzell theory [19, 38]) describe the family of solutions when dW_t above is replaced by ϵdW_t (or equivalently, the Brownian motion is run at speed $\epsilon^2 t$). Closely related are the Varadhan asymptotics for diffusions which have been used in the context of the implied volatility smile in [5, 6, 13].

In general, asymptotic probabilities as $\epsilon \to 0$ are unrelated to the behavior of spacial asymptotic probabilities of the form $\{S_T > K\}$ with $K \to \infty$. In the CEV model, however, one can switch from the $K \to \infty$ regime to the $\epsilon \to 0$ regime by a scaling property. To wit,

$$d\tilde{S} \equiv d(S/K) = \sigma(S/K)^{1-\beta}\epsilon dW = \sigma \tilde{S}^{1-\beta}\epsilon dW,$$

with $\epsilon = 1/K^\beta \to 0$ for K large. From Freidlin-Wentzell's estimate, now writing S^ϵ for $\tilde{S}$,

$$\epsilon^2 \log \mathbb{P}(S_T^\epsilon > 1) \sim -\frac{1}{2T}d^2(S_0^\epsilon, 1) \sim -\frac{1}{2T}d^2(0, 1)$$

as $S_0^\epsilon \to 0$, where $d(0, 1)$ is the Riemannian distance from 0 to 1 given by

$$d(0, 1) = \int_0^1 \frac{1}{\sigma x^{1-\beta}}dx = \frac{1}{\beta\sigma}.$$

The geodesic connecting S_0^ϵ and 1 stays away from the boundary at zero. Hence, we don't expect boundary conditions at zero to play a role for the right tail. Unwrapping the definition leads to

$$\log \mathbb{P}(S_T > K) \sim -\frac{K^{2\beta}}{2\beta^2\sigma^2 T}, \tag{2.6.1}$$

which can alternatively be derived, rigorously, from the explicitly known density of S_T. As a consistency check, note that (2.6.1) recovers normal "Bachelier" asymptotics in the case $\beta = 1$.

If we express this in terms of moneyness $k = \log(K/S_0)$ then $\{S_T > K\} = \{\log(S_T/S_0) > k\}$ and the probability of this event decays exponentially fast as $k \to \infty$, so that the CCDF is *not* of regular variation. This is one of the rare examples we are aware of where an application of the tail-wing formula as stated in section 3 is not justified.

What *does* apply here is Theorem 2.12, which completes rigorously the proof of

$$V^2(k)/k \sim k(S_0 e^k)^{-2\beta}\sigma^2\beta^2 T \text{ as } k \to \infty, \tag{2.6.2}$$

a relationship reported in [22].

2.6.2 SABR Model

Combining the CEV model with stochastic volatility, the SABR model is defined by the dynamics

$$dS_t = \sigma_t S_t^c dW_t^1 \tag{2.6.3}$$

$$d\sigma_t = \varepsilon\sigma_t dW_t^2 \tag{2.6.4}$$

where ε and $c \leq 1$ are constants, and W^1 and W^2 are Brownian motions with correlation ρ. This model is popular partly because it has an explicit solution for call prices in the limit as time to maturity tends to 0, and this can be used to produce an expansion in time to maturity for the implied volatility that is accurate as long as log strike and time are not too large.

The expansion for annualized implied volatility in the case $c = 1$ is as follows (see [26]):

$$\frac{V(k)}{\sqrt{T}} \approx \sigma_{SABR}(k, T) := \frac{\sigma_0 z}{x(z)}\left(1 + \left(\frac{1}{4}\rho\varepsilon\sigma_0 + \frac{2 - 3\rho^2}{24}\varepsilon^2\right)T\right),$$

$$x(z) := \log\left(\frac{\sqrt{1 - 2\rho z + z^2} + z - \rho}{1 - \rho}\right)$$

where $z := -\varepsilon k/\sigma_0$. After some simplification it becomes clear that, as $|k| \to \infty$,

$$\sigma_{SABR}(k, T) \sim \frac{\varepsilon|k|}{\sigma_0 \log|k|} \left(1 + \left(\frac{1}{4}\rho\varepsilon\sigma_0 + \frac{2 - 3\rho^2}{24}\varepsilon^2\right) T\right)$$

which is incompatible with Theorems 2.1 and 2.2, and so the approximation $\sigma_{SABR}(k, T)$ cannot be accurate in the large $|k|$ regime. Interestingly, it was proved in [13] that $\sigma_{SABR}(k, 0)$ equals the $T \to 0$ limit of implied volatility, which demonstrates that the limits $T \to 0$ and $k \to \pm\infty$ are not interchangeable in general.

For large $|k|$, therefore, we turn to the techniques presented in this article. However, because neither the moment generating function nor the distribution function is known for SABR, we need to approximate one of these to apply our results. Let us consider the MGF.

The expression for $c < 1$ is similar, but uses a power series expansion in k, which diverges in the limits we are looking at, so we will not discuss it here. The tail behavior in this model depends on the value of c. When $c = 1$, we can determine which moments of S_T are finite, and use the moment formula. Solving 2.6.3 and 2.6.4, we have

$$S_t = S_0 \exp\left(\int_0^t \sigma_s \mathrm{d}W_s^1 - \frac{1}{2}\int_0^t \sigma_s^2 \, \mathrm{d}s\right)$$

$$\sigma_t = \sigma_0 \exp(\varepsilon W_t^2 - \varepsilon^2 t/2)$$

Taking the expectation of S_T^p conditional on W^2, we have

$$\mathbb{E}[S_T^p] = \mathbb{E}[\mathbb{E}[S_T^p | W^2]]$$

$$= S_0^p \exp\left(p\rho\int_0^T \sigma_s \, \mathrm{d}W_s^2 + \frac{p^2(1 - p^2) - p}{2}\int_0^T \sigma_s^2 \, \mathrm{d}s\right)$$

$$= S_0^p \mathbb{E} \exp\left(\frac{p\rho(\sigma_T - \sigma_0)}{\varepsilon} + \frac{p^2(1 - p^2) - p}{2}\int_0^T \sigma_s^2 \, \mathrm{d}s\right). \quad (2.6.5)$$

Because $\mathbb{E}\exp(a\int_0^T \sigma_s^2 \mathrm{d}s) = \infty$ for any positive a and T (see for example [3]), we would expect 2.6.5 to be infinite whenever the coefficient of $\int_0^T \sigma_s^2 \mathrm{d}s$ (which we would expect to dominate the σ_T term) in 2.6.5 is positive. This would imply that, for $\rho \leq 0$, we have

$$\mathbb{E}[S_T^p] = \infty \text{ iff } p > 1/(1 - \rho^2) \text{ or } p < 0. \quad (2.6.6)$$

For $p > 1, \rho < 0$, this is indeed proved in [32], Theorem 2.3; the case $p > 1, \rho = 0$ follows directly from 2.6.5 as does the case $p < 0, \rho \leq 0$ since in that case the coefficients of σ_T and $\int_0^T \sigma_s^2 ds$ appearing in 2.6.5 are ≥ 0 resp. > 0. In summary, the moment formula then implies

$$\limsup_{k \to \infty} V^2(k)/k = \psi \left(\frac{1}{1 - \rho^2} - 1 \right)$$

and

$$\limsup_{k \to \infty} V^2(-k)/k = \psi(0) = 2$$

which concludes the analysis of the case $c = 1$. By [29, 37], if $\rho > 0$ and $c = 1$, then S would not be a martingale.

Now consider the case $c < 1$. Because S can reach 0 with positive probability, we assume, as usual, an absorbing boundary condition at 0, which leads to

$$\lim_{k \to \infty} V^2(-k)/k = 2.$$

Note that for $c \in (1/2, 1)$ this is the only possible boundary condition, and for $c \leq 1/2$ this is the only possibility that ensures that S_t is a martingale.

The lim sup statement is clear. To see that one has a genuine lim it suffices to compare put prices (in the small strike limit) with those obtained from a model where returns decay like $exp(-p|k|)$ as $k \to \infty$. By monotonicity of the Black-Scholes prices in volatility, and the tail-wing formula applied to the "comparison-model," this leads to

$$\liminf_{k \to \infty} V^2(-k)/k \to \psi(p),$$

for all $p > 0$. As p tends to zero, the right-hand-side approaches 2, which finishes the argument.

To calculate the right wing, we need a sufficiently good approximation for the distribution function of S_T, which we will obtain below (via Kasahara's Tauberian theorem) from a sufficiently good approximation of the moment generating function of $\log S_T$ (equivalently, the moments of S_T). Andersen and Piterbarg [3, Prop 5.2] calculated the upper bounds

$$\mathbb{E}[S_t^p] \leq \left[S_0^{2(1-c)} + (1-c)(p-1) \int_0^t \mathbb{E}(\sigma_s^{p/(1-c)})^{2(1-c)/p} ds \right]^{\frac{p}{2(1-c)}}$$

Therefore, we have

$$\limsup_{p \to \infty} \frac{\log \mathbb{E}[S_T^p]}{p^2} \leq \limsup_{p \to \infty} \frac{1}{2p(1-c)} \log \int_0^T \mathbb{E}(\sigma_s^{p/(1-c)})^{2(1-c)/p} ds$$

$$= \limsup_{p \to \infty} \frac{1}{2p(1-c)} \log \int_0^T e^{(p^2/(1-c)^2 - p/(1-c))\varepsilon^2 s(1-c)/p} ds$$

$$\leq \limsup_{p \to \infty} \frac{1}{2p(1-c)} \left(\frac{p}{1-c} - 1 \right) \varepsilon^2 T = \frac{\varepsilon^2 T}{2(1-c)^2}$$

$$(2.6.7)$$

To apply the tail-wing formula, we need to show that this bound is sharp enough. We can do so, at least when the correlation ρ is 0, which we shall assume from here on. We do emphasize, however, that $\rho = 0$ still allows for skew in the implied volatility.

Proposition 2.14. *Assume $\rho = 0$. For $n \in \mathbb{N}$ define $p_n = 1 + 2(1-c)n$. Then we have the lower bound*

$$\mathbb{E}[S_T^{p_n}] \geq S_0 \sigma_0^{2n} \varepsilon^{-2n} e^{(4n^2 - 2n)\varepsilon^2 T/2} (1 + O(e^{-n})) \prod_{i=1}^n \frac{p_i(p_i - 1)}{2n^2 - n - 2(i-1)^2 + (i-1)}$$

Proof. By Itô's formula,

$$S_t^p - S_0^p = \int_0^t p S_s^{p-1} S_s^c \sigma_s dW_s^1 + \int_0^t p \frac{p-1}{2} S_s^{p-2} S_s^{2c} \sigma_s^2 ds.$$

We now take expectations conditional on the second Brownian motion W^2 and see that

$$E[S_t^p | W^2] \geq \int_0^t p \frac{p-1}{2} E[S_s^{p-2+2c} | W^2] \sigma_s^2 ds$$

Note that the first integral disappeared because it is a martingale, on the filtration of W^1 which is independent of W^2, using the fact that σ and S have finite moments of all orders. Then

$$\mathbb{E}[S_t^{p_1} | W^2] \geq \int_0^t p_1 \frac{p_1 - 1}{2} \mathbb{E}[S_s | W^2] \sigma_s^2 ds = \int_0^t p_1 \frac{p_1 - 1}{2} S_0 \sigma_s^2 ds$$

and the same reasoning yields the recurrence relation

$$\mathbb{E}[S_t^{p_n}|W^2] \geq \int_0^t p_n \frac{p_n - 1}{2} \mathbb{E}[S_s^{p_{n-1}}|W^2]\sigma_s^2 ds$$

By iteration and taking the total expectation, we can therefore bound the p_n^{th} moments. Moreover, because σ_s/σ_u and σ_u are independent for $s > u$, it is relatively easy to do so. This leads us to

$$\mathbb{E}[S_T^{p_n}] \geq S_0\sigma_0^{2n}\varepsilon^{-2n}e^{(4n^2-2n)\varepsilon^2 T/2}(1 + O(e^{-n})) \prod_{i=1}^{n} \frac{p_i(p_i - 1)}{2n^2 - n - 2(i-1)^2 + (i-1)}$$

where $O(e^{-n})$ depends tacitly on T.

Now, for each p, define $N(p)$ to be the integer such that

$$p \in [p_{N(p)}, p_{N(p)+1}) \equiv [1 + 2(1 - c)N(p), 1 + 2(1 - c)(N(p) + 1))$$

Then

$$\liminf_{p\to\infty} \frac{\log \mathbb{E}[S_T^p]}{p^2} \geq \liminf_{p\to\infty} \frac{\log \mathbb{E}[S_T^{p_{N(p)}}]}{p^2}$$

$$= \liminf_{p\to\infty} \frac{2[N(p)]^2\varepsilon^2 T}{p^2} = \frac{\varepsilon^2 T}{2(1 - c)^2}$$

Combining this with (2.6.7), we obtain

$$\log \mathbb{E}[S_T^p] = \log \mathbb{E}[\exp(p\log S_T)] \sim \frac{\varepsilon^2 T}{(1 - c)^2} \times \frac{p^2}{2}$$

which matches the growth of the MGF of a standard Gaussian with variance $\varepsilon^2 T/(1 - c)^2$. One suspects that the CCDF of $\log S_T$, denoted by $\bar{F}_{\log S_T}$, has (at least at logarithmic scale) a matching Gaussian tail, that is,

$$-\log \bar{F}_{\log S_T}(k) \sim \frac{(1 - c)^2}{2\varepsilon^2 T}k^2$$

We now make this rigorous via *Kasahara's exponential Tauberian theorem* [14, Theorem 4.12.7, p. 253].

Theorem 2.15. (Kasahara). *Let μ be a measure on $(0, \infty)$ such that*

$$M(\lambda) := \int_0^\infty e^{\lambda x} d\mu(x) < \infty$$

for all $\lambda > 0$. If $0 < \alpha < 1$, $\phi \in R_\alpha$, put $\theta(\lambda) := \lambda/\phi(\lambda) \in R_{1-\alpha}$.
   Then, for $B > 0$,

$$-\log \mu(x, \infty) \sim B\phi^{\leftarrow}(x) \text{ as } x \to \infty$$

if and only if

$$\log M(\lambda) \sim (1 - \alpha)(\alpha/B)^{\alpha/(1-\alpha)}\theta^{\leftarrow}(\lambda) \text{ as } \lambda \to \infty$$

where $f^{\leftarrow}$ denotes the generalized inverse of f.

   If we let $\mu(x, y) = \mathbb{P}[S_T \in (x, y)]$, $\phi(x) = x^{1/2} = \theta(x)$, $B = (1 - c)^2/(2\varepsilon^2 T)$, and $\alpha = 1/2$, then

$$\log M(p) \sim \log \mathbb{E}\left[\exp\left(p \log S_T\right)\right] \sim \frac{\varepsilon^2 T}{(1 - c)^2} \times \frac{p^2}{2},$$

and so

$$-\log \bar{F}_{\log S_T}(k) \sim -\log \mu(k, \infty) \sim \frac{(1 - c)^2}{2\varepsilon^2 T}k^2,$$

as expected.
   The right-tail wing formula now leads immediately to the following result as conjectured by Piterbarg in [33].

Proposition 2.16. ([10]). *Let $V(k)$ denote the (unannualized) implied volatility for the SABR model with $\rho = 0$ and $c < 1$. Then*

$$\lim_{k\to\infty} V^2(k) = \frac{\varepsilon^2 T}{(1 - c)^2}$$

Remark 2.17. *Hagan, Lesniewski, and Woodward [27] (see also [13, 4]) find that the pdf of S_t is "approximately" Gaussian with respect to distance:*

$$d(S_0, S) = \frac{1}{\varepsilon} \log \frac{\sqrt{\zeta^2 - 2\rho\zeta + 1} + \zeta - \rho}{1 - \rho},$$

$$\zeta = \frac{\varepsilon}{\sigma_0} \int_{S_0}^{S} \frac{1}{u^c} du \sim \frac{\varepsilon}{\sigma_0} \frac{S^{1-c}}{1 - c}.$$

To compare with our result above, let $\rho = 0$. Then, as $S \to \infty$,

$$d(S_0, S) \sim \frac{1}{\varepsilon} \log \zeta \sim \frac{1-c}{\varepsilon} \log S$$

and

$$-\log \mathbb{P}\left(S_T \in dS\right) \approx \frac{1}{2T} d\left(S_0, S\right)^2 \sim \frac{(1-c)^2}{2\varepsilon^2 T}\left(\log S\right)^2$$

If f denotes the pdf of $\log S_t$, this easily implies that

$$-\log f(k) \sim \frac{(1-c)^2}{2\varepsilon^2 T} k^2$$

and the tail-wing formula gives the same asymptotic implied volatility as Kasahara's Tauberian theorem above. Heat-kernel estimates may provide the key to make such heuristics rigorous and extend the discussion to arbitrary stochastic volatility models. For stochastic volatility models with specific structure, smile asymptotics have been discussed early on, see [24, 7]. We also note that heat-kernel bounds have been explored (e.g.,[22]) toward large strike asymptotics of implied volatility in local volatility models.

ACKNOWLEDGEMENT

The first two authors gratefully acknowledge financial support from the Cambridge Endowment for Research in Finance (CERF) and would like to thank Chris Rogers and Nick Bingham for related discussions. All of us would like to thank Jim Gatheral and Marco Avellaneda. Finally, it is our pleasure to thank Peter Laurence for suggesting final improvements.

REFERENCES

1. Albin, J. M. P., and M. Bengtsson. On the asymptotic behaviour of Levy processes. Part I: Subexponential and exponential processes. To appear in *Stochastic Processes and Their Applications*.
2. Albin, J. M. P., and M. Bengtsson. (2005). On the asymptotic behaviour of Levy processes. Part II: Superexponential Processes. Preprint.
3. Andersen, L. B. G., and V. V. Piterbarg. (2005). Moment explosions in stochastic volatility models. Available at Social Science Research Network: http://ssrn.com/abstract=559481.

4. Avellaneda, M. (2005). From SABR to geodesics. Presentation.

5. Avellaneda, M., D. Boyer-Olson, J. Busca, and P. K. Friz. (2003). Application of large deviation methods to the pricing of index options in finance. *Comptes Rendus Mathematique* 336(3): 263–266.

6. Avellaneda, M., D. Boyer-Olson, J. Busca, and P. K. Friz. (2003). Reconstruction of volatility: pricing index options using the steepest-descent approximation. *Risk* 91–95.

7. Avellaneda, M., and Y. Zhu. (1998). A risk-neutral stochastic volatility model. *International Journal of Theoretical and Applied Finance* 1(2): 289–310, April.

8. Barndorff-Nielsen, O. E. (1998). Processes of normal inverse Gaussian type. *Finance and Stochastics* 2(1): 41–68.

9. Barndorff-Nielsen, O., J. Kent, and M. Sorensen. (1982). Normal variance—mean mixtures and z distributions. *International Statistical Review* 50(2): 145–159.

10. Benaim, S. (2007). Regular variation and smile asymptotics. PhD thesis, Cambridge University.

11. Benaim, S., and P. K. Friz. Regular variation and smile asymptotics. *Mathematical Finance* (to appear).

12. Benaim, S., and P. K. Friz. Smile asymptotics II: Models with known MGFs. *Journal of Applied Probability* (to appear).

13. Berestycki, H., J. Busca, and I. Florent. (2004). Computing the implied volatility in stochastic volatility models. *Communications on Pure and Applied Mathematics* 57: 0001–0022.

14. Bingham, N. H., C. M. Goldie, and J. L. Teugels. (1987). *Regular Variation*. Cambridge: Cambridge University Press.

15. Carr, P., and D. Madan. (1999). Option valuation using the fast Fourier transform. *Journal of Computational Finance* 3: 463–520.

16. Cont, R., and P. Tankov. (2004). *Financial Modelling with Jump Processes*. London: CRC Press.

17. Carr, P., and L. Wu. (2004). The finite moment log stable process and option pricing. *Journal of Finance* 58(2): 753–778.

18. Davydov, D., and V. Linetsky. (2001). Pricing and hedging path-dependent options under the CEV process. *Management Science* 47(7): 949–965.

19. Deuschel, J.-D., and D. W. Stroock. (1989). Large Deviations. Boston: Academic Press.

20. Dragulescu, A. A., and V. M. Yahovenko. (2002). Probability distribution of returns in the Heston model with stochastic volatility. *Quantitative Finance* 2(6): 443–453.

21. Embrechts, P., J. L. Jensen, M. Maejima, and J. L. Teugels. (1985). Approximations for compound Poisson and Pólya processes. *Advances in Applied Probability* 17: 623–637.

22. Forde, M. (2006). Tail asymptotics for diffusion processes, with applications to local volatility and CEV-Heston models. Available at http://arxiv.org/pdf/math/0608634.

23. Feigin, Y. Z. (1983). On a strong Tauberian result. *Zeitschrift für Wahrscheinlichkeitstheorie und verwandte Gebiete* 65: 35–48.
24. Gatheral, J. (2000). Rational shapes of the volatility surface. Presentation.
25. Gatheral, J. (2006). *The Volatility Surface: A Practitioner's Guide*. Hoboken, NJ: John Wiley & Sons.
26. Hagan, P., D. Kumar, A. Lesniewski, and D. Woodward. (2002). Managing smile risk. Available at www.wilmott.com/pdfs/021118_smile.pdf.
27. Hagan, P., A. Lesniewski,, and D. Woodward. (2005). Probability distribution in the SABR model of stochastic volatility. Preprint.
28. Henry-Labordere, P. (2005). A general asymptotic implied volatility for stochastic volatility models. April. Available at Social Science Research Network: http://ssrn.com/abstract=698601.
29. Jourdain, B. (2004). Loss of martingality in asset price models with lognormal stochastic volatility. CERMICS preprint no. 27.
30. Lee, R. (2004). The moment formula for implied volatility at extreme strikes. *Mathematical Finance* 14(3): 469–480.
31. Lee, R. (2004). Option pricing by transform methods: Extensions, unification, and error control. *Journal of Computational Finance* 7(3) (Spring): 51–86.
32. Lions, P. L., and M. Musiela. (2007). Correlations and bounds for stochastic volatility models. *Annales de l'Institut Henri Poincaré* 24: 1–16.
33. Piterbarg, V. V. (2004). Implied volatility smile asymptotics when all moments are finite. Working paper.
34. Revuz, D., and M. Yor. (1989). *Continuous Martingales and Brownian Motion*. New York: Springer, 1989.
35. Schoutens, W. (2003). *Lévy Processes in Finance*. Hoboken, NJ: John Wiley & Sons.
36. Schoutens, W., E. Simons, and J. Tistaert. 2004. A perfect calibration! Now what? *Wilmott*, March.
37. Sin, C. A. (1998). Complications with stochastic volatility models. *Advances in Applied Probability* 30(1): 256–268.
38. Varadhan, S. R. S. (1984). *Large Deviations and Applications*. Philadelphia: SIAM.

CHAPTER 3

Dynamic Properties of Smile Models

Lorenzo Bergomi

This chapter summarizes two presentations given in 2003 and 2005 in the *Petits Déjeuners de la Finance* seminar in Paris, on the subject of smile modeling for equity derivatives.

In the first section we use the example of the Napoleon option to motivate modeling issues that are the subject of the following sections. The Napoleon option is a typical case among the recent breed of exotic options, which embed new types of risks, such as:

- The volatility of implied volatilities
- The correlation between spot and implied volatilities
- The forward skew

to a degree not seen before in familiar exotic options such as barrier options and simple cliquets. The second section deals with the dynamic properties of popular standard smile models such as the Heston model and Levy-based models. Traditionally, smile models have been assessed according to how well they fit market option prices across strikes and maturities. However, the pricing of recent exotic structures is more dependent on the assumptions made for the future dynamics of implied volatilities than on today's vanilla option prices. We thus choose to address here the dynamic properties of popular models, rather than their smile-fitting abilities. Our aim is not to conduct an extensive survey of these models, but to characterize some of their salient properties and highlight structural features and limitations that are shared by classes of models.

In the third section we propose a new class of models that allows for much more flexibility in the specification of the joint dynamics of the spot and the implied volatilities. We illustrate the capabilities of this new model by using the examples of the Napoleon, the reverse cliquet, the accumulator, and the option on realized variance.

3.1   INTRODUCTION

In the Black-Scholes model, by construction, (1) implied volatilities for different strikes are equal, and (2) they are also frozen. Over the years several alternate models, starting with local volatility, have appeared with the aim of fitting market implied volatilities across strikes and maturities.

This capability is a desirable feature of any smile model: the model price then incorporates by construction the cost of trading vanilla options to hedge the exotic option's vega risk—at least for the initial trade. Otherwise, the price has to be manually adjusted to reflect hedging costs, that is, the difference between market and model prices of vanilla options used for the hedge. This may be sufficient if the vega hedge is stable, which is usually the case for barrier options.

However, most of the recent exotic structures, such as Napoleons and reverse cliquets,[1] require rebalancing of the vega hedge when the underlier or its implied volatilities move substantially. To ensure that future hedging costs are priced-in correctly, the model has to be designed so that it incorporates from the start a dynamics for implied volatilities which is consistent with the historically experienced one.

Stated differently, for this type of options, $\frac{\partial^2 P}{\partial \hat{\sigma}^2}$ and $\frac{\partial^2 P}{\partial S \partial \hat{\sigma}}$ are sizeable and a suitable model needs to price in a theta to match these gammas. In our view this issue is far more important than the model's ability to exactly reproduce today's smile surface.

As an illustration, let us consider the following example of a Napoleon option of maturity 6 years. The client initially invests 100, then gets a 6 percent coupon for the first 2 years and at the end of years 3, 4, 5, 6, an annual coupon of 8 percent augmented by the worst of the 12 monthly performances of the Eurostoxx 50 index observed each year, with the coupon floored at zero. At maturity, he also gets his 100 back. The payoff for the last four coupons is designed so that their value at inception is very small, thereby financing the "large" fixed initial coupons[2] which we remove from the option in what follows.

---

[1] See review article by C. Jeffery [8].
[2] As well as the distributor's fee, typically 1 percent per year.

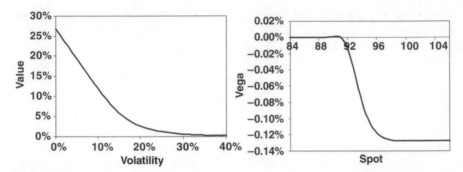

FIGURE 3.1 Left: Initial value of coupons of years 3, 4, 5, 6, as a function of volatility. Right: Vega of a coupon at the end of the first month, as a function of the spot price.

Figure 3.1 shows on the left the Black-Scholes value of the option at time $t = 0$, as a function of volatility. As we can see, the Napoleon is in substance a put option on long (1-year) forward volatility, for which no time value has been appropriated in the Black-Scholes price (no theta matching $\frac{\partial^2 P}{\partial \hat{\sigma}^2}$).

Now let us move to the end of the first month of year 3. The graph on the right pictures the vega of the coupon of year 3 at 20 percent volatility, as a function of the spot price, assuming the spot value at the beginning of the year was 100: it is a decreasing function of the spot, and goes to zero for low spot values, as the coupon becomes worthless. Now, as the spot decreases, the options' seller will need to buy back vega; however, moves in spot prices are historically negatively correlated with moves in implied volatilities, resulting in a negative profit and loss (P&L) to the seller, not accounted for in the Black-Scholes price (no theta matching $\frac{\partial^2 P}{\partial S \partial \hat{\sigma}}$).

The Black-Scholes price should thus be adjusted for the effect of the two cross-gammas mentioned, as well as for the one-month forward skew contribution.

Local volatility models [3], whose *raison d'être* is their ability to exactly fit observed market smiles, have historically been used to price skew-sensitive options. Even though implied volatilities do move in these models, their motion is purely driven by the spot and is dictated by the shape of the market smile used for calibration. This also materializes in the fact that forward smiles depend substantially on the forward date and the spot value at the forward date.

It would be desirable to be able to independently (1) calibrate today's market smile and (2) specify its future dynamics. One can attempt to directly specify an *ab initio* joint process for implied volatilities and the spot. This approach has been explored [8] and is hampered by the difficulty to ensure no-arbitrage in future smiles.

Alongside the local volatility model, other types of models have been proposed, capable of generating both spot skew and forward skew, as candidates for calibrating market smiles and endowing implied volatilities with non-trivial dynamics. We review in the next section the properties of two classes of models:

- One-factor stochastic volatility models, among which the Heston model, which we pick as an example, is the most popular.
- Exponential Lévy models and their stochastic volatility extensions.

3.2 SOME STANDARD SMILE MODELS

3.2.1 Stochastic Volatility—the Heston Model

In this section we examine the Heston model, a typical example within the class of one-factor stochastic volatility models. First, we characterize its static properties. Next we compare the model-generated dynamics of implied volatilities with their historical dynamics. We then comment on the pricing of forward-start options and end with a discussion of the delta and a comparison with local volatility models.

In the Heston model [4], the dynamics for the spot process is:

$$dS_t = (r - q) S_t dt + \sqrt{V_t} S_t dZ_t$$
$$dV_t = -k(V_t - V_0)dt + \sigma \sqrt{V_t} dW_t \qquad (3.2.1)$$

and the delta—the position in the underlying security that minimizes the variance of the hedging error—is given by:

$$\Delta = \frac{\partial P}{\partial S} + \frac{\rho \sigma}{S} \frac{\partial P}{\partial V} \qquad (3.2.2)$$

The Risk-Neutral Drift of *V* In most early work on stochastic volatility models much confusion has surrounded the issue of the "risk-neutral" drift of V. There are, however, no restrictions on the drift of V. Indeed, forward variances can be locked in by trading (or synthesizing) variance swaps at no cost. The pricing drift of forward variances is thus zero.

In stochastic volatility models built on a process for the instantaneous variance V, the expression of the forward variance at time T, conditional on the information available at time t, is:

$$\xi_t^T = E\left[V_T \mid V_t\right]$$

By definition, ξ_t^T is a martingale and as such has no drift, irrespective of the drift of V_t. The effect of the drift of V_t—besides affecting the dynamics of forward variances—is to set the value of the slope of the variance curve for short maturities. This implies, for the Heston model, the following identity:

$$\left.\frac{d\xi_t^T}{dT}\right|_{T=t} = -k\left(V_t - V_0\right)$$

In this respect, the issue of the drift of the instantaneous variance in stochastic volatility models echoes that of the drift of the instantaneous rate in short–rate models. It is well known that the drift of the short rate can be arbitrary—it is usually chosen so as to match the shape of the yield curve at $t = 0$.

The Heston model has five parameters V, V_0, ρ, σ, k among which k plays a special role: $\tau = 1/k$ is a cutoff that separates short and long maturities. The Heston model is homogeneous: implied volatilities are a function of V and moneyness: $\hat{\sigma} = f(\frac{K}{F}, V)$, where F is the forward. Perturbation of the pricing equation at first order in σ yields the following expressions for the skew and at-the-money-forward (ATMF) volatility:

- $T \ll \tau$, at order zero in T:

$$\hat{\sigma}_F = \sqrt{V}, \qquad \left.\frac{d\hat{\sigma}}{d\ln K}\right|_F = \frac{\rho\sigma}{4\sqrt{V}} \tag{3.2.3}$$

- $T \gg \tau$, at order 1 in $\frac{1}{T}$:

$$\hat{\sigma}_F = \sqrt{V_0}\left(1 + \frac{\rho\sigma}{4k}\right) + \frac{\sqrt{V_0}}{2kT}\left(\frac{V - V_0}{V_0} + \frac{\rho\sigma}{4k}\frac{V - 3V_0}{V_0}\right),$$

$$\left.\frac{d\hat{\sigma}}{d\ln K}\right|_F = \frac{\rho\sigma}{2kT\sqrt{V_0}} \tag{3.2.4}$$

The long-term behavior of the skew is what we expect: in a stochastic volatility model with mean reversion, increments of $\ln(S)$ become stationary and independent at long times. Thus, the *skewness* of $\ln(S)$ decays like $1/\sqrt{T}$; consequently[3] the *skew* decays like $1/T$.

Let us write the expression of the variance swap volatility $\hat{\sigma}_{VS}(T)$, defined such that $T\hat{\sigma}^2_{VS}(T)$ is the expectation of the realized variance for maturity T:

$$\hat{\sigma}^2_{VS}(T) = V_0 + (V - V_0)\frac{1 - e^{-kT}}{kT} \tag{3.2.5}$$

Dynamics of Implied Volatilities   We have calibrated market implied volatilities of the Eurostoxx 50 index from March 12, 1999, to March 12, 2004, for options of maturities 1 month, 3 months, 6 months, and 1 year.

Although the dynamics of both short and long implied volatilities in the model is driven by V, Equation 3.2.5 shows that the dynamics of V is mostly reflected in that of short volatilities. We thus choose $k = 2$ and fit all other parameters. The daily historical values for V, V_0, σ, ρ are shown in Figure 3.2.

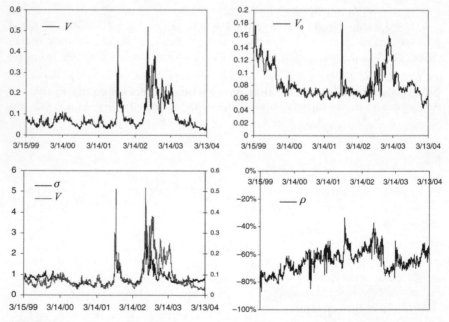

FIGURE 3.2   Fitted values of V, V_0, σ, ρ.

---

[3] See [1].

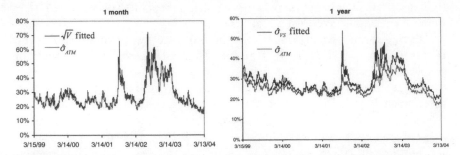

FIGURE 3.3 Left: $\sqrt{V}$ and 1-month ATM vol. Right: $\hat{\sigma}_{VS}$ and 1-year ATM vol.

We can see surges in volatility on September 11, 2001, then again in the summer of 2002, following the WorldCom collapse, and in the spring of 2003 at the beginning of the second Gulf war.

Figure 3.3 illustrates how well levels of short and long implied volatilities are tracked. The graph on the left shows the at-the-money (ATM) 1-month implied volatility and $\sqrt{V}$: $\sqrt{V}$ is a good proxy for the 1-month ATM volatility.

The right-hand graph in Figure 3.3 pictures the 1-year ATM volatility as well as the 1-year variance swap volatility, computed from V and V_0 using Equation 3.2.5. We see that, as we would expect for equity smiles, the variance swap volatility lies higher than the ATM volatility. Here, too, the calibration is satisfactory.

Discussion In the Heston model, while S and V are dynamic, V_0, ρ, σ are supposed to be constant: their dynamics is not priced-in by the model. Figure 3.2 shows that:

- V_0 moves, but this is expected as we are asking the model to fit both short and long implied volatilities.
- ρ is fairly stable, and does not seem correlated with other parameters.
- σ is the most interesting parameter: we have superimposed the graph of V with a scale 10 times larger. We see that σ varies substantially and seems very correlated with V.

The last observation can be accounted for by looking at the approximate expression for the short-term skew. Equation 3.2.3 shows that in the Heston model it is inversely proportional to $\sqrt{V}$, which is approximately equal to the ATM volatility. The fact that fitted values for σ are roughly proportional to V suggests that market skews are proportional to ATM volatilities, rather than inversely proportional.

In this respect the model is misspecified, since it is not pricing in the observed correlation between V and σ. This correlation is very visible in graphs for V and σ, mostly for extreme events. However, it is high even in more normal regimes. For example, daily *variations* of V and σ measured from March 15, 1999, to September 10, 2001, have a correlation of 59 percent.

The last portion of our sample shows a different behavior: starting in the summer of 2003, while ATM volatilities decreased, skews steepened sharply, an effect that the Heston model naturally generates. Figure 3.2 indeed shows that during that period σ remains stable while V decreases. Study of a larger historical data sample would have evidenced an even wider variety of regimes.

Let us now turn to the dynamics of implied volatilities generated by the model, as compared to the historical one. In the Heston model, the implied volatility dynamics is determined, by construction, by that of S and V.

We can use daily values for the couple (S, V) to check whether their dynamics is consistent with the model specification 3.2.1. Let us compute the following averages, which in theory should all be equal to 1:

$$R_S = \left\langle \frac{\delta S^2}{S^2 V \delta t} \right\rangle = 0.75$$

$$R_V = \left\langle \frac{\delta V^2}{\sigma^2 V} \right\rangle = 0.4$$

$$R_{SV} = \left\langle \frac{\delta S \delta V}{\rho \sigma S V \delta t} \right\rangle = 0.6$$

where brackets denote historical averages using daily variations.

From these numbers we estimate that

$$\frac{\sigma_{realized}}{\sigma_{implied}} = \sqrt{R_V} = 0.63$$

$$\frac{\rho_{realized}}{\rho_{implied}} = \frac{R_{SV}}{\sqrt{R_V R_S}} = 1.1$$

suggesting that calibration on market smiles overestimates the volatility of volatility σ by 40 percent, while the value of the spot/volatility correlation ρ is captured with acceptable accuracy.

Surprisingly, R_S is notably different than 1, showing that short implied volatilities overrestimated historical volatility by 13 percent on our historical sample, possibly accounting for the enduring popularity of dispersion trades.

It is possible that these global averages are excessively impacted by extreme events. Let us then look at running monthly averages. Figure 3.4 shows the results for the six following quantities:

$$V_{\frac{\delta S}{S}}^{real} = \left\langle \frac{\delta S^2}{S^2} \right\rangle \quad \text{and} \quad V_{\frac{\delta S}{S}}^{impl} = \langle V\delta t \rangle$$

$$V_{\delta V}^{real} = \langle \delta V^2 \rangle \quad \text{and} \quad V_{\delta V}^{impl} = \langle \sigma^2 V\delta t \rangle$$

$$C_{\frac{\delta S}{S}\delta V}^{real} = \left\langle \frac{\delta S}{S}\delta V \right\rangle \quad \text{and} \quad C_{\frac{\delta S}{S}\delta V}^{impl} = \langle \rho\sigma V\delta t \rangle$$

where brackets now denote running monthly averages. The sign of $C_{\frac{\delta S}{S}\delta V}^{real}$ and $C_{\frac{\delta S}{S}\delta V}^{impl}$ has been changed.

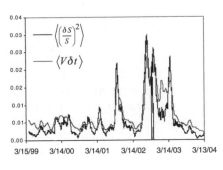

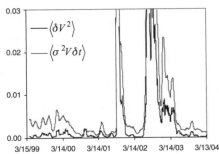

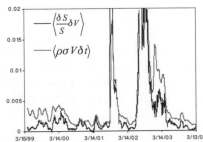

FIGURE 3.4 $V_{\frac{\delta S}{S}}^{real}$ and $V_{\frac{\delta S}{S}}^{imp}$, $V_{\delta V}^{real}$ and $V_{\delta V}^{impl}$, $C_{\frac{\delta S}{S}\delta V}^{real}$ and $C_{\frac{\delta S}{S}\delta V}^{impl}$.

We see that even during "normal" market conditions, the difference between "realized" and "implied" quantities is substantial. For example, using monthly running averages estimated on data from March 15, 1999, to September 10, 2001, gives the following numbers:

$$R_S = 0.73, \quad R_V = 0.30, \quad R_{SV} = 0.44$$

corresponding to the following ratios:

$$\frac{\sigma_{realized}}{\sigma_{implied}} = 0.54, \qquad \frac{\rho_{realized}}{\rho_{implied}} = 0.95$$

again showing that, while the "spot/volatility correlation" ρ is well captured by market smiles, the "volatility of volatility" σ is overestimated by roughly a factor of 2.

Concretely this means that the model is pricing in a "volatility of volatility" for 1-month ATM volatilities which is twice larger than its historical value: future vega rehedging costs are not properly priced in. It also implies that the model's delta given by Equation 3.2.2 is not efficient, as it overhedges the systematic impact of spot moves on volatility moves.

The main results of our historical analysis are: (1) σ and V are very correlated, and (2) the value of σ determined from calibration on market smiles is a factor of 2 larger than its historical value.

While (1) could be solved by altering the model's specification, (2) is structural. Indeed, we have only one device in the model—namely, the volatility of volatility σ—to achieve two different objectives, one static, the other dynamic: (1) create skewness in the distribution of $\ln(S)$ so as to match market smiles, and (2) drive the dynamics of implied volatilities in a way which is consistent with their historical behavior. It is natural that we are unable to fulfill both objectives. We view this as a structural limitation of any one-factor stochastic volatility model.

The Term Structure of the Volatility of Volatility   The preceding discussion has focussed on the dynamics of short-term volatilities. We now briefly consider the issue of the term structure of the volatility of volatility: how does the motion of implied volatilities—and its amplitude—depend on their maturity? Let us look at variance swap volatilities, which, in contrast to ATM volatilites, are known in closed form in the Heston model:

$$\hat{\sigma}_{VS}^2(T) = V_0 + (V - V_0)\frac{1 - e^{-kT}}{kT}$$

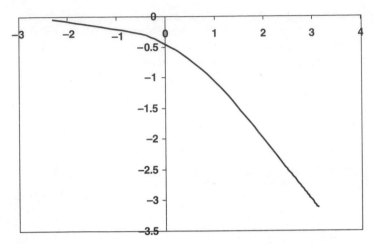

FIGURE 3.5   Log-log plot of $\frac{1-e^{-kT}}{kT}$ as a function of kT.

Their dynamics is given by:

$$d\left[\hat{\sigma}_{VS}^2(T)\right] = \frac{1 - e^{-kT}}{kT} dV_t \qquad (3.2.6)$$

Thus, locally, the dependence on T of the instantaneous volatility of $\hat{\sigma}_{VS}(T)$ is proportional to the factor $\frac{1-e^{-kT}}{kT}$ and thus set by the value of k. We could imagine choosing k so as to match as well as possible the historical levels of volatility of volatility for a range of maturities T, however:

- The choice of k impacts the time dependence of the spot skew and the forward skew, leading to an unwanted dependence of the term structure of the skew on the term structure of volatility of volatility.
- More importantly, it turns out that, historically, the term structure of the volatility of volatility has a dependence on T that is well approximated by a power law, a behavior inconsistent with the expression in Equation 3.2.6. This is made clear in Figure 3.5: only for large values of kT does $\frac{1-e^{-kT}}{kT}$ resemble a power law, albeit with an exponent set to 1.

Forward Start Options   Here we consider a one-period forward call option which pays $(\frac{S_{T_1+\theta}}{S_{T_1}} - \xi)^+$ at date $T_1 + \theta$, for different values of moneyness ξ. From the model-generated price of the forward start option we imply Black-Scholes volatilities to get what is generally termed the "forward smile" $\hat{\sigma}(\xi)$.

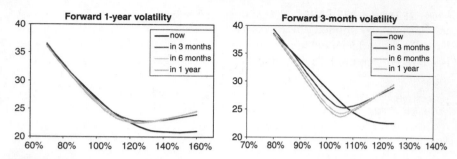

FIGURE 3.6 $\hat{\sigma}(\xi)$ for a 1-year maturity (left) and a 3-month maturity (right).

Figure 3.6 shows the forward smile computed using the following typical values: $V = V_0 = 0.1$, $\sigma = 1$, $\rho = -0.7$, $k = 2$, for two values of θ: 0.25 (3 months) and 1 (1 year). Today's smile ($T_1 = 0$) is also plotted for reference.

Note that forward smiles are more convex than today's smile: since the price of a call option is an increasing and convex function of its implied volatility, uncertainty in the value of future implied volatility increases the option price.

As T_1 is more distant, the distribution for V becomes stationary in the Heston model. Thus, forward smiles collapse onto a single curve for $T_1 \gg$ 6 months in our example. This is manifest in Figure 3.6.

The graphs also show that the increased convexity with respect to today's smile is larger for strikes $\xi > 100$ percent than for strikes $\xi < 100$ percent. This can be traced to the dependence of the skew to the level of ATM volatility. Since the short-term skew is inversely proportional to the ATM volatility, implied volatilities for strikes lower than 100 percent will move more than those for symmetrical strikes in the money. This is specific to the Heston model.

While the forward smile is a global measure of the distribution of implied volatilities at a forward date it is instructive to look at the distribution itself. Let $T_1 \gg \frac{1}{k}$. The density of V has the following stationary form:

$$\rho(V) \propto V^{\left(\frac{2kV_0}{\sigma^2}-1\right)} e^{-\frac{2k}{\sigma^2}V}$$

Using the parameter values listed above, we find that $\frac{2kV_0}{\sigma^2} - 1 = -0.6$; that is, the density for V *diverges* for small values of V.

Thus, even simple cliquets are substantially affected by the model specification: the practical conclusion for pricing is that, for short-term forward-start options, the Heston model is likely to overemphasize low-ATM-volatility/high-skew scenarios.

Local Dynamics and Delta   We here study the local dynamics of the Heston model: how do implied volatilities move when the spot moves? This sheds light on the model's delta since its deviation from the Black-Scholes value is related to the model's expected shift in implied volatilities when the spot moves.

In local volatility models, the motion of implied volatilities is driven by the spot. From the expression of the local volatility [3], for short maturities and weak skew, one can derive the following well-known relationship linking the skew to the dynamics of the ATM volatility as a function of the spot:

$$\frac{d\hat{\sigma}_{K=S}}{d\ln S} = 2 \left.\frac{d\hat{\sigma}}{d\ln K}\right|_{K=S}$$

showing that $\hat{\sigma}_{K=S}$ moves "twice as fast" as the skew.

In stochastic volatility models, while implied volatilities are not a function of S, they are correlated with S: this is what the second piece of the delta in Equation 3.2.2 hedges against. Conditional on a small move of the spot δS, V moves on average by $\delta V = \frac{\rho\sigma}{S}\delta S$.

Let us compute the expected variation in $\hat{\sigma}_F$, for short and long maturities:

- For $T \ll \tau$ we use expression 3.2.3, correct at order 0 in T. At this order, F and S can be identified. The expression for σ_F gives: $E[\delta\hat{\sigma}_{K=S}] = \frac{\rho\sigma}{2\sqrt{V}}\frac{\delta S}{S}$. Looking at the expression for the skew, we notice that:

$$\frac{E[\delta\hat{\sigma}_{K=S}]}{\delta\ln S} = 2 \left.\frac{d\hat{\sigma}}{d\ln K}\right|_{K=S} \tag{3.2.7}$$

This shows that, locally, the shift in implied volatilities expected by the Heston model when the spot moves is identical to that of a local volatility model; thus, the deltas of vanilla options for strikes near-the-money will be the same for both models—at order one in σ. This result is generic and holds for all stochastic volatility models.

- For $T \gg \tau$ we use expression 3.2.4, correct at order 1 in $\frac{1}{T}$. We get, keeping only terms linear in σ:

$$E[\delta\hat{\sigma}_{K=F}] = \frac{\rho\sigma}{2kT\sqrt{V_0}}\frac{\delta S}{S}$$

Comparing with the expression of the skew in Equation 3.2.4 we see that:

$$\frac{E[\delta\hat{\sigma}_{K=F}]}{\delta \ln S} = \left.\frac{d\hat{\sigma}}{d \ln K}\right|_{K=F}$$

The ATMF volatility slides on the smile and the Heston model behaves like a *sticky-strike* model: implied volatilities for fixed strikes do not move as the spot moves. Thus the deltas of vanilla options for strikes near the forward will be equal to their Black-Scholes deltas—again at order 1 in σ.

These results are obtained for the Heston model at first order in σ and are relevant for equity smiles. If ρ is small, as is the case for currency smiles, the contribution from terms of order σ^2 dominates, altering the conclusions: for example, the similarity to local volatility models for short maturities will be lost.

3.2.2 Models Based on Lévy Processes

Here we look at models built using Lévy processes. We assume that the relative size of jumps does not depend on the spot level. For a jump model, we use the following historical dynamics:

$$dS_t = \mu S dt + \sigma S dZ_t + J_t S_t dQ_t$$

where Q_t is a Poisson counting with an intensity λ. J_t is the relative size of the jump, itself a random variable, uncorrelated with Z_t. In models based on a jump or Lévy process, it is not possible to bring the variance of the hedging error down to zero, even when delta hedging in continuous time. The issue of which delta should be used is then open and the pricing equation depends on the choice of delta. One could choose the delta so as to minimize the variance of the hedging error, or to immunize the hedger locally at order one in small moves of S, irrespective of the cause of the move (volatility or jumps). This is the choice we make here. This yields the following pricing equation:

$$\frac{\partial P}{\partial t} + (r-q)S\frac{\partial P}{\partial S} + \lambda\left(\overline{\delta P} - \overline{J}S\frac{\partial P}{\partial S}\right) + \frac{\sigma^2 S^2}{2}\frac{\partial^2 P}{\partial S^2} = rP \qquad (3.2.8)$$

where we have used the following notation: $\delta m = m(S(1+J), t) - m(S, t)$ and $\overline{f} = E[f]$, where the expectation is taken over J, the amplitude of the jump. The delta we use, which is consistent with the above pricing equation, is:

$$\Delta = \frac{\partial P}{\partial S} \qquad (3.2.9)$$

The pricing equation for an exponential Lévy model is analogous, with the difference that λ and the density of J are replaced by the Lévy density.

Because the relative size of jumps in the spot price does not depend on the spot level these models are homogeneous: implied volatilities are a function of moneyness $\hat{\sigma}(K, S) = \hat{\sigma}\left(\frac{K}{S}\right)$.

The spot is the only degree of freedom in the model. As it moves the smile experiences a translation along with it: for a fixed moneyness, implied volatilities are frozen. This has two main consequences:

- Forward smiles do not depend on the forward date and are the same as today's smile: a graph similar to Figure 3.6 would show all smiles collapsing onto a single curve. When pricing a cliquet, this is equivalent to impacting all forward-start options by the same smile cost.
- The deltas for vanilla options are model independent and can be read off the smile directly. The delta for strike K is given by:

$$\Delta_K = \Delta_K^{BS} - \frac{1}{S}\text{Vega}_K^{BS}\frac{d\hat{\sigma}_K}{d\ln K}$$

where Δ_K^{BS} and Vega_K^{BS} are the Black-Scholes delta and vega of the vanilla option of strike K computed with its implied volatility $\hat{\sigma}_K$.

In exponential Lévy models, increments of $\ln(S)$ are independent, thus the skewness of the distribution of $\ln(S_T)$ decays as $\frac{1}{\sqrt{T}}$, and, at first order in the skewness, the *skew* decays as $\frac{1}{T}$, too fast in comparison with market smiles.

Stochastic volatility models generate a smile by starting with a process for $\ln(S)$ which is Gaussian at short time scales and making volatility stochastic and correlated with the spot process. In contrast, jump/Lévy models generate a skew without additional degrees of freedom by starting with a process for $\ln(S)$ at short time scales with sufficient embedded skewness and kurtosis so that both are still large enough at longer time scales to generate a smile, even though they decay as $\frac{1}{\sqrt{T}}$ and $\frac{1}{T}$, respectively.

In the next section we use the example of variance swaps to illustrate how the behavior of exponential Lévy models at short time scales impacts the price of very path-dependent options.

Variance Swaps   A variance swap (VS) is a contract that pays at maturity the realized variance of the spot, measured as the sum of squared returns observed at discrete dates, usually daily.

If the observations are frequent enough, its price P_{VS} is just the discounted expected variance by construction:

$$P_{VS} = e^{-rT}\hat{\sigma}_{VS}^2$$

We now introduce the log swap volatility $\hat{\sigma}_{LS}(T)$. $\hat{\sigma}_{LS}(T)$ is the implied volatility of the log swap, which is the European payoff $-2\ln(S)$. This profile, when delta hedged, generates a gamma P&L that is exactly equal[4] to the squared return of the spot between two rehedging dates. Because this statically replicates the payout of a variance swap, variance swaps are usually priced using $\hat{\sigma}_{LS}(T)$. In the Black-Scholes model, in the limit of very frequent observations, $\hat{\sigma}_{LS} = \hat{\sigma}_{VS} = \sigma$.

The value of $\hat{\sigma}_{LS}(T)$ is the implied volatility of a European payoff; it is thus model independent and is derived from the market smile. For equity smiles, $\hat{\sigma}_{LS}(T)$ usually lies higher than the ATM volatility—typically a few points of volatility.

In the Heston model, direct computation yields $\hat{\sigma}_{VS}(T) = \hat{\sigma}_{LS}(T)$. This self-consistence can be shown to hold for all diffusive models.

In jump/Lévy models, however, $\hat{\sigma}_{VS}$ is usually *lower* than $\hat{\sigma}_{LS}$ and even *lower* than $\hat{\sigma}_{ATM}$. For example, in the limit of frequent jumps of small amplitude, the following relationship can be derived, at first order in the skewness:

$$\hat{\sigma}_{K=F} - \hat{\sigma}_{VS} = 3(\hat{\sigma}_{LS} - \hat{\sigma}_{K=F})$$

where $\hat{\sigma}_{K=F}$ is the volatility for a strike equal to the forward.

The question then is: to price variance swaps, should we use $\hat{\sigma}_{VS}$, or $\hat{\sigma}_{LS}$ or yet another volatility?

To understand the difference, imagine hedging the profile $-2\ln(S)$ with the Black-Scholes delta computed with an implied volatility $\hat{\sigma}$. If there are no dividends, the delta is independent on the volatility, equal to $\frac{-2}{S}$. The gamma portion of the gamma/theta P&L realized during Δt, stopping at third-order terms in ΔS reads:

$$\left(\frac{\Delta S}{S}\right)^2 - \frac{2}{3}\left(\frac{\Delta S}{S}\right)^3$$

---

[4] Except if dividends are modelled as discrete cash amounts.

Introducing the volatility σ, given by $\sigma^2 \Delta t = E[(\frac{\Delta S}{S})^2]$, and the skewness $\mathcal{S}_{\Delta t}$ of $\frac{\Delta S}{S}$, we can write the expectation of this P&L as:

$$\sigma^2 \Delta t \left(1 - \frac{2\mathcal{S}_{\Delta t}}{3} \sigma \sqrt{\Delta t} \right)$$

Let us take the limit $\Delta t \to 0$.

- In stochastic volatility models, as $\Delta t \to 0$, returns become Gaussian and $\mathcal{S}_{\Delta t} \to 0$. Thus, the P&L generated by delta-hedging the log swap profile is exactly the realized variance. This explains why $\hat{\sigma}_{LS}$ and $\hat{\sigma}_{VS}$ are the same.
- In exponential Lévy models, because $\mathcal{S}_{\Delta t} \propto \frac{1}{\sqrt{\Delta t}}$, the third-order term contribution tends to a finite constant as $\Delta t \to 0$: delta hedging the log swap profile generates an additional contribution from third-order terms.[5]

    For equity smiles $\mathcal{S}$ is negative. Delta hedging the log swap profile then generates in addition to the realized variance a spurious *positive* P&L. Thus, the variance swap should be priced using a volatility lower than $\hat{\sigma}_{LS}$: $\hat{\sigma}_{VS} < \hat{\sigma}_{LS}$.

If real underliers behaved according to the exponential Lévy model specification, we should then price variance swaps using $\hat{\sigma}_{VS}$. Inspection of daily returns of the Eurostoxx 50 index shows however that for daily returns $\mathcal{S}_{\Delta t}$ is a number of order 1. Using a daily volatility of 2 percent gives an estimation of the contribution of the third-order term ≈ 50 times smaller than that of the second-order term, in sharp contrast with the model's estimation.

The practical conclusion for the pricing of variance swaps is that it will be more appropriate to use $\hat{\sigma}_{LS}$.

More generally, we have to be aware of the fact that, once their parameters are calibrated to market smiles, exponential Lévy models will predict excessive skews at shorter time scales; this behavior is structural.

Stochastic Volatility Extensions to Jump/Lévy Models A simple way of adding dynamics to implied volatilities in a jump/Lévy model is to make the flow of time stochastic: replace t with a nondecreasing process τ_t and

---

[5] Higher-order terms also yield at each order a nonvanishing contribution. This is due to the discontinuous nature of the spot process: even at short time scales, the P&L involves nonlocal terms.

evaluate the Lévy process L at τ. This is a particular case of a subordinated process. If the characteristic functions of both L_t and τ_t are known, then the characteristic function of L_τ is also known and an inverse Laplace transform yields European option prices. [2] choose τ_t as the integral of a CIR process:

$$\tau_t = \int_0^t \lambda_u du$$

$$d\lambda = -k(\lambda - \lambda_0)dt + \sigma\sqrt{\lambda}dZ_t$$

What is the dynamics of implied volatilities in such a model? Here we look at short-term options. The shape of the smile for maturity T is determined by the distribution of $\ln(S_T)$. Given the variance $\mathcal{V}$ and the skewness $\mathcal{S}$ of a distribution for $\ln(S_T)$, perturbation at first order in $\mathcal{S}$ gives [1]:

$$\hat{\sigma}_{K=F} = \sqrt{\frac{\mathcal{V}}{T}} \tag{3.2.10}$$

$$K\left.\frac{d\hat{\sigma}}{dK}\right|_{K=F} = \frac{\mathcal{S}}{6\sqrt{T}} \tag{3.2.11}$$

where F is the forward of maturity T.

Because λ_t is a continuous process, for short maturities: $L_{\tau_T} \approx L_{\lambda T}$; in other words, λ acts as a pure scale factor on time. Since the cumulants of L all scale linearly with time, we have

$$\mathcal{V} \propto \lambda T$$

$$\mathcal{S} \propto \frac{1}{\sqrt{\lambda T}}$$

Plugging these expressions in equations (3.2.10), (3.2.11), we get the following form for the ATMF volatility and skew, for short maturities:

$$\hat{\sigma}_{K=F} \propto \sqrt{\lambda}$$

$$K\left.\frac{d\hat{\sigma}}{dK}\right|_{K=F} \propto \frac{1}{\sqrt{\lambda T}}$$

Let us examine the scaling behavior of these expressions. The dependence of volatility and skew on T is what we would expect; more interesting is the dependence on λ: combining both equations yields the following result:

$$K \left.\frac{d\hat{\sigma}}{dK}\right|_{K=F} \propto \frac{1}{\hat{\sigma}_{K=F}}$$

Thus, for short maturities, the skew is approximately inversely proportional to the ATMF volatility.

This result is interesting in that it is general for the class of models considered: it depends neither on the choice of Lévy process nor the process for λ. Thus, impacting time with a stochastic scale factor allows implied volatilities to move but with a fixed dependence of the short-term skew on the level of the ATMF volatility. As noted in section 3 of Part I this feature is also shared by the Heston model, for very different reasons. To get different behavior, we would need to make the parameters of the Lévy process λ dependent, probably losing the analytical tractability of the model.

3.3 A NEW CLASS OF MODELS FOR SMILE DYNAMICS

In the preceding section we have analyzed the Heston model and the class of Lévy process models and have pointed out that, although these models produce prices that include an estimation of the effects of

- The dynamics of implied volatilities
- The forward skew
- The spot/volatility correlation

they impose structural constraints on how these features of the joint dynamics of the spot and implied volatilities are related. This is mostly due to the fact that they are based on an *a priori* specification of the spot process, from which the dynamics—not just of the spot, but also of implied volatilities—ensues.

While no-arbitrage conditions on vanilla option implied volatilities make it difficult to design a model that will accommodate any specification for their dynamics, forward variances are simpler objects, which moreover can be traded using variance swaps. It is then natural to shift our focus to endowing forward variances with their own dynamics, in addition to that of the spot process.

In this section we propose a new model which aims at pricing both standard exotic options and general options on variance in a consistent manner, and lets us independently set requirements on:

- The dynamics of variance swap volatilities.
- The level of short-term forward skew.
- The correlation between the underlying and short and long variance swap volatilities.

We first set up a general framework for the dynamics of forward variance swap variances, which we call simply *variances*. Then we specify a dynamics for the underlying which is consistent with that of variances. Next we specify a particular choice for the dynamics of FVs and the underlying. We then focus on practical features of the model such as the term structure of the volatility of volatility and the term structure of the skew. We then turn to using the model for pricing a reverse cliquet, a Napoleon, an accumulator and a call on variance, to demonstrate how the model makes it possible to separately measure the contributions of the three types of risks listed above to the price of a derivative.

3.3.1 Modeling Realized Variance

A variance swap pays at maturity $V_{tT}^b - V_t^T$ where V_{tT}^b is the annualized variance of the spot, realized over the interval $[t, T]$ and V_t^T is the implied variance swap variance, observed at time t for maturity T. Because variance swaps are statically replicable by vanilla options, V_t^T depends only on the implied volatilities seen at time t for maturity T.[6] Because of the definition of V_t^T, the variance swap contract has zero value at inception.

Now consider the variance $V_t^{T_1, T_2}$ defined as:

$$
V_t^{T_1, T_2} = \frac{(T_2 - t)V_t^{T_2} - (T_1 - t)V_t^{T_1}}{T_2 - T_1}
$$

where $T_1, T_2 > t$.

To write a pricing equation for an option on $V_t^{T_1, T_2}$ we first need to know the cost of entering a trade whose payoff at time $t + dt$ is linear in $V_{t+dt}^{T_1, T_2} - V_t^{T_1, T_2}$. Let us buy $\frac{T_2 - t}{T_2 - T_1} e^{r(T_2 - t)}$ VS of maturity T_2 and sell

---

[6] As well as on how dividends are modeled and assumptions on interest rate volatility.

$\frac{T_1-t}{T_2-T_1}e^{r(T_1-t)}$ VS of maturity T_1. This is done at no cost; our P&L at time $t' = t + dt$ is:

$$P\&L = \frac{T_2 - t}{T_2 - T_1}\left(\frac{V_{tt'}^b(t'-t) + V_{t'}^{T_2}(T_2 - t')}{T_2 - t} - V_t^{T_2}\right)e^{r(T_2-t)}e^{-r(T_2-t')}$$

$$-\frac{T_1 - t}{T_2 - T_1}\left(\frac{V_{tt'}^b(t'-t) + V_{t'}^{T_1}(T_1 - t)}{T_1 - t} - V_t^{T_1}\right)e^{r(T_1-t)}e^{-r(T_1-t')}$$

$$= \left(V_{t'}^{T_1,T_2} - V_t^{T_1,T_2}\right)e^{-r(t'-t)} = \left(V_{t+dt}^{T_1,T_2} - V_t^{T_1,T_2}\right)(1 - rdt)$$

This position generates a P&L linear in $V_{t+dt}^{T_1,T_2} - V_t^{T_1,T_2}$ at lowest order in dt, at zero initial cost: thus the pricing drift of any forward FV $V_t^{T_1,T_2}$ is zero.[7]

We now specify a dynamics for the variance swap curve. Let us introduce $\xi_t^T = V_t^{T,T}$, the value of the variance for date T, observed at time t.

3.3.2 A One-Factor Model

We are free to specify any dynamics on the $\xi^T(t)$ that complies with the requirement that $\xi^T(t)$ be driftless. However, for practical pricing purposes, we would like to drive the dynamics of all of the $\xi^T(t)$ with a small number of factors. In this paragraph we show how this can be done by carefully choosing the volatility function of $\xi^T(t)$.

Let us assume $\xi^T(t)$ is lognormally distributed and that its volatility is a function of $T - t$ so that the model is translationally invariant through time:

$$d\xi^T = \omega(T - t)\xi^T dU_t$$

where U_t is a Brownian motion. Let us choose the form $\omega(\tau) = \omega e^{-k_1 \tau}$.
$\xi^T(t)$ can be written as:

$$\xi^T(t) = \xi^T(0)e^{(\omega e^{-k_1(T-t)}X_t - \frac{\omega^2}{2}e^{-2k_1(T-t)}E[X_t^2])} \tag{3.3.1}$$

---

[7] The driftless nature of forward variance swap variances had been noticed before—see [4]. In diffusive models it is dictated by the definition of forward variance as a martingale.

where X_t is an Ornstein-Ühlenbeck process

$$X_t = \int_0^t e^{-k_1(t-u)} dU_u$$

whose dynamics reads:

$$dX_t = -k_1 X_t dt + dU_t$$
$$X_0 = 0$$

$\xi^T(t)$ is driftless by construction. Knowing X_t, we can generate $X_{t+\delta}$ through:

$$X_{t+\delta} = e^{-k_1\delta} X_t + x_\delta$$

where x_δ is a centered Gaussian random variable such that $E[x_\delta^2] = \frac{1-e^{-2k_1\delta}}{2k_1}$.

Starting from known values for X_t and $E\left[X_t^2\right]$ at time t we can generate the FV curve $\xi^T(t+\delta)$ at time $t+\delta$ by using the following relationship:

$$X_{t+\delta} = e^{-k_1\delta} X_t + x_\delta$$
$$E\left[X_{t+\delta}^2\right] = e^{-2k_1\delta} E\left[X_t^2\right] + \frac{1-e^{-2k_1\delta}}{2k_1}$$

and expression (3.3.1).

Thus by choosing an exponentially decaying form for $\omega(\tau)$ the model becomes Markovian: all $\xi^T(t)$ are functions of just one Gaussian factor X_t.

3.3.3 A Two-Factor Model

To achieve greater flexibility in the range of term structures of volatilities of variances that can be generated, we prefer to work with two factors. We then write:

$$d\xi^T = \omega\xi^T(e^{-k_1(T-t)} dU_t + \theta e^{-k_2(T-t)} dW_t)$$

where W_t is a Brownian motion. Its correlation with U_t is ρ. We can run through the same derivation as above. $\xi^T(t)$ now reads:

$$\xi^T(t) = \xi^T(0) \exp \left(\begin{array}{c} \omega \left[e^{-k_1(T-t)} X_t + \theta e^{-k_2(T-t)} Y_t \right] \\ -\frac{\omega^2}{2} \left[e^{-2k_1(T-t)} E[X_t^2] + \theta^2 e^{-2k_2(T-t)} E[Y_t^2] \right] \\ +2\theta e^{-(k_1+k_2)(T-t)} E[X_t Y_t]] \end{array} \right) \quad (3.3.2)$$

As in the one-factor case, if X_t, Y_t, $E[X_t^2]$, $E[Y_t^2]$, $E[X_t Y_t]$ are known at time t, they can be generated at time $t + \delta$ through the following relationships:

$$X_{t+\delta} = e^{-k_1\delta} X_t + x_\delta$$

$$Y_{t+\delta} = e^{-k_2\delta} Y_t + y_\delta$$

and

$$E\left[X_{t+\delta}^2\right] = e^{-2k_1\delta} E\left[X_t^2\right] + \frac{1 - e^{-2k_1\delta}}{2k_1}$$

$$E\left[Y_{t+\delta}^2\right] = e^{-2k_2\delta} E\left[Y_t^2\right] + \frac{1 - e^{-2k_2\delta}}{2k_2}$$

$$E\left[X_{t+\delta} Y_{t+\delta}\right] = e^{-(k_1+k_2)\delta} E\left[X_t Y_t\right] + \rho \frac{1 - e^{-(k_1+k_2)\delta}}{k_1 + k_2}$$

where, in the right-hand terms, the second component is, respectively, the variance of x_δ, the variance of y_δ and the covariance of x_δ and y_δ. Starting from time $t = 0$ we can easily generate a FV curve at any future time t by simulating two Gaussian factors. We choose $k_1 > k_2$ and call X_t the short factor, Y_t the long factor.

3.3.4 A Discrete Formulation

Instead of modeling the set of all instantaneous forward variances, it may be useful to set up a tenor structure and model the dynamics of forward variances for discrete time intervals, in a way which is analogous to London Interbank Offered Rate (LIBOR) market models.

In fixed income this is motivated by the fact that forward LIBOR rates are the actual underliers over which options are written. In our case, it is motivated by the fact that we want to control the skew for a given time scale.

Let us define a set of equally spaced dates $T_i = t_0 + i\Delta$, starting from t_0, today's date. We will model the dynamics of FVs defined over intervals of width Δ: define $\xi^i(t) = V_t^{t_0+i\Delta, t_0+(i+1)\Delta}$, for $t \le t_0 + i\Delta$. $\xi^i(t)$ is the value at time t of the FV for the interval $[t_0 + i\Delta, t_0 + (i+1)\Delta]$.

$\xi^i(t)$ is a random process until $t = t_0 + i\Delta$. When t reaches $t_0 + i\Delta$, the variance swap variance for time interval $[t, t + \Delta]$ is known and is equal to $\xi^i(t = t_0 + i\Delta)$.

We model the ξ^i in the same way as their continuous counterparts:

$$\xi^i(t) = \xi^i(0) \exp\left(\begin{array}{c} \omega\left[e^{-k_1(T_i-t)}X_t + \theta e^{-k_2(T_i-t)}Y_t\right] \\ -\frac{\omega^2}{2}\left[e^{-2k_1(T_i-t)}E[X_t^2] + \theta^2 e^{-2k_2(T_i-t)}E[Y_t^2]\right] \\ +2\theta e^{-(k_1+k_2)(T_i-t)}E[X_t Y_t]] \end{array} \right) \quad (3.3.3)$$

where we use the same recursions as above for X_t, Y_t, $E[X_t^2]$, $E[Y_t^2]$, $E[X_t Y_t]$.

While this setup for the dynamics of the ξ^i is reminiscent of the LIBOR market models used in fixed income, there are as yet no market quotes for prices of caps/floors and swaptions on forward variances, on which to calibrate volatilities and correlations for the ξ^i.[8]

An *N*-Factor Model   Rather than limiting ourselves to a small set of driving processes for the dynamics of the discrete variances ξ^i, we could use as many processes as there are forward variances, and choose an arbitrary correlation structure. We may generally write

$$\xi^i(t) = \xi^i(0)\, e^{\omega_i Z_t^i - \frac{\omega_i^2 t}{2}}$$

where ω_i and $\rho(Z_i, Z_j)$ are chosen at will. Further in this article we will compare pricing results obtained in the two-factor model with those obtained in an N–factor model for which $\omega_i = \omega$, a constant, and the correlation structure of the Z^i is:

$$\rho(Z_i, Z_j) = \theta\rho_0 + (1 - \theta)\beta^{|j-i|} \quad (3.3.4)$$

where $\theta, \rho_0, \beta \in [0, 1]$.

It should be noted that, when pricing an option of maturity T, in contrast to the two-factor model, the number of factors driving the dynamics of

---

[8] This was the case when this piece of work was originally done. Nowadays, market prices for options on VIX futures provide information on the smile of forward *volatilities*.

variances in the N-factor model is proportional to T, thus the pricing time will grow like T^2.

3.3.5 Specifying a Joint Dynamics for the Spot

A Continuous Setting   Let use the dynamics of instantaneous forward variances specified in Equation 3.3.2 and write the following lognormal dynamics on the underlying:

$$dS = (r - q) S dt + \sqrt{\xi^t (t)} S dZ_t$$

with correlations ρ_{SX} and ρ_{SY} between Z and, respectively U and W. This yields a stochastic volatility model whose differences with standard models are:

- It has two factors.
- It is calibrated by construction to the term-structure of variance swap volatilities.

In such a model the level of forward skew is determined by $\rho_{SX}, \rho_{SY}, \rho,$ ω, k_1, k_2, θ. Just as in standard stochastic, it will not be possible to change the level of forward skew without changing the correlation between spot and implied volatilities. However, in contrast with one-factor stochastic volatility models, we can use the two factors at our disposal to either control the term structure of the vanilla skew and make its decay compatible with market smiles, or control the term structure of volatilities of volatilities.

The continuous time version of our model can thus be used in its own right. However, by using the discrete tenor structure defined above for forward variances, it is possible to achieve our objective of independently controlling the forward skew for time scale Δ.

A Discrete Setting   At time $t = T_i$, the variance swap volatility $\hat{\sigma}_{VS}$ for maturity $T_i + \Delta$ is known: it is given by $\hat{\sigma}_{VS} = \sqrt{\xi^i(T_i)}$. To be able to specify the spot process over the interval $[T_i, T_i + \Delta]$ we make a few more assumptions:

- The spot process over the time interval $[T_i, T_i + \Delta]$ is homogeneous: the distribution of $\frac{S_{T_i+\Delta}}{S_{T_i}}$ does not depend on S_{T_i}. The reason for this requirement is that we want to decouple the short forward skew and the spot/volatility correlation. Imposing this condition makes the skew of maturity Δ independent on the spot level. Thus, prices of cliquets of period Δ will not depend on the level of spot-volatility correlation.

- We impose that the ATMF skew $\frac{d\hat{\sigma}_K}{d\ln K}|_F$ for maturity $T_i + \Delta$ be a deterministic function of $\hat{\sigma}_{VS}$ or $\hat{\sigma}_{ATMF}$. Here we impose that it is constant or proportional to $\hat{\sigma}_{ATMF}$. Other specifications for the dependence of the ATMF skew on $\hat{\sigma}_{VS}$ or $\hat{\sigma}_{ATMF}$ are easily accommodated in our framework.

There are many processes available for fulfilling our objective—note that we also need to correlate the spot process with that of forward variances ξ^j for $j > i$. We could use a Lévy process, especially one of those that has an expression in terms of a subordinated Brownian motion.[9] Here we decide to use a constant elasticity of variance (CEV) form of local volatility: over the interval $[T_i, T_i + \Delta]$ the dynamics of S_t reads:

$$dS = (r_t - q_t)\,S dt + \sigma_0 \left(\frac{S}{S_{T_i}}\right)^{1-\beta} S dZ_t \qquad (3.3.5)$$

where $\sigma_0(\hat{\sigma}_{VS})$, $\beta(\hat{\sigma}_{VS})$ are functions of $\hat{\sigma}_{VS} = \sqrt{\xi^i(T_i)}$ calibrated so that the variance swap volatility of maturity $T_i + \Delta$ is $\hat{\sigma}_{VS}$ and the condition on the ATMF skew is fulfilled. r_t and q_t are, respectively, the interest rate and the repo, inclusive of dividend yield. Note that instead of—or in addition to—controlling the skew we could have controlled the convexity of the smile near the money—this would be relevant in the forex or fixed income world. In this article we restrict our attention to the skew.

This completely specifies our model and the pricing algorithm. We can write the corresponding pricing equation as:

$$\frac{dP}{dt} + (r_t - q_t)\,S\frac{dP}{dS} + \frac{\sigma\left(S_{T_{i_0}},\xi^{i_0},S\right)^2}{2}S^2\frac{d^2P}{dS^2}$$

$$+ \frac{1}{2}\sum_{i,j>i_0}\rho_{ij}\omega_i\omega_j\xi^i\xi^j\frac{d^2P}{d\xi^i d\xi^j} + \sum_{i>i_0}\rho_{Si}\omega_i\sigma\left(S_{T_{i_0}},\xi^{i_0},S\right)S\xi^i\frac{d^2P}{dSd\xi^i} = rP$$

where $i_0(t)$ is such that $t \in [T_{i_0}, T_{i_0} + \Delta]$, ω_i is the volatility of the ξ^i and ρ_{ij} their correlations.

---

[9] For example, the variance gamma and normal inverse Gaussian processes.

In the N-factor model, $\omega_i = \omega$ and $\rho_{ij} = \rho(Z_i, Z_j)$. In the two-factor model, the dynamics of the ξ^i is driven by the processes X and Y. The pricing equation can then be written more economically as:

$$
\frac{dP}{dt} + (r_t - q_t) S \frac{dP}{dS} - k_1 X \frac{dP}{dX} - k_2 Y \frac{dP}{dY} + \frac{\sigma(\cdots, S)^2}{2} S^2 \frac{d^2 P}{dS^2}
$$
$$
+ \frac{1}{2} \left(\frac{d^2 P}{dX^2} + \frac{d^2 P}{dY^2} + 2\rho \frac{d^2 P}{dXdY} \right)
$$
$$
+ \sigma(\cdots, S) S \left(\rho_{SX} \frac{d^2 P}{dSdX} + \rho_{SY} \frac{d^2 P}{dSdY} \right) = rP
$$

where ρ_{SX} and ρ_{SY} are, respectively, the correlation between Brownian motions U_t and Z_t and the correlation between W_t and Z_t. $\sigma(\cdots, S)$ is a shorthand notation for:

$$
\sigma(\cdots, S) \equiv \sigma \left(S_{T_{i_0}}, \xi^{i_0} \left(X_{T_{i_0}}, Y_{T_{i_0}} \right), S \right)
$$

3.3.6 Pricing

We now turn to using the model for pricing, focussing on the two-factor model. In what follows we choose as time scale $\Delta = 1$ month. By construction the model is calibrated at time t_0 to the FV curve for all maturities $t_0 + i\Delta$. We specify, in this order:

- Values for $k_1, k_2, \omega, \rho, \theta$.
- A value for the forward ATMF skew.
- Values for ρ_{SX} and ρ_{SY}.

These steps are discussed in the next three sections.

Setting a Dynamics for Implied Variance Swap Volatilities Our aim is to price options whose price is a very nonlinear function of volatility; as we roll toward the option's maturity, the maturity of the volatilities we are sensitive to shrinks as well: we thus need the ability to control the term structure of the volatilities of volatilities, be they ATMF or variance swap volatilities. In our framework, it is more natural to work with variance swap volatilities.

In our model the dynamics of variance swap volatilities is controlled by $k_1, k_2, \omega, \rho, \theta$. As there is presently no active market for options on forward ATM or variance swap volatility, these parameters cannot be calibrated on market prices. Thus, their values have to be chosen so that the level and

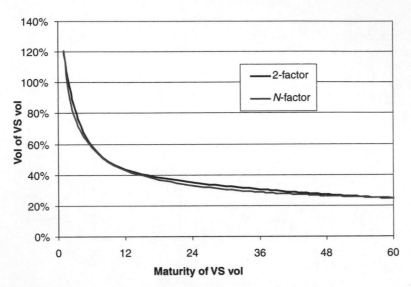

FIGURE 3.7 Term-structure of the vols of variance swap vols for a 1 month interval.

term structure of volatility of volatility are reasonably conservative when compared to historically observed volatilities of implied volatilities.[10] Here we choose the following values:

$$\omega = 2.827, \ \rho = 0, \ \theta = 30\%, \ k_1 = 6 \ (2 \ \text{months}), \ k_2 = 0.25 \ (4 \ \text{years})$$

$$(3.3.6)$$

so that the volatility of volatility for a 1-month horizon is about 120 percent for the 1-month variance swap vol, 45 percent for the one-year vol, and 25 percent for the 5-year volatility. Figure 3.7 displays the term structure of the volatilities of variance swap volatilities generated by the two-factor model with a flat initial VS term-structure at 20 percent using these parameter values. We graph

$$\frac{1}{\sqrt{\Delta t}} \text{StDev} \left[\ln \left(\frac{\sqrt{V_{\Delta t}^{\Delta t, \Delta t + \tau}}}{\sqrt{V_0^{\Delta t, \Delta t + \tau}}} \right) \right]$$

---

[10] Dealers trading Napoleons and reverse cliquets usually accumulate a negative gamma position on volatility. In practice, bid and offer term structures of volatility of volatility are used for pricing.

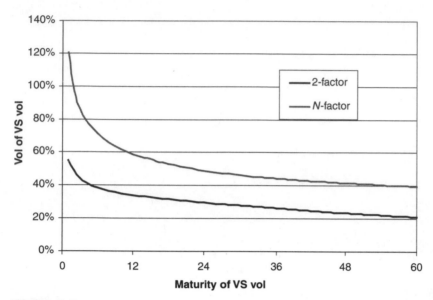

FIGURE 3.8 Term-structure of the vol of VS vols, for a 1-year interval.

for a range of values of τ from 1 month to 5 years. We have picked $\Delta t = 1$ month. The value of ω is chosen so that, over the interval of $\Delta t = 1$ month, the volatility of the one-month variance swap volatility is 120 percent.

We also display the term structure generated by the N-factor model using the following parameters

$$\sigma = 240\%, \theta = 40\%, \rho_0 = 5\%, \beta = 10\%$$

These values are chosen so that, for $\Delta t = 1$ month, the term structure of the two-factor model is matched. Now let us measure volatilities over a time interval of one year, instead of one month (Figure 3.8).

They are very different; although both models would yield similar prices for options on variance swap variances observed 1 month from now, they would price differently options on variance swap variances observed in 1 year. In the two-factor model volatilities of volatilities will tend to decrease as the time scale over which they are measured increases, due to the mean-reverting nature of the driving processes. In the N-factor model, by contrast, they increase: this is due to the fact that forward variances are lognormal—the term structure would be constant if forward variances were normal.

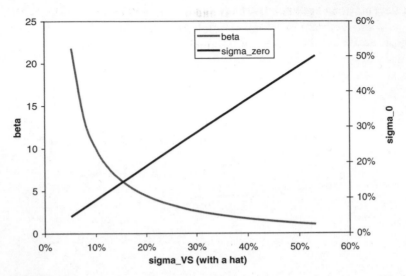

FIGURE 3.9 β and σ_0 as a function of $\hat{\sigma}_{VS}$ in the case of a constant 5% skew.

Setting the Short Forward Skew We calibrate the dependence of σ_0 and β to $\hat{\sigma}_{VS}$ so that the 1-month ATMF skew has a constant value—say 5 percent; we use the 95 percent to 105 percent skew:

$$\hat{\sigma}_{95\%} - \hat{\sigma}_{105\%} \simeq -\frac{1}{10} \left. \frac{d\hat{\sigma}_K}{d \ln K} \right|_F$$

instead of the local derivative $\frac{d\hat{\sigma}_K}{d \ln K}$. This defines the functions $\sigma_0(\hat{\sigma}_{VS})$ and $\beta(\hat{\sigma}_{VS})$. This calibration is easily done numerically; we can also use analytical approximations.[11]

If needed, individual calibration of $\sigma_0(\hat{\sigma}_{VS})$ and $\beta(\hat{\sigma}_{VS})$ can be performed for each interval $[T_i, T_i + \Delta]$. Typically, the same calibration will be used for all intervals except the first one, for which a specific calibration is performed so as to match the short vanilla skew. Here we use the same calibration for all intervals. Figure 3.9 shows functions $\sigma_0(\hat{\sigma}_{VS})$ and $\beta(\hat{\sigma}_{VS})$ for the case of a constant 95 percent to 105 percent skew equal to 5 percent.

The level of 95 percent to 105 percent skew can either be selected by the trader or chosen so that market prices of call spread cliquets of period Δ (here 1 month) are matched.

---

[11] See, for example, [9].

Setting Correlations between the Spot and Short/Long Factors—the Term Skew ρ_{SX} and ρ_{SY} cannot be chosen independently, since X and Y have correlation ρ. We use the following parametrization:

$$\rho_{SY} = \rho_{SX}\,\rho + \chi\sqrt{1 - \rho_{SX}^2}\sqrt{1 - \rho^2}$$

with $\chi \in [-1, 1]$. ρ_{SX} and ρ_{SY} control both the correlation between spot and short and long variance swap volatilities and the term structure of the skew of vanilla options. They can be chosen, calibrated to the market prices of call spread cliquets of period larger than Δ or calibrated to the market skew for the maturity of the option considered. The dependence of the term skew on ρ_{SX} and ρ_{SY} is made explicit in the following section.

In the N-factor model, we need to specify correlations between the spot process and all forward variances, in a manner which is consistent with correlations specified in Equation 3.3.4, a nontrivial task that we leave outside the scope of this chapter.

The Term Skew To shed light on how our model generates skew, we derive an approximate expression for the ATMF skew as a function of maturity, for the case of a flat term structure of variance swap volatilities, at order 1 in both ω and the skew $\frac{d\hat{\sigma}_K}{d\ln K}|_F$ at time scale Δ, which we denote Skew$_\Delta$.

Given the skewness $\mathcal{S}_T$ of the distribution of $\ln(\frac{S_T}{F_T})$ the ATMF skew is given, at first order in $\mathcal{S}_T$ by [1]:

$$\text{Skew}_T = \frac{\mathcal{S}_T}{6\sqrt{T}} \tag{3.3.7}$$

where F_T is the forward for maturity T.

Consider a maturity $T = N\Delta$ and let us compute the second and third moments of $\ln(\frac{S_T}{F_T}) = \sum_{i=1}^{N} r_i$ where returns r_i are defined as $r_i = \ln(\frac{S_{i\Delta}}{F_{i\Delta}}) - \ln(\frac{S_{(i-1)\Delta}}{F_{(i-1)\Delta}})$. While returns are not independent, they are uncorrelated. Thus, assuming that Δ is small, so that the drift term in $E[r_i]$ is negligible with respect to the random term:

$$M_3^T = \left\langle \left(\sum_{i=1}^{N} r_i \right)^3 \right\rangle = \sum_i \langle r_i^3 \rangle + 3 \sum_{j>i} \langle r_i r_j^2 \rangle$$

Let us work at lowest order in Δ: for the purpose of deriving an expression of the third moment at order 1 in ω and S$_\Delta$ we can use the following approximations:

$$r_j^2 = \Delta \xi^j (T_j)$$

$$r_i = \sqrt{\xi^i (T_i)} \int_{T_i}^{T_i+\Delta} dZ_t$$

Let us denote ξ the constant value of the variance swap volatilities at time 0. We get, at order 1 in ω:

$$M_3^T = \sum_i \langle r_i^3 \rangle + 3 \sum_{j>i} \Delta \left\langle \sqrt{\xi^i (T_i)} \int_{T_i}^{T_i+\Delta} dZ_t \xi^j (T_j) \right\rangle$$

$$= \sum_i \langle r_i^3 \rangle + 3 \sum_{j>i} \Delta \left\langle \sqrt{\xi^i (T_i)} \int_{T_i}^{T_i+\Delta} dZ_t \xi^j (0) \begin{pmatrix} 1 + \omega \int_0^{T_j} e^{-k_1(T_j-u)} dU_u \\ + \theta\omega \int_0^{T_j} e^{-k_2(T_j-u)} dW_u \end{pmatrix} \right\rangle$$

$$= \sum_i \langle r_i^3 \rangle + 3 \sum_{j>i} \Delta\omega\xi^j (0) \sqrt{\xi^i (0)}$$

$$\times \left\langle \left(\int_{T_i}^{T_i+\Delta} dZ_t \int_0^{T_j} \left(e^{-k_1(T_j-u)} dU_u + \theta e^{-k_2(T_j-u)} dW_u \right) \right) \right\rangle$$

$$= \sum_i \langle r_i^3 \rangle + \rho\omega\xi^{\frac{3}{2}} \Delta^2 N^2 \left[\rho_{SX} \zeta (k_1\Delta, N) + \theta\rho_{SY} \zeta (k_2\Delta, N) \right]$$

where $\zeta(x, N)$ is defined by:

$$\zeta (x, N) = \left(\frac{1 - e^{-x}}{x} \right) \frac{\sum_{\tau=1}^{N-1} (N - \tau) e^{-(\tau-1)x}}{N^2} \tag{3.3.8}$$

Since we have set the short skew to a value which is independent on the level of variance, expression 3.3.7 shows that the skewness of r_i is constant. Thus:

$$\sum_i \langle r_i^3 \rangle = S_\Delta \sum_i \left\langle (\Delta\xi^i (T_i))^{\frac{3}{2}} \right\rangle = N S_\Delta (\Delta\xi)^{\frac{3}{2}}$$

where $\mathcal{S}_\Delta$ is the skewness at time scale Δ. We then get:

$$M_3^T = N\mathcal{S}_\Delta (\xi\Delta)^{\frac{3}{2}} + \rho\omega\sqrt{\Delta} (\xi\Delta)^{\frac{3}{2}} N^2 (\rho_{SX}\zeta (k_1\Delta, N) + \theta\rho_{SY}\zeta (k_2\Delta, N))$$

At order zero in $\mathcal{S}_\Delta$ and ω

$$M_2^T = \left\langle \left(\sum_{i=1}^n r_i\right)^2\right\rangle = N\xi\Delta$$

hence, the following expression for $\mathcal{S}_T = \dfrac{M_3^T}{(M_2^T)^{\frac{3}{2}}}$

$$\mathcal{S}_T = \frac{\mathcal{S}_\Delta}{\sqrt{N}} + \sqrt{N}\omega\sqrt{\Delta}\,[\rho_{SX}\zeta (k_1\Delta, N) + \theta\rho_{SY}\zeta (k_2\Delta, N)]$$

Using Equation 3.3.7 again we finally get the expression of Skew$_{N\Delta}$ at order 1 in Skew$_\Delta$ and ω:

$$\text{Skew}_{N\Delta} = \frac{\text{Skew}_\Delta}{N} + \frac{\omega}{2}\,[\rho_{SX}\zeta (k_1\Delta, N) + \theta\rho_{SY}\zeta (k_2\Delta, N)] \qquad (3.3.9)$$

This expression is instructive as it makes apparent how much of the skew for maturity T is contributed on the one hand by the instrinsic skewness of the spot process at time scale Δ, and on the other hand by the spot/volatility correlation.

When $\omega = 0$, the skew decays as $\frac{1}{T}$, as expected for a process of independent increments. The fact that volatility is stochastic and correlated with the spot alters this behavior. Inspection of the definition of function ζ in Equation 3.3.8 shows that for $N\Delta \gg \frac{1}{k1}, \frac{1}{k_2}$, $\zeta(x, N) \propto \frac{1}{N}$, so that Skew $_{N\Delta} \propto \frac{1}{N}$, again what we would expect.

Equation 3.3.9 also shows how ρ_{SX} and ρ_{SY} can naturally be used to control the term structure of the skew.

Figure 3.10 shows how the approximate skew in Equation 3.3.9 compares to the actual skew. We have chosen the following values: $\Delta = 1$ month, the 1-month 95 percent/105 percent skew is 5 percent, $\omega = 2.827$, $\rho = 0$, $\theta = 30$ percent, $k_1 = 6$, $k_2 = 0.25$. The spot/volatility correlations are: $\rho_{SX} = -70$ percent, $\rho_{SY} = -35.7$ percent ($\chi = -50$ percent). Even though ω and Skew$_\Delta$ are both large, the agreement is very satisfactory.

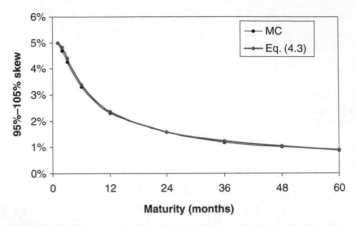

FIGURE 3.10 The 95%–105% skew as a function of maturity.

The two contributions to $\text{Skew}_{N\Delta}$ in Equation 3.3.9 are graphed in Figure 3.11: "intrinsic" denotes the first piece, "spot/volatility correlation" denotes the second piece in Equation 3.3.9. While the contribution of Skew_Δ to $\text{Skew}_{N\Delta}$ is monotonically decreasing, the contribution of the spot/volatility correlation is not, as it starts from zero at short time scales. Depending on

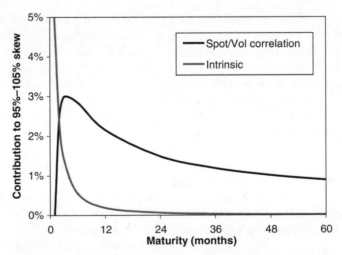

FIGURE 3.11 The two contributors to the 95%–105% skew in eq. (3.3.9).

the relative magnitude of both terms, the term structure of the skew can be nonmonotonic.

While we have derived expression 3.3.9 for the case of a flat VS term structure, the general case poses no particular difficulty.

3.4 PRICING EXAMPLES

Here we use our model to price a reverse cliquet, a Napoleon, an accumulator, and a call on realized variance, and analyze the relative contribution of forward skew, volatility of volatility and spot/volatility correlation to prices. We use zero interest rates and dividend yield.

For the sake of comparing prices we need to specify how we calibrate model parameters. While it is natural to calibrate to the vanilla smile when pricing options that can be reasonably hedged with a static position in vanilla options, it is more natural to calibrate to call spread cliquets and ATM cliquets when pricing Napoleons and reverse cliquets, which have a large sensitivity to forward volatility and skew.

These products are also very sensitive to volatility of volatility. They are usually designed so that their price at inception is small but increases significantly if implied volatility decreases.[12] As there is as yet no active market for options on variance we use the volatility of volatility parameter values listed in 3.3.6.

Unless forward skew is turned off, the constant 95 percent to 105 percent 1-month skew is calibrated so that the price of a 3-year 95 percent to 105 percent 1-month call spread cliquet has a constant value, equal to its price when volatility of volatility is turned off and the 1-month 95 percent to 105 percent skew is 5 percent, which is equal to 191.6 percent.

In all cases the level of the flat variance swap volatility has been calibrated so that the implied volatility of the 3-year 1-month ATM cliquet is 20 percent.

The values for ρ_{SX} and ρ_{SY} are $\rho_{SX} = -70$ percent, $\rho_{SY} = -35.7$ percent ($\chi = -50$ percent). The corresponding term skew is that of Figure 3.10.

In addition to the BS price, we compute three other prices by switching on either the 1-month forward skew ($\hat{\sigma}_{95\%} - \hat{\sigma}_{105\%} \neq 0$, $\omega = 0$), or the volatility of volatility ($\hat{\sigma}_{95\%} - \hat{\sigma}_{105\%} = 0$, $\omega \neq 0$), or both (full). These prices are listed in Table 3.1. We give the definition of each product and comment on pricing results in the following paragraphs (also see Table 3.2).

---

[12] See Figure 3.1.

TABLE 3.1   A. Model Prices

Model	Reverse Cliquet	Napoleon	Accumulator
Black-Scholes	0.25%	2.10%	1.90%
With forward skew	0.56%	2.13%	4.32%
With Vol of vol	2.92%	4.71%	1.90%
Full	3.81%	4.45%	5.06%

TABLE 3.2   B. Model Prices

Model	Reverse Cliquet	Napoleon	Accumulator
Full—correlations halved	3.10%	4.01%	5.04%
Full—proportional skew	3.05%	4.30%	4.15%

3.4.1   Reverse Cliquet

Here we consider a globally floored locally capped cliquet, which pays once at maturity:

$$\max\left(0, C + \sum_{i=1}^{N} r_i^-\right)$$

The maturity is 3 years, returns r_i are observed on a monthly basis ($N = 36$), $r_i^- = \min(r_i, 0)$ and the value of the coupon is $C = 50$ percent.

Notice that corrections to the Black-Scholes price are by no means small, the contribution of volatility of volatility being the largest. The fact that volatility of volatility makes the reverse cliquet more expensive is expected: this option, as well as the Napoleon, is in essence a put on volatility.

To understand why forward skew increases the price, consider first that, in the four cases listed above, $E[\sum_{i=1}^{N} r_i^-]$ is constant, by calibration on the ATM cliquet. Next consider the last period of the reverse cliquet: the final payoff is a function of the final return; it is a call spread whose low and high strikes are, respectively, $-C + \sum_{i<N} r_i^-$—if it is negative—and zero. When forward skew is turned on, the implied volatility of the ATM strike is unchanged, by calibration, while the implied volatility for lower strikes increases, making the call spread more expensive. The same argument holds for returns prior to the last one.

3.4.2 Napoleon

The maturity is still 3 years and the option pays at the end of each year a coupon given by:

$$\max\left(0,\ C + \min_i r_i\right)$$

where r_i are the 12 monthly returns observed each year. Here we use $C = 8$ percent.

Again, we notice that volatility of volatility accounts for most of the price. Forward skew seems to have no sizeable impact; however, this is not generic—its magnitude and sign depend on the coupon size. While the payoff is still a call spread as a function of the final return, both strikes lie below the money. Also, in contrast to the case of the reverse cliquet, $E[\min_i r_i]$ is not constant in the four cases considered.

3.4.3 Accumulator

The maturity is again 3 years with one final payout, given as a function of the 36 monthly returns r_i by:

$$\max\left(0, \sum_{i=1}^{N} \max(\min(r_i, \text{cap}), \text{floor})\right)$$

where floor $= -1\%$ and cap $= 1\%$—a standard product.

The largest contribution comes from forward skew. Notice that switching on the volatility of volatility in the case when there is no skew has no material impact on the price while it does when forward skew is switched on. To understand this, observe that, in Black-Scholes, when both strikes are priced with the same volatility, a 99 percent to 101 percent 1-month call spread has negligible vega. However, when the call spread is priced with a downward sloping skew, it acquires positive convexity with respect to volatility shifts.

3.4.4 Effect of Spot/Volatility Correlation— Decoupling of the Short Forward Skew

In standard stochastic volatility models, changing the spot/volatility correlation changes the forward skew and thus the price of cliquets. In our model, because of the specification chosen for the spot dynamics in Equation 3.3.5, changing the spot/volatility correlation does not change the value of cliquets of period 1 month. It alters only the term skew.

Prices quoted above have been computed using $\rho_{SX} = -70$ percent, $\rho_{SY} = -35.7$ percent. With these values the 3-year 95 percent to 105 percent skew is 1.25 percent.

Let us now halve the spot/volatility correlation: $\rho_{SX} = -35$ percent, $\rho_{SY} = -18$ percent ($\chi = -19.2$ percent). The 3-year 95 percent to 105 percent skew is now 0.75 percent—almost halved. The implied volatility of the 3-year cliquet of 1-month ATM calls remains 20 percent and the price of a 95 percent to 105 percent one–month call spread cliquet is unchanged, at 191.6 percent. The corresponding prices appear on first line of Table 3.2. The difference with prices on line four of Table 3.1 measures the impact of the term skew, all else—in particular cliquet prices—being kept constant. The fact that prices decrease when the spot/volatility correlation is less negative is in line with the shape of the Black-Scholes vega as a function of the spot value (see Figure 3.1).

3.4.5 Making Other Assumptions on the Short Skew

Here we want to highlight how a different model for the short skew alters prices, using the three payoff examples studied above. We now calibrate functions $\sigma_0(\hat{\sigma}_{VS})$ and $\beta(\hat{\sigma}_{VS})$ so that, instead of being constant, the 95 percent to 105 percent skew for maturity Δ is proportional to the ATMF volatility for maturity Δ.

We have calibrated the proportionality coefficient so that the 3-year cliquet of 1-month 95 percent to 105 percent call spreads has the same value as before. The flat variance swap volatility is still chosen so that the implied volatility of the 3-year cliquet of 1-month ATM call is 20 percent. Prices are listed on the second line of Table 3.2.

The accumulator is now sizeably cheaper. One can check that, in Black-Scholes, the value of a symmetrical call spread as a function of ATM volatility, when the skew is kept proportional to the ATM vol, is almost a linear function of volatility—in contrast to the case when volatilities are shifted in parallel fashion, where it is a convex function of volatility—thus explaining why the volatility of volatility has much less impact than in the constant skew case.

3.4.6 Option on Realized Variance

Here we consider a call option that pays at maturity:

$$\frac{1}{2\hat{\sigma}_K} \max\left(\sigma_b^2 - \hat{\sigma}_K^2, \, 0\right)$$

where volatility $\hat{\sigma}_K$ is the strike, and σ_h^2 is the annualized variance measured using daily log-returns. We assume there are 250 daily observations in a year, equally spaced. The variance of the distribution of σ_h^2 has two sources:

- The dynamics of variance swap variances.
- The fact that observations are discrete: in the case when variance swap variances are static it is the only contribution and it is determined by the distribution of spot returns, in particular its kurtosis, which depends on assumptions made for the short-maturity smile—in our context, the value of β. In the general case, it affects short-maturity options most noticeably.

Prices are expressed as implied volatilities computed with the Black-Scholes formula with zero rate and repo. The underlying is the variance swap variance for the maturity of the option, whose intial value is given by the variance swap term structure observed at the pricing date.

In our model, daily returns are generated by the volatility function form in Equation (3.3.5). Their conditional kurtosis is a function of β, a parameter we use to control the short-term skew. The prices of options on variance will thus depend on assumptions we make for the skew at time scale Δ. Figure 3.12 shows implied volatilities of call options on variance, using a flat term structure of variance swap volatilities at 20 percent, the same correlations as in the examples above ($\rho_{SX} = -70\%$, $\rho_{SY} = -35.7\%$), for the two cases: $\hat{\sigma}_{95\%} - \hat{\sigma}_{105\%} = 5\%$ and $\hat{\sigma}_{95\%} - \hat{\sigma}_{105\%} = 0\%$.

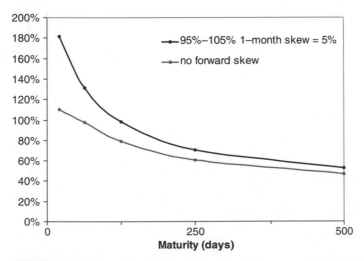

FIGURE 3.12 Implied volatility of a call option on realized variance as a function of maturity in the two-factor model.

Figure 3.12 illustrates how assumptions for the forward skew significantly affect the distribution of returns and thus the price of options on
variance, mostly for short options. The shortest maturity in the graph corresponds to options of maturity 1 month (20 days): since we have taken $\Delta = 1$
month, the distribution of σ_h^2 does not depend on the dynamics of variances
ξ^i—it only depends on β.

Note that, in this model, variance swap volatilities for maturities shorter
than Δ are not frozen: instead of being driven by Equation 3.3.3, their
dynamics is set by the value of β.

3.4.7 Using the *N*-Factor Model

It is instructive to compare prices of options on realized variance generated
by the two-factor and N-factor models. As Figures 3.7 and 3.8 illustrate,
even though the short-term dynamics of variance swap volatilities in both
models are similar, they become different for longer horizons.

Here we price the same option on variance considered above using the
N-factor model of forward variances. Parameter values for the dynamics
of forward variances are the same as those used in Figures 3.7 and 3.8.
We have taken no forward skew: $(\hat{\sigma}_{95\%} - \hat{\sigma}_{105\%} = 0)$. Also, to make prices
comparable with those obtained in the two-factor model, we have taken
zero correlation between spot and forward variances. Implied volatilities for
both models are shown in Figure 3.13.

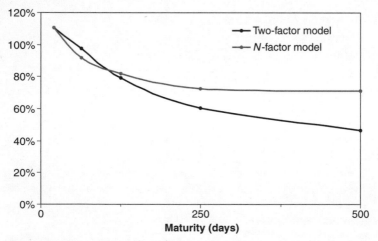

FIGURE 3.13   Implied volatility of a call option on realized variance as a function
of maturity in the two-factor and N-factor models.

Because $\Delta = 1$ month, for the shortest maturity considered—20 days—the implied volatilities for both models coincide. For longer maturities the fact that implied volatilities are higher in the N-factor model is in agreement in Figure 3.8, which shows that, for longer horizons, the volatilities of forward variances in the N-factor model are larger than in the two-factor model.

Finally, in addition to the effects discussed above, prices of calls on variance have to be adjusted to take into account bid/offer spreads on the VS hedge. These can be approximately included by shifting the level of volatility of volatility [7].

3.5 CONCLUSION

We have analyzed the dynamical properties of stochastic volatility and exponential Lévy models. While, historically, these models have been promoted on the grounds of their ability to generate skews and match market smiles, we have pointed out that the joint dynamics they generate for the spot and implied volatilities is very constrained. Moreover, most of the limitations we have highlighted are of a structural nature and could not be remedied by marginally altering the models' specification.

It is our assessment that, in the light of the complexity of the recent exotic structures that have come to the market, the issue of designing models that make it possible to separately control:

- The term-structure of the volatility of volatility
- The short-term skew
- The correlation of spot and volatilities

has acquired more relevance than the ability of accurately fitting market smiles, as these options cannot be hedged with vanilla options during most of their life.

Contrary to most popular smile models, which usually lump together risks of a different nature into a single parameter (think, for example, of the role of the volatility-of-volatility parameter in the Heston model), the modeling framework we propose makes it possible to measure the separate contributions of the three effects listed above to a the price of a derivative.

When this work was first done, options on realized variance had only been trading for a short time and choosing a value for model parameters affecting the term structure of the volatility of volatility was a trading decision.

The market of options on realized variance has since then grown considerably, and new derivatives—such as options on VIX futures—provide a sharper view on smiles of forward volatilities. In our view these new developments will favor the development of models that are able to accurately split risks of a different nature and price them appropriately. As more sophisticated models are able to calibrate to a wider variety of hedging instruments, the issue of choosing the instruments whose market prices should be calibrated to will become ever more relevant.

REFERENCES

1. Backus, D., S. Foresi, K. Li, and L. Wu. (1997). Accounting for biases in Black-Scholes. Unpublished.
2. Carr, P., H. Geman, D. Madan, and M. Yor. (2003). Stochastic volatility for Levy processes. *Mathematical Finance* 13(3) (July): 345–382.
3. Dupire, B. (1994). Pricing with a smile. *Risk* (January): 18–20.
4. Dupire, B. (1996). A unified theory of volatility. Unpublished.
5. Heston, S. (1993). A closed-form solution for options with stochastic volatility with applications to bond and currency options. *Review of Financial Studies* 6: 327–343.
6. Jeffery, C. (2004). Reverse cliquets: End of the road? *Risk* (February): 20–22.
7. Leland, H. (1985). Option replication with transaction costs. *Journal of Finance* 40 (5), 1283–1301.
8. Schönbucher P. (1999). A market model for stochastic implied volatility. *Philosophical Transactions of the Royal Society,* Series A, 357(1758) (August): 2071–2092.
9. Zhou, F. (2003). Black Smirks. *Risk* January 2003: 87–91.

CHAPTER 4

A Geometric Approach to the Asymptotics of Implied Volatility

Pierre Henry-Labordère

Since 1973, the Black-Scholes formula [5] has been extensively used by traders in financial markets to price options. However, the original Black-Scholes derivation is based on several unrealistic assumptions which are not satisfied under real market conditions. For example, in the original Black-Scholes framework, assets are assumed to follow lognormal processes (i.e., with constant volatilities). This hypothesis can be relaxed by introducing more elaborate models called local and stochastic volatility models (see [12] for a nice review).

On the one hand, local volatility models assume that the volatility $\sigma_L(t, f)$ depends only on the underlying f and on the time t. The market is still complete and, as shown by [9], prices of European call-put options determine the diffusion term $\sigma_L(t, f)$ uniquely. On the other hand, stochastic volatility models assume that the volatility itself follows a stochastic process [23]: in this case, the market becomes incomplete as it is not possible to hedge and trade the volatility with a single underlying asset. It can be shown that the local volatility function represents some kind of average over all possible instantaneous volatilities in a stochastic volatility model [10].

For these two types of models (local volatility and stochastic volatility), the resulting Black-Scholes partial differential equation becomes complicated and only a few exact solutions are known. The most commonly used solutions are the constant elasticity of variance model (CEV) [6], which assumes that the local volatility function is given by $\sigma_L(t, f) = \sigma_0 f^\beta$ with σ_0 and β constant, and the Heston model [21], which assumes a mean-reverting square-root process for the variance.

In all other cases, analytical solutions are not available and singular perturbation techniques have been used to obtain asymptotic expressions for the price of European-style options. These singular perturbation techniques can also be used to derive an implied volatility (i.e., *smile*). By definition, this implied volatility is the value of the volatility that when put in the Black-Scholes formula, reproduces the market price for a European call option.

In this chapter, we obtain asymptotic solutions for the conditional probability and the implied volatility up to the first-order in the maturity with any kind of stochastic volatility models using the heat kernel expansion on a Riemannian manifold. This asymptotic smile is very useful for calibration purposes. The smile at zero order (no dependence on the expiry date) is connected to the geodesic distance on a Riemann surface. This relation between the smile at zero order and the geodesic distance has already been obtained in [3, 4] and used in [1] to compute an asymptotic smile for an equity basket. Starting from this nice geometric result, we show how the first-order correction (linear in the expiry date) depends on an Abelian connection which is a nontrivial function of the drift processes.

We derive the asymptotics of implied volatility in two steps: First, we compute the local volatility function associated to our general stochastic volatility model. It corresponds to the mean value of the square of the stochastic volatility. This expression depends on the conditional probability which satisfies by definition a backward Kolmogorov equation. Rewriting this equation in a covariant way (i.e., independent of a system of coordinates), we find a general asymptotic solution in the short-time limit using the heat kernel expansion on a Riemannian manifold. Then, an asymptotic local volatility at first-order is obtained using a saddle-point method. In this geometric framework, stochastic (local) volatility models will correspond to the geometry of (real) complex curves (i.e., Riemann surfaces). In particular, the SABR model can be associated to the geometry of the (hyperbolic) Poincaré plane $\mathbb{H}^2$. This connection between $\mathbb{H}^2$ and the SABR model has also been obtained in an unpublished paper [20]. Similar results can be found in [4].

The second step consists in using a one-to-one asymptotic correspondence between a local volatility function and the implied volatility. This relation is derived using the heat kernel on a time-dependent real line.

Next, we focus on a specific example and derive an asymptotic implied volatility at the first-order for a SABR model with a mean-reversion term which we call λ-SABR. The computation for the smile at the zero-order is already presented in [4] and a similar computation for the implied volatility at the first-order (without a mean-reversion term) is done in [20].

Furthermore, in order to show the strength of this geometric approach, we obtain *two exact solutions* for the conditional probability in the SABR model (with $\beta = 0, 1$). The $\beta = 0$ solution has also been obtained in an unpublished paper [20] and presented by the author in [22]. For $\beta = 1$, an extra dimension appears and in this case, the SABR model is connected to the three-dimensional hyperbolic space $\mathbb{H}^3$. This extra dimension appears as a (hidden) Kaluza-Klein dimension.

As a final comment for the reader not familiar with differential geometry, we have included a short appendix explaining some key notions such as manifold, metric, line bundle and Abelian connection (see [11] for a quick introduction). The saddle-point method is also described in the appendix.

4.1 VOLATILITY ASYMPTOTICS IN STOCHASTIC VOLATILITY MODELS

A (time-homogeneous) stochastic volatility model depends on two stochastic differential equations (SDEs), one for the asset f and one for the volatility a. Let denote $x = (x^i)_{i=1,2} = (f, a)$, with initial conditions $\alpha = (\alpha^i)_{i=1,2} = (f_0, \alpha)$. These variables x^i satisfy the following SDEs

$$dx^i = b^i(x)dt + \sigma^i(x)dW_i$$

$$dW_i dW_j = \rho_{ij}dt \tag{4.1.1}$$

with the initial condition $x^i(t = 0) = \alpha^i$ (with $b^f = 0$ in the forward measure as f is a traded asset). Here $[\rho_{ij}]_{i,j=1,2}$ is a correlation matrix.

We have that the square of the local volatility function is the mean value of the square of the stochastic volatility when the forward x^1 is fixed to f [10]

$$\sigma^2(\tau, f) = \frac{\int_0^\infty \sigma^1(x)^2 p(\tau, x|\alpha)dx_2}{\int_0^\infty p(\tau, x|\alpha)dx_2}$$

with $p(\tau, x|\alpha)$ the conditional probability. In order to obtain an asymptotic expression for the local volatility function, we will use an asymptotic expansion for the conditional probability $p(\tau, x|\alpha)$. This density satisfies the backward Kolmogorov equation:

$$\frac{\partial p}{\partial \tau} = b^i \partial_i p + g^{ij} \partial_{ij} p, \, (i, j) = a, f \tag{4.1.2}$$

with the initial condition $\lim_{\tau \to 0} p(\tau, x|\alpha) = \delta(x - \alpha)$. Here $g^{ij} \equiv \frac{1}{2}\rho_{ij}\sigma^i\sigma^j$ and $\partial_i \equiv \frac{\partial}{\partial \alpha^i}$.

In (4.1.2), we have used the Einstein summation convention, meaning that two identical indices are summed.

For example, $b^i \partial_i p = \sum_{i=1}^{2} b^i \partial_i p$. Note that in the relation $g^{ij} \equiv \frac{1}{2} \rho_{ij} \sigma^i \sigma^j$ although two indices are repeated, there are no implicit summation over i and j. As a result, g^{ij} is a symmetric tensor precisely dependent on these two indices. We will adopt this Einstein convention throughout this chapter.

In the next section, we will show how to derive an asymptotic conditional probability for any multidimensional stochastic volatility models (4.1.1) using the heat kernel expansion on a Riemannian manifold (we will assume here that n is not necessarily equal to 2 as it is the case for a stochastic volatility model). In particular, we will explain the DeWitt's theorem which gives the asymptotic solution to the heat kernel. An extension to the time-dependent heat kernel will be also given as this solution is particularly important in finance to include term structure.

4.2 HEAT KERNEL EXPANSION

Note that the coordinates $\{\alpha^i\}$ (resp. $\{x^i\}$) will be noted $\{x^i\}$ (resp. $\{y^i\}$) below in order to be consistent with our (geometric) notation.

4.2.1 Heat kernel on a Riemannian manifold

In this section, the partial differential equation (PDE) (4.1.2) will be interpreted as a heat kernel on a general smooth n-dimensional manifold M (here we have that $i, j = 1 \cdots n$) without a boundary, endowed with the metric g_{ij} (see Appendix A for definitions and explanations of the terms in this section). The inverse of the metric g^{ij} is defined by

$$g^{ij} = \frac{1}{2} \rho_{ij} \sigma^i \sigma^j$$

and the metric (ρ^{ij} inverse of ρ^{ij}, i.e. $\rho^{ij} \rho_{jk} = \delta_k^i$)

$$g_{ij} = 2 \frac{\rho^{ij}}{\sigma^i \sigma^j} \tag{4.2.1}$$

The differential operator

$$D = b^i \partial_i + g^{ij} \partial_{ij}$$

which appears in (4.1.2) is a second-order elliptic operator of Laplace type. We can then show that there is a unique connection ∇ on $\mathcal{L}$, a line bundle over M, and Q a unique smooth section of $End(\mathcal{L}) = \mathcal{L} \otimes \mathcal{L}^*$ such that

$$D = g^{ij}\nabla_i\nabla_j + Q$$
$$= g^{-\frac{1}{2}}(\partial_i + \mathcal{A}_i)g^{\frac{1}{2}}g^{ij}(\partial_j + \mathcal{A}_j) + Q$$

Using this connection ∇, (4.1.2) can be written in the covariant way, that is,

$$\frac{\partial}{\partial\tau}p(\tau, x|y) = Dp(\tau, x|y) \tag{4.2.2}$$

If we take $\mathcal{A}_i = 0$ and $Q = 0$ then D becomes the Laplace-Beltrami operator (or Laplacian) $\Delta = g^{-\frac{1}{2}}\partial_i(g^{\frac{1}{2}}g^{ij}\partial_j)$. For this configuration, (4.2.2) will be called the Laplacian heat kernel.

We may express the connection $\mathcal{A}^i$ and Q as a function of the drift b^i and the metric g_{ij} by identifying in (4.2.2) the terms ∂_i and ∂_{ij} with those in (4.1.2). We find

$$\mathcal{A}^i = \frac{1}{2}\left(b^i - g^{-\frac{1}{2}}\partial_j\left(g^{1/2}g^{ij}\right)\right) \tag{4.2.3}$$

$$Q = g^{ij}\left(\mathcal{A}_i\mathcal{A}_j - b_j\mathcal{A}_i - \partial_j\mathcal{A}_i\right) \tag{4.2.4}$$

Note that the Latin indices $i, j \ldots$ can be lowered or raised using the metric g_{ij} or its inverse g^{ij}. For example $\mathcal{A}_i = g_{ij}\mathcal{A}^j$ and $b_i = g_{ij}b^j$. The components $\mathcal{A}_i = g_{ij}\mathcal{A}^j$ define a local one-form $\mathcal{A} = \mathcal{A}_i dx^i$. We deduce that under a change of coordinates $x^{i'}(x^j)$, $\mathcal{A}_i$ undergoes the co-vector transformation $\mathcal{A}_{i'}\partial_i x^{i'} = \mathcal{A}_i$. Note that the components b^i don't transform as a vector. This results from the fact that the SDE (4.1.1) has been derived using the Itô calculus and not the Stratonovich one.

Next, let's introduce the Christoffel's symbol Γ^k_{ij} which depends on the metric and its first derivatives

$$\Gamma^k_{ij} = \frac{1}{2}g^{kp}(\partial_j g_{ip} + \partial_i g_{jp} - \partial_p g_{ji}) \tag{4.2.5}$$

Equation 4.2.3 can be rewritten as

$$A^i = \frac{1}{2}(b^i - g^{pq}\Gamma^i_{pq})$$

Note that if we define

$$p' = e^{\chi(\tau,x)-\chi(\tau=0,x=\alpha)}\, p \tag{4.2.6}$$

then p' satisfies the same equation as p (4.2.2) but with

$$\mathcal{A}'_i \equiv \mathcal{A}_i - \partial_i \chi \tag{4.2.7}$$

$$Q' \equiv Q + \partial_\tau \chi \tag{4.2.8}$$

The transformation (4.2.6) is called a *gauge transformation*. The reader should be aware that the transformation (4.2.7) only applies to the connection $\mathcal{A}_i$ with lower indices. The constant phase $e^{\chi(x=\alpha,\tau=0)}$ has been added in (4.2.6) so that p and p' satisfy the same boundary condition at $\tau = 0$. Mathematically, (4.2.6) means that p is a section of the line bundle $\mathcal{L}$ and when we apply a (local) Abelian gauge transformation, this induces an action on the connection $\mathcal{A}$ (4.2.7) (see Appendix A). In particular, if the one-form $\mathcal{A}$ is exact, meaning that there exists a smooth function χ such that $\mathcal{A} = d\chi$ then the new connection $\mathcal{A}'$ (4.2.7) vanishes.

The asymptotic resolution of the heat kernel (4.2.2) in the short time limit is an important problem in theoretical physics and in mathematics. In physics, it corresponds to the solution of the Euclidean Schrödinger equation on a fixed space-time background [7] and in mathematics, the heat kernel—corresponding to the determination of the spectrum of the Laplacian—can give topological information (e.g., the Atiyah-Singer's index theorem) [13]. The following theorem proved by Minakshisundaram-Pleijel-De Witt-Gilkey gives the complete asymptotic solution for the heat kernel on a Riemannian manifold.

Theorem 4.1. *Let M be a Riemannian manifold without a boundary. Then for each $x \in M$, there is a complete asymptotic expansion:*

$$p(\tau, x|y) = \frac{\sqrt{g(y)}}{(4\pi\tau)^{\frac{n}{2}}} \sqrt{\Delta(x,y)}\, \mathcal{P}(y,x) e^{-\frac{\sigma(x,y)}{2\tau}} \sum_{n=1}^{\infty} a_n(x,y)\tau^n, \quad \tau \to 0 \tag{4.2.9}$$

- Here, $\sigma(x, y)$ is the Synge world function equal to one half of the square of geodesic distance $|x - y|_g$ between x and y for the metric g. This distance is defined as the minimizer of

$$|x - y|_g = \min_C \int_0^T \sqrt{g_{ij}\frac{dx^i}{dt}\frac{dx^j}{dt}}\, dt$$

and t parameterizes the curve C. The Euler-Lagrange equation gives the following geodesic differential equation, which depends on the Christoffel's coefficients Γ^i_{jk} (4.2.5):

$$\frac{d^2 x^i}{dt^2} + \Gamma^i_{jk}\frac{dx^j}{dt}\frac{dx^k}{dt} = 0 \qquad (4.2.10)$$

- $\Delta(x, y)$ is the so-called Van Vleck–Morette determinant

$$\Delta(x, y) = g(x)^{-\frac{1}{2}} \det\left(-\frac{\partial^2 \sigma(x, y)}{\partial x \partial y}\right) g(y)^{-\frac{1}{2}} \qquad (4.2.11)$$

with $g(x) = \det[g_{ij}(x, x)]$
- $\mathcal{P}(y, x)$ is the parallel transport of the Abelian connection along the geodesic from the point y to x

$$\mathcal{P}(y, x) = e^{-\int_{C(y,x)} A_i dx^i} \qquad (4.2.12)$$

- The $a_i(x, y)$, called the heat kernel coefficients, are smooth sections $\Gamma(M \times M, \mathcal{L} \times \mathcal{L}^*)$. The first coefficient is simple

$$a_0(x, y) = 1, \ \forall\, (x, y) \in M \times M$$

The other coefficients are more complex. However, when evaluated on the diagonal $x = y$, they depend on geometric invariants such as the scalar curvature R. The nondiagonal coefficients can then be computed as a Taylor series when x is in a neighborhood of y. The first diagonal coefficients are fairly easy to compute by hand. Recently $a_n(x, x)$ has been computed up to order $n = 8$. These formulas become exponentially more complicated as n increases. For example, the formula for a_6 has 46 terms. The first diagonal coefficients are given below:

$$a_1(x, x) = P \equiv \frac{1}{6}R + Q$$

$$a_2(x, x) = \frac{1}{180}\left(R_{ijkl}R^{ijkl} - R_{ij}R^{ij}\right) + \frac{\Delta Q}{6} + \frac{\Delta R}{30}$$

$$+ \frac{1}{2}P^2 + \frac{1}{12}\mathcal{R}_{ij}\mathcal{R}^{ij}$$

with R_{ijkl} the Riemann tensor, R_{ij} the Ricci tensor and R the scalar curvature given by

$$R^i_{jkl} = \partial_l \Gamma^i_{jk} - \partial_k \Gamma^i_{jl} + \Gamma^p_{jk} \Gamma^i_{pl} - \Gamma^p_{jl} \Gamma^i_{pk}$$

$$R_{jl} = R^i_{jil}$$

$$R = g^{ij} R_{ij}$$

and

$$\mathcal{R}_{ij} = [\nabla_i, \nabla_j]$$

Let's now explain how to use the heat kernel expansion (4.2.9) with a simple example, namely a lognormal process.

Example 4.2 (log-normal process). The *SDE* is $df = \sigma_0 f dW$ and using the Definition 4.2.1, we obtain the following one-dimensional metric:

$$g_{ff} = \frac{2}{\sigma_0^2 f^2}$$

When written with the coordinate $s = \sqrt{2} \frac{\ln(f)}{\sigma_0}$, the metric is flat $g_{ss} = 1$ and all the heat kernel coefficients depending on the Riemann tensor vanish. The geodesic distance between two points s and s' is given by the classical Euclidean distance $d(s, s') = |s - s'|$ and the Synge function is $\sigma(s, s') = \frac{1}{2}(s - s')^2$. In the old coordinate [f], σ is

$$\sigma(f, f_0) = \frac{1}{\sigma_0^2} \ln\left(\frac{f}{f_0}\right)^2 \tag{4.2.13}$$

Furthermore, the connection $\mathcal{A}$ (4.2.3) and the function Q (4.2.4) are given by

$$\mathcal{A} = -\frac{1}{2f} df$$

$$Q = -\frac{\sigma_0^2}{8}$$

Therefore, the parallel transport $\mathcal{P}(f_0, f)$ is given by $\mathcal{P}(f_0, f) = e^{\frac{1}{2}\ln(\frac{f}{f_0})}$. Plugging these expressions into 4.2.9, we obtain the following first-order asymptotic solution for the lognormal process

$$p_1(\tau, f \mid f_0) = \frac{1}{f\left(2\pi\sigma_0^2\tau\right)^{\frac{1}{2}}} e^{-\frac{\ln\left(\frac{f}{f_0}\right)^2}{2\sigma_0^2\tau} - \frac{1}{2}\ln\left(\frac{f}{f_0}\right)} \left(1 - \frac{\sigma_0^2}{8}\tau + \cdots\right)$$

Note the sign minus in front of $\ln(\frac{f}{f_0})$ as the coordinates f_0 was noted f above.

At the second order, the second heat kernel coefficient is given by $a_2 = \frac{1}{2}Q^2 = \frac{\sigma_0^4\tau^2}{128}$ and the asymptotic solution is

$$p_2(\tau, f \mid f_0) = \frac{1}{f\left(2\pi\sigma_0^2\tau\right)^{\frac{1}{2}}} e^{-\frac{\ln\left(\frac{f}{f_0}\right)^2}{2\sigma_0^2\tau} - \frac{1}{2}\ln\left(\frac{f}{f_0}\right)} \left(1 - \frac{\sigma_0^2\tau}{8} + \frac{\sigma_0^4\tau^2}{128}\right)$$

This should be compared with the exact solution:

$$p(f, \tau \mid f_0) = \frac{1}{f\left(2\pi\sigma_0^2\tau\right)^{\frac{1}{2}}} e^{-\frac{\left(\ln\left(\frac{f}{f_0}\right)+\frac{\sigma_0^2\tau}{2}\right)^2}{2\sigma_0^2\tau}}$$

Note that this exact solution can be found using a gauge transformation which reduces the Kolmogorov equation to the heat kernel on $\mathbb{R}$. Indeed the connection $\mathcal{A}$ and the section Q are exact, meaning that $\mathcal{A} = d\chi$, $Q = -\partial_\tau\chi$, with $\chi = -\frac{1}{2}\ln(f) + \frac{\sigma_0^2\tau}{8}$. Modulo a gauge transformation $p' = e^{-\frac{1}{2}\ln(\frac{f_0}{f})+\frac{\sigma_0^2\tau}{8}}p$, p' satisfies the (Laplacian) heat kernel on $\mathbb{R}$

$$\partial_s^2 p' = \partial_\tau p' \tag{4.2.14}$$

whose solution is the normal distribution.

To be thorough, we conclude this section with a brief overview of the derivation of the heat kernel expansion.

We start with the Schwinger-DeWitt antsaz:

$$p(\tau, x \mid y) = \frac{\sqrt{g(y)}}{(4\pi\tau)^{\frac{n}{2}}} \Delta(x, y)^{\frac{1}{2}} e^{-\frac{\sigma(x,y)}{2\tau}} \mathcal{P}(y, x)\Omega(\tau, x \mid y) \tag{4.2.15}$$

Plugging 4.2.15 into the heat kernel equation (4.2.2), we derive a PDE satisfied by the function $\Omega(\tau, x|y)$

$$\partial_\tau \Omega = \left(-\frac{1}{\tau}\sigma^i \nabla_i + \mathcal{P}^{-1}\Delta^{-\frac{1}{2}}(D+Q)\Delta^{\frac{1}{2}}\mathcal{P} \right)\Omega \qquad (4.2.16)$$

with $\nabla_i = \partial_i + \mathcal{A}_i$ and $\sigma_i = \nabla_i \sigma$, $\sigma^i = g^{ij}\sigma_j$. The regular boundary condition is $\Omega(\tau, x|y) = 1$. We solve this equation by writing the function Ω as a formal series in τ:

$$\Omega(\tau, x|y) = \sum_{n=0}^{\infty} a_n(x, y)\tau^n \qquad (4.2.17)$$

Plugging this series 4.2.17 into 4.2.16 and identifying the coefficients in τ^n, we obtain an infinite system of ordinary coupled differential equations:

$$a_0 = 1$$

$$\left(1 + \frac{1}{k}\sigma^i \nabla_i\right)a_k = \mathcal{P}^{-1}\Delta^{-\frac{1}{2}}(D+Q)\Delta^{\frac{1}{2}}\mathcal{P}\frac{a_{k-1}}{k}, \quad \forall k \neq 0$$

The calculation of the heat kernel coefficients in the general case of arbitrary background offers a complex technical problem. The Schwinger-DeWitt's method is quite simple but it is not effective at higher orders. By means of it only the two lowest-order terms were calculated. For other advanced methods, see [2].

4.2.2 Heat Kernel on a Time-Dependent Riemannian Manifold

In most financial models, the volatility diffusion-drift terms can explicitly depend on time. In this case, we obtain a time-dependent metric and connection. It is therefore useful to generalize the heat kernel expansion from the previous section to the case of a time-dependent metric defined by

$$g_{ij}(t) = 2\frac{\rho^{ij}(t)}{\sigma^i(t)\sigma^j(t)}$$

This is the purpose of this section.
The differential operator

$$\mathcal{D} = b^i(t)\partial_i + g^{ij}(t)\partial_{ij} \qquad (4.2.18)$$

which appears in 4.1.2 is a time-dependent family of operators of Laplace type. Let $(, t)$ denote the multiple covariant differentiation according to the Levi-Cevita connection (t). We can expand $\mathcal{D}$ in a Taylor series expansion in t to write $\mathcal{D}$ invariantly in the form

$$\mathcal{D}u = Du + \sum_{r>0} t^r \left(\mathcal{G}_r^{ij} u_{;ij} + \mathcal{F}_r^i u_{;i} + \mathcal{Q}_r \right) \tag{4.2.19}$$

with the operator D depending on a connection $\mathcal{A}_i$ and a smooth section $\mathcal{Q}$ $(b^i \equiv b^i(t = 0)$, $g_{ij} \equiv g_{ij}(t = 0))$ given by (4.2.2). The tensor $\mathcal{G}_1^{ij}$ is given by

$$\mathcal{G}_1^{ij} = g_{,t}^{ij}(0) = \frac{\rho_{ij,t}(0)}{2} \sigma^i(0) \sigma^j(0) + \rho_{ij}(0) \sigma_{,t}^i(0) \sigma^j(0) \tag{4.2.20}$$

Using this connection, 4.1.2 can be written in the covariant way, that is,

$$\frac{\partial}{\partial t} p(t, x|y) = \mathcal{D} p(t, x|y) \tag{4.2.21}$$

with $\mathcal{D}$ given by (4.2.19). The asymptotic resolution of the heat kernel (4.2.21) in the short time limit in a time-dependent background is an important problem in quantum cosmology. When the spacetime slowly varies, the time-dependent metric describing the cosmological evolution can be expanded in a Taylor series with respect to t. The index r in this situation is related to the adiabatic order [8]. The following expression obtained in [14, 15] gives the complete asymptotic solution for the heat kernel on a Riemannian manifold.

Theorem 4.3. *Let M be a Riemannian manifold (without a boundary) with a time-dependent metric. Then for each $x \in M$, there is a complete asymptotic expansion:*

$$p(t, x|y) = \frac{\sqrt{g(y)}}{(4\pi t)^{\frac{n}{2}}} \sqrt{\Delta(x, y)} \mathcal{P}(y, x) e^{-\frac{\sigma(x,y)}{2t}} \sum_{n=0}^{\infty} a_n(x, y) t^n \tag{4.2.22}$$

The $a_i(x, y)$ are smooth functions on M and depend on geometric invariants such as the scalar curvature R. The diagonal coefficients a_n have been computed up to the fourth order $(a_0(x, y) = 1)$. The first coefficient is given below:

$$a_1(x, x) = P \equiv \frac{1}{6} R + Q - \frac{1}{4} \mathcal{G}_{1,ii} \tag{4.2.23}$$

4.3 GEOMETRY OF COMPLEX CURVES AND ASYMPTOTIC VOLATILITY

In our geometric framework, a stochastic volatility model (SVM) corresponds to a complex curve, also called Riemann surfaces. Using the classification of conformal metric on a Riemann surface, we will show that the SVM falls into three classes. In particular, the λ-SABR corresponds to the Poincare hyperbolic plane. This connection between the SABR model and $\mathbb{H}^2$ has already been presented in [4, 20, 22, 26]. This identification allows us to find an exact solution to the SABR model ($\lambda = 0$) with $\beta = 0, 1$. The $\beta = 0$ solution has also been obtained in an unpublished paper [20] and rederived by the author in [22]. Furthermore, we will derive a general asymptotic implied volatility for any stochastic volatility model. This expression only depends on the geometric objects that we have introduced before (i.e., metric, connection).

4.3.1 Complex Curves

On a Riemann surface we can show that the metric can always be written locally in a neighborhood of a point (using the right system of coordinates):

$$g_{ij} = e^{\phi(x)}\delta_{ij}, \quad i, j = 1, 2$$

and it is therefore locally conformally flat. The coordinates x_i are called the isothermal coordinates. Furthermore, two metrics on a Riemann surface, g_{ij} and h_{ij} (in local coordinates), are called conformally equivalent if there exists a smooth function $\phi(x)$ such that

$$g_{ij} = e^{\phi(x)}h_{ij} \tag{4.3.1}$$

The following theorem follows from the preceding observations:

Theorem 4.4 (Uniformization). *Every metric on a simply connected Riemann surface[1] is conformally equivalent to a metric of constant scalar curvature R:*

1. *$R = +1$: the Riemann sphere S^2.*
2. *$R = 0$: the complex plane $\mathbb{C}$.*
3. *$R = -1$: the upper half plane $\mathbb{H}^2 = \{z \in \mathbb{C} | Im(z) > 0\}$.*

---

[1] The nonsimply connected Riemann surfaces can also be classified by taking the double cover.

By the uniformization theorem, all surfaces fall into these three types, and we conclude that there are *a priori* three types of stochastic volatility models (modulo the conformal equivalence). In the following, we compute the metric associated with the λ-SABR model and find the corresponding metric on $\mathbb{H}^2$ [26]. In this way, we will show that the λ-SABR model englobes these universality classes and thus is a generic framework allowing all possible behaviors of the implied volatility.

In the next section, we present our general asymptotic implied volatility at the first-order and postpone the derivation to subsection 4.3.3.

4.3.2 Unified Asymptotic Implied Volatility

The general asymptotic implied volatility at the first order (for any [time-independent] stochastic volatility models), depending implicitly on the metric g_{ij} (4.2.1) and the connection $\mathcal{A}_i$ (4.2.3) on our Riemann surface, is given by

$$
\sigma_{BS}(K, \tau, g_{ij}, \mathcal{A}_i)
$$

$$
= \frac{\ln(\frac{K}{f_0})}{\int_{f_0}^{K} \frac{df'}{\sqrt{2g^{ff}(c)}}} \left\{ 1 + \frac{g^{ff}(c)\tau}{12} \left(-\frac{3}{4} \left(\frac{\partial_f g^{ff}(c)}{g^{ff}(c)} \right)^2 + \frac{\partial_f^2 g^{ff}(c)}{g^{ff}(c)} + \frac{1}{f^2} \right) \right.
$$

$$
\left. + \frac{\tau g^{ff'}(c)}{2\phi''(c)} \left(\ln\left(\Delta g \mathcal{P}^2 \right)'(c) - \frac{\phi'''(c)}{\phi''(c)} + \frac{g^{ff''}(c)}{g^{ff'}(c)} \right) \right\} \tag{4.3.2}
$$

Here c is the volatility a which minimizes the geodesic distance $d(x, \alpha)$ on the Riemann surface ($\phi(x, \alpha) = d^2(x, \alpha)$). Δ is the Van Vleck–Morette determinant (4.2.11), g is the determinant of the metric, and $\mathcal{P}$ is the parallel gauge transport, (4.2.12). The prime symbol ($'$) indicates a derivative according to a.

This formula (4.3.2) is particularly useful as we can use it to calibrate rapidly any SVM. In section 5, we will apply it to the λ-SABR model. In order to use the above formula, the only computation needed is the calculation of the geodesic distance. For example, for a n-dimensional hyperbolic space $\mathbb{H}^n$, the geodesic distance is known. We will see that $\mathbb{H}^2$ corresponds to a SABR model with a mean-reversion drift.

4.3.3 Derivation

Asymptotic Probability We now have the necessary data to apply the heat kernel expansion and deduce the asymptotic formula for the probability density at the first order for any (time-independent) stochastic volatility model. We obtain

$$p(\tau, x|y) = \frac{\sqrt{g(y)}}{(4\pi\tau)} \sqrt{\Delta(x, y)} \mathcal{P}(y, x) e^{-\frac{d^2(x,y)}{4\tau}} \left(1 + a_1(x, y)\tau + o(\tau^2)\right)$$

$$(4.3.3)$$

We will now derive an asymptotic expression for the implied volatility. The computation involves two steps. The first step as illustrated in this section consists in computing the local volatility $\sigma(\tau, f)$ associated to the SVM. In the second step (see next section), we will deduce the implied volatility from the local volatility using the heat kernel on a time-dependent real line.

We know that the local volatility associated to a SVM is given by [10]

$$\sigma^2(\tau, f) = \frac{2 \int_0^\infty g^{ff} p \, da}{\int_0^\infty p \, da} \tag{4.3.4}$$

when the forward $x_1 = f$ is fixed. p is the conditional probability given in the short time limit at the first order by 4.3.3. Plugging our asymptotic expression for the conditional probability 4.3.3 in 4.3.4, we obtain

$$\sigma^2(\tau, f) = \frac{2 \int_0^\infty f(a) e^{\epsilon\phi(a)} da}{\int_0^\infty h(a) e^{\epsilon\phi(a)} da} \tag{4.3.5}$$

with $\phi(a) = d^2(x, y)$, $h(a) = \sqrt{g}\sqrt{\Delta(x, y)}\mathcal{P}(y, x)(1 + a_1(x, y)\tau)$, $f(a) = h(a)g^{ff}$ and $\epsilon = -\frac{1}{4\tau}$. Using a saddle-point method, we can find an asymptotic expression for the local volatility. For example, at the zero order, σ^2 is given by $2g^{ff}(c)$ with c the stochastic volatility, which minimizes the geodesic distance on our Riemann surface:

$$c \equiv a | \min_a \phi \tag{4.3.6}$$

Using the saddle-point method at the first-order, we find the following expression for the numerator in 4.3.5 (see Appendix B for a sketch of the proof):

$$\int_0^\infty f(a) e^{\epsilon\phi(a)} da = \sqrt{\frac{2\pi}{-\epsilon\phi''(c)}} e^{\epsilon\phi(c)} f(c)$$

$$\left(1 + \frac{1}{\epsilon}\left(-\frac{f''(c)}{2f(c)\phi''(c)} + \frac{\phi^{(4)}(c)}{8\phi''(c)^2} + \frac{f'(c)\phi'''(c)}{2\phi''(c)^2 f(c)} - \frac{5\phi'''(c)}{24(\phi''(c))^3}\right)\right)$$

Computing the denominator in 4.3.5 in a similar way, we obtain a first-order correction of the local volatility:

$$\sigma(\tau, f)^2 = 2g^{ff}(c)$$
$$\left(1 + \frac{1}{\epsilon}\left(-\frac{1}{2\phi''(c)}\left(\frac{f''(c)}{f(c)} - \frac{h''(c)}{h(c)}\right) + \frac{\phi'''(c)}{2\phi''(c)^2}\left(\frac{f'(c)}{f(c)} - \frac{h'(c)}{h(c)}\right)\right)\right)$$

Plugging the expression for f and g, we finally obtain

$$\sigma(\tau, f) = \sqrt{2g^{ff}(c)}$$
$$\left(1 + \frac{\tau}{\phi''(c)}\left(\frac{g^{ff'}(c)}{g^{ff}(c)}\left(\ln(\Delta g \mathcal{P}^2)'(c) - \frac{\phi'''(c)}{\phi''(c)}\right) + \frac{g^{ff''}(c)}{g^{ff}(c)}\right)\right) \qquad (4.3.7)$$

Here the prime symbol ($'$) indicates a derivative according to a. This expression depends only on the geodesic distance and the parallel gauge transport on our Riemann surface.

Remark 4.5. *Note that in our discussion we have disregarded the boundary conditions. In the heat kernel expansion, these boundary conditions affect only the heat kernel coefficients. As a result, our formula (4.3.7) does not depend on some specific boundary conditions.*

The final step is to obtain a relation between the local volatility function $\sigma(\tau, f)$ and the implied volatility. We will show in the next section how to obtain such a relation using the heat kernel expansion on a time-dependent one-dimensional real line (4.2.22).

Local Volatility Model and Implied Volatility   Let's assume we have a local volatility model

$$df = C(t, f)dW_t \; ; \; f(t = 0) = f_0 \qquad (4.3.8)$$

The fair value of a European call option (with maturity date τ and strike K) is given by (using the Itô-Tanaka lemma and assuming that τ is small):

$$\mathcal{C}(K, \tau, f_0) = (f_0 - K)^+ + \frac{C^2(t = 0, K)}{2}\int_0^\tau dT(1 + 2\partial_t \ln C(0, K))p(T, K| f_0)$$

$$(4.3.9)$$

with $p(T, K | f_0)$ the conditional probability associated to the process (4.3.8). In our framework, this model corresponds to a (one-dimensional) real curve endowed with the time-dependent metric $g_{ff} = \frac{2}{C(t, f)^2}$. For $t = 0$ and for the new coordinate $u = \sqrt{2} \int \frac{df'}{C(f')}$ (with $C(0, f) \equiv C(f)$), the metric is flat: $g_{uu} = 1$. The distance is then given by the classical Euclidean distance

$$d(u, u') = |u - u'|$$

Furthermore, the connection $\mathcal{A}$ (4.2.3) and the function Q (4.2.4) are given by

$$\mathcal{A}_f = -\frac{1}{2} \partial_f \ln(C(f))$$

$$Q = \frac{C^2(f)}{4} \left(\left(\frac{C''(f)}{C(f)} \right) - \frac{1}{2} \left(\frac{C'(f)}{C(f)} \right)^2 \right)$$

The parallel transport is then given by $\mathcal{P}(f, f_0) = \sqrt{\frac{C(f_0)}{C(f)}}$. Furthermore, $\mathcal{G}$ (4.2.20) is given by

$$\mathcal{G}(K) = 2 \partial_t \ln(C(t, K))|_{t=0} \tag{4.3.10}$$

To compute the conditional probability density $p(T, K | f_0)$ using the heat kernel expansion, we need the nondiagonal coefficient $a_1(f, f_0)$. From the diagonal heat kernel coefficient (4.2.23), we will use the following approximation for the nondiagonal term

$$a_1(f, f_0) \simeq a_1(f_{av}, f_{av})$$

with $f_{av} = \frac{f_0 + K}{2}$. The first-order conditional probability (using the heat kernel expansion on a time-dependent manifold (4.2.22)) is then

$$p(T, K | f_0, t) = \frac{1}{C(K)\sqrt{2\pi T}} \sqrt{\frac{C(f_0)}{C(K)}} e^{-\frac{\sigma(f_0, K)^2}{2T}} \left(1 + \left(Q(f_{av}) - \frac{\mathcal{G}(f_{av})}{4} \right) T \right)$$

Plugging this expression in (4.3.9), the integration over T can be performed and we obtain

Proposition 4.6.

$$C(K, \tau, f_0) = (f_0 - K)^+ + \frac{\sqrt{C(K)C(f_0)\tau}}{2\sqrt{2\pi}}$$

$$\times \left(H_1(\omega) + \left(Q(f_{av}) + \frac{3\mathcal{G}(f_{av})}{4} \right) \tau H_2(\omega) \right) \quad (4.3.11)$$

with

$$H_1(\omega) = 2(e^{-\omega^2} + \sqrt{\pi\omega^2}(N(\sqrt{2}|\omega|) - 1))$$

$$H_2(\omega) = \frac{2}{3}(e^{-\omega^2}(1 - 2\omega^2) - 2|\omega|^3\sqrt{\pi}(N(\sqrt{2}|\omega|) - 1))$$

$$\omega = \int_{f_0}^{K} \frac{df'}{\sqrt{2\tau}C(f')}$$

Here $N(\cdot)$ is the cumulative normal distribution.

In the case of a constant volatility $C(t, f) = \sigma_0 f$, the above formula reduces to

Example 4.7 (Black-Scholes Vanilla option).

$$C(K, \tau, f_0) = (f_0 - K)^+ + \frac{\sqrt{Kf_0\sigma_0^2\tau}}{2\sqrt{2\pi}} \left(H_1(\bar{\omega}) - \frac{\sigma_0^2}{8}\tau H_2(\bar{\omega}) \right) \quad (4.3.12)$$

with $\bar{\omega} = \frac{\ln\left(\frac{K}{f_0}\right)}{\sqrt{2\tau}\sigma_0}$.

By identifying the formula (4.3.11) with the same formula obtained with an implied volatility $\sigma_0 = \sigma_{BS}(\tau, K)$ (4.3.12), we deduce

$$\sigma_{BS}(\tau, K) = \frac{\sqrt{C(K)C(f_0)}}{\sqrt{Kf_0}} \frac{H_1(\omega)}{H_1(\bar{\omega})} \left(1 + \left(Q(K) + \frac{3\mathcal{G}(K)}{4} \right) \tau \frac{H_2(\omega)}{H_1(\omega)} \right)$$

$$+ \frac{\sigma_{BS}^2(\tau, K)\tau}{8} \frac{H_2(\bar{\omega})}{H_1(\bar{\omega})} \quad (4.3.13)$$

At the zero order, we obtain $\omega = \bar{\omega}$, that is,

$$\lim_{\tau \to 0} \sigma_{BS}(\tau, K) = \frac{\ln\left(\frac{K}{f_0}\right)}{\int_{f_0}^{K} \frac{df'}{C(f')}} \tag{4.3.14}$$

The formula (4.3.14) has already been found in [3] and we will call it the *BBF* relation in the following. Then using the recurrence equation (4.3.13), we obtain at the first order

$$\sigma_{BS}(\tau, K) = \frac{\ln\left(\frac{K}{f_0}\right)}{\int_{f_0}^{K} \frac{df'}{C(f')}} \left(1 + \frac{\tau}{3}\left(\frac{1}{8}\left(\frac{\ln\left(\frac{K}{f_0}\right)}{\int_{f_0}^{K} \frac{df'}{C(f')}}\right)^2 + Q(f_{av}) + \frac{3\mathcal{G}(f_{av})}{4}\right)\right)$$

$$\simeq \frac{\ln\left(\frac{K}{f_0}\right)}{\int_{f_0}^{K} \frac{df'}{C(f')}} \left(1 + \frac{C^2(f_{av})\tau}{24}\left(2\frac{C''(f_{av})}{C(f_{av})} - \left(\frac{C'(f_{av})}{C(f_{av})}\right)^2\right.\right.$$

$$\left.\left. + \frac{1}{f_{av}^2} + 12\frac{\partial_t C}{C^3(f_{av})}\right)\right) \tag{4.3.15}$$

In the case $C(t, f) = C(f)$, we reproduce the asymptotic implied volatility obtained in [18]. Now plugging the local volatility (4.3.7) into the implied volatility (4.3.15), we obtain 4.3.2 and this achieves our derivation of an asymptotic implied volatility at the first order.

4.4 λ-SABR MODEL AND HYPERBOLIC GEOMETRY

4.4.1 λ-SABR Model

The volatility a is not a tradable asset. Therefore, in the risk-neutral measure, a can have a drift. A popular choice is to make the volatility process mean reverting. Therefore, we introduce the λ-SABR model defined by the following SDE [4]:

$$df = a C(f) dW_1$$
$$da = \lambda(a - \bar{\lambda})dt + vadW_2$$
$$C(f) = f^\beta, \ a(0) = \alpha, \ f(0) = f_0$$

where W_1 and W_2 are two Brownian processes with correlation $\rho \in]-1, 1[$. The stochastic Black volatility is $\sigma_t = af^{\beta-1}$. In the following section, we present our asymptotic smile for the λ-SABR model and postpone the derivation to the next section.

4.4.2 Asymptotic Smile for the λ-SABR

The first-order asymptotic smile (with strike f, maturity date τ, and spot f_0) associated to the stochastic λ-SABR model is

$$\sigma_{BS}(f_0, f, \tau) = \frac{\ln\left(\frac{f_0}{f}\right)}{\text{vol}(q(f))}\left(1 + \sigma_1\left(\frac{f + f_0}{2}\right)\tau\right) \qquad (4.4.1)$$

with

$$\sigma_1(f) = \frac{(a_{\min}(q)C(f))^2}{24}$$

$$\times \left(\frac{1}{f^2} + \frac{2\partial_{ff}(C(f)a_{\min}(q(f)))}{C(f)a_{\min}(q(f))} - \left(\frac{\partial_f(C(f)a_{\min}(q(f)))}{C(f)a_{\min}(q(f))}\right)^2\right)$$

$$+ \frac{\alpha v^2 \ln(\mathcal{P})'(a_{\min}(q(f)))(1 - \rho^2)\sqrt{\cosh(d(a_{\min}(q(f))))^2 - 1}}{2d(a_{\min}(q(f)))}$$

with $\quad q(f) = \int_{f_0}^f x^{-\beta}dx, \quad \text{vol}(q) = \frac{1}{v}\log\left(\frac{-qv - \alpha\rho + \sqrt{\alpha^2 + q^2v^2 + 2q\alpha v\rho}}{\alpha(1-\rho)}\right) \quad$ and $a_{\min}(q) = \sqrt{\alpha^2 + 2\alpha v\rho q + v^2q^2}$. Moreover, we have

$$\ln\left(\frac{\mathcal{P}}{\mathcal{P}^{SABR}}\right)'(a_{\min}(q(f)))$$

$$= \frac{\lambda}{v^2}(G_0(\theta_2(a_{\min}(q(f))), A_0(a_{\min}(q(f))), B)\theta_2'(a_{\min}(q(f)))$$

$$- G_0(\theta_1(a_{\min}(q(f))), A_0(a_{\min}(q(f))), B)\theta_1'(a_{\min}(q(f)))$$

$$+ A_0'(a_{\min}(q(f)))(G_1(\theta_2(a_{\min}(q(f))), B) - G_1(\theta_1(a_{\min}(q(f))), B)))$$

$$\qquad (4.4.2)$$

$$d(a_{\min}(q(f))) = \cosh^{-1}\left(\frac{-q(f)v\rho - \alpha\rho^2 + a_{\min}(q(f))}{\alpha(1 - \rho^2)}\right)$$

with

$$\ln(\mathcal{P}^{SABR})'(a_{min}(q)) = \frac{\beta}{2(1 - \rho^2)(1 - \beta)}$$
$$\times \left(F_0(\theta_2(a_{min}(q)), A(a_{min}(q)), B)\theta_2'(a_{min}(q)) \right.$$
$$- F_0(\theta_1(a_{min}(q)), A(a_{min}(q)), B)\theta_1'(a_{min}(q))$$
$$- A'(a_{min}(q))F_1(\theta_2(a_{min}(q)), A(a_{min}(q)), B)$$
$$\left. - F_1(\theta_1(a_{min}(q)), A(a_{min}(q)), B)) \right)$$

and with

$$G_1(x, b) = -\csc(x) + b \, Re\left(\log\left(\tan\left(\frac{x}{2}\right)\right)\right)$$

$$G_0(x, a, b) = \cot(x)\csc(x)\,(a + \sin(x))\,(1 + b\tan(x))$$

$$A_0(a_{min}(q)) = -\left(\frac{\bar{\lambda}\sqrt{1 - \rho^2}}{C(f)}\right)$$

$$A_0'(a_{min}(q)) = \frac{\bar{\lambda}\sqrt{1 - \rho^2}\,(\alpha\rho + vq(f))}{C(f)^2\,(\rho\,(\alpha - C(f)) + vq(f))}$$

$$F_0(x, a, b) = \frac{\sin(x)}{a + \cos(x) + b\sin(x)}$$

$$F_1(x, a, b) = \frac{-2b\arctan\left(\frac{b+(-1+a)\tan\left(\frac{x}{2}\right)}{\sqrt{-1+a^2-b^2}}\right)}{(-1 + a^2 - b^2)^{\frac{3}{2}}}$$
$$+ \frac{-1 + a^2 + ab\sin(x)}{(-1 + a^2 - b^2)\,(a + \cos(x) + b\sin(x))}$$

$$\theta_2(a_{min}(q)) = \pi - \arctan\left(\frac{\sqrt{1 - \rho^2}}{\rho}\right)$$

$$\theta_1(a_{min}(q)) = -\arctan\left(\frac{\alpha\sqrt{1 - \rho^2}}{\alpha\rho + vq(f)}\right) + \pi\mathbf{1}_{(\alpha\rho+vq(f))\geq 0}$$

$$\theta_2'(a_{min}(q)) = \frac{\alpha\theta_1'(a_{min}(q))}{a_{min}(q)}$$

$$\theta_1'(a_{min}(q)) = \frac{\alpha\,(vq(f) + \rho\,(\alpha + a_{min}(q)))}{v\sqrt{1 - \rho^2}q(f)\,(2\alpha\rho + vq(f))\,a_{min}(q)}$$

$$A(a_{\min}(q)) = -\left(\frac{\nu(f_0 - f_0^\beta(-1 + \beta)q(f))}{f_0^\beta(-1 + \beta)a_{\min}(q)}\right)$$

$$A'(a_{\min}(q)) = \frac{f_0\nu(\alpha\rho + \nu q(f)) + f_0^\beta\alpha(-1 + \beta)(\alpha + \nu\rho q(f))}{f_0^\beta(-1 + \beta)a_{\min}(q)^2(\nu q(f) + \rho(\alpha - a_{\min}(q)))}$$

$$B = \frac{\rho}{\sqrt{1 - \rho^2}}$$

4.4.3 Derivation

In order to use our general formula (4.3.2) for the implied volatility, we will compute the metric and the connection associated to the λ-SABR model in the next subsection. We will show that the λ-SABR metric is diffeomorphic equivalent to the metric on $\mathbb{H}^2$, the hyperbolic Poincaré plane [22, 26].

Hyperbolic Poincaré Plane   The metric associated to the λ-SABR model is (using 4.2.1)

$$ds^2 = g_{ij}dx^i dx^j$$

$$= \frac{2}{a^2 C^2 \nu^2(1 - \rho^2)}[\nu^2 df^2 - 2\nu\rho C(f)dadf + C(f)^2 da^2]$$

By introducing the new coordinates $x = \nu q(f) - \rho a$ (with $q(f) = \int_{f_0}^f \frac{df'}{C(f')}$) and $y = (1 - \rho^2)^{\frac{1}{2}}a$, the metric becomes (after some algebraic manipulations) the standard hyperbolic metric on the Poincaré half-plane $\mathbb{H}^2$ in the coordinates $[x, y]$ [2]

$$ds^2 = \frac{2}{\nu^2}\left(\frac{dx^2 + dy^2}{y^2}\right) \qquad (4.4.3)$$

---

[2] How can we prove that this is the correct metric on $\mathbb{H}^2$? By applying a Möbius transformation (see above), the upper half plane is mapped to the Poincaré disk $\mathcal{D} = \{z \in C||z| \le 1\}$. Then if we define $x_1 = \frac{1+|z|^2}{1-|z|^2}$, $x_1 = \frac{2\Re(z)}{1-|z|^2}$, $x_3 = \frac{2\Re(z)}{1-|z|^2}$, we obtain that $\mathcal{D}$ is mapped to the Minskowski pseudo-sphere $-x_0^2 + x_1^2 + x_2^2 = 1$. On this space, we have the metric $ds^2 = -dx_0^2 + dx_1^2 + dx_3^2$. We can then deduce the induced metric on the Minskowki model. On the upper-half plane, this gives (4.4.3) (without the scale factor $\frac{2}{\nu^2}$).

The unusual factor $\frac{2}{v^2}$ in front of the metric (4.4.3) can be eliminated by scaling the time $\tau' = \frac{v^2}{2}\tau$ in the heat kernel (4.2.2) (and Q becomes $\frac{2}{v^2}Q$). This is what we will use in the following.

Remark 4.8 (Heston model). *The Heston model is a stochastic volatility model given by the following SDEs [21]:*

$$df = af dW_1$$

$$da = -\left(\frac{\eta^2}{8a} + \frac{\lambda a}{2}\left(1 - \left(\frac{\bar{a}}{a}\right)^2\right)\right) dt + \frac{\eta}{2} dW_2$$

Let's introduce the variable $x = \frac{\eta}{2}\ln(f) - \rho\frac{a}{2}$, $y = (1 - \rho^2)^{\frac{1}{2}}\frac{a}{2}$. Then, in the coordinates $[x, y]$, the metric becomes

$$ds^2 = \frac{4}{\eta^2(1 - \rho^2)^{\frac{1}{2}}} y ds_{\mathbb{H}^2}^2$$

One can show that the the scalar curvature diverges at $y = 0$ and therefore the metric has a true singularity at $y = 0$.

As this connection between the λ-SABR model and $\mathbb{H}^2$ is quite intriguing, we investigate some of the useful properties of the hyperbolic space (for example the geodesics). First, by introducing the complex variable $z = x + iy$, the metric becomes

$$ds^2 = \frac{dz d\bar{z}}{\Im(z)^2}$$

In this coordinate system, it can be shown that $PSL(2, \mathbb{R})^3$ is an isometry, meaning that the distance is preserved. The action of $PSL(2, \mathbb{R})$ on z is transitive and given by

$$z' = \frac{az + b}{cz + d}$$

Furthermore, let's define the Möbius transformation T as an element of $PSL(2, \mathbb{R})$ which is uniquely given by its values at 3 points: $T(0) = 1$,

---

[3] $PSL(2, \mathbb{R}) = SL(2, \mathbb{R})/\mathbb{Z}_2$ with $SL(2, \mathbb{R})$ the group of two-by-two real matrices with determinant one. $\mathbb{Z}_2$ acts on $A \in SL(2, \mathbb{R})$ by $\mathbb{Z}_2 A = -A$.

$T(i) = 0$ and $T(\infty) = -1$. If $\Im(z) > 0$ then $|T(z)| < 1$ so T maps the upper half-plane on the Poincaré disk $\mathcal{D} = \{z \in \mathcal{C} | |z| \leq 1\}$. In the upper half-plane, the geodesics correspond to vertical lines and to semicircles centered on the horizon $\Im(z) = 0$, and in $\mathcal{D}$ the geodesics are circles orthogonal to $\mathcal{D}$ (Figure 4.1).

Solving the Euler-Lagrange equation (4.2.10), it can be proven that the (hyperbolic) distance (invariant under $PSL(2, \mathbb{R})$) between the points $z = x + iy$, $z' = x' + iy'$ on $\mathbb{H}^2$ is given by

$$d(z, z') = \cosh^{-1}\left(1 + \frac{|z - z'|^2}{2yy'}\right) \tag{4.4.4}$$

Using this explicit expression for the hyperbolic distance, the Van Vleck-Morette determinant is

$$\Delta(z, z') = \frac{d(z, z')}{\sqrt{\cosh^2(d(z, z')) - 1}} \tag{4.4.5}$$

Using our specific expression for the geodesic distance (4.4.4), we find that $a_{\min}(q)$, the saddle-point, is the following expression

$$a_{\min}(q) = \sqrt{\alpha^2 + 2\alpha v \rho q + v^2 q^2} \tag{4.4.6}$$

As Δ depends only on the geodesic distance d and d is minimized for $a = a_{\min}(q)$, we have $\ln(\Delta)'(a_{\min}(q)) = 0$.

Furthermore, we have (using Mathematica)

$$a_{\min}(q)\phi''(a_{\min}(q)) = \frac{2d(a_{\min}(q))}{\alpha(1 - \rho^2)\sqrt{\cosh(d(a_{\min}(q)))^2 - 1}} \tag{4.4.7}$$

$$\frac{\phi'''(a_{\min}(q))}{\phi''(a_{\min}(q))} = -\frac{3}{a_{\min}(q)} \tag{4.4.8}$$

$$d(a_{\min}(q)) = \cosh^{-1}\left(\frac{-qv\rho - \alpha\rho^2 + a_{\min}(q)}{\alpha(1 - \rho^2)}\right) \tag{4.4.9}$$

The above formula (4.4.9) has already been obtained in [4].

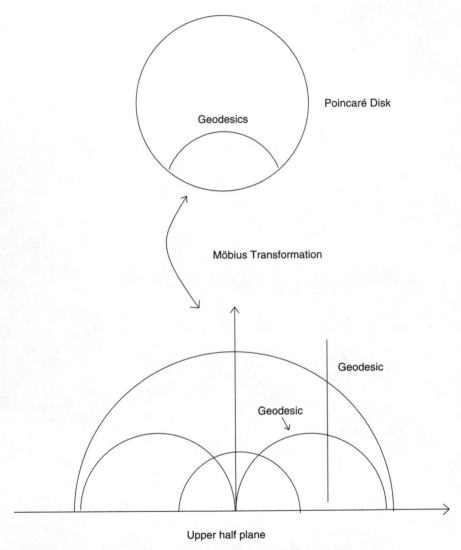

FIGURE 4.1 Poincaré disk $\mathcal{D}$ and upper half-plane $\mathbb{H}$ with some geodesics. In the upper half-plane, the geodesics correspond to vertical lines and to semicircles centered on the horizon $\Im(z) = 0$. In $\mathcal{D}$ the geodesics are circles orthogonal to $\mathcal{D}$.

Connection for the λ-SABR   In the coordinates $[a, f]$, the connection $\mathcal{A}$ is

$$\mathcal{A} = \frac{1}{2(1-\rho^2)} \left(\frac{(2\lambda\bar{\lambda}\rho - 2\lambda\rho a - va^2 C'(f))}{vC(f)a^2} df \right.$$

$$\left. + \frac{(-2\lambda\bar{\lambda} + 2\lambda a + v\rho a^2 C'(f))}{v^2 a^2} da \right) \qquad (4.4.10)$$

In the new coordinates $[x, y]$, the above connection is given by

$$\mathcal{A} = \mathcal{A}^{SABR} + \frac{\lambda(\bar{\lambda}\sqrt{1-\rho^2} - y)}{v^2 y^2 \sqrt{1-\rho^2}} (\rho dx - \sqrt{1-\rho^2} dy)$$

with

$$\mathcal{A}^{SABR} = -\frac{\beta}{2(1-\rho^2)(1-\beta)} \frac{dx}{\left(x + \frac{\rho}{\sqrt{1-\rho^2}} y + \frac{v f_0^{1-\beta}}{(1-\beta)} \right)} \qquad \text{for } \beta \neq 1$$

$$\mathcal{A}^{SABR} = -\frac{dx}{2(1-\rho^2)v} \quad \text{for } \beta = 1$$

The pullback of the connection on a geodesic $\mathcal{C}$ satisfying $(x - x_0)^2 + y^2 = R^2$ is given by $(\beta \neq 1$ [4] $)$

$$i^*\mathcal{A} = i^*\mathcal{A}^{SABR} + \frac{\lambda\left(-\bar{\lambda}\sqrt{1-\rho^2} + y\right)}{v^2 y^2} \left(\frac{\rho y}{\sqrt{(R^2 - y^2)(1-\rho^2)}} + 1 \right) dy$$

and with

$$i^*\mathcal{A}^{SABR} = \frac{\beta}{2(1-\rho^2)(1-\beta)} \frac{ydy}{\sqrt{R^2 - y^2} \left(\hat{x}_0 + \sqrt{R^2 - y^2} + \frac{\rho}{\sqrt{1-\rho^2}} y \right)}$$

$$(4.4.11)$$

with $i : \mathcal{C} \to \mathbb{H}^2$ the embedding of the geodesic $\mathcal{C}$ on the Poincaré plane and $\hat{x}_0 = x_0 + \frac{v f_0^{1-\beta}}{(1-\beta)}$. We have used that $i^*dx = -\frac{ydy}{\sqrt{R^2-y^2}}$. Note that the two constants x_0 and R are determined by using the fact that the two points

---

[4] The case $\beta = 1$ will be treated in the next section.

$z_1 = -\rho\alpha + i\sqrt{1-\rho^2}\alpha$ and $z_2 = v\int_{f_0}^{f} \frac{df'}{C(f')} - \rho a + i\sqrt{1-\rho^2}a$ pass through the geodesic curves. The algebraic equations given R and x_0 can be exactly solved:

$$x_0 = \frac{x_1^2 - x_2^2 + y_1^2 - y_2^2}{2(x_1 - x_2)}$$

$$R = \frac{1}{2}\sqrt{\frac{((x_1-x_2)^2 + y_1^2)^2 + 2((x_1-x_2)^2 - y_1^2)y_2^2 + y_2^4}{(x_1-x_2)^2}}$$

Using polar coordinates $x - x_0 = R\cos(\theta)$, $y = R\sin(\theta)$, we obtain that the parallel gauge transport is

$$\ln(\mathcal{P}) = \ln(\mathcal{P}^{SABR}) + \frac{\lambda}{v^2}\int_{\theta_1(a)}^{\theta_2(a)} (1 + B\tan(\theta))(\sin(x) + A_0)\frac{\cos(x)}{\sin(x)^2}dx$$

with

$$\mathcal{P}^{SABR} = \exp\left(\int_{\theta_1}^{\theta_2} \frac{\beta}{2(1-\rho^2)(1-\beta)} \frac{\sin(\theta)d\theta}{(\cos(\theta) + \frac{\hat{x}_0}{R} + \frac{\rho}{\sqrt{1-\rho^2}}\sin(\theta))}\right)$$

with $\theta_i(a, f) = \arctan(\frac{y_i}{x_i - x_0})$, $i = 1, 2$, $A(a, f) = \frac{\hat{x}_0}{R}$, $B = \frac{\rho}{\sqrt{1-\rho^2}}$ and $A_0 = -\frac{\hat{\lambda}\sqrt{1-\rho^2}}{R}$. The two integration bounds θ_1 and θ_2 explicitly depend on a and the coefficient $\frac{\hat{x}_0}{R}$. Doing the integration, we obtain 4.4.2.

Plugging all these results (4.4.7, 4.4.8, 4.4.9, 4.4.2) in 4.3.2, we obtain our final expression for the asymptotic smile at the first-order associated to the stochastic λ-SABR model (4.4.1).

Remark 4.9 (SABR original formula). *We can now see how the classical Hagan-al asymptotic smile [19] formula can be obtained in the case $\lambda = 0$ and show that our formula gives a better approximation. First, we approximate $a_{\min}(q)$ by the following expression*

$$a_{\min}(q) \simeq \alpha + q\rho v \tag{4.4.12}$$

In the same way, we have

$$\frac{\sqrt{\cosh(d(a_{\min}(q)))^2 - 1}}{d(a_{\min}(q))} \simeq 1$$

Furthermore, for $\lambda = 0$, the connection (4.4.10) reduces to

$$\mathcal{A} = \frac{1}{2(1 - \rho^2)} \left(-d \ln(C(f)) + \frac{\rho}{\nu} \partial_f C da \right)$$

Therefore, the parallel gauge transport is obtained by integrating this one-form along a geodesic C

$$\mathcal{P} = \exp\left(\frac{1}{2(1 - \rho^2)} \left(-\ln\left(\frac{C(f)}{C(f_0)}\right) + \int_C \frac{\rho}{\nu} \partial_f C da \right) \right)$$

The component f of the connection is an exact form and therefore has easily been integrated. The result doesn't depend on the geodesic but only on the endpoints. However, this is not the case for the component $\mathcal{A}_a$. But by approximating $\partial'_f C(f') \simeq \partial_f C(f)$, the component $\mathcal{A}_a$ becomes an exact form and can therefore be integrated:

$$\int_C \frac{\rho}{\nu} \partial_f C da \simeq \frac{\rho}{\nu} \partial_f C(f)(a - \alpha)$$

Finally, plugging these approximations into our formula (4.3.2), we reproduce the Hagan-al original formula [19]

$$\sigma_{BS}(f_0, f, \tau) = \frac{\ln(\frac{f_0}{f})}{\text{vol}(q)} \left(1 + \sigma_1 \left(\frac{f + f_0}{2} \right) \tau \right)$$

with

$$\sigma_1(f) = \frac{(\alpha C(f))^2}{24} \left(\frac{1}{f^2} + \frac{2 \partial_{ff}(C(f))}{C(f)} - \left(\frac{\partial_f(C(f))}{C(f)} \right)^2 \right)$$

$$+ \frac{\alpha \nu \partial_f(C(f)) \rho}{4} + \frac{2 - 3\rho^2}{24} \nu^2$$

Therefore, the Hagan-al's formula corresponds to the approximation of the Abelian connection by an exact form. The latter can be integrated outside the parametrization of the geodesic curves.

Remark 4.10. ($\mathbb{H}^2$-model) *In the previous section, we have seen that the λ-SABR mode corresponds to the geometry of $\mathbb{H}^2$. This space is particularly nice in the sense that the geodesic distance and the geodesic curves are known. A similar result holds if we assume that $C(f)$ is a general function ($C(f) = f^\beta$ for λ-SABR). In the following, we will try to fix this arbitrary function in order to fit the short-term smile. In this case, we can use our unified asymptotic smile formula at the zero order. The short-term smile will be automatically calibrated by construction if*

$$\sigma_{loc}(f) = C(f)a_{\min}(q)$$

$$a_{\min}(q) = \alpha^2 + 2\rho\alpha v q + v^2 q^2$$

$$q = \int_{f_0}^{f} \frac{df'}{C(f')} \tag{4.4.13}$$

with $\sigma_{loc}(f)$ the short-term local volatility. By short-term, we mean a maturity date less than $\simeq 1$ year. Solving 4.4.13 according to q, we obtain

$$vq = -\rho\alpha v + \sqrt{\alpha^2(-1 + \rho^2) + \frac{\sigma_{loc}(f)^2}{C(f)^2}} \tag{4.4.14}$$

and if we derive under f, we have $\left(\psi(f) = \frac{\sigma_{loc}(f)}{C(f)} \right)$

$$\frac{d\psi}{\sqrt{\psi^2 - \alpha^2(1 - \rho^2)}} = \frac{v}{\sigma_{loc}(f)} df$$

Solving this ODE, we obtain that C(f) is fixed to

$$C(f) = \frac{\sigma_{loc}(f)}{\alpha\sqrt{1 - \rho^2} \cosh\left[v \int_{f_0}^{f} \frac{df'}{\sigma_{loc}(f')} \right]}$$

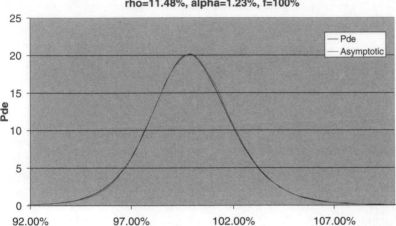

FIGURE 4.2 Pdf $p(K, T| f_0) = \frac{\partial^2 C}{\partial^2 K}$. Asymptotic solution vs numerical solution (PDE solver). In some cases, Hagan et al's formula has been plotted to see the impact of the mean-reversion term.

Using the BBF formula, we have

$$C(f) = \frac{f \sigma_{BS}(f)(1 - f \ln(\frac{f}{f_0}) \frac{\sigma'_{BS}(f)}{\sigma_{BS}(f)})}{\alpha \sqrt{1 - \rho^2} \cosh[v \frac{\ln(\frac{f}{f_0})}{\sigma_{BS}(f)}]}$$

Using this function for the λ-SABR model, the short term smile is then automatically calibrated. (Refer to Figure 4.2 for illustration.)

4.5 SABR MODEL WITH $\beta = 0, 1$

4.5.1 SABR Model with $\beta = 0$ and $\mathbb{H}^2$

For the SABR model, the connection $\mathcal{A}$ and the function Q are given by

$$\mathcal{A} = \frac{1}{2(1 - \rho^2)} \left(-\partial_f \ln(C) df + \frac{\rho}{v} \partial_f C da \right) \qquad (4.5.1)$$

$$Q = \frac{a^2}{4} \left(C \partial_f^2 C - \frac{(\partial_f C)^2}{2(1 - \rho^2)} \right) \qquad (4.5.2)$$

For $\beta = 0$, the function Q and the potential A vanish. Then p satisfies a heat kernel where the differential operator D reduces to the Laplacian on $\mathbb{H}^2$:

$$\frac{\partial p}{\partial \tau'} = \Delta_{\mathbb{H}^2} p$$

$$= y^2(\partial_x^2 + \partial_y^2)p$$

Therefore, solving the Kolmogorov equation for the SABR model with $\beta = 0$ (called SAR0 model) is equivalent to solving this (Laplacian) heat kernel on $\mathbb{H}^2$. Surprisingly, there is an analytical solution for the heat kernel on $\mathbb{H}^2$ (4.5.3) found by McKean [24]. It is connected to the Selberg trace formula [17]. The *exact conditional probability* density p depends on the hyperbolic distance $d(z, z')$ and is given by (with $\tau' = \frac{v^2\tau}{2}$)

$$p(d, \tau') = 2^{-\frac{5}{2}}\pi^{-\frac{3}{2}}\tau'^{-\frac{3}{2}}e^{-\frac{\tau'}{4}} \int_{d(z,z')}^{\infty} \frac{be^{-\frac{b^2}{4\tau'}}}{(\cosh b - \cosh d(z, z'))^{\frac{1}{2}}} db$$

The conditional probability in the old coordinates $[a, f]$ is

$$p(f, a, \tau')df da = \frac{2v}{(1-\rho^2)^{\frac{1}{2}}} \frac{df da}{a^2} 2^{-\frac{5}{2}}\pi^{-\frac{3}{2}}\tau'^{-\frac{3}{2}}e^{-\frac{\tau'}{4}}$$

$$\int_{d(z,z')}^{\infty} \frac{be^{-\frac{b^2}{4\tau'}}}{(\cosh b - \cosh d(z, z'))^{\frac{1}{2}}} db$$

We have compared this exact solution (Figure 4.3) with a numerical PDE solution of the SAR0 model and found agreement. A similar result was obtained in [20] for the conditional probability.

The value of a European option is (after an integration by parts)

$$C(f, K) = (f - K)^+ + \frac{1}{2}\int_0^\tau d\tau \int_0^\infty da\, a^2 p(x_1 = K, a, \tau|\alpha)$$

In order to integrate over a we use a small trick: we interchange the order of integration over b and a. The half space $b \geq d$ with a arbitrary is

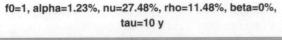

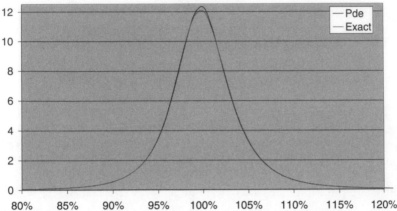

FIGURE 4.3 Conditional probability for the SABR model with $\beta = 0$ versus numerical PDE.

then mapped to the half-strip $a_{min}(q) \leq a \leq a_{max}(q)$ and $b \geq l_{min}$ where[5]

$$
\begin{aligned}
&a_{max}(q) - a_{min}(q) \\
&\quad = 2\sqrt{(\alpha(\cosh(b) + \rho^2 - \cosh(b)\rho^2) - v\rho q)^2 - (\alpha^2 - 2\alpha v\rho q + v^2 q^2)} \\
&a_{min}(q) + a_{max} = 2\alpha \cosh(b) + 2\alpha\rho^2(1 - \cosh(b)) + 2v\rho q \\
&\cosh(l_{min}) = \frac{\text{num}}{\text{den}}
\end{aligned}
$$

with

$$
\begin{aligned}
\text{num} &= -\alpha^2 - 2\alpha^2\rho^2 - 2\alpha^2\rho^4 + 4\alpha^2\rho^6 - 6\alpha v\rho^3 s \\
&\quad + 4\alpha v\rho^5 s - 3v^2\rho^2 s^2 + 2v^2\rho^4 s^2 + \rho\left(-1 + 2\rho^2\right) \\
&\quad \times (\alpha\rho + vs)\sqrt{\alpha^2 + 2\alpha v\rho\left(-1 + 2\rho^2\right)s + v^2\left(-1 + 2\rho^2\right)s^2} \\
\text{den} &= \alpha\left(-1 + \rho^2\right)\left(1 + 2\rho^2\right)\left(2\rho\left(\alpha\rho + vs\right)\right. \\
&\quad \left. + \sqrt{\alpha^2 + 2\alpha v\rho\left(-1 + 2\rho^2\right)s + v^2\left(-1 + 2\rho^2\right)s^2}\right)
\end{aligned}
$$

---

[5] All these algebraic computations have been done with Mathematica.

Performing the integration according to a leads to an *exact solution* for the fair value of a call option with strike K and maturity τ:

$$C(\tau, f, K) = (f - K)^+ + \frac{1}{v(1 - \rho^2)^{\frac{1}{2}}} 2^{-\frac{5}{2}} \pi^{-\frac{3}{2}} \int_0^{\frac{v^2\tau}{2}} dt\, t^{-\frac{3}{2}} e^{-\frac{t}{4}}$$

$$\times \int_{l_{\min}}^{\infty} \frac{b(a_{\max} - a_{\min}(q)) e^{-\frac{b^2}{4t}}}{\sqrt{(\cosh b - \cosh l_{\min})}} db$$

4.5.2 SABR Model with $\beta = 1$ and the Three-Dimensional Hyperbolic Space $\mathbb{H}^3$

A similar computation can be carried out for $\beta = 1$. Using 4.5.1, we can show that the connection $\mathcal{A}$ is exact, meaning there exists a smooth function Λ such that $\mathcal{A} = d\Lambda$ with $\Lambda = \frac{1}{2(1-\rho^2)}(-\ln(f) + \frac{\rho}{v}a)$. Furthermore, using 4.5.2, we have $Q = -\frac{a^2}{8(1-\rho^2)} = -\frac{y^2}{8(1-\rho^2)^2}$.

Applying an Abelian gauge transformation $p' = e^{\Lambda} p$ (4.2.6), we find that p' satisfies the following equation:

$$y^2 \left(\partial_x^2 + \partial_y^2 - \frac{1}{4v^2(1 - \rho^2)^2} \right) p' = \partial_{\tau'} p'$$

How do we solve this equation? It turns out that the solution corresponds in some fancy way to the solution of the (Laplacian) heat kernel on the three-dimensional hyperbolic space $\mathbb{H}^3$. This space can be represented as the upper-half space $\mathbb{H}^3 = \{x = (x_1, x_2, x_3)|x_3 > 0\}$. In these coordinates, the metric takes the following form:

$$ds^2 = \frac{(dx_1^2 + dx_2^2 + dx_3^2)}{x_3^2}$$

and the geodesic distance between two points x and x' in $\mathbb{H}^3$ is given by[6]

$$\cosh(d(x, x')) = 1 + \frac{|x - x'|^2}{2x_3 x_3'}$$

---

[6] $|\cdot|$ is the Euclidean distance in $\mathbb{R}^3$.

As in $\mathbb{H}^2$, the geodesics are straight vertical lines or semicircles orthogonal to the boundary of the upper-half space. An interesting property, useful to solve the heat kernel, is that the group of isometries of $\mathbb{H}^3$ is $PSL(2, \mathcal{C})$.[7] If we represent a point $p \in \mathbb{H}^3$ as a quaternion[8] whose fourth components equal zero, then the action of an element $g \in PSL(2, \mathcal{C})$ on $\mathbb{H}^3$ can be described by the formula

$$p' = g.p = \frac{ap + b}{cp + d}$$

with $p = x_1 1 + x_2 i + x_3 j$.

The Laplacian on $\mathbb{H}^3$ in the coordinates $[x_1, x_2, x_3]$ is given by

$$\Delta_{\mathbb{H}^3} = x_3^2 (\partial_{x_1}^2 + \partial_{x_2}^2 + \partial_{x_3}^2)$$

and the (Laplacian) heat kernel is

$$\partial_{\tau'} p' = \Delta_{\mathbb{H}^3} p'$$

The exact solution for the conditional probability density $p'(d(x, x'), t)$, depending on the geodesic distance $d(x, x')$, is [16]

$$p'(d(x, x'), \tau') = \frac{1}{(4\pi\tau')^{\frac{3}{2}}} \frac{d(x, x')}{\sinh(d(x, x'))} e^{-\tau' - \frac{d(x,x')^2}{4\tau'}}$$

Let's apply a Fourier transformation on p along the coordinate x_1 (or equivalently x_2):

$$p'(x_1, x_2, x_3, x', \tau') = \int_{-\infty}^{\infty} \frac{dk}{\sqrt{2\pi}} e^{ikx_1} \hat{p}'(k, x_2, x_3, x', t)$$

Then $\hat{p}'$ satisfies the following PDE:

$$\partial_{\tau'} \hat{p}' = x_3^2 (-k^2 + \partial_{x_2}^2 + \partial_{x_3}^2) \hat{p}'$$

---

[7] $PSL(2, \mathcal{C})$ is identical to $PSL(2, \mathbb{R})$, except that the real field is replaced by the complex field.

[8] The quaternionic field is generated by the unit element 1 and the basis i, j, k, which satisfy the multiplication table $i.j = k$ and the other cyclic products.

By comparing (4.5.3) with (4.5.3), we deduce that the exact solution for the conditional probability for the SABR model with $\beta = 1$ is (with $x \equiv x_2$, $y \equiv x_3$, $k \equiv \frac{1}{2v(1-\rho^2)}$, $x_1' = 0$)

$$p'(x, y, x', y', \tau') = e^{-\frac{1}{2(1-\rho^2)}(\ln(\frac{f}{k}) - \frac{\rho}{v}(a-\alpha))} \int_{-\infty}^{\infty} \frac{dx_1}{\sqrt{2\pi}}$$

$$\times \frac{1}{(4\pi\tau')^{\frac{3}{2}}} \frac{d(x, x')}{\sinh(d(x, x'))} e^{-\tau' - \frac{d(x,x')^2}{4\tau'}} e^{-\frac{ix_1}{2v(1-\rho^2)}}$$

A previous solution for the SABR model with $\beta = 1$ was obtained by [25], although only in terms of Gauss hypergeometric series.

4.6   CONCLUSIONS AND FUTURE WORK

Let's summarize our findings. By using the heat kernel expansion, we have explained how to obtain a general first-order asymptotic smile formula. As an application, we have derived the smile formula for a SABR model with a mean-reversion term. Furthermore, we have shown how to reproduce [18, 19]. In the case of the SABR model with $\beta = 0, 1$, exact solutions have been found, corresponding to the geometries of $\mathbb{H}^2$ and $\mathbb{H}^3$, respectively. These solutions are not easy to obtain without exploiting this connection with hyperbolic geometry.

ACKNOWLEDGEMENTS

I would like to thank Dr. C. Waite and Dr. G. Huish for stimulating discussions. I would also like to acknowledge Prof. Avramidi for bringing numerous references on the heat kernel expansion to my attention. Moreover, I would like to thank Dr. A. Lesniewski and Prof. H. Berestycki for bringing their respective papers [4, 20, 26] to my attention.

4.7   APPENDIX A: NOTIONS IN DIFFERENTIAL GEOMETRY

4.7.1   Riemannian Manifold

A real n-dimensional manifold is a space which looks like $\mathbb{R}^n$ around each point. More precisely, M is covered by open sets $\mathcal{U}_i$ (topological space) which are homeomorphic to $\mathbb{R}^n$ meaning that there is a continuous map ϕ_i

(and its inverse) from $\mathcal{U}_i$ to $\mathbb{R}^n$ for each i. Furthermore, we impose that the map $\phi_{i,j} = \phi_i^{-1} o \phi_j$ from $\mathbb{R}^n$ to $\mathbb{R}^n$ is $C^\infty(\mathbb{R}^n)$.

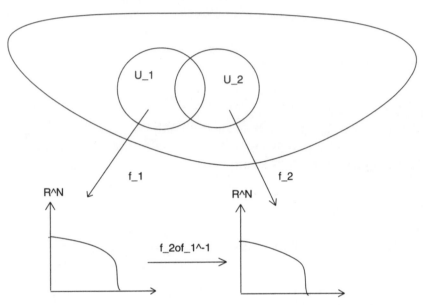

As an example, a two-sphere S^2 can be covered with two patches: $\mathcal{U}_N$ and $\mathcal{U}_S$, defined respectively as S^2 minus the north pole, and the south pole. We obtain the map ϕ_N (ϕ_S) by doing a stereographic projection on $\mathcal{U}_N$ ($\mathcal{U}_S$). This projection consists in taking the intersection of a line passing through the North (South) Pole and a point p on S^2 with the equatorial plane. We can show that $\phi_{SN}(x, y) = (\frac{x}{(x^2+y^2)}, -\frac{y}{(x^2+y^2)})$ is C^∞ and even holomorphic. So S^2 is a *complex manifold*.

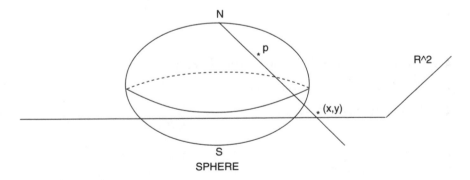

4.7.2 Metric

A metric g_{ij} written with the local coordinates x_i (corresponding to a particular chart $\mathcal{U}_i$) allows us to measure the distance between infinitesimally nearby points x^i and $x^i + dx^i$: $ds^2 = g_{ij}dx^i dx^j$. If a point p belongs to two charts then the distance can be computed using two different systems of coordinates x^i and $x^{i'} = f(x^i)$. However, the result of the measure should be the same, meaning that $g_{ij}dx^i dx^j = g_{ij}dx^{i'} dx^{j'}$. We deduce that under a change of coordinates, the metric is not invariant but changes in a contravariant way by $g_{ij} = g_{i'j'}\partial_i x^{i'}\partial_j x^{j'}$.

A manifold endowed with an Euclidean metric is called a *Riemannian manifold*.

On a n-dimensional Riemannian manifold, the measure $\sqrt{g}\Pi_{i=1}^n dx^i$ is invariant under an arbitrary change of coordinates. Indeed, the metric changes as $g_{ij} = g_{i'j'}\frac{\partial x^{i'}}{\partial x^i}\frac{\partial x^{j'}}{\partial x^j}$ and therefore $g = \det(g_{ij})$ changes as $\sqrt{g} = \det(\frac{\partial x^{i'}}{\partial x^i})\sqrt{g'}$. Furthermore, the element $\Pi_{i=1}^n dx^i$ changes as $\Pi_{i=1}^n dx^i = \det^{-1}(\frac{\partial x^{i'}}{\partial x^i})\Pi_{i'=1}^n dx^{i'}$ and we deduce the result.

4.7.3 Line Bundle and Abelian Connection

Line Bundle

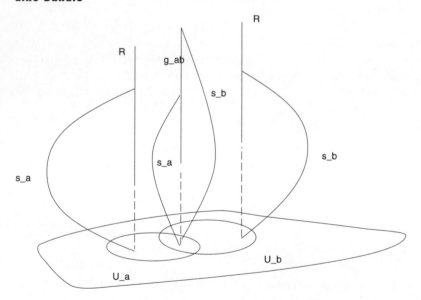

Line Bundle

A line bundle $\mathcal{L}$ is defined by an open covering of M, $\{\mathcal{U}_\alpha\}$, and for each (α, β), a smooth transition function $g_{\alpha\beta} : \mathcal{U}_\alpha \cap \mathcal{U}_\beta \to \mathbb{R}$ which satisfies the "cocycle condition"

$$g_{\alpha\beta} g_{\beta\gamma} g_{\gamma\alpha} = 1 \text{ on } \mathcal{U}_\alpha \cap \mathcal{U}_\beta \cap \mathcal{U}_\gamma$$

A section σ of $\mathcal{L}$ is defined by its local representatives σ on each $\mathcal{U}_\alpha$:

$$\sigma|_{\mathcal{U}_\alpha} \equiv \sigma_\alpha : \mathcal{U}_\alpha \to \mathbb{R}$$

and they are related to each other by the formula $\sigma_\alpha = g_{\alpha\beta} \sigma_\beta$ on $\mathcal{U}_\alpha \cap \mathcal{U}_\beta$.

Abelian Connection An Abelian connection ∇ on the line bundle $\mathcal{L}$ is a collection of differential operator $\partial_i + \mathcal{A}_i^\alpha$ on each open set $\mathcal{U}_\alpha$ which transforms according to

$$\mathcal{A}_i^\alpha = \mathcal{A}_i^\beta + g_{\alpha\beta} \partial_i g_{\alpha\beta}^{-1} \text{ on } \mathcal{U}_\alpha \cap \mathcal{U}_\beta$$

4.8 APPENDIX B: LAPLACE INTEGRALS IN MANY DIMENSIONS

Let ω be a bounded domain on $\mathbb{R}^n$, $S : \Omega \to \mathbb{R}$, $f : \Omega \to \mathbb{R}$ and $\lambda > 0$ be a large positive parameter. The Laplace's method consists in studying the asymptotic as $\lambda \to \infty$ of the multidimensional Laplace integrals:

$$F(\lambda) = \int_\Omega f(x) e^{\lambda S(x)} dx$$

Let S and f be smooth functions and the function S have a maximum only at one interior nondegenerate critical point $x_0 \in \Omega$. Then in the neighborhood at x_0 the function S has the following Taylor expansion:

$$S(x) = S(x_0) + \frac{1}{2}(x - x_0)^2 \partial_x^2 S(x_0)(x - x_0) + o((x - x_0)^3)$$

As $\lambda \to \infty$, the main contribution of the integral comes from the neighborhood of x_0. Replacing the function f by its value at x_0, we obtain a Gaussian integrals where the integration over x can be performed. One gets the leading asymptotic of the integral as $\lambda \to \infty$:

$$F(\lambda) \sim e^{\lambda S(x_0)} \left(\frac{2\pi}{\lambda}\right)^{\frac{n}{2}} [-\det(\partial_x^2 S(x_0))]^{\frac{-1}{2}} f(x_0)$$

More generally, doing a Taylor expansion at the nth order for S (resp. $n-2$-order for $f(x)$) around $x = x_0$, we obtain

$$F(\lambda) \sim e^{\lambda S(x_0)} \left(\frac{2\pi}{\lambda}\right)^{\frac{n}{2}} [-\det(\partial_x^2 S(x_0))]^{\frac{-1}{2}} \sum_{k=0}^{\infty} a_k \lambda^{-k}$$

with the coefficients a_k are expressed in terms of the derivatives of the functions f and S at the point x_0. For example, at the first order (in one dimension), we find

$$F(\lambda) \sim \sqrt{\frac{2\pi}{-\lambda S''(c)}} e^{\lambda S(x_0)} \left(f(x_0) + \frac{1}{\lambda} \left(-\frac{f''(x_0)}{2S''(x_0)} + \frac{f(x_0)S^{(4)}(x_0)}{8S''(x_0)^2} \right. \right.$$
$$\left. \left. + \frac{f'(x_0)S^{(3)}(x_0)}{2S''(x_0)^2} - \frac{5S'''(x_0)f(x_0)}{24S''(x_0)^3} \right) \right)$$

REFERENCES

1. Avellaneda, M., D. Boyer-Olson, J. Busca, and P. Fritz. (2002). Reconstructing the smile. *Risk* (October).
2. Avramidi, I. V., and R. Schimming. (1996). Algorithms for the Calculation of the Heat Kernel Coefficients. *Proceedings of the 3rd Workshop "Quantum Theory under the Influence of External Conditions,"* M. Bordag (ed.), *Teubner-Texte zur Physik*, vol. 30. Stuttgart: Teubner, pp. 150–162.
3. Berestycki, H., J. Busca, and I. Florent. 1998. Asymptotics and calibration of local volatility models. *Quantitative Finance* 2: 31–44.
4. Berestycki, H., J. Busca, and I. Florent. (2004). Computing the implied volatility in stochastic volatility models. *Communications on Pure and Applied Mathematics* 57 (10): 1352–1373.
5. Black, F., and M. Scholes. (1973). The pricing of options and corporate liabilities. *Journal of Political Economy* 81: 637–659.
6. Cox, J. C. (1975). Notes on option pricing I: Constant elasticity of variance diffusions. Working paper, Stanford University. Reprinted in *Journal of Portfolio Management* 22 (1996): 15–17.

7. DeWitt, B. S. (1975). Quantum field theory in curved spacetime. *Physics Report* 19C(6).
8. Birrell, N. D., and P. C. W. Davies. (1982). *Quantum Fields in Curved Space.* Cambridge: Cambridge University Press.
9. Dupire, B. (1994). Pricing with a smile. *Risk* 7 (1): 18–20.
10. Dupire, B. (2004). A unified theory of volatility. In Peter Carr (ed.), *Derivatives Pricing: The Classic Collection.* London: Risk Publications.
11. Eguchi, T., P. B. Gilkey, and A. J. Hanson. (1980). Gravitation, gauge theories, and differential geometry. *Physics Report* 66(6) (December).
12. Gatheral, J. (2006). *The Volatility Surface: A Practitioner's Guide.* Hoboken, NJ: John Wiley & Sons.
13. Gilkey, P. B. (1984). *Invariance Theory, the Heat Equation, and the Atiyah-Singer Index Theorem*, Mathematics Lecture Series, vol. 11. Wilmington, DE: Publish or Perish, Inc.
14. Gilkey, P. B., K. Kirsten, J. H. Park, and D. Vassilevich. (2002). Asymptotics of the heat equation with "exotic" boundary conditions or with time dependent coefficients. *Nuclear Physics B (Proceedings Supplement)* 104: 63–70, math-ph/0105009.
15. Gilkey, P. B., K. Kirsten, and J. H. Park. (2001). Heat trace asymptotics of a time dependent process. *Journal of Physics A: Mathematical and General* 34: 1153–1168, hep-th/0010136.
16. Grigor'yan, A., and M. Noguchi. (1998). The heat kernel on hyperbolic space. *Bulletin of the London Mathematical Society* 30: 643–650.
17. Gutzwiller, M. C. (1990). *Chaos in Classical and Quantum Mechanics.* New York: Springer.
18. Hagan, P. S., and D. E. Woodward. (1999). Equivalent black volatilities. *Applied Mathematical Finance* 6: 147–157.
19. Hagan, P. S., D. Kumar, A. S. Lesniewski, and D. E. Woodward. (2002). Managing smile risk. Available at www.wilmott.com/pdfs/021118_smile.pdf.
20. Hagan, P. S., A. S. Lesniewski, and D. E. Woodward. (2005). Probability distribution in the SABR model of stochastic volatility. Unpublished.
21. Heston, S. (2007). A closed-for solution for options with stochastic volatility with applications to bond and currency options. *Review of Financial Studies* 6: 327–343.
22. Henry-Labordere, P. (2005). General asymptotic implied volatility for stochastic volatility models. Available at Social Science Research Network: http://srn.com/abstract=698601.
23. Hull, J., and A. White. (1987). The pricing of options on assets with stochastic volatilities. *Journal of Finance* 42: 281–300.
24. McKean, H. P. (1970). An upper bound to the spectrum of Δ on a manifold of negative curvature. *Journal of Differential Geometry* 4: 359–366.
25. Lewis, A. L. (2000). *Option Valuation under Stochastic Volatility with Mathematica Code.* Newport Beach, CA: Finance Press.
26. Lesniewski, A. (2002). Swaption smiles via the WKB method. Math Finance Seminar, Courant Institute of Mathematical Sciences, February.

CHAPTER 5

Pricing, Hedging, and Calibration in Jump-Diffusion Models

Peter Tankov and Ekaterina Voltchkova

Starting with Merton's seminal paper [34] and up to the present date, financial models with jumps have been studied in the academic finance community (see [11] for a list of almost 400 references on the subject). In the last decade, also the risk management and trading teams of major banks started to accept jump diffusions as a valuable tool in their day-to-day modeling. This increasing interest to jump models in finance is mainly due to the following reasons.

First, in a model with continuous paths like a diffusion model, the price process behaves locally like a Brownian motion and the probability that the stock moves by a large amount over a short period of time is very small, unless one fixes an unrealistically high value of volatility. Therefore, in such models the prices of short-term out-of-the-money options should be much lower than what one observes in real markets. On the other hand, if stock prices are allowed to jump, even when the time to maturity is very short, there is a nonnegligible probability that after a sudden change in the stock price the option will move in the money. Recently, the market participants started trading *gap notes*, which provide a specific protection against jumps in the underlying. A typical gap note pays a predetermined amount to its holder if, on any single day within the lifetime of the contract, the underlying moves by more than a fixed percentage, say, 20 percent. Since such moves are all but impossible in diffusion models, gap notes cannot be traded using a model without a jump component.

Second, from the point of view of hedging, continuous models of stock price behavior generally lead to a complete market or to a market, which can be made complete by adding one or two additional instruments, like in stochastic volatility models. Since in such a market every terminal payoff can be exactly replicated, options are redundant assets, and the very existence of traded options becomes a puzzle. The mystery is easily solved by allowing for discontinuities: in real markets, due to the presence of jumps in the prices, perfect hedging is impossible, and options enable the market participants to hedge risks that cannot be hedged by using the underlying only.

From a risk management perspective, jumps allow to quantify and take into account the risk of strong stock price movements over short time intervals, which appears nonexistent in the diffusion framework.

The last and probably the strongest argument for using discontinuous models is simply the presence of jumps in observed prices. Figure 5.1 depicts the evolution of stock price of Respironics Inc. (RESP ticker on Nasdaq) over a 3-week period in 2006, and one can see at least two points where the price moved by over 50 cents within a 1-minute period. Price moves like these clearly cannot be accounted for in a diffusion model with continuous paths, but they must be dealt with if the market risk is to be measured and managed correctly.

In this chapter we give a brief introduction to jump-diffusion models and review various mathematical and numerical tools needed to use these models for option pricing and hedging. Since we are focusing on explanations rather than technical details, no proofs are given, but the reader will always be able to find complete proofs in the references we provide.

FIGURE 5.1 Jumps in the stock price of Respironics Inc. (Nasdaq), sampled at 1-minute intervals.

The chapter is structured as follows. In section 5.1 we provide a brief mathematical introduction to jump diffusions and define several important parametric and nonparametric classes. Section 5.2 discusses the Fourier-transform methods for European option pricing, based on the explicit knowledge of the characteristic function in many jump-diffusion models. Section 5.3 discusses the partial integro-differential equations which play the role of the Black-Scholes equation in jump-diffusion models and can be used to value American and barrier options. Finally, section 5.4 discusses hedging in presence of jumps and section 5.5 explains how jump-diffusion models can be calibrated to market data.

5.1 OVERVIEW OF JUMP-DIFFUSION MODELS

5.1.1 Compound Poisson Process

Take a sequence $\{\tau_i\}_{i \geq 1}$ of independent exponential random variables with parameter λ, that is, with cumulative distribution function $P[\tau_i \geq y] = e^{-\lambda y}$ and let $T_n = \sum_{i=1}^{n}$. The process

$$N_t = \sum_{n \geq 1} 1_{t \geq T_n}$$

is called the *Poisson process* with parameter λ. The trajectories of a Poisson process are piecewise constant (right continuous with left limits or RCLL), with jumps of size 1 only. For financial applications, it is of little interest to have a process with a single possible jump size. The *compound Poisson process* is a generalization where the waiting times between jumps are exponential but the jump sizes can have an arbitrary distribution. More precisely, let N be a Poisson process with parameter λ and $\{Y_i\}_{i \geq 1}$ be a sequence of independent random variables with law f. The process

$$X_t = \sum_{i=1}^{N_t} Y_i$$

is called *compound Poisson process*. Its trajectories are RCLL and piecewise constant but the jump sizes are now random with law f (cf. Fig. 5.2). Its law at a given time t is not known explicitly but the characteristic function is known and has the form

$$E[e^{iuX_t}] = \exp\left\{ t\lambda \int_{\mathbb{R}} (e^{iux} - 1) f(dx) \right\}$$

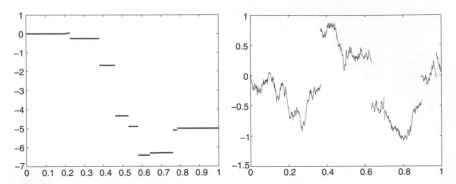

FIGURE 5.2 Left: Sample path of a compound Poisson process with Gaussian distribution of jump sizes. Right: Sample path of a jump-diffusion process (Brownian motion + compound Poisson).

The compound Poisson process shares with the Brownian motion the very important property of independence and stationarity of increments, that is, for every $t > s$ the increment $X_t - X_s$ is independent from the history of the process up to time s and has the same law as X_{t-s}. The processes with independent and stationary increments are called Lévy processes after the French mathematician Paul Lévy.

5.1.2 Jump Diffusions and Lévy Processes

Combining a Brownian motion with drift and a compound Poisson process, we obtain the simplest case of a jump diffusion—a process that sometimes jumps and has a continuous but random evolution between the jump times (cf. Figure 5.2):

$$X_t = \mu t + \sigma B_t + \sum_{i=1}^{N_t} Y_i. \qquad (5.1.1)$$

The best-known model of this type in finance is the Merton model [34], where the stock price is $S_t = S_0 e^{X_t}$ with X_t as above and the jumps $\{Y_i\}$ have Gaussian distribution.

In Kou's model [26], the jump size distribution has a density of the form

$$f(x) = \frac{(1-p)}{\eta_+} e^{-x/\eta_+} 1_{x>0} + \frac{p}{\eta_-} e^{-|x|/\eta_-} 1_{x<0}. \qquad (5.1.2)$$

Here p is the probability that a given jump is negative and η_- and η_+ are characteristic lengths of respectively negative and positive jumps.

The process (5.1.1) is again a Lévy process and its characteristic function can be computed by multiplying the CF of the Brownian motion and that of the compound Poisson process (since the two parts are independent):

$$E[e^{iuX_t}] = \exp\left\{t\left(i\mu u - \frac{\sigma^2 u^2}{2} + \lambda \int_{\mathbb{R}} (e^{iux} - 1) f(dx)\right)\right\}$$

The class of Lévy processes is not limited to jump diffusions of the form (5.1.1): there exist Lévy processes with infinitely many jumps in every interval. Most of such jumps are very small and there is only a finite number of jumps with absolute value greater than any given positive number. One of the simplest examples of this kind is the gamma process, a process with independent and stationary increments such that for all t, the law p_t of X_t is the gamma law with parameters λ and ct:

$$p_t(x) = \frac{\lambda^{ct}}{\Gamma(ct)} x^{ct-1} e^{-\lambda x}$$

The gamma process is an increasing Lévy process (also called subordinator). Its characteristic function has a very simple form:

$$E[e^{iuX_t}] = (1 - iu/\lambda)^{-ct}$$

The gamma process is the building block for a very popular jump model, the variance gamma process [30, 31], which is constructed by taking a Brownian motion with drift and changing its time scale with a gamma process:

$$Y_t = \mu X_t + \sigma B_{X_t}$$

Using Y_t to model the logarithm of stock prices can be justified by saying that the price is a geometric Brownian motion if viewed on a stochastic time scale given by the gamma process [20]. The variance gamma process is another example of a Lévy process with infinitely many jumps and has characteristic function

$$E[e^{iuY_t}] = \left(1 + \frac{\sigma^2 u^2}{2} - i\mu\kappa u\right)^{-\kappa t}$$

The parameters have the following (approximate) interpretation: σ is the variance parameter, μ is the skewness parameter and κ is responsible for the kurtosis of the process.

In general, every Lévy process can be represented in the form

$$X_t = \gamma t + \sigma B_t + Z_t,$$

where Z_t is a jump process with (possibly) infinitely many jumps. A detailed description of this component is given by the Lévy-It decomposition [11] and the characteristic function of a Lévy process is known from the Lévy-Khintchine formula:

$$E[e^{iuX_t}] = \exp\left\{ t\left(i\gamma u - \frac{\sigma^2 u^2}{2} + \int_{\mathbb{R}} (e^{iux} - 1 - iux1_{|x|\leq 1})\nu(dx) \right) \right\}$$

where ν is a positive measure on $\mathbb{R}$ describing the jumps of the process: the Lévy measure. If X is compound Poisson, then $\nu(\mathbb{R}) < \infty$ and $\nu(dx) = \lambda f(dx)$ but in the general case ν need not be a finite measure. It must satisfy the constraint

$$\int_{\mathbb{R}} (1 \wedge x^2)\nu(dx) < \infty$$

and describes the jumps of X in the following sense: for every closed set $A \subset \mathbb{R}$ with $0 \notin A$, $\nu(A)$ is the average number of jumps of X in the time interval $[0, 1]$, whose sizes fall in A.

In the rest of this chapter we will mostly focus on Lévy jump-diffusions, that is, Lévy processes with finite jump intensity of the form (5.1.1), but with the new notation $\nu(dx) = \lambda f(dx)$ for the Lévy measure. The characteristic function of such a process therefore takes the form

$$E[e^{iuX_t}] = \exp\left\{ t\left(i\mu u - \frac{\sigma^2 u^2}{2} + \int_{\mathbb{R}} (e^{iux} - 1)\nu(dx) \right) \right\} \tag{5.1.3}$$

5.1.3 Exponential Lévy Models

To ensure positivity as well as the independence and stationarity of log-returns, stock prices are usually modeled as exponentials of Lévy processes:

$$S_t = S_0 e^{X_t} \tag{5.1.4}$$

In the jump-diffusion case, this gives

$$S_t = S_0 \exp\left(\mu t + \sigma B_t + \sum_{i=1}^{N_t} Y_i\right)$$

Between the jumps, the process evolves like a geometric Brownian motion, and after each jump, the value of S_t is multiplied by e^{Y_i}. This model can therefore be seen as a generalization of the Black-Scholes model:

$$\frac{dS_t}{S_{t-}} = \tilde{\mu}dt + \sigma dB_t + dJ_t \tag{5.1.5}$$

Here, J_t is a compound Poisson process such that the i-th jump of J is equal to $e^{Y_i} - 1$. For instance, if Y_i has Gaussian distribution, S will have lognormally distributed jumps. The notation S_{t-} means that whenever there is a jump, the value of the process *before the jump* is used on the left-hand side of the formula. The forms (5.1.4) and (5.1.5) are equivalent: for a model of the first kind, one can always find a model of the second kind with the same law [21]. In the rest of the chapter, unless explicitly stated otherwise, we will use the exponential form (5.1.4).

For option pricing, we will explicitly include the interest rate into the definition of the exponential Lévy model:

$$S_t = S_0 e^{rt+X_t} \tag{5.1.6}$$

While the forms (5.1.4) and (5.1.6) are equivalent, the second one leads to a slightly simpler notation. In this case, under the risk-neutral probability, e^{X_t} must be a martingale and from the Lévy-Khintchine formula (5.1.3) combined with the independent increments property we conclude that this is the case if

$$b + \frac{\sigma^2}{2} + \int_{\mathbb{R}} (e^x - 1)\nu(dx) = 0 \tag{5.1.7}$$

The model (5.1.6) admits no arbitrage opportunity if there exists an equivalent probability under which e^{X_t} is a martingale. For Lévy processes it can be shown that this is almost always the case, namely an exponential Lévy model is arbitrage free if and only if the trajectories of X are not almost surely increasing nor almost surely decreasing.

If a Brownian component is present, the martingale probability can be obtained by changing the drift as in the Black-Scholes setting. Otherwise, in finite-intensity models, the drift must remain fixed under all equivalent probabilities since it can be observed from a single stock price trajectory. To satisfy the martingale constraint (5.1.7), one must therefore change the Lévy measure, that is, the intensity of jumps. To understand how this works, suppose that X is a Poisson process with drift:

$$X_t = N_t - at, \quad a > 0.$$

We can obtain a martingale probability by changing the intensity of N to $\lambda_{mart} = \frac{a}{e-1}$. If, however, X is a Poisson process without drift (increasing trajectories), one cannot find a value of $\lambda > 0$ for which e^{X_t} is a martingale.

5.1.4 Beyond Lévy Processes

Although the class of Lévy processes is quite rich, it is sometimes insufficient for multiperiod financial modeling for the following reasons:

- Due to the stationarity of increments, the stock price returns for a fixed time horizon always have the same law. It is therefore impossible to incorporate any kind of new market information into the return distribution.
- For a Lévy process, the law of X_t for any given time horizon t is completely determined by the law of X_1. Therefore, moments and cumulants depend on time in a well-defined manner, which does not always coincide with the empirically observed time dependence of these quantities [6].

For these reasons, several models combining jumps and stochastic volatility appeared in the literature. In the Bates [5] model, one of the most popular examples of the class, an independent jump component is added to the Heston stochastic volatility model:

$$dX_t = \mu dt + \sqrt{V_t} dW_t^X + dZ_t, \qquad S_t = S_0 e^{X_t}, \qquad (5.1.8)$$

$$dV_t = \xi(\eta - V_t)dt + \theta\sqrt{V_t} dW_t^V, \quad d\langle W^V, W^X \rangle_t = \rho dt$$

where Z is a compound Poisson process with Gaussian jumps. Although X_t is no longer a Lévy process, its characteristic function is known in closed form [11, Chapter 15] and the pricing and calibration procedures are similar to those used for Lévy processes.

5.2 PRICING EUROPEAN OPTIONS VIA FOURIER TRANSFORM

In the Black-Scholes setting, the prices of European calls and puts are given explicitly by the Black-Scholes formula. In the case of Lévy jump diffusions, closed formulas are no longer available but a fast deterministic algorithm, based on Fourier transform, was proposed by Carr and Madan [10]. Here we present a slightly improved version of their method, due to [35, 11].

Let $\{X_t\}_{t\geq0}$ be a Lévy process and, for simplicity, take $S_0 = 1$. We would like to compute the price of a European call with strike K and maturity T in the exponential Lévy model (5.1.6). Denote $k = \log K$ the logarithm of the strike. To compute the price of a call option

$$C(k) = e^{-rT}E[(e^{rT+X_T} - e^k)^+]$$

we would like to express its Fourier transform in log strike in terms of the characteristic function $\Phi_T(v)$ of X_T and then find the prices for a range of strikes by Fourier inversion. However, we cannot do this directly because $C(k)$ is not integrable (it tends to 1 as k goes to $-\infty$). The idea is to subtract the Black-Scholes call price with nonzero volatility and compute the Fourier transform of the resulting function which is integrable and smooth:[1]

$$z_T(k) = C(k) - C_{BS}^\Sigma(k),$$

where $C_{BS}^\Sigma(k)$ is the Black-Scholes price of a call option with volatility Σ and log-strike k for the same underlying value and the same interest rate.

Proposition 5.1. *Let* $\{X_t\}_{t\geq0}$ *be a real-valued Lévy process such that* (e^{X_t}) *is a martingale, and*

$$\int_{x>1} e^{(1+\alpha)x}\nu(dx) < \infty$$

for some $\alpha > 0$. *Then the Fourier transform in log-strike* k *of* $z_T(k)$ *is given by:*

$$\zeta_T(v) = e^{ivrT}\frac{\Phi_T(v-i) - \Phi_T^\Sigma(v-i)}{iv(1+iv)},$$

---

[1] Carr and Madan proposed to subtract the (nondifferentiable) intrinsic value of the price $(1 - e^{k-rT})^+$, but this leads to a slower convergence.

where $\Phi_T^\Sigma(v) = \exp(-\frac{\Sigma^2 T}{2}(v^2 + iv))$ is the characteristic function of log-stock price in the Black-Scholes model.

The optimal value of Σ is the value for which $\zeta_T(0) = 0$. However, the convergence is good for any $\Sigma > 0$. One can take, for example, $\Sigma = 0.2$ for practical calculations.

5.2.1 Numerical Fourier Inversion

Option prices can be computed by evaluating numerically the inverse Fourier transform of ζ_T:

$$z_T(k) = \frac{1}{2\pi} \int_{-\infty}^{+\infty} e^{-ivk} \zeta_T(v) dv. \tag{5.2.1}$$

This integral can be efficiently computed for a range of strikes using the fast Fourier transform. Recall that this algorithm allows to calculate the discrete Fourier transform $\text{DFT}[f]_{n=0}^{N-1}$, defined by

$$\text{DFT}[f]_n := \sum_{k=0}^{N-1} f_k e^{-2\pi i n k/N}, \quad n = 0 \ldots N-1$$

using only $O(N \log N)$ operations.

To approximate option prices, we truncate and discretize the integral (5.2.1) as follows:

$$\frac{1}{2\pi} \int_{-\infty}^{\infty} e^{-ivk} \zeta_T(v) dv = \frac{1}{2\pi} \int_{-L/2}^{L/2} e^{-ivk} \zeta_T(v) dv + \varepsilon_{\text{trunc}}$$

$$= \frac{L}{2\pi(N-1)} \sum_{m=0}^{N-1} w_m \zeta_T(v_m) e^{-ikv_m} + \varepsilon_{\text{trunc}} + \varepsilon_{\text{discr}},$$

where $\varepsilon_{\text{trunc}}$ is the truncation error, $\varepsilon_{\text{discr}}$ is the discretization error, $v_m = -L/2 + m\Delta$, $\Delta = L/(N-1)$ is the discretization step and w_m are weights, corresponding to the chosen integration rule (for instance, for the Simpson's rule $w_0 = 1/3$, and for $k = 1, \ldots, N/2$, $w_{2k-1} = 4/3$ and $w_{2k} = 2/3$).[2] Now,

---

[2] We use the FFT with $N = 2^p$, so N is even.

choosing $k_n = k_0 + \frac{2\pi n}{N\Delta}$ we see that the sum in the last term becomes a discrete Fourier transform:

$$\frac{L}{2\pi(N-1)} e^{ik_n L/2} \sum_{m=0}^{N-1} w_m \zeta_T(k_m) e^{-ik_0 m\Delta} e^{-2\pi i nm/N}$$

$$= \frac{L}{2\pi(N-1)} e^{ik_n L/2} \mathrm{DFT}_n[w_m \zeta_T(k_m) e^{-ik_0 m\Delta}]$$

Therefore, the FFT algorithm allows to compute z_T and option prices for the log strikes $k_n = k_0 + \frac{2\pi n}{N\Delta}$. The log strikes are thus equidistant with the step d satisfying

$$d\Delta = \frac{2\pi}{N}.$$

This relationship implies that if we want to computed option prices on a fine grid of strikes, and at the same time keep the discretization error low, we must use a large number of points.

Figure 5.3 shows typical option price profiles computed in the Merton model using the Fourier transform method. This method applies to all

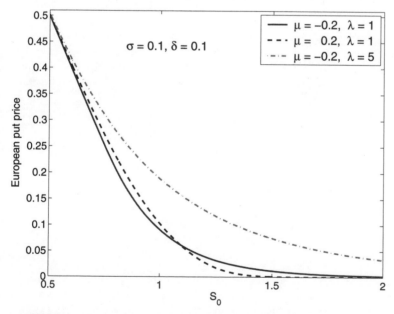

FIGURE 5.3 European put price as a function of stock for three choices of parameters in the Merton model. Other parameters: $K = 1$, $T = 1$, $r = 0$.

TABLE 5.1 Examples of Characteristic Functions of Jump-Diffusion Processes
Used in Financial Modeling (For further examples, see [11, Chapter 4])

Model	$f(dx)$	$\Phi_T(u) = \mathbb{E}[e^{iuX_T}]$
Merton	$\dfrac{\exp(-(x-\mu)^2)}{\sqrt{2\pi\delta^2}}dx$	$e^{T(-\frac{\sigma^2}{2}+ibu+\lambda\{e^{-\delta^2u^2/2+i\mu u}-1\})}$
Kou	$(p\lambda_+e^{-\lambda_+x}1_{x>0} +$ $(1-p)\lambda_-e^{-\lambda_-\|x\|}1_{x<0})dx$	$e^{T(-\frac{\sigma^2}{2}+ibu+iu\lambda\{\frac{p}{\lambda_+-iu}-\frac{1-p}{\lambda_-+iu}\})}$

models where the characteristic function of log-stock price is known or easy to compute. This is the case for exponential Lévy models (see, e.g., Table 5.1) but also holds for a more general class of *affine* processes [17, 18], which includes in particular the Bates model mentioned in section 5.1.

5.3 INTEGRO-DIFFERENTIAL EQUATIONS FOR BARRIER AND AMERICAN OPTIONS

The Fourier-transform based algorithm of the preceding section is very efficient for European vanilla options, but less so for more complicated contracts with barriers or American-style exercise.[3] In diffusion models their prices are usually expressed as solutions of the Black-Scholes partial differential equation

$$\frac{\partial P}{\partial t} + \frac{1}{2}\sigma^2 S^2 \frac{\partial^2 C}{\partial S^2} = rC - rS\frac{\partial C}{\partial S} \tag{5.3.1}$$

with appropriate boundary conditions. In this section, we show how this method can be generalized to models with jumps by introducing partial integro-differential equations (PIDEs). A complete presentation with proofs,

---

[3] Fourier-transform based methods for pricing single-barrier options can be found in the literature [8, 28, 40] but except for some particular models [27], the numerical complexity of the resulting formulae is prohibitive. Efficient Fourier-based methods were recently developed for Bermudan options (several exercise dates) [29] but the extension to American contracts remains problematic.

as well as the general case of possibly infinite Lévy measure, can be found in [38, 15].

5.3.1 Barrier "Out" Options

We start with *up-and-out*, *down-and-out*, and *double barrier* options, which have, respectively, an upper barrier $U > S_0$, a lower barrier $L < S_0$, or both. If the stock price S_t has not crossed any of the barriers before maturity T, then the payoff of the option is $H(S_T)$; otherwise, the option expires worthless or pays out a rebate $G(\tau^*, S_{\tau^*})$ where τ^* is the moment when the stock price first touches the barrier (usually, the rebate is simply a constant amount).

The barrier options are said to be *weakly path dependent*, because at any given time t, their price does not depend on the entire trajectory of the stock price prior to t but only on the current value S_t and on the event $\{t < \tau^*\}$, that is, on the information, whether the barrier has already been crossed. If the price of a barrier option is denoted by C_t then $C_t 1_{t<\tau^*} = C_b(t, S_t) 1_{t<\tau^*}$ where C_b is a deterministic function, which satisfies a generalized Black-Scholes equation given below.

To obtain an equation with constant coefficients we switch to log-prices and denote:

- $\tau = T - t$ (time to maturity), $x = \log(S/S_0)$ (log-price)
- $l = \log(L/S_0)$, $u = \log(U/S_0)$ (barriers in terms of log-price)
- $h(x) = H(S_0 e^x)$ (payoff function after the change of variables)
- $g(\tau, x) = e^{r\tau} G(T - \tau, S_0 e^x)$ (rebate after the change of variables)
- $v(\tau, x) = e^{r\tau} C_b(T - \tau, S_0 e^x)$ (option's forward price)

Then the transformed option price $v(\tau, x)$ satisfies

$$\frac{\partial v}{\partial \tau}(\tau, x) = Lv(\tau, x), \quad (\tau, x) \in (0, T] \times (l, u), \tag{5.3.2}$$

$$v(0, x) = h(x), \qquad x \in (l, u), \tag{5.3.3}$$

$$v(\tau, x) = g(\tau, x), \qquad \tau \in [0, T], \quad x \notin (l, u), \tag{5.3.4}$$

where L is an integro-differential operator:

$$Lf(x) = \frac{\sigma^2}{2} f''(x) - \left(\frac{\sigma^2}{2} - r\right) f'(x) + \int_{\mathbb{R}} \nu(dy) f(x + y) - \lambda f(x) - \alpha f'(x),$$

$$\tag{5.3.5}$$

with $\lambda = \int_{\mathbb{R}} \nu(dy)$, $\alpha = \int_{\mathbb{R}} (e^y - 1)\nu(dy)$. By convention, we set $l = -\infty$ if there is no lower barrier and $u = \infty$ if there is no upper barrier. So, (5.3.2)–(5.3.4) covers all types of barrier options above, as well as the European vanilla case.

In the case of the Black-Scholes model ($\nu \equiv 0$), equation (5.3.2)–(5.3.4) is nothing more than the standard heat equation

$$\frac{\partial v}{\partial \tau} = \frac{\sigma^2}{2} \frac{\partial^2 v}{\partial x^2} - \left(\frac{\sigma^2}{2} - r \right) \frac{\partial v}{\partial x},$$

which can be obtained from the Black-Scholes equation (5.3.1) by an exponential change of variable.

Note, that (5.3.4) is different from usual boundary conditions for differential equations: it gives the values of the solution not only *at* the barriers but also *beyond* the barriers. It is an important consequence of the *nonlocal* character of the operator L due to the integral part.

5.3.2 Numerical Solution of the Integro-Differential Equation

To solve numerically the problem (5.3.2)–(5.3.4), we proceed with the following steps:

- *Truncation of large jumps*. This corresponds to truncating the integration domain in (5.3.5).
- *Localization*. If the problem was initially stated on an unbounded interval (as in the European or one-barrier cases), we must choose a bounded computational domain and, consequently, impose artificial boundary conditions.
- *Discretization*. The derivatives of the solution are replaced by usual finite differences and the integral terms are approximated using the trapezoidal rule. The problem is then solved using an explicit-implicit scheme.

Let us now consider these steps in detail.

Truncation of Large Jumps Since we cannot calculate numerically an integral on the infinite range $(-\infty, \infty)$, the domain is truncated to a bounded interval (B_l, B_r). In terms of the process, this corresponds to removing the large jumps. Usually, the tails of ν decrease exponentially, so the probability of large jumps is very small. Therefore, we don't change much the solution by truncating the tails of v.

Localization Similarly, for the computational purposes, the domain of definition of the equation has to be bounded. For barrier options, the barriers are the natural limits for this domain and the rebate is the natural boundary condition. In the absence of barriers, we have to choose artificial bounds $(-A_l, A_r)$ and impose artificial boundary conditions. Recall that "boundary" conditions in this case must extend the solution beyond the bounds as well: $v(\tau, x) = g(\tau, x)$ for all $x \notin (-A_l, A_r)$, $\tau \in [0, T]$.

In [38], it is shown that a good choice for the boundary conditions is $g(\tau, x) = h(x + r\tau)$ where h is the payoff function. For example, for a put option, we have $h(x) = (K - S_0 e^x)^+$ and thus $g(\tau, x) = (K - S_0 e^{x+r\tau})^+$.

In the case of one barrier, we need this boundary condition only on one side of the domain: the other is zero or given by the rebate.

Discretization We consider now the localized problem on $(-A_l, A_r)$:

$$\frac{\partial v}{\partial \tau} = Lv, \qquad \text{on } (0, T] \times (-A_l, A_r) \qquad (5.3.6)$$

$$v(0, x) = h(x), \qquad x \in (-A_l, A_r), \qquad (5.3.7)$$

$$v(\tau, x) = g(\tau, x), \qquad x \notin (-A_l, A_r). \qquad (5.3.8)$$

where L is the following integro-differential operator:

$$Lv = \frac{\sigma^2}{2} \frac{\partial^2 v}{\partial x^2} - \left(\frac{\sigma^2}{2} - r \right) \frac{\partial v}{\partial x} + \int_{B_l}^{B_r} v(dy) v(\tau, x + y) - \lambda v - \alpha \frac{\partial v}{\partial x}$$

with $\lambda = \int_{B_l}^{B_r} v(dy)$, $\alpha = \int_{B_l}^{B_r} (e^y - 1) v(dy)$. Let us introduce a uniform grid on $[0, T] \times \mathbb{R}$:

$$\tau_n = n \Delta t, \quad n = 0 \dots M, \quad x_i = -A_l + i \Delta x, \quad i \in \mathbb{Z}$$

with $\Delta t = T/M$, $\Delta x = (A_r + A_l)/N$. The values of v on this grid are denoted by $\{v_i^n\}$. The space derivatives of v are approximated by finite differences:

$$\left(\frac{\partial^2 v}{\partial x^2} \right)_i \approx \frac{v_{i+1} - 2v_i + v_{i-1}}{(\Delta x)^2} \qquad (5.3.9)$$

$$\left(\frac{\partial v}{\partial x} \right)_i \approx \frac{v_{i+1} - v_i}{\Delta x}, \qquad \text{or} \qquad \left(\frac{\partial v}{\partial x} \right)_i \approx \frac{v_i - v_{i-1}}{\Delta x} \qquad (5.3.10)$$

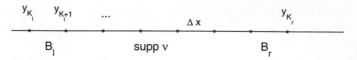

FIGURE 5.4   The Support of v Is Discretized with the Same Step Δx as $[-A_l, A_r]$.

The choice of the approximation of the first order derivative—forward or backward difference—depends on the parameters σ, r, and α (see below).

To approximate the integral term, we use the trapezoidal rule with the same discretization step Δx. Choose integers K_l, K_r such that $[B_l, B_r]$ is contained in $[(K_l - 1/2)\Delta x, (K_r + 1/2)\Delta x]$ (Figure 5.4). Then,

$$\int_{B_l}^{B_r} v(dy)v(\tau, x_i + y) \approx \sum_{j=K_l}^{K_r} v_j v_{i+j}, \quad \text{where} \quad v_j = \int_{(j-1/2)\Delta x}^{(j+1/2)\Delta x} v(dy).$$

$$(5.3.11)$$

Using (5.3.9)–(5.3.11) we obtain an approximation for $Lv \approx D_\Delta v + J_\Delta v$, where $D_\Delta v$ and $J_\Delta v$ are chosen as follows.

5.3.3 Explicit-Implicit Scheme

Without loss of generality, suppose that $\sigma^2/2 - r < 0$. Then

$$(D_\Delta v)_i = \frac{\sigma^2}{2} \frac{v_{i+1} - 2v_i + v_{i-1}}{(\Delta x)^2} - \left(\frac{\sigma^2}{2} - r\right) \frac{v_{i+1} - v_i}{\Delta x}$$

If $\sigma^2/2 - r > 0$, to ensure the stability of the algorithm, we must change the discretization of $\partial v/\partial x$ by choosing the backward difference instead of the forward one. Similarly, if $\alpha < 0$ we discretize J as follows:

$$(J_\Delta v)_i = \sum_{j=K_l}^{K_r} v_j v_{i+j} - \lambda v_i - \alpha \frac{v_{i+1} - v_i}{\Delta x} \qquad (5.3.12)$$

Otherwise, we change the approximation of the first derivative. Finally, we replace the problem (5.3.6)–(5.3.8) with the following *explicit-implicit scheme*:

Initialization:

$$v_i^0 = h(x_i), \quad \text{if } i \in \{0, \ldots, N-1\}, \tag{5.3.13}$$

$$v_i^0 = g(0, x_i), \qquad \text{otherwise.} \tag{5.3.14}$$

For n = 0, ..., M − 1:

$$\frac{v_i^{n+1} - v_i^n}{\Delta t} = (D_\Delta v^{n+1})_i + (J_\Delta v^n)_i, \quad \text{if } i \in \{0, \ldots, N-1\} \tag{5.3.15}$$

$$v_i^{n+1} = g((n+1)\Delta t, x_i), \quad \text{otherwise} \tag{5.3.16}$$

Here, the nonlocal operator J is treated explicitly to avoid the inversion of the dense matrix J_Δ, while the differential part D is treated implicitly. At each time step, we first evaluate vector $J_\Delta v^n$ where v^n is known from the previous iteration,[4] and then solve the tridiagonal system (5.3.15) for $v^{n+1} = (v_0^{n+1}, \ldots, v_{N-1}^{n+1})$. This scheme is stable if

$$\Delta t < \frac{\Delta x}{|\alpha| + \lambda \Delta x}$$

5.3.4 Other Approaches

In [36, 23, 39, 33, 37], fully implicit or Crank-Nicolson finite difference schemes are used which are unconditionally stable. To solve the resulting dense linear systems, the authors use iterative methods which require only matrix-vector multiplication performed using FFT.

Another way to solve the problem of the dense matrix is proposed in [33]. The authors use a finite element method with a special basis of wavelet functions. In this basis, the most of entries in the matrix operator are very small, so that they can be replaced by zeros without affecting much the solution.

We can use a non-uniform grid with, for example, more nodes near the strike and maturity [2, 37]. In this case, an interpolation at each time step is needed in order to apply FFT [23].

---

[4] The particular form of the sum in (5.3.12) (discrete convolution of two vectors) allows to compute it efficiently and simultaneously for all i using Fast Fourier transform.

In [4], the operator is also split into differential and integral parts, and then an alternating direction implicit (ADI) time stepping is used.

5.3.5 Pricing American Options

The simplest way to adapt the above method to pricing American options is to use the dynamic programming. If we approximate continuous time by a discrete grid of exercise dates $t_n = n\Delta t$, the value of the American option at t_n is the maximum between profits from exercising immediately and holding the option until t_{n+1}:

$$V_n = \max\{H(S_{t_n}), V_n^e\}, \tag{5.3.17}$$

where $V_n^e = e^{-r\Delta t}\mathbb{E}[V_{n+1}|\mathcal{F}_{t_n}]$ may be interpreted as the value of a European option with payoff V_{n+1} and maturity t_{n+1}. Therefore, at each time step, we can compute V_n^e as above and then adjust the result by taking the maximum as in (5.3.17).

More precisely, after the same change of variables, localization and discretization procedures, we end up with the following scheme:

Initialization:

$$v_i^0 = h(x_i), \qquad \text{for all } i,$$

For n = 0, ..., M − 1:

$$\frac{\tilde{v}_i^{n+1} - v_i^n}{\Delta t} = (D_\Delta \tilde{v}^{n+1})_i + (J_\Delta v^n)_i, \quad \text{if } i \in \{0, \ldots, N-1\}$$

$$\tilde{v}_i^{n+1} = g((n+1)\Delta t, x_i), \qquad \text{otherwise}$$

$$v_i^{n+1} = \max\{h(x_i), \tilde{v}_i^{n+1}\}, \qquad \text{for all } i$$

Alternatively, American option price may be represented as solution of a linear complementarity problem (LCP) of the following form:

$$\frac{\partial v}{\partial \tau} - Lv \geq 0, \tag{5.3.18}$$

$$v - h \geq 0, \tag{5.3.19}$$

$$\left(\frac{\partial v}{\partial \tau} - Lv\right)(v - h) = 0, \tag{5.3.20}$$

where L is the same integro differential operator as in the PIDE (5.3.2) and h is the payoff received upon exercise. Pricing American options in Lévy-driven models based on (5.3.18)–(5.3.20) is considered, for example, in [25, 32, 22, 23, 39, 1, 2, 3]. Numerical solution of the integro differential problem (5.3.18)–(5.3.20) faces globally the same difficulties as that of PIDEs. The dense and nonsymmetric matrix of the operator makes unfeasible or inefficient standard methods for solving LCPs. The solutions proposed rely on similar ideas as in the European case: splitting the operator [1], wavelet compression [32], using iterative methods with suitable preconditioning. In [22, 23, 39], the LCP is replaced by an equation with a nonlinear penalty term. We refer to the references cited above for the details on these methods.

5.4 HEDGING JUMP RISK

In the Black-Scholes model, the delta-hedging strategy completely eliminates the risk of an option position. This strategy consists in holding the amount of stock equal to $\frac{\partial C}{\partial S}$, the sensitivity of the option price with respect to the underlying. However, in presence of jumps, delta hedging is no longer optimal. Suppose that a portfolio contains ϕ_t stock, with price S_t, and a short option position. After a jump ΔS_t, the change in the stock position is $\phi_t \Delta S_t$, and the option changes by $C(t, S_t + \Delta S_t) - C(t, S_t)$. The jump will be completely hedged if and only if

$$\phi_t = \frac{C(t, S_t + \Delta S_t) - C(t, S_t)}{\Delta S_t}.$$

Since the option price is a nonlinear function of S, $\phi_t \neq \frac{\partial C}{\partial S}$ and delta-hedging does not offset the jump risk completely.

Thus, to hedge a jump of a given size, one should use the sensitivity to movements of the underlying of this size rather than the sensitivity to infinitesimal movements. Since typically the jump size is not known in advance, the risk associated to jumps cannot be hedged away completely: we are in an incomplete market. In this setting, the hedging becomes an approximation problem: instead of *replicating* an option, one tries to *minimize* the residual hedging error.

In this section we show how to compute the optimal hedging strategies in presence of jumps and answer, using empirical data, the following two questions.

- How and when is the optimal strategy different from delta hedging, that is, under what market conditions does it really make sense to use the optimal strategy rather than the usual delta hedging?
- If the optimal strategy is used, how big is the residual hedging error and what can be done to improve its performance?

5.4.1 Computing the Optimal Strategy

First, we treat the case when the hedging portfolio contains only stock and the risk-free asset. Let S_t denote the stock price and ϕ the quantity of stock in the hedging portfolio, and suppose that S satisfies (5.1.4) with volatility σ and Lévy measure of the jump part denoted by ν. Then the (self-financing) portfolio evolves as

$$dV_t = (V_t - \phi_t S_t) r\,dt + \phi_t dS_t$$

We would like to compute the strategy which minimizes the expected squared residual hedging error under the martingale probability:

$$\phi^* = \arg\inf_{\phi} E[(V_T - H_T)^2]$$

with H_T the option's payoff. We suppose that this payoff only depends on the terminal stock price (no path dependency) and denote by $C(t, S)$ the price of the option at time t expressed as a function of the stock price at this time:

$$C(t, S) = e^{-r(T-t)} E[H_T | S_t = S]$$

We now reproduce the main results on the optimal hedging strategy and refer the reader to [14] for details of computation.

- The initial capital minimizing the hedging error is

$$V_0 = e^{-rT} E[H_T] \tag{5.4.1}$$

- If the initial capital is given by (5.4.1), the residual hedging error is zero (and the market is complete) only in the following two cases:
  - No jumps in the stock price ($\nu \equiv 0$). This case corresponds to the Black-Scholes model and the optimal hedging strategy is

$$\phi_t^* = \frac{\partial C}{\partial S}$$

  - No diffusion component ($\sigma = 0$) and only one possible jump size ($\nu = \delta_{z_0}(z)$). In this case, the optimal hedging strategy is

$$\phi_t^* = \frac{C(S_t e^{z_0}) - C(S_t)}{S_t(e^{z_0} - 1)}$$

- In all other cases, the residual hedging error is nonzero (and the market is incomplete) and is minimized by

$$\phi^*(t, S_t) = \frac{\sigma^2 \frac{\partial C}{\partial S} + \frac{1}{S_t} \int \nu(dz)(e^z - 1)(C(t, S_t e^z) - C(t, S_t))}{\sigma^2 + (e^z - 1)^2 \nu(dz)} \qquad (5.4.2)$$

5.4.2 Delta Hedging versus Optimal Strategy

How far is the optimal strategy from delta hedging? To answer this question, for jump diffusions, if jumps are small, we can perform a Taylor expansion with respect to the jump size in (5.4.2), obtaining

$$\phi_t^* = \frac{\partial C}{\partial S} + \frac{S_t}{2\Sigma^2} \frac{\partial^2 C}{\partial S^2} \int \nu(dz)(e^z - 1)^3$$

where

$$\Sigma^2 = \sigma^2 + \int (e^z - 1)^2 \nu(dz)$$

Typically in equity markets the jumps are negative and small, therefore $\phi_t < \frac{\partial C}{\partial X}$ and the optimal strategy represents a small (of the order of third power of jump size) asymmetry correction. This situation is represented in Figure 5.5. On the other hand, for pure-jump processes such as variance gamma, we cannot perform the Taylor expansion, because the second derivative $\frac{\partial^2 C}{\partial X^2}$

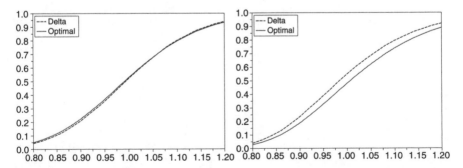

FIGURE 5.5 Hedging with stock in Kou model: Delta hedging vs. optimal strategy. Left: parameters estimated from market data (MSFT). Right: Here the jump intensity is the same, but all jumps are supposed to be negative: we see that the optimal strategy is a negative correction to delta hedging.

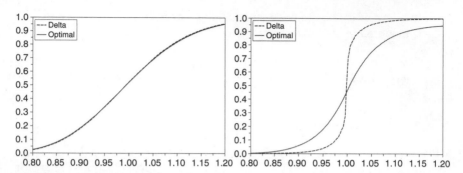

FIGURE 5.6 Hedging with stock in variance gamma model: Delta hedging vs. optimal strategy. Left: Parameters estimated from market data (same series as in Figure 5.5), the option maturity is $T = 1$ month. Right: The mean jump size parameter was changed to 7 percent and the option maturity to $T = 2$ days.

may not even exist, and the correction may therefore be quite large (see Figure 5.6).

5.4.3 How Big Is the Hedging Error?

To answer this question, we simulated the terminal value of the hedging portfolio and that of the option's payoff over 10,000 trajectories for different strategies and different parameter sets.

In the first case study, Kou model with parameters estimated from market data (MSFT) was used, and the option to hedge was a European put with strike $K = 90\%$ of the spot price and time to maturity $T = 1$ year. The hedging errors are given in Table 5.2 and the left graph in Figure 5.7 shows the profit-and-loss (P&L) histograms. For this parameter set, the optimal strategy is very close to delta hedging (see the left graph in Figure 5.5), and consequently, the hedging error is the same for delta hedging as for the optimal strategy. On the other hand, this error is very low, it is only

TABLE 5.2 Hedging Errors for Different Strategies in Kou Model Expressed in Percentage of the Initial Stock Price (model parameters were estimated from MSFT time series)

Strategy	Root of Mean Squared Error
Delta-hedging	0.0133
Optimal 1 asset	0.0133
Black-Scholes (due to discrete hedging)	0.0059
No hedging	0.107

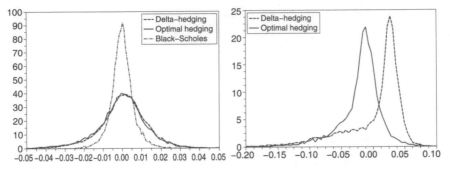

FIGURE 5.7 Histograms of the residual hedging error in Kou model. Left: parameters estimated from MSFT time series. Right: strong negative jumps.

twice as big as what we would get in the Black and Scholes model with equivalent volatility (this error in the Black-Scholes model is due to the fact that in the simulations, the portfolio is only rebalanced once a day and not continuously).

In the second case study, Kou model, with unfrequent large negative jumps (10%) was used, and we wanted once again to hedge an out-of-the-money (OTM) European put ($K = 90\%$, $T = 1$). The hedging errors are given in Table 5.3 and the P&L histograms in Figure 5.7, right graph. Here we see that first, the optimal strategy has a much better performance than delta hedging, and second, even this performance may not be sufficient, since the residual error is still of order of 4 percent of the initial stock price.

5.4.4 Hedging with Options

To reduce the hedging error in the presence of strong jumps, additional assets such as liquid European options can be included in the hedging portfolio, and [14] give explicit formulas for computing the hedge ratios. Here we

TABLE 5.3 Hedging Errors for Different Strategies in Kou Model Expressed in Percentage of the Initial Stock Price (a parameter set ensuring the presence of large negative jumps was taken)

Strategy	Root of Mean Squared Error
Delta-hedging	0.051
Optimal 1 asset	0.041
No hedging	0.156

TABLE 5.4   Hedging Errors for Different Strategies in Kou Model
Expressed in Percentage of the Initial Stock Price. A parameter set
ensuring the presence of large negative jumps was taken. The hedging
portfolio contains stock and another option.

Strategy	Root of Mean Squared Error
Delta-hedging	0.051
Optimal 1 asset	0.041
Optimal 2 assets	0.015

present numerical results in the case where we want to hedge an OTM
European put (strike $K = 90\%$ of the initial stock price and time to maturity
$T = 1$ year) with stock and an OTM European call ($K = 110\%$ and $T = 1$).
The hedging errors for the same model parameters as in case 2 above are
given in Table 5.4 and the P&L histograms in Figure 5.8, right graph. We see
that the use of options for hedging allows to reduce the residual hedging error
by a further factor of three, making it compatible to the (good) performance

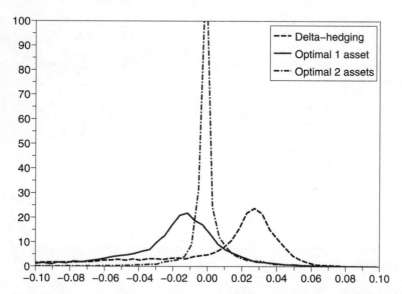

FIGURE 5.8   Histograms of the residual hedging error in Kou model with strong
negative jumps. The hedging portfolio contains stock and another option.

observed for the first parameter set (Table 5.2). To summarize our empirical findings, in models with jumps:

- If the jumps are small, delta hedging works well and its performance is close to optimal.
- In the presence of a strong jump component, the optimal strategy is superior to delta hedging both in terms of hedge stability and residual error.
- If jumps are strong, the residual hedging error can be further reduced by adding options to the hedging portfolio.

5.5 MODEL CALIBRATION

In the Black-Scholes setting, the only model parameter to choose is the volatility σ, originally defined as the annualized standard deviation of logarithmic stock returns. The notion of model calibration does not exist, since after observing a trajectory of the stock price, the pricing model is completely specified. On the other hand, since the pricing model is defined by a single volatility parameter, this parameter can be reconstructed from a single option price (by inverting the Black-Scholes formula). This value is known as the implied volatility of this option.

If the real markets obeyed the Black-Scholes model, the implied volatility of all options written on the same underlying would be the same and equal to the standard deviation of returns of this underlying. However, empirical studies show that this is not the case: implied volatilities of options on the same underlying depend on their strikes and maturities (Figure 5.9).

Jump-diffusion models provide an explanation of the implied volatility smile phenomenon since in these models the implied volatility is both different from the historical volatility and changes as a function of strike and maturity. Figure 5.10 shows possible implied volatility patterns (as a function of strike) in the Merton jump-diffusion model.

The results of calibration of the Merton model to Standard & Poor's (S&P) index options of different maturities are presented in Figure 5.11 (calibration to a single maturity) and Figure 5.12 (simultaneous calibration to several maturities). The calibration was carried out using the routine [7] from Premia software. In this program, the vector of unknown parameters θ is found by minimizing numerically the squared norm of the difference between market and model prices:

$$\theta^* = \arg\inf\|P^{obs} - P^{\theta}\|^2 \equiv \arg\inf \sum_{i=1}^{N} w_i (P_i^{obs} - P^{\theta}(T_i, K_i))^2, \qquad (5.5.1)$$

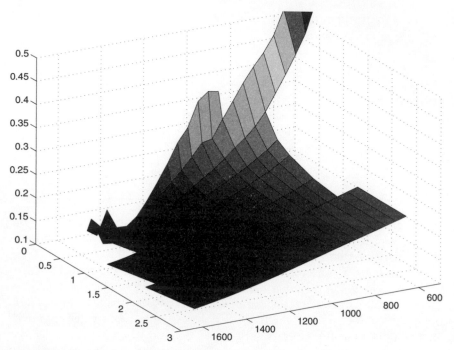

FIGURE 5.9 Implied volatilities of options on S&P 500 Index as a function of their strikes and maturities.

where P^{obs} denotes the prices observed in the market and $P^{\theta}(T_i, K_i)$ is the Merton model price computed for parameter vector θ, maturity T_i and strike K_i. Here, the weights $w_i := \frac{1}{(P_i^{obs})^2}$ were chosen to ensure that all terms in the minimization functional are of the same order of magnitude. The model prices were computed simultaneously for all strikes present in the data using the FFT-based algorithm described in section 5.2. The functional in (5.5.1) was then minimized using a quasi-Newton method (LBFGS-B described in [9]). In the case of Merton model, the calibration functional is sufficiently well behaved, and can be minimized using this convex optimization algorithm. To test this, we ran the calibration procedure 20 times with starting parameter values chosen at random. In 19 tests out of 20, the parameter values found by the algorithm coincided up to a relative precision of 10^{-6}, and in the remaining case the precision was still of the order of 5×10^{-3}. In more complex jump-diffusion models, in particular, when no parametric shape of the Lévy measure is assumed, a penalty term must be added to the distance functional in (5.5.1) to ensure convergence and stability. This procedure is described in detail in [12, 13, 35].

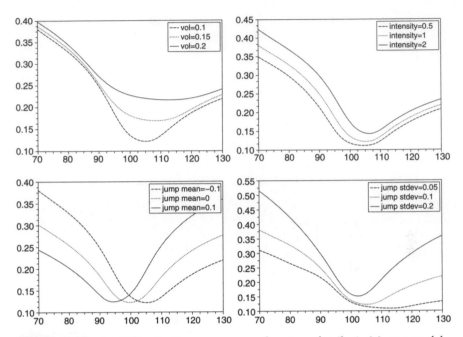

FIGURE 5.10 Implied volatility patterns as a function of strike in Merton model.

As seen from Figure 5.11, the calibration to a single maturity is quite good, especially for short-term options. For long-term options, the model has more difficulty in reproducing the skew correctly. Although the options of different maturities correspond to the same trading day and the same underlying, the parameter values for each maturity are different, as seen

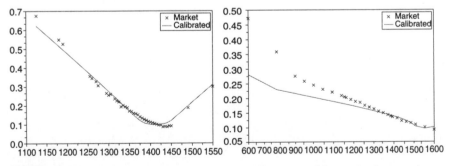

FIGURE 5.11 Calibration of Merton jump-diffusion model to a single maturity. Left: maturity 8 days. Right: maturity 188 days.

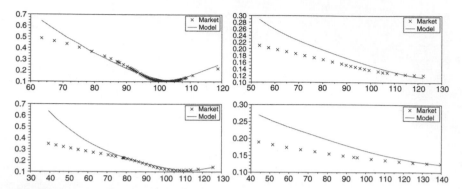

FIGURE 5.12 Calibration of Merton jump-diffusion model simultaneously to 4 maturities (calibrated parameter values: $\sigma = 9.0\%$, $\lambda = 0.39$, jump mean -0.12 and jump standard deviation 0.15. Top left: maturity 1 month. Bottom left: maturity 5 months. Top right: maturity 1.5 years. Bottom right: maturity 3 years).

from Table 5.5. In particular, the behavior for short (1 to 5 months) and long (1 to 3 years) maturities is qualitatively different, and for longer maturities the mean jump size tends to increase while the jump intensity decreases with the length of the holding period.

Figure 5.12 shows the result of simultaneous calibration of Merton model to options of four different maturities, ranging from 1 month to 3 years. As we see, the calibration error is quite big. This happens because, as already observed in section 5.1, for processes with independent and stationary increments (and the log-price in Merton model is an example of such process), the law of the entire process is completely determined by its law at any given time t (cf. Equation 5.1.3). If we have calibrated the model

TABLE 5.5 Calibrated Merton Model Parameters for Different Times to Maturity

Maturity	σ	λ	Jump Mean	Jump Std. Dev.
1 month	9.5%	0.097	−1.00	0.71
2 months	9.3%	0.086	−0.99	0.63
5 months	10.8%	0.050	−0.59	0.41
11 months	7.1%	0.70	−0.13	0.11
17 months	8.2%	0.29	−0.25	0.12
23 months	8.2%	0.26	−0.27	0.15
35 months	8.8%	0.16	−0.38	0.19

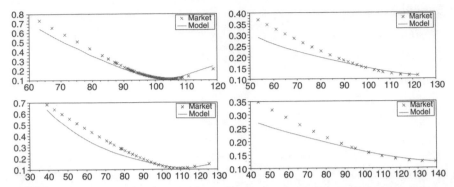

FIGURE 5.13   Calibration of the Bates stochastic volatility jump-diffusion model simultaneously to four maturities. (Top left: maturity 1 month. Bottom left: maturity 5 months. Top right: maturity 1.5 years. Bottom right: maturity 3 years. Calibrated parameters (see Equation 5.1.8): initial volatility $\sqrt{V_0} = 12.4\%$, rate of volatility mean reversion $\xi = 3.72$, long-run volatility $\sqrt{\eta} = 11.8\%$, volatility of volatility $\theta = 0.501$, correlation $\rho = -48.8\%$, jump intensity $\lambda = 0.038$, mean jump size -1.14, jump standard deviation 0.73).

parameters for a single maturity T, this fixes completely the risk-neutral stock price distribution for all other maturities. A special kind of maturity dependence is therefore hard-wired into every Lévy jump-diffusion model, and Table 5.5 shows that it does not always correspond to the term structures of market option prices.

To calibrate a jump-diffusion model to options of several maturities at the same time, the model must have a sufficient number of degrees of freedom to reproduce different term structures. This is possible for example in the Bates model (5.1.8), where the smile for short maturities is explained by the presence of jumps whereas the smile for longer maturities and the term structure of implied volatility is taken into account using the stochastic volatility process. Figure 5.13 shows the calibration of the Bates model to the same data set as in Figure 5.12. As we see, the calibration quality has improved and is now almost as good as if each maturity was calibrated separately. The calibration was once again carried out using the tool [7] from Premia. In the case of Bates model, the calibration functional is less well behaved than in Merton model. To ensure convergence, one can either add a penalty term to the calibration functional, or calibrate separately the jump component and the stochastic volatility component (this method is used in [7]). A variant of the second method is described in detail in [19].

REFERENCES

1. Almendral, A. (2005). Numerical valuation of American options under the CGMY process. In A. Kyprianou, W. Schoutens, and P. Wilmott (eds.), *Exotic Options Pricing and Advanced Levy Models*. Hoboken, NJ: John Wiley & Sons.
2. Almendral, A., and C. W. Oosterlee. (2006). Accurate evaluation of European and American options under the variance gamma process. *Journal of Computational Finance* 10 (1): 21–42.
3. Almendral, A., and C. W. Oosterlee. (2007). Accurate evaluation of European and American options under the CGMY process. *SIAM Journal on Scientific Computing* 29: 93–117.
4. Andersen, L., and J. Andreasen. (2000). Jump-diffusion models: Volatility smile fitting and numerical methods for pricing. *Review of Derivatives Research* 4 (3): 231–262.
5. Bates, D. (1996). Jumps and stochastic volatility: The exchange rate processes implicit in Deutschemark options. *Review of Financial Studies* 9: 69–107.
6. Bates, D. S. (1996). Testing option pricing models. In G. S. Maddala and C. R. Rao (eds.), *Statistical Methods in Finance, vol. 14 of Handbook of Statistics*. Amsterdam: North-Holland, pp. 567–611.
7. Ben Haj Yedder, A. (2004). Calibration of stochastic volatility model with jumps. A computer program, part of Premia software, www.premia.fr.
8. Boyarchenko, S., and S. Levendorskii. (2002). *Non-Gaussian Merton-Black-Scholes Theory*. River Edge, NJ: World Scientific.
9. Byrd, R., P. Lu, and J. Nocedal. (1995). A limited memory algorithm for bound constrained optimization. *SIAM Journal on Scientific and Statistical Computing* 16: 1190–1208.
10. Carr, P., and D. Madan. (1998). Option valuation using the fast Fourier transform. *Journal of Computational Finance* 2: 61–73.
11. Cont, R., and P. Tankov. (2004). *Financial Modelling with Jump Processes*. Boca Raton, FL: Chapman & Hall/CRC Press.
12. Cont, R., and P. Tankov. (2004). Non-parametric calibration of jump-diffusion option pricing models. *Journal of Computational Finance* 7.
13. Cont, R., and P. Tankov. (2006). Retrieving Lévy processes from option prices: Regularization of an ill-posed inverse problem. *SIAM Journal on Control and Optimization* 45: 1–25.
14. Cont, R., P. Tankov, and E. Voltchkova. (2005). Hedging with options in models with jumps. *Proceedings of the 2005 Abel Symposium in Honor of Kiyosi Itô*.
15. Cont, R., and E. Voltchkova. (2005). A finite difference scheme for option pricing in jump-diffusion and exponential Lévy models. *SIAM Journal on Numerical Analysis* 43.
16. Devroye, L. (1986). *Nonuniform Random Variate Generation*. New York: Springer.
17. Duffie, D., D. Filipovic, and W. Schachermayer. (2003). Affine processes and applications in finance. *Annals of Applied Probability* 13: 984–1053.

18. Duffie, D., J. Pan, and K. Singleton. (2000). Transform analysis and asset pricing for affine jump-diffusions. *Econometrica* 68: 1343–1376.
19. Galluccio, S., and Y. Le Cam. (2007). Implied calibration of stochastic volatility jump diffusion models. Available at ssrn.com.
20. Geman, H., D. Madan, and M. Yor. (2001). Asset prices are Brownian motion: Only in business time. In M. Avellaneda (ed.), *Quantitative Analysis in Financial Markets*. River Edge, NJ: World Scientific, pp. 103–146.
21. Goll, T., and J. Kallsen. (2000). Optimal portfolios for logarithmic utility. *Stochastic Processes and Their Applications* 89: 31–48.
22. D'Halluin, Y., P. Forsyth, and G. Labahn. A penalty method for American options with jump diffusion processes. *Numerische Mathematik* 97: 321–352.
23. D'Halluin, Y., P. Forsyth, and K. Vetzal. (2005). Robust numerical methods for contingent claims under jump diffusion processes. *IMA Journal on Numerical Analysis* 25: 87–112.
24. D'Halluin, Y., P. Forsyth, and G. Labahn. (2005). A semi-Lagrangian approach for American Asian options under jump diffusion. *SIAM Journal on Scientific Computing* 27: 315–345.
25. Hirsa, A., and D. B. Madan. (2003). Pricing American options under variance gamma. *Journal of Computational Finance* 7 (2): 63–80.
26. Kou, S. (2002). A jump-diffusion model for option pricing. *Management Science* 48: 1086–1101.
27. Kou, S., and H. Wang. (2004). Option pricing under a double exponential jump-diffusion model. *Management Science* 50: 1178–1192.
28. Kyprianou, A., W. Schoutens, and P. Wilmott (eds.). (2005). *Exotic Option Pricing and Advanced Lévy Models*. Hoboken, NJ: John Wiley & Sons.
29. Lord, R., F. Fang, F. Bervoets, and C. W. Oosterlee. (2007). A fast and accurate FFT-based method for pricing early-exercise options under Levy processes. Available at http://ssrn.com/paper=966046.
30. Madan, D., P. Carr, and E. Chang. (1998). The variance gamma process and option pricing. *European Finance Review* 2: 79–105.
31. Madan, D., and F. Milne. (1991). Option pricing with variance gamma martingale components. *Mathematical Finance* 1: 39–55.
32. Matache, A.-M., P.-A Nitsche, and C. Schwab. (2005). Wavelet galerkin pricing of American on Lévy-driven assets. *Quantitative Finance* 5 (4): 403–424.
33. Matache, A.-M., T. von Petersdorff, and C. Schwab. (2004). Fast deterministic pricing of options on Lévy driven assets. M2AN. *Mathematical Modelling and Numerical Analysis* 38 (1): 37–71.
34. Merton, R. (1976). Option pricing when underlying stock returns are discontnuuous. *Journal of Financial Economics* 3: 125–144.
35. Tankov, P. (2004). Lévy processes in finance: Inverse problems and dependence modelling. PhD thesis, Ecole Polytechnique, France.
36. Tavella, D., and C. Randall. *Pricing Financial Instruments: The Finite Difference Method*. New York: John Wiley & Sons.

37. Toivanen, J. (2006). Numerical valuation of European and American options under Kou's jump-diffusion model. Report B11/2006, Department of Mathematical Information Technology, University of Jyväskylä.
38. Voltchkova, E. (2005). Integro-differential evolution equations: Numerical methods and applications in finance. PhD thesis, Ecole Polytechnique, France.
39. Wang, I. R., J. W. Wan, and P. Forsyth. (2007). Robust numerical valuation of European and American options under the CGMY process. *Journal of Computational Finance* 10: 31–69.
40. Yor, M., and L. Nguyen-Ngoc. (2007). Lookback and barrier options under general Lévy processes. In Y. At-Sahalia and L.-P. Hansen (eds.), *Handbook of Financial Econometrics*. Amsterdam: North-Holland.

CHAPTER 6

Modeling Credit Risk

L. C. G. Rogers

The notes that follow were originally prepared for a course given in 1999, and in the intervening years the whole subject of credit has boomed; accordingly, though in parts the material of these notes is timeless, elsewhere it appears distinctly dated. At the end of the chapter, I will make some remarks on the subject more recently, and where it might look in the future.

6.1 WHAT IS THE PROBLEM?

The first and most important thing to realize about modeling of credit risk is that we may be trying to answer questions of *two different types*, and the links between the two are somewhat tenuous.

To fix some notation, let's suppose that the value of a firm's assets at time t are denoted by V_t, and that these evolve as

$$dV_t = V_{t-}(\sigma_t dW_t + (\mu_t - c_t)dt - dJ_t) \qquad (6.1.1)$$

where W is a standard Brownian motion, μ is some process, the *rate of return* process, c is the dividend process, and J is some jumping process. The volatility process σ can be quite general. The value at time t of the total equity of the firm is denoted by S_t, and so the value at time t of all debt must be simply $V_t - S_t$. Default happens at some time τ; upon default, the control of the firm passes from the shareholders to the bondholders, and there may be restructuring losses incurred. Default may happen because of some failure of the firm to fulfill its obligations to its creditors, or it may happen because the shareholders decide to surrender control by declaring bankruptcy. For now, we will not be specific about the circumstances of default.

We might be interested in questions of *risk management*: What is the probability that the firm will default in the next 5 years? What is the expected loss on default if that happens? What are our expected losses from all the defaults of our obligors over the next 5 years? To answer these, we would presumably need to know the dividend policy, and the statistics of the rate of return. We would also need to know under what conditions default happens; if we make the simplifying assumption that it happens when V falls to some level, then we are dealing with a first-passage problem for a continuous process, which we may or may not be able to solve. Our approach to the problem would involve our estimating the dynamics of various processes, as well as the dependence of μ on them. This would require historical data and perhaps some judgemental inputs.

Contrast this with the situation we face if we are trying to answer *pricing* questions. This time, we are working in the *risk-neutral* or *pricing* measure, and so 6.1.1 is modified to make the rate of return equal to the riskless spot-rate r. To estimate this model, we would be looking to market prices—prices of equity, and credit-sensitive instruments. In the extreme case of $J = 0$, we would simply have $\mu = r$, and all structural dependence of the rate of return on economic fundamentals washes out!

The two situations involve working in two different measures, and they are linked only rather indirectly; if we had built a good model for one class of questions, we would have to make some (usually quite arbitrary) assumptions on risk premia to translate to a model for the other class of questions. We shall study in some detail below an example which displays clearly the kinds of difficulty involved.

We posed the problem in the generality of 6.1.1 because this form embraces the two main types of approach in the literature: the *structural* approach, and the *hazard rate* or *reduced form* approach. Typically in the first, the term dJ is absent, the value of the firm is modeled as a continuous process, with default occurring when the value reaches some (possibly time-dependent) barrier. In the second, the emphasis is on the jump process dJ, and default will occur at the first jump time of J.

It seems that we really need to include both components in our analysis.[1] The structural approach fails to match the observed evidence that corporate spreads do not decrease to zero as maturity decreases to zero; even for short maturities, the market does not neglect the possibility that some disaster may strike. On the other hand, the reduced-form approach can struggle

---

[1] The paper [4] is a first (rather simple-minded) step in this direction.

to capture the dependency between defaults of different firms; in principle, by making the hazard rate depend on a range of other processes we can incorporate this, but this is rather artificial—we still need to understand the other processes on which the hazard rate depends.

6.1.1 Data Issues

Let's first consider the risk-management questions. In order to estimate the probability of default of the firm, we would like to know as much as possible about the rate-of-return process. This may be affected by:

- Costs of labor and raw materials.
- Interest rates in countries where the firm produces and sells.
- Exchange rates between countries where the firm produces and sells.
- Recent and projected sales of the corporation.
- Other debt issues outstanding, their priority, maturity, and other characteristics.
- Failure of obligors.
- Perceived creditworthiness of the corporation.
- Taxation levels in various countries.
- Technological progress and new products of the firm and competitors.
- Possible major falls in value (e.g., litigation).
- Continuity and competence of management.
- Major political and market changes.

If we were well informed about all these things (as we would be if the corporation had approached us for a $5 billion loan, or for a credit rating), most of the uncertainty about default would be removed. On the other hand, much of this information about the firm would be very difficult for individual investors to discover, so most would be relying on coarser information, such as credit ratings, share prices and prices of the firm's bonds. We must be cautious in using *all* of these!

To begin with, credit ratings are obtained by some gross aggregation of many diverse corporations in order to make some estimates of (unlikely) changes in credit class, or default, and then all corporations with the same credit rating are treated the same for the purpose of assessing default risk. Now this is clearly too simplified; Hershey's will be significantly affected by the price of cocoa, Ford will not. Also, the moves between credit classes are often modelled as a continuous-time Markov chain, which means that the times in ratings classes will be exponentially distributed, but more importantly, the probability of a downgrade given that a firm has just experienced one is higher than for a firm that has been in that class for some time. This is not supported by evidence. Credit ratings convey only very crude information about the riskiness of a firm's debt—it would be tempting to omit them entirely from any modeling effort, were it not for the fact that there are various credit-sensitive products whose payoffs depend on the credit class to which the firm is assigned!

As far as share and bond prices go, these are calculated using the pricing measure, so we can't expect them to tell us much of use for risk management, apart from information about volatility.

How about the pricing questions? This time the useful data is the data relating to the pricing measure, so the prices of shares and corporate bonds; empirical estimates of ratings class transitions will not tell us anything we can use directly here. One point to note is that for sovereign debt, we do not have any share prices, so the range of usable data is much less; we would like our models to work without share price data, therefore.

Is there no useable link between the pricing measure and the real-world measure? Not entirely; the dividend policy of the firm will presumably depend on various economic fundamentals as well as the value of the firm, and the share price is just the net present value of all future dividends, so there is a link here. However, we still have to understand the law of the fundamentals in the pricing probability, so the matter is not ended.

6.2 HAZARD RATE MODELS

There are two broad classes of models, the *structural* models (characterized by an attempt to model default by modeling the dynamics of the assets of the firm) and the *hazard rate* models, where the idea is that the default comes "by surprise" in some sense, and we merely try to model the infinitesimal likelihood of a default. Hazard rate models are also called *reduced form* models by some authors.

In hazard rate models, the fundamental modeling tool is the Poisson process, and we begin by recalling the definition and some properties.

Definition 6.1. A Poisson counting process $(N_t)_{t \geq 0}$ is a nondecreasing process with right-continuous paths and values in $\mathbb{Z}^+$ such that

(i) $N_0 = 0$;
(ii) for any $0 \leq s_1 \leq t_1 \leq s_2 \leq t_2 \leq \ldots \leq s_n \leq t_n$, the random variables $X_i \equiv N(t_i) - N(s_i)$ are independent, and the distribution of each X_i depends only on the length $t_i - s_i$;
(iii) for all $t \geq 0$, $N_t - N_{t-}$ is either 0 or 1.

The definition of the Poisson process uniquely determines its distribution to within a single positive parameter λ. When $\lambda = 1$, we speak of a standard Poisson process. Here are other key properties, in which the positive parameter λ appears explicitly.

(2.2) the process $\tilde{N}_t \equiv N_t - \lambda t$ is a martingale;

(2.3) the interevent times $T_n - T_{n-1}$ are independent with common exponential(λ) distribution:

$$P[T_n - T_{n-1} > t] = \exp(-\lambda t)$$

for all $t \geq 0$; (Here, $T_n \equiv \inf\{t \geq 0 | N_t = n\}$.)

(2.4) For any $s \leq t$, $N_t - N_s \sim \mathcal{P}(\lambda(t-s))$, the Poisson distribution with mean λ:

$$P[N_t - N_s = k] = e^{-\lambda(t-s)}\lambda^k(t-s)^k/k!$$

for $k \in \mathbb{Z}^+$;

This much is known from any introductory text on stochastic processes, where the Poisson process will be motivated by descriptions of the arrivals of radioactive particles at a Geiger counter, or customers at a post office counter. But suppose we were counting the radioactive particles arriving from some source at the Geiger counter, and after one minute we halved the distance from source to counter. Physics tells us that the intensity of counts would be multiplied by four, but how would we model it? We could suppose that we have two independent Poisson processes N' and N'' with intensities λ and 4λ respectively, and set up the counting process

$$\tilde{N}_t = N'(t \wedge 1) + N''(t \vee 1) - N''(1)$$

but a neater way to do it is to suppose we have a standard Poisson process N and define the counting process

$$N_t^* \equiv N(H_t),$$

where

$$H_t = \lambda(t + 3(t-1)^+)$$

$$= \int_0^t h_s \, ds \tag{6.2.1}$$

where $h_s = \lambda(I_{\{s<1\}} + 4I_{\{s\geq1\}})$. The function h is the *intensity* or *hazard rate* function of the counting process N^*; the bigger it is, the faster the events (the jumps of N^*) are coming. This way of looking at the problem is powerful, because it permits immediate generalization to intensity functions which are allowed to be stochastic, and this is really all that is going on in the hazard rate approach to credit risk modeling. In more detail, we model the time τ of default as the first time that N^* jumps, so we shall have

$$H(\tau) = T_1 \qquad (6.2.2)$$

This is true for stochastic hazard rate processes as well, of course. In our modeling, we shall suppose that we have defined the hazard rate process in some way, and then take an *independent* standard Poisson process N and define τ by way of (6.2.1) and (6.2.2). From this, we have immediately the key relation

$$P[\tau > t] = P[T_1 > H(t)]$$

$$= E\left[\exp\left(-\int_0^t h_s ds\right)\right] \qquad (6.2.3)$$

using property (6.2.2) and the independence assumption.[2] Differentiating (6.2.3) gives us an expression for the density of τ:

$$P[\tau \in dt] = E\left[h_t \exp\left(-\int_0^t h_s ds\right)\right] dt$$

Once this is understood, deriving expressions for prices of various credit-sensitive instruments becomes a straightforward application of the arbitrage-pricing principle. For example, if we wish to find the time-t price $P_C(t, T)$ of a zero-coupon corporate bond with expiry T, which delivers 1 at time T if there were no default before T and delivers δ_τ at time T if default occurred at time $\tau \leq T$, then we have simply

$$P_C(t, T) = E_t\left[e^{-R_{tT}}(I_{\{\tau > T\}} + \delta_\tau I_{\{\tau \leq T\}})\right]$$

$$= P(t, T) - E_t\left[e^{-R_{tT}}(1 - \delta_\tau)I_{\{\tau \leq T\}}\right], \qquad (6.2.4)$$

---

[2] It is worth emphasizing that we *do* need independence here; to derive (6.2.3) we use the argument $P[T_1 > H(t)] = E[P[T_1 > H(t)|\mathcal{G}]] = E[\exp(-H(t))]$, where $\mathcal{G}$ is a σ-field with respect to which h is measurable but which is independent of N. The independence assumption is key to a number of the expressions which are derived in the literature of the subject.

$$= P(t, T) - E_t \left[e^{-R_{tT}} \int_t^T (1 - \delta_s) h_s e^{-H_{ts}} ds \right] \qquad (6.2.5)$$

where $P(t, T)$ is the time-t price of a riskless zero-coupon bond with expiry T, and $R_{st} \equiv \int_s^t r_u du$, $H_{st} \equiv \int_s^t h_u du$.

Expression (6.2.5) for the price of a risky zero-coupon bond appears in various places at various levels of generality; it appears in modified guises according to the assumptions made about what happens on default (Is payment made immediately? Is the loss proportional to the value of the asset immediately prior to default?), and we shall shortly discuss some of the papers where it features. For the moment, though, notice that the key components of the pricing problem are to model the riskless interest rate, the timing of default, and the recovery process; and notice also that without some very strong assumptions about the dynamics of these processes, simple closed-form prices for corporate bonds are unlikely to arise.

Example 6.1. If the recovery process is identically zero, the price of the corporate bond becomes

$$P_C(t, T) = E_t \left[e^{-R_{tT}} I_{\{\tau > T\}} \right] = E_t \left[e^{-R_{tT} - H_{tT}} \right]$$

so what we see is like a riskless zero-coupon bond with spot rate $R + H$. We can now view the problem as similar to the problem of pricing index-linked bonds, or bonds denominated in a foreign currency, thus making an existing literature available. It seems, however, that we may get further by exploiting the additional structure of the credit interpretation.

Example 6.2. If we assume that the recovery process δ is constant, and that the hazard rate takes the constant value μ, then the price given by (6.2.5) for the corporate bond simplifies to

$$P_C(t, T) = P(t, T)(\delta + (1 - \delta)e^{-\mu(T-t)} I_{\{\tau > t\}}) \qquad (6.2.6)$$

In this case, the credit spread (if $\tau > t$) is given simply by

$$(T - t)^{-1} \log(P(t, T)/P_C(t, T)) = \mu - \frac{1}{T - t} \log(1 + \delta(e^{\mu(T-t)} - 1)) \qquad (6.2.7)$$

which is a decreasing function of $T - t$; if $\delta = 0$ then the spread is constant. The paper [11] presents a fairly general framework for credit modeling, and then specializes to this example with a Gaussian Heath-Jarrow-Morton (HJM) interest rate model. The choice of the Gaussian HJM description obscures the simplicity and generality of their work, in my view.

Example 6.3. In a more recent work, [12] extend their earlier paper by considering a situation where the Vasicek interest rate process is used, and where the hazard function h_t is some linear function of r_t and Z_t, where Z is some Brownian motion which may be correlated with the interest rate process. More specifically,

$$dr_t = \sigma\, dW_t + \beta(r_\infty - r_t)dt,$$
$$dW_t\, dZ_t = \rho\, dt,$$
$$h_t = a_0(t) + a_1(t)r_t + a_2(t)Z_t$$

As with the Vasicek model itself, the use of a process which may take negative values for the intrinsically nonnegative process h is questionable, but if we close our eyes to this problem, then simple formulae result for the price of the corporate bond:

$$P_C(0, T) = \delta P(0, T) + (1 - \delta)\exp\left(-\mu_T + \tfrac{1}{2}v_T\right),$$

where μ_T and v_T are the mean and variance of $R_{0T} + H_T$, respectively:

$$\mu_T = \int_0^T \{(1 + a_1(s))(r_\infty + e^{-\beta s}(r_0 - r_\infty) + a_0(s))\}ds$$

$$v_T = 2E \int_0^T ds \int_s^T dv \left[(1 + a_1(s))(1 + a_1(v))e^{\beta(s-v)} f(2\beta, s)\right.$$
$$+\rho a_2(v)(a + a_1(s))f(\beta, s) + \rho a_2(s)(1 + a_1(v))e^{\beta(s-v)} f(\beta, s)$$
$$\left. + s a_2(s)a_2(v)\right]$$

where $f(\lambda, t) = (1 - e^{-\lambda t})/l$. The freedom to choose the three functions a_i gives a great deal of flexibility in fitting the model, and the involvement of the spot rate and another Brownian motion (for which Jarrow and Turnbull offer the interpretation of the log of some index price) certainly incorporates a desirable dependence of credit risk on economic fundamentals.

Example 6.4. This example (see [10]) is again in the same spirit as the earlier Jarrow and Turnbull paper, with various structural assumptions on the hazard-rate process. The idea is to model moves between credit classes as a time-homogeneous Markov chain X in the real-world measure (which facilitates estimation from historical data). One then assumes that in the pricing measure the riskless rate and the transitions are *independent*, and additionally that the recovery rate is *constant*. This leads to a neat formula for the price of risky bonds:

$$P_C(t, T) = E\left[e^{-R_{tT}}(\delta + (1 - \delta)\tilde{P}(\tau > T \mid X_t, \tau > t))\right]$$

$$= P(t, T) - E\left[e^{-R_{tT}}(1 - \delta)\right]\tilde{P}(\tau > T \mid X_t, \tau > t) \quad (6.2.8)$$

$$= P(t, T) - (1 - \delta)P(t, T)\tilde{P}(\tau > T \mid X_t, \tau > t) \quad (6.2.9)$$

The probability $\tilde{P}$ is the law governing the Markov chain of credit class transitions under the pricing measure. The link between the law of X under the two measures is achieved by assuming that the intensity matrix $\tilde{Q}(t)$ in the pricing measure may be expressed as $\tilde{Q}(t) = U(t)Q$, where $U(t)$ is diagonal, and Q is the Q-matrix in the real-world measure.

It is worth following through in some detail the steps of the analysis, because among all reduced-form models, this one is making perhaps the most sophisticated use of the most readily-available information about the riskiness of a firm's debt, namely credit ratings. The difficulties we encounter along the way will arise in any similar model.

Our goal is to estimate the model for the default process under the pricing measure, and the expression *( )* for the price of a risky zero-coupon bond is the starting point. We assume that we know the riskless bond prices $P(t, T)$; finding these from market data is a non-trivial but well-studied problem. Next we need to know the risky zero-coupon bond prices $P_C(t, T)$. These are harder to tease out of market data, because most bonds are coupon-bearing, and many have convertible features. The procedure advocated by Jarrow, Lando, and Turnbull goes as follows:

- Separate bonds into buckets by maturity and credit class.
- Within each bucket, compute the market value–weighted average (MVWA) coupon, and the MVWA yield-to-worst.[3]
- Treat each bucket as if it were a single bond with the MVWA coupon and MVWA yield-to-worst, and recursively compute $P_C(t, T_i)$, $i = 1, \ldots, n$, from these synthesized bond prices. The treatment of convertible bonds is rather crude, and Jarrow, Lando, and Turnbull find that the procedure sometimes results in a lower-rated bond being worth more than a higher-rated one! They comment that this problem is accentuated when there are comparatively few bonds in a bucket (apart from A and BAA1 grades, few of the buckets contain more than 30 bonds, and in many cases the number is less than 10).

---

[3] For a nonconvertible bond, this is the yield; for a convertible bond, it is the yield calculated under the assumption that the bond will be called at the earliest allowable date.

Having got this far, there remains only the estimation of δ between us and estimates of the default probabilities in the pricing measure. The method used in the paper is to take for δ the MVWA of recovery rates over all classes of debt in 1991. This takes the value 0.3265; the values for the five classes of debt are 0.6081, 0.4550, 0.3368, 0.1658, and 0.0363, which we see varies very considerably, so this is a significant simplification. We now are able to use (6.2) to give us estimates of $\tilde{P}(\tau > T_j | X_t = i, \tau > t)$ for a range of maturities T_j, and for each credit class i.

If we knew the jump intensities $Q \equiv (q_{ij})$ between credit classes, we could compute the matrix of transition probabilities over time Δt as $\exp(Q\Delta t)$; assuming that Δt is small enough that we can ignore the possibility of more than one jump, we then have an approximation for the Δt-transition probabilities given by

$$p_{ij}(\Delta t) = q_{ij}(1 - e^{-q_i \Delta t})/q_i, \quad (i \neq j) \tag{6.2.10}$$

where $q_i = \int_{j \neq i} q_{ij}$. The Standard & Poor's Credit Review provides an estimate of the one-year transition probabilities, and using these for the left-hand side of (6.2.10) it is easy to deduce the values of q_{ij} corresponding. This then deals with the estimation of the transitions between credit classes in the real-world probability, and now it remains to estimate the transformation from real-world to pricing probability.

This last step must of course use information from prices, and we use the risky zero-coupon bond prices $P_C(t, T)$ for each of the credit classes, and each of the maturities T_j. Using (6.2), we transform this into $\tilde{P}(\tau > T_j | X_t = i, \tau > t)$ for each j, and each credit class $i = 1, \ldots, K$, where credit class K is the default state. Now recall that we are going to write the jump-rate matrix $\tilde{Q}(s)$ in continuous time as $U(s)Q$ for some diagonal matrix $U(s)$, and so the transitions in the pricing probability will be approximately

$$\tilde{P}(X_{s+\Delta t} = j | X_s = i) \doteq \delta_{ij} + \Delta t U_{ii}(s) q_{ij}$$

Supposing that we knew the diagonal matrices $U(T_j)$ for $j = 1, \ldots, m - 1$, we would then know $\tilde{P}(X_{T_m} = j | X_t = i)$, and so we could use the identity

$$\tilde{P}(\tau \leq T_{m+1} | X_t = i, \tau > t)$$
$$= \sum_k \tilde{P}(X_{T_m} = k | X_t = i)\{\delta_{kK} + (T_{m+1} - T_m)U_{kk}(T_m)q_{kK}\}$$

to find the unknown $U_{kk}(T_m)$—we have $K - 1$ linear equations in $K - 1$ unknowns. This way, we build up recursively the estimates of the transition rates between states in the pricing probability, and can in principle answer any credit-sensitive pricing question in this framework.

There are several features of this modelling approach which pose problems (most of them signalled by Jarrow, Lando, and Turnbull in their paper):

- By inspection of (6.2), we see that the ratio $P_C(t, T)/P(t, T)$ of the price of risky to riskless zero-coupon bonds depends only on t, T, and the current credit class. This seems an improbable feature, and disappears in the extension of [5], who allow the recovery rate to be random and correlated with the assumed Vasicek term structure.
- It appears hard to deal realistically with convertible bonds. There are also problems related to estimation issues:
- The estimation of risk premia described above actually leads to some extremely negative values of $U_{kk}(t)$, so Jarrow, Lando, and Turnbull find that it is better to make a best-fit estimate subject to the constraint that all the $U_{kk}(t)$ are nonnegative. This certainly cures the negative values problem, but we end up (of course!) with zero values for some of the $U_{kk}(t)$—in fact, for quite a lot of them—which would have the unacceptable consequence that transitions out of some classes in some years would be impossible. In particular, an AA-rated firm would stay AA rated after the third year of their study going out 14 years, which seems difficult to accept.
- Can we accurately estimate the transition intensities of the Markov chain? If we have a Poisson random variable, and we want to be 95 percent certain that we know the mean of that random variable to within 5 percent, we would need the mean to be of the order of 1,500. In terms of transitions between credit classes, this is quite a large number, and in terms of defaults of investment-grade bonds it is a very large number! If we had observed 100 changes of credit class of a certain type, we would be 95 percent certain only that we knew the transition rate to within about 20 percent.

In addition to these features of the chosen modeling framework, that framework itself is open to question:

- Are transitions between credit classes really governed by a Markov chain? If so, then we would see that the times spent in different credit classes would have exponential distributions independent of the jumps, and there would be no tendency for a company to continue to fall through credit classes, contrary to some empirical evidence.
- Can we justify the assumed independence of the ratings transitions and everything else in the pricing probabilities?

Despite these difficulties, the approach is a sensible attempt to make use of widely available credit ratings to model the default of corporate bonds.

Example 6.5. [8] assume in contrast to the situation in [11] that at the moment τ that default occurs, the corporate bond loses a fraction L_τ of its value. Denoting the hazard rate for default by h_t, and the payment at the maturity T of the bond by X, they find that the value at time $t < \tau$ of the bond is given by

$$S_t = E_t\left[\exp\left(-\int_t^T (r_s + h_s L_s)ds\right)X\right] \tag{6.2.11}$$

Duffie and Singleton present a proof of this result using Itô's formula for jumping processes, but this is unnecessarily complicated. First, observe that if the fraction lost on default were 1, the expression for the bond price if $t < \tau$ is

$$E_t\left[\exp\left(-\int_t^T r_s ds\right)XI_{\{\tau > T\}}\right] = E_t\left[\exp\left(-\int_t^T (r_s + h_s)ds\right)X\right] \tag{6.2.12}$$

This establishes the result (6.2.11) in the special case $L \equiv 1$. Now suppose that the default time happens exactly as before, at intensity h_t, but that now when default happens at time t, with probability L_t the bond becomes worthless, while with probability $1 - L_t$ the value of the bond is unchanged. It is clear that the predefault value of the bond is not changed by this way of thinking; just prior to default, the expected value of the bond is $S_{\tau-}(1 - L_\tau)$ in either case. However, we now can think of two types of default, harmless (with intensity $h_t(1 - L_t)$), and lethal (with intensity $h_t L_t$). As far as valuing the bond prior to default is concerned, we may simply ignore the harmless defaults, and price using the intensity hL of the lethal defaults. This reduces the problem to the simple situation where the bond loses all value on default, which we solved at (6.2.12). As Duffie and Singleton observe, the model does not allow for the effects of h and L separately, only for the product hL; estimation of the two terms would require other data.

Duffie and Singleton offer various forms for the "adjusted" default-rate process $r + hL$ (which they also allow may include a spread for convenience yield.) In a subsequent paper (1997), they examine the situation for an affine diffusion model in some depth, using interest rate swap data for credit-risky counterparties.

Note that it is *essential* that we have independence of the Poisson process governing default, and the intensity h and loss-on-default L; if this were not the case, any processes h and L which agreed up to the default time could be used, and the value of (6.2.11) could be varied at will!

In this approach, the bond loses L_τ of its value on default, which contrasts with the assumption of Jarrow and Turnbull mentioned earlier, namely that on default the bond is replaced with $1 - L_\tau$ riskless bonds with the promised payout; under which assumption will the price of the bond be larger?

Summary of the Reduced-Form Approach
- The existence of convertible bonds really forces one to consider firm value—so maybe we should go for a structural approach anyway?
- Bucketing complicates the estimation procedure. If we allow default rates to depend on economic fundamentals and certain gross features of the firm, then we may well end up estimating fewer parameters—and in particular, making some structural assumptions valid for all firms, the estimates are based on the whole sample, which would be advantageous for AAA, where the credit event data is so scarce.
- Modeling the moves between credit classes as a fundamental process leads to issues of estimation and interpretation. Perhaps it would be better to regard the credit class as a noisy observation of some more informative underlying process describing the creditworthiness of the firm, and then to use a filtering approach.

6.3 STRUCTURAL MODELS

The hallmark of a structural model is some attempt to model the value of the assets of the firm, and deduce the value of corporate debt from this. The paper of [16] is the first and simplest approach of this kind that we shall discuss.

Example 6.1. The model of Merton assumes a fixed rate of interest $r > 0$, and that the value V_t of the firm's assets at time t may be described by

$$dV_t = V_t(\sigma\, d W_t + r\, dt) \qquad (6.3.1)$$

It is assumed that the firm is financed in part by the issue of bonds, and the face value B of the bonds must be repaid in full at time T. The shareholders are not allowed to pay dividends nor issue debt of equal or higher rank in the meantime. At time T, the bondholders will receive $\min\{V_T, B\}$, so the value of the bonds at time $t < T$ will be simply

$$E_t \left[e^{-r(T-t)} \min\{V_T, B\} \right] = Be^{-r(T-t)} - P(t, V_t, B)$$

where $P(t, V_t, B)$ is the value at time t of a put option with strike B if the current value of the firm's assets is V_t. But this is just the familiar Black-Scholes formula:

$$Be^{-r(T-t)}\Phi(-d_2) - V_t\Phi(-d_1)$$

where Φ is the cumulative distribution function of the standard normal distribution, and

$$d_1 = \frac{\log(V_t/B) + (r + \sigma^2/2)(T-t)}{\sigma\sqrt{T-t}},$$

$$d_2 = \frac{\log(V_t/B) + (r - \sigma^2/2)(T-t)}{\sigma\sqrt{T-t}} = d_1 - \sigma\sqrt{T-t}$$

The spread on corporate debt is

$$-\frac{1}{T-t}\log\left[\Phi(-d_2) - \frac{1}{d}\Phi(-d_1)\right]$$

where we have written $d \equiv Be^{-r(T-t)}/V$ for the debt-equity ratio, expressed in terms of the current value of the debt. It is easy to see that in fact the spread depends only on d, the time and the volatility. Merton studies the comparative statics of this model, and shows among other things that the spread is a decreasing function of maturity if $d \geq 1$, but for $d < 1$ it is humped.

Example 6.2. In one of the most intellectually satisfying papers in the literature, [13] consider the impact of the maturity of debt on the optimal exercise of the default option by the shareholders. The assumptions of the model are:

- Constant interest rate r.
- The value V_t of the firm's assets at time t evolves as

$$dV_t = V_t(\sigma dW_t + (r - \delta)dt)$$

where δ is the constant rate of dividends paid to the shareholders, and σ is a positive constant.

- Upon default, a fraction α of the value of the firm is lost through restructuring.
- There is a constant rolling debt structure, with total outstanding principal of P and maturity T, with new debt being issued (and old debt retired) at rate P/T, and coupons being paid continuously at rate C annually.
- Tax benefits accrue at rate γC on the coupon payments.
- The shareholders declare bankruptcy when the value of the firm's assets falls to V_B.

The value of the firm is given by the expression

$$v(V, V_B) = V + \frac{\gamma C}{r}\left[1 - \left(\frac{V}{V_B}\right)^{-x}\right] - \alpha V_B \left(\frac{V}{V_B}\right)^{-x} \qquad (6.3.2)$$

where x is the larger root of $\sigma^2\theta^2/2 + (r - \delta - \sigma^2/2)\theta - r = 0$. Noticing that $E\exp(-r\tau) = (V/V_B)^{-x}$, we may interpret the three terms in (6.3.2) as the value of the firm's assets, the net present value of all future tax refunds, and the net present value of the loss on default. A bondholder who will receive a coupon at fixed rate c, and will be repaid p at time t provided this was before default, but who receives ρV_B at the default time (if this was earlier than t) has an asset worth

$$d(V, V_B, t) = \int_0^t ce^{-rs}\,[1 - F(s)[\,ds + e^{-rt}p\,[1 - F(t)[\, + \int_0^t e^{-rs}\rho V_B F(ds)$$
$$(6.3.3)$$

where F is the distribution function of the default time, which depends of course on the values of V and V_B (in fact, only through their ratio). The total value $D(V, V_B, T)$ of the firm's debt is obtained by integrating (6.3.3) from 0 to T, using $c = C/T$, $p = P/T$, and $\rho = (1 - \alpha)/T$. The value of the firm's equity is therefore the difference:

$$eq(V, V_B, T) = v(V, V_B) - D(V, V_B, T)$$
$$= v(V, V_B) - \int_0^T d(V, V_B, t)dt$$

A closed-form expression is available for D in terms of the normal distribution function.

The level V_B is determined endogenously as the level which maximises the value of equity subject to $eq \geq 0$, and Leland and Toft obtain a closed-form expression for V_B. Assuming that the coupon on debt is chosen so that new debt is issued at par, they go on to examine various comparative statics of the optimal solution, and they find (among other things) that:

- The longer the maturity of the debt, the higher the value of the firm, and the greater the optimal leverage.
- Bond values are humped for low to moderate leverage, but for high leverage the bond sells below par for long time to maturity and above for short time to maturity, the effect becoming more pronounced as T increases.
- The credit spreads are increasing with T for low leverage, but become humped for moderate to large leverages.
- Credit spreads for values of T up to 2 years are negligible.

Example 6.3. [13] assume that the interest rate is constant, which is a reasonable assumption in order to get insight into the influence of various effects, but the assumption of constant interest rates is too restrictive for a working model. [15] embrace the possibility of stochastic interest rates, modeling the spot rate as a Vasicek process correlated with the log-Brownian share price process. They assume that there is some threshold value K such that if the value of the firm ever falls to that level, then restructuring takes place, and the bond is replaced by $(1 - w)$ riskless bonds of the same maturity. Longstaff and Schwartz derive an expression for the price of the risky bond, but their derivation contains a flaw; they apply results of [3] concerning the first-passage distributions of one-dimensional diffusions to the log of the discounted firm value, but this process is not a diffusion. It appears, therefore, that the pricing of a corporate bond in this modeling framework remains an open question.

Example 6.4. [2] consider a variant of the problem dealt with by Merton; control of the firm passes to the bondholders not only if the value of the firm is below some value B at the maturity T of the debt but also if in the meantime the value of the firm falls below some value (which depends on time as $Ce^{-\gamma(T-t)}$). They derive a closed-form expression for the value of the corporate bond, under the assumption of zero restructuring costs on default. They also derive the values of two bond issues, the senior and junior bonds, by identifying the prices in terms of the solution to the first problem.

Example 6.5. The KMV method for pricing risky debt relies on a structural-type approach. The description that follows is vague, not least because the details of the methodology are proprietary. The value of the firm's assets are modeled by a log-Brownian motion, $V_t = V_0 \exp(\sigma W_t + (m - \sigma^2/2)t)$, and the probability of default at time T is the probability that the value of the firm does not cover the liabilities K of the firm at that time, namely,

$$\Phi(-d_2)$$

where

$$d_2 = (\log(V_0/K) + (m - \sigma^2/2)T)/\sigma\sqrt{T}$$

is the so-called *distance to default*. In common with other structural approaches, the estimation of the parameters is a difficult matter, and the identification of the equity as a call option on the value of the firm allows an estimate of the volatility to be made. The total liabilities and market value of equity need to be observed or estimated. It is not clear how m is determined. The distance to default is used in conjunction with empirical data on the relation of defaults to the distance-to-default to estimate the probability of default.

The use of widely available equity price data is an appealing feature of this approach (though this would render it unsuitable for pricing sovereign debt). The assumption of constant interest rates is a limitation also.

Example 6.6. Another structural approach to credit risk is given by [14], who assume that the value of the firm's assets obeys the SDE

$$dV_t = V_t(\sigma\,dW_t + (\alpha - \gamma)dt)$$

for constants σ, α, and γ. They assume that the interest rate process is a Cox-Ingersoll-Ross model, and that the bondholders must be paid coupons at constant rate c. Bankruptcy is triggered when the cash flow γV_t from the firm is no longer sufficient to cover the coupon payments which have to be made, that is, when V drops to c/γ. The authors compute values of convertible and nonconvertible bonds in this model, and assert that the spreads which result are consistent with market values.

6.4 SOME NICE IDEAS

This short section gathers some neat ideas which do not fit obviously in any of the preceding sections.

The paper of [9] contains some simple but attractive ideas for dealing with credit risk. They present a general characterization of the time-t price of some risky contingent claim paying off X at time T if there is no default before time T, and otherwise paying $\delta_\tau Y_\tau$ at default time τ, where Y_t is the time-t price of a riskless asset paying X at time T. Their expression is

$$E_t \left[e^{-R_{tT}} w_{tT} X \right] \tag{6.4.1}$$

where w_{tT} is the expectation of δ_τ conditional on the interest rate process between t and T, and on the final contingent claim X. Of course, this is too general to be of much use as such; we could think of this expression as an alternative description of the price in a hazard-rate model, so until we have been much more specific about the hazard rate, we can go no further. Nevertheless, Hull and White use (6.4.1) quite effectively to bound the price of a credit-risky call option on a log-Brownian stock, assuming constant interest rate. In this situation, we shall have that w_T is a function of S_T, $w_T = u(S_T)$. The price of the risky option is

$$e^{-r(T-t)} E_t \left[u(S_T)(S_T - K)^+ \right] \tag{6.4.2}$$

which has to be consistent with the market price of the credit-risky zero-coupon bond of the call writer,

$$P_C(t, T) = e^{-r(T-t)} E_t \left[u(S_T) \right] \tag{6.4.3}$$

Since $0 \le u(S) \le 1$, we maximize the value of the risky option by taking $u(S) = I_{\{S > s_1\}}$ for a constant s_1 chosen to make (6.4.3) hold, and we minimize it similarly by taking $u(S) = I_{\{S < s_2\}}$ for suitable s_2. Numerical examples using a call writer with log-Brownian asset value process and bankruptcy when the value falls to some trigger level show that these bounds are not very tight, but perhaps by incorporating the information from other market prices they could be improved.

Hull and White also remark that a credit-risky American option will be exercised no later than its credit-risk-free counterpart; the reason is easy to see on a moment's reflection.

For a very quick and dirty approach, Hull and White also discuss the situation where the default process is independent of the interest rate and the payoff of the contingent claim in the pricing probability. Then using the market prices of credit-risky and default-free bonds, it is immediate that

$$P_C(t, T)/P(t, T) = E(w_{tT}), \tag{6.4.4}$$

and so the price of the risky contingent claim would be simply

$$Y_t P_C(t, T)/P(t, T),$$

where Y_t is as before the time-t price of the default-free contingent claim. This approach can be extended to deal with swaps by using (6.4.4) for a range of values of T.

One neat idea, to be found in [1] and [19], is to try to hedge out all credit risk, using a single credit-sensitive instrument. The idea is very simple. If your portfolio is vunerable to default of a counterparty, and if there is a liquid asset which is also sensitive to the default of the same counterparty, then you take up a dynamically adjusted position in the liquid asset so that upon default, the loss to your portfolio is zero. Thus, you choose the holding of the liquid asset to exactly cancel out the loss that the rest of your portfolio will make on default. This done, there are no jumps in the value of your combined portfolio and (under Brownian market assumptions) you may therefore hedge the combined portfolio perfectly.

As a parting remark, it may be of interest to note that formally the reduced-form approach may be thought to include the structural form approach, in that the default intensity becomes infinite at the moment that the asset price in the structural description reaches the default boundary. This does not (of course!) mean that we can throw away the structural approach.

6.5 CONCLUSION

Each of the two main classes of approach has its strengths and weaknesses. For the *structural approach*, we have:

- A clear link between economic fundamentals and defaults. This helps to understand losses on default, and the correlation of defaults of different firms.
- Reliance on economic fundamentals and the value of the firm's assets which may be hard to estimate with any accuracy.

On the other hand, features of the reduced-form approach are:

- A model which is sufficiently close to the data that it is always possible to fit *some* version of the model.
- The fitted model may not perform well "out of sample."
- In the case of proportional losses, it is hard to distinguish the hazard rate and the percentage loss on default.
- Pricing of convertible bonds does not fit well into this framework.

Where might the modeling of credit risk be going now? Within the reduced-form framework, it seems that there is little one may do except explore further parametric forms of the intensity and loss-on-default processes. In the structural approach, we need to incorporate jumps in the value of the firm in a reasonable way, and we need to develop a filtering approach to the estimation; realistically, we cannot assume that we know the value of the firm with precision, nor how its rate of return will depend on the economic fundamentals, so we have to confront that uncertainty honestly. Ultimately, the quality of what we can create will be constrained by the quality of the data to calibrate it, so we probably should not be trying to do anything too sophisticated!

And yet we have! Since 1999, we have seen the improbable rise and overdue demise of the "industry-standard" Gaussian copula, we have seen the publication of excellent monographs on the subject, such as [18], and vigorous development of new modeling ideas. We have, for example, seen developments of filtering ideas, such as in [7], and in works of Monique Jeanblanc and her coworkers; and we have seen enormous effort expended in modeling and fitting collateralized debt obligations and other derivatives which depend on the defaults of more than one name. Most attention has focused on the reduced-form approach, and while it is regrettable that we are not able to offer a structural story that really works in practice, it is inevitable that we will not be able to build something that could handle the complexities and heterogeneities of the practical world. Ease of calibration has been the overriding consideration, and many quite strange models (in reality, fits) have been pressed into service because they were easy to align to market data, without possessing any other virture, such as intertemporal consistency.

This is an area which I have stood back from since these notes were first prepared, with one exception, the paper [6]. The approach adopted there is, I believe, quite simple; it is self-consistent; it can handle corporate and government debt in one model; and it can in principle embrace foreign exchange also, and therefore offers a sensible approach to hybrid pricing. Indeed, the whole modeling approach can be thought of in terms of the potential approach [17].

In the markets, we have experienced the liquidity drought following from the subprime fallout of the summer of 2007, exacerbated by the profusion of repackaged credit risks, and understanding these presents huge challenges for the industry and the academic profession. Credit risks are more similar to insurance risks than to market risks, as the range of useable hedging instruments is far more restricted, and in the end if everything goes sour at once, no portfolio of market instruments will save you. Ratings agencies have been criticized in the wake of the subprime disaster, and I feel that some more rational characterization of corporate creditworthiness is required. The very granular nature of credit ratings causes corporations a lot of difficulty if a downgrade should occur, and probably some index of creditworthiness which is real-valued would make more sense. Even better would be some index of exposure of the firm to a number of major macro-economic indicators; this would prevent the meaningless comparison of one company's being "riskier" than another.

REFERENCES

1. Beumee, J. G. B., B. Hilberink, and M. H. Vellekoop. (2001). Pricing and hedging options on defaultable assets. Available at SSRN: http://ssrn.com/abstract=934781.
2. Black, F., and J. C. Cox. (1976). Valuing corporate securities: Some effects of bond indenture provisions. *Journal of Finance* 31: 351–367.
3. Buonocore, A., A. G. Nobile, and L. M. Ricciardi. (1987). A new integral equation for the evaluation of first-passage-time probability densities. *Advances in Applied Probability* 19: 784–800.
4. Cathcart, L., and L. El-Jahel. (2006). Pricing defaultable bonds: A middle way approach between strucutral and reduced form models. *Quantitative Finance* 6: 243–253.
5. Das, S. R., and P. Tufano. (1996). Pricing credit-sensitive debt when interest rates, credit ratings, and credit spreads are stochastic. *Journal of Financial Engineering* 5: 161–198.
6. Di Graziano, G., and L. C. G. Rogers. (2005). A dynamic approach to the modelling of correlation credit derivatives using Markov chains. Technical report, University of Cambridge.
7. Duffie, J. D., and D. Lando. (2001). Term structure of credit spreads with incomplete accounting information. *Econometrica* 69: 633–644.
8. Duffie, J. D., and K. J. Singleton. (1999). Modelling term structures of defaultable bonds. *Review of Financial Studies* 12: 687–720.
9. Hull, J., and A. White. (1995). The impact of default risk on the prices of options and other derivative securities. *Journal of Banking and Finance* 19: 299–322.
10. Jarrow, R. A., D. Lando, and S. M. Turnbull. (1997). A Markov model for the term structure of credit risk spreads. *Review of Financial Studies* 10: 481–523.
11. Jarrow, R. A., and S. M. Turnbull. (1995). Pricing derivatives on financial securities subject to credit risk. *Journal of Finance* 50: 53–85.
12. Jarrow, R. A., and S. M. Turnbull. (2000). The intersection of market and credit risk. *Journal of Banking and Finance* 24: 271–299.
13. Leland, H. E., and K. Toft. (1996). Optimal capital structure, endogenous bankruptcy, and the term structure of credit spreads. *Journal of Finance* 51: 987–1019.
14. Lim, I. J., K. Ramaswamy, and S. Sundaresan. (1993). Does default risk in coupons affect the valuation of corporate bonds? A contingent claims model. *Financial Management* 22: 117–131.
15. Longstaff, F. A., and E. S. Schwartz. (1995). A simple approach to valuing risky fixed and floating rate debt. *Journal of Finance* 50.

16. Merton, R. C. (1974). On the pricing of corporate debt: The risk structure of interest rates. *Journal of Finance* 29: 449–470.
17. Rogers, L. C. G. (1997). The potential approach to the term structure of interest rates and foreign exchange rates. *Mathematical Finance* 7: 157–176.
18. Schoenbucher, P. (2003). *Credit Derivatives Pricing Models: Models, Pricing, Implementation*. New York: Wiley Finance.
19. Wong, D. (1998). A unifying credit model. PhD thesis, Carnegie-Mellon University.

CHAPTER 7

An Overview of Factor Modeling for CDO Pricing

Jean-Paul Laurent and Areski Cousin

We review in the pricing of synthetic collateralized debt obligation (CDO) tranches from the point of view of factor models. Thanks to the factor framework, we can handle a wide range of well-known pricing models. This includes pricing approaches based on copulas, but also structural, multivariate Poisson and affine intensity models. Factor models have become increasingly popular since they are associated with efficient semianalytical methods and parsimonious parametrization. Moreover, the approach is not restrictive at all to the case of homogeneous credit portfolios. Easy-to-compute and -handle large portfolio approximations can be provided. In factor models, the distribution of conditional default probabilities is the key input for the pricing of CDO tranches. These conditional default probabilities are also closely related to the distribution of large portfolios. Therefore, we can compare different factor models by simply comparing the distribution functions of the corresponding conditional default probabilities.

7.1 PRICING OF PORTFOLIO CREDIT DERIVATIVES

7.1.1 Pricing Models for Credit Derivatives

When one looks at the pricing methodologies for credit derivatives, a striking feature is the profusion of competing approaches; none of them could be seen as an academic and practitioner's standard. This contrasts with equity or interest rate derivatives to set some examples. Despite rather negative appreciation from the academic world, the industry relies on the one-factor Gaussian copula for the pricing of CDO tranches, possibly amended with

185

base correlation approaches. Among the usual critics, one can quote the poor dynamics of the credit loss process and the credit spreads, and the disconnection between the pricing and the hedging, while pricing at the cost of the hedge is a cornerstone of modern finance. Given the likelihood of plain static arbitrage opportunities when "massaging" correlations without caution, the variety and complexity of mapping procedures for the pricing of bespoke portfolios, a purist might assert that base correlations are simply a way to express CDO tranche quotes. Even from that minimal view, the computation of base correlations from market quotes is not an easy task due to the amortization scheme of premium legs and the dependence on more or less arbitrary assumptions on recovery rates.

Unsurprisingly, there are many ways to assess model quality, such as the ability to fit market quotes, tractability, parsimony, hedging efficiency, and, of course, economic relevance and theoretical consistency. One should keep in mind that different models may be suitable for different payoffs. As discussed below, standard CDO tranche premiums depend only on the marginal distributions of portfolio losses at different dates, and not on the temporal dependence between losses. This may not be the case for more exotic products such as leverage tranches and forward-starting CDOs. Therefore, copula models might be well suited for the former plain vanilla products, while a direct modeling of the loss process, as in the top-down approach, tackles the latter. Standard tranches on ITRAXX or CDX have almost become asset classes on their own. Though the market directly provides their premium at the current date, a modeling of the corresponding dynamics might be required when risk managing nonstandard tranches. Let us remark that the informational content of standard tranches is not fully satisfactory, especially when considering the pricing of tranchelets corresponding to first losses (e.g., a [0, 1 percent] tranche) or senior tranches associated with the right tail of the loss distribution. There are also some difficulties when dealing with short-maturity tranches. Whatever the chosen approach, a purely numerical smoothing of base correlations or a pricing model–based interpolation, there is usually a lot of model risk: models that are properly calibrated to liquid tranche prices may lead to significantly different prices for nonstandard tranches.

In the remainder of the chapter, we will focus on pricing models for typical synthetic CDO tranches, either based on standard indexes or related to bespoke portfolios, and we will not further consider products that involve the joint distribution of losses and credit spreads such as options on tranches. We will focus on model-based pricing approaches, such that the premium of the tranche can be obtained by equaling the present value of the premium and the default legs of the tranches, computed under a given risk-neutral measure. At least, this rules out static arbitrage opportunities, such as negative tranchelet prices. Thus, we will leave aside comparisons between base correlation and model-based approaches that might be important in some cases. Though we will discuss the ability of different models to be well calibrated to standard liquid tranches, we will not further consider the various and sometimes rather proprietary mapping methodologies that aim at pricing bespoke CDO tranches given the correlation smiles on standard indexes. Such practical issues are addressed in [42] and in the references therein.

Fortunately, there remain enough models to leave anyone with an encyclopedic tendency more than happy. When so many academic approaches contest, there is a need to categorize, which obviously does not mean to write down a catalog.

Recently, there has been a discussion about the relative merits of bottom-up and top-down approaches. In the actuarial field, these are also labeled as the individual and the collective models. In a bottom-up approach, also known as a name-per-name approach, one starts from a description of the dynamics (credit spreads, defaults) of the names within a basket, from which the dynamics of the aggregate loss process is derived. Some aggregating procedure involving the modeling of dependence between the default events is required to derive the loss distribution. The bottom-up approach has some clear advantages over the top-down approach, such as the possibility to easily account for name heterogeneity: for instance, the trouble with GMAC and the corresponding widening of spreads had a salient impact on CDX equity tranche quotes. It can be easily seen that the heterogeneity of individual default probabilities breaks down the Markov property of the loss process. One needs to know the current structure of the portfolio, for example, the proportion of risky names, and not only the current losses to further simulate appropriately further losses. This issue is analogous to the well-known burnout effect in mortgage prepayment modeling. The random thinning approach provides only a partial answer to the heterogeneity issue: names with higher marginal default probabilities actually tend to default first, but the change in the loss intensity does not depend on the defaulted name, as one would expect. The concept of idiosyncratic gamma, which is quite important in the applied risk management of equity tranches, is thus difficult to handle in a top-down approach. Also, a number of models belonging to this class do not account for the convergence to zero of the loss intensity as the portfolio is exhausted. This leads to positive, albeit small, probabilities that the loss exceeds the nominal of the portfolio. Another practical and paramount topic is the risk management of CDO tranches at the book level. Since most investment banks deal with numerous credit portfolios, they need to model a number of aggregate loss processes, which obviously are not independent. While such a global risk management approach is amenable to the bottom-up approach, it remains an open issue for its contender.

There are some other major drawbacks when relying on bottom-up approaches. A popular family within the bottom-up approaches, relying on Cox processes, bears its own burden. On theoretical grounds, it fails to account for contagion effects, also known as informative defaults: default of one name may be associated with jumps, usually of positive magnitude, of the credit spreads of the surviving names. Though some progress has recently been completed, the numerical implementation, especially with respect to calibration on liquid tranches, is cumbersome. In factor copula approaches, the dynamics of the aggregate loss are usually quite poor, with high dependence between losses at different time horizons and even comonotonic losses in the large portfolio approximation. Thus, factor copula approaches fall into disrepute when dealing with some forward-starting tranches where the dependence between losses at two different time horizons is a key input.

Nevertheless, the pricing of synthetic CDO tranches involves only marginal distribution of losses and is likely to be better handled in the bottom-up approach. Since this chapter is focused on CDO tranches, when discussing pricing issues, we will favor the name-per-name perspective.

As mentioned above, due to the number of pricing models at hand,[1] a unifying perspective is needed, especially with respect to the dependence between default dates. In the following, we will privilege a factor approach: default dates will be independent given a low dimensional factor. This framework is not that restrictive since it encompasses factor copulas, but also multivariate Poisson, structural models, and some intensity models within the affine class. Moreover, in the homogeneous case, where the names are indistinguishable, on a technical ground this corresponds to the exchangeability assumption; the existence of a single factor is a mere consequence of de Finetti's theorem, as explained below. From a theoretical point of view, the key inputs in a single-factor model are the distributions of the conditional (on the factor) default probabilities. Given these, one can unambiguously compute CDO tranche premiums in a semianalytical way. It is also fairly easy to derive large portfolio approximations under which the pricing of CDO tranche premiums reduces to a simple numerical integration. The factor approach also allows some model taxonomy by comparing the conditional default probabilities through the so-called convex order. This yields some useful results on the ordering of tranche premiums. The factor assumption is also almost necessary to deal with large portfolios and avoid overfitting. As

---

[1] See [23], [68], [8], or [53] for a detailed account of the different approaches to credit risk.

an example, let us consider the Gaussian copula; the number of correlation parameters evolves as n^2, where n is the number of names, without any factor assumption, while it increases linearly in a one-factor model.

In Section 7.2, we will present some general features of factor models with respect to the pricing of CDO tranches. This includes the derivation of CDO tranche premiums from marginal loss distributions, the computation of loss distributions in factor models, the factor representation associated with de Finetti's theorem for homogeneous portfolios, large portfolio approximations, and an introduction to the use of stochastic orders as a way to compare different models. Section 7.3 details various factor pricing models, including factor copula models as well as structural, multivariate Poisson and Cox process–based models. As for the factor copula models, we deal with additive factor copula models and some extensions involving stochastic or local correlation. We also consider Archimedean copulas and eventually "perfect" copulas that are implied from market quotes. Multivariate Poisson models include the so-called common shock models. Examples based on Cox processes are related to affine intensities, while structural models are multivariate extensions of the Black and Cox first hitting time of a default barrier.

7.2 FACTOR MODELS FOR THE PRICING OF CDO TRANCHES

Factor models have been used for a long time with respect to stock or mutual fund returns. As far as credit risk management is concerned, factor models also appear as an important tool. They underlie the IRB approach in the Basel II regulatory framework: see [16], [27], [39], [40], [76], [77] or [29] for some illustrations. The idea of computing loss distributions from the associated characteristic function in factor models can be found in [65]. The application of such ideas to the pricing of CDOs is discussed in [36], [3], [46], [4], and [54]. Various discussions and extensions about the factor approach for the pricing of CDO tranches can be found in a number of papers, including [28] and [11].

7.2.1 Computation of CDO Tranche Premiums from Marginal Loss Distributions

A synthetic CDO tranche is a structured product based on an underlying portfolio of equally weighted reference entities subject to credit risk.[2] Let

---

[2] We refer the reader to [17] or [50] for a detailed analysis of the CDO market and credit derivatives cash flows.

us denote by n the number of references in the credit portfolio and by $(\tau_1, \ldots, \tau_n)$ the random vector of default times. If name i defaults, it drives a loss of $M_i = E(1 - \delta_i)$ where E denotes the nominal amount (which is usually name independent for a synthetic CDO) and δ_i the recovery rate. M_i is also referred as the loss given default of name i. The key quantity for the pricing of CDO tranches is the cumulative loss $L_t = \sum_{i=1}^{n} M_i D_i$, where $D_i = 1_{\{\tau_i \leq t\}}$ is a Bernoulli random variable indicating whether name i defaults before time t. L_t is a pure jump process and follows a discrete distribution at any time t.

The cash flows associated with a synthetic CDO tranche depend only on the realized path of the cumulative losses on the reference portfolio. Default losses on the credit portfolio are split along some thresholds (attachment and detachment points) and allocated to the various tranches. Let us consider a CDO tranche with attachment point a, detachment point b and maturity T. It is sometimes convenient to see a CDO tranche as a bilateral contract between a protection seller and a protection buyer. We describe below the cash flows associated with the default payment leg (payments received by the protection buyer) and the premium payment leg (payments received by the protection seller).

Default Payments Leg The protection seller agrees to pay the protection buyer default losses each time they impact the tranche $[a, b]$ of the reference portfolio. More precisely, the cumulative default payment $L_t^{[a,b]}$ on the tranche $[a, b]$ is equal to zero if $L_t \leq a$, to $L_t - a$ if $a \leq L_t \leq b$ and to $b - a$ if $L_t \geq b$. Let us remark that $L_t^{[a,b]}$ has a call spread payoff with respect to L_t (see Figure 7.1) and can be expressed as $L_t^{[a,b]} = (L_t - a)^+ - (L_t - b)^+$.

Default payments are simply the increment of $L_t^{[a,b]}$: there is a payment of $L_t^{[a,b]} - L_{t-}^{[a,b]}$ from the protection seller at every jump time of $L_t^{[a,b]}$ occurring

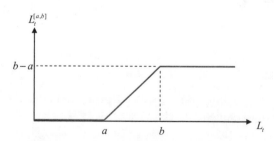

FIGURE 7.1 Cumulative Loss on CDO Tranche $[a, b]$ with respect to L_t.

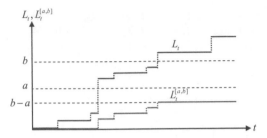

FIGURE 7.2 A realized path of the reference portfolio losses (top line) and the corresponding path of losses affecting CDO tranche $[a, b]$ (bottom line) (jumps occur at default times).

before contract maturity T. Figure 7.2 shows a realized path of the loss process L_t and consequences on CDO tranche $[a, b]$ cumulative losses.

For simplicity, we further assume that the continuously compounded default free interest rate r_t is deterministic and denote by $B_t = \exp(-\int_0^t r_s ds)$ the discount factor. Then, the discounted payoff corresponding to default payments can written as:

$$\int_0^T B_t dL_t^{[a,b]} = \sum_{i=1}^n B_{\tau_i} \left(L_{\tau_i}^{[a,b]} - L_{\tau_i-}^{[a,b]} \right) 1_{\{\tau_i \leq T\}}$$

Thanks to Stieltjes integration by parts formula and Fubini theorem, the price of the default payment leg can be expressed as:

$$E \left[\int_0^T B_t dL_t^{[a,b]} \right] = B_T E \left[L_T^{[a,b]} \right] - \int_0^T r_t B_t E \left[L_t^{[a,b]} \right] dt$$

Premium Payments Leg The protection buyer has to pay the protection seller a periodic premium payment (quarterly for standardized indexes) based on a fixed spread or premium S and proportional to the current outstanding nominal of the tranche $b - a - L_t^{[a,b]}$. Let us denote by $t_i, i = 1, \ldots, I$ the premium payment dates with $t_I = T$ and by Δ_i the length of the ith period $[t_{i-1}, t_i]$ (in fractions of a year and with $t_0 = 0$). The CDO premium payments are equal to $S\Delta_i(b - a - L_{t_i}^{[a,b]})$ at regular payment dates $t_i, i = 1, \ldots, I$. Moreover, when a default occurs between two premium payment dates and when it affects the tranche, an additional payment (the accrued coupon) must be made at default time to compensate the change in value of the tranche outstanding nominal. For example, if name j defaults between t_{i-1} and t_i, the associated accrued coupon is equal to $S(\tau_j - t_{i-1})(L_{\tau_j}^{[a,b]} - L_{\tau_j-}^{[a,b]})$. Eventually, the discounted payoff corresponding to premium payments can be expressed as:

$$\sum_{i=1}^{I} \left(B_{t_i} S \Delta_i \left(b - a - L_{t_i}^{[a,b]} \right) + \int_{t_{i-1}}^{t_i} B_t S \left(t - t_{i-1} \right) dL_t^{[a,b]} \right)$$

Using same computational methods as for the default leg, it is possible to derive the price of the premium payment leg, that is

$$S \sum_{i=1}^{I} \left(B_{t_i} \Delta_i \left(b - a - E\left[L_{t_i}^{[a,b]} \right] \right) + B_{t_i} \left(t_i - t_{i-1} \right) E\left[L_{t_i}^{[a,b]} \right] \right.$$

$$\left. - \int_{t_{i-1}}^{t_i} B_t \left(r_t \left(t - t_{i-1} \right) + 1 \right) E\left[L_t^{[a,b]} \right] dt \right)$$

The CDO tranche premium S is chosen such that the contract is fair at inception, that is, such that the default payment leg is equal to the premium payment leg. S is quoted in basis point per annum.[3] Figure 7.3 shows the dynamics of credit spreads on the five year ITRAXX index (series 7) between May and November 2007. It is interesting to observe a wide bump corresponding to the summer 2007 crisis.

Let us remark that the computation of CDO tranche premiums only involves the expected losses on the tranche, $E[L_t^{[a,b]}]$ at different time horizons. These can readily be derived from the marginal distributions of the aggregate loss on the reference portfolio. In the next section, we describe some numerical methods for the computation of the aggregate loss distribution within factor models.

---

[3] Let us remark that market conventions are quite different for the pricing of equity tranches (CDO tranches [0, b] with $0 < b < 1$). Due to the high level of risk embedded in these "first losses tranches," the premium S is fixed beforehand at 500 bps per annum and the protection seller receive an additional payment at inception based on an "up-front premium" and proportional to the size b of the tranche. This "up-front premium" is quoted in percentage.

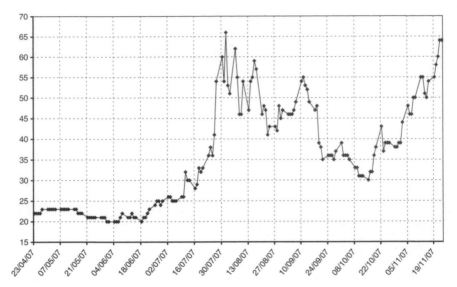

FIGURE 7.3 Credit spreads on the five years ITRAXX index (Series 7) in bps.

7.2.2 Computation of Loss Distributions

In a factor framework, one can easily derive marginal loss distributions. We will assume that default times are conditionally independent given a one-dimensional factor V. The key inputs for the computation of loss distribution are the conditional default probabilities $p_t^{i|V} = P(\tau_i \leq t | V)$ associated with names $i = 1, \ldots, n$. Extensions to multiple factors are straightforward but are computationally more involved. However, the one-factor assumption is not that restrictive as explained in [36], where computation of the loss distribution is performed with an admissible loss of accuracy [0] using some dimensional reduction techniques. In some examples detailed below, the factor V may be time dependent. This is of great importance when pricing correlation products that involve the joint distribution of losses at different time horizons such as leverage tranches or forward starting CDOs. Since this chapter is focused on the pricing of standard CDO tranches, which involve only marginal distributions of cumulative losses, omitting the time dependence is a matter of notational simplicity.

Unless otherwise stated, we will thereafter assume that recovery rates are deterministic and concentrate upon the dependence among default times.

Two approaches can be used for the computation of loss distributions, one based on the inversion of the characteristic function and another based on recursions.

Fast Fourier Transform (FFT) Approach The first approach deals with the characteristic function of the aggregate loss L_t, which can be derived thanks to the conditional independence assumption:

$$\varphi_{L_t}(u) = E\left[e^{iuL_t}\right] = E\left[\prod_{1 \leq i \leq n} \left(1 + p_t^{i|V}\left(e^{iuM_i} - 1\right)\right)\right].$$

The previous expectation can be computed using a numerical integration over the distribution of the factor V. This can be achieved for example using a Gaussian quadrature. The computation of the loss distribution can then be accomplished thanks to the inversion formula and some fast Fourier transform algorithm. Let us remark that the former approach can be adapted without extra complication when losses given default M_i, $i = 1, \ldots, n$ are stochastic but (jointly) independent together with default times. This method is described in [40] or [54]. [41] investigate a richer correlation structure in which credit references are grouped in several sectors. They specify an intersector and an intrasector dependence structure based on a factor approach and show that the computation of the loss distribution can be performed easily using the FFT approach.

Recursion Approaches An alternative approach, based on recursions is discussed in [3] and [46].[4]

The first step is to split up the support of the loss distribution into constant width loss units. The width u of each loss unit is chosen such that each potential loss given default M_i can be approximated by a multiple of u. The support of the loss distribution is thus turned into a sequence $l = 0, u, \ldots, n_{max}u$ where $n_{max} > n$ and $n_{max}u$ corresponds to the maximal potential loss $\sum_{1 \leq i \leq n} M_i$. Clearly, the simplest case is associated with constant losses given default, for instance $M_i = \frac{1-\delta}{n}$ with $\delta = 40\%$ and $n = 125$, which is a reasonable assumption for standard tranches. We can then choose $n_{max} = n$.

The second step is performed thanks to the conditional independence of default events given the factor V. The algorithm starts from the conditional loss distribution associated with a portfolio set up with only one name,

---

[4] Let us remark that similar recursion methods have first been investigated by actuaries to compute the distribution of aggregate claims within individual life models. Several recursion algorithms originated from [74] have been developed such as the Z-method or the Newton method based on development of the loss generating function.

then it performs the computation of the conditional loss distribution when another name is added, and so on. Let us denote by $q_t^k(i)$, $i = 0, \ldots, n$ the conditional probability that the loss is equal to iu in the kth portfolio where names $1, 2, \ldots, k$ $(k \leq n)$ have been successively added. Let us start with a portfolio set up with only name number 1 with conditional default probability $p_t^{1|V}$, then

$$
\begin{cases}
q_t^1(0) = 1 - p_t^{1|V}, \\
q_t^1(1) = p_t^{1|V}, \\
q_t^1(i) = 0, i > 1.
\end{cases}
$$

Assume now that $q_t^k(.)$ has been computed after successive inclusion of names $2, \ldots, k$ in the pool. We then add firm $k + 1$ in the portfolio with conditional default probability $p_t^{k+1|V}$. The loss distribution of the $(k + 1)^{\text{th}}$ portfolio can be computed with the following recursive relation:

$$
\begin{cases}
q_t^{k+1}(0) = \left(1 - p_t^{k+1|V}\right)q_t^k(0), \\
q_t^{k+1}(i) = \left(1 - p_t^{k+1|V}\right)q_t^k(i) + p_t^{k+1|V}q_t^k(i - 1), i = 1, \ldots, k + 1, \\
q_t^{k+1}(i) = 0, i > k + 1.
\end{cases}
$$

In the new portfolio, the loss can be iu either by being iu in the original portfolio if firm $k + 1$ has not defaulted or by being $(i - 1)u$ if firm $k + 1$ has defaulted. The required loss distribution is the one obtained after all names have been added in the pool. It corresponds to $q_t^n(i)$, $i = 0, \ldots, n$. Let us remark that even though intermediate loss distributions obviously depend on the ordering of names added in the pool, the loss distribution associated to the entire portfolio is unique.

The last step consists of computing the unconditional loss distribution using a numerical integration over the distribution of the factor V. It is straightforward to extend the latter method to the case of stochastic and name-dependent recovery rates. However, one of the key issues is to find a loss unit u that allows both getting enough accuracy on the loss distribution and driving low computational time. [46] present an extension of the former approach in which computation efforts are focused on pieces of the loss distribution associated with positive CDO tranche cash flows, allowing the algorithm to cope with nonconstant width loss subdivisions.

Other approximation methods used by actuaries in the individual life model have also been adapted to the pricing of CDO tranches. For example, [20] investigate the compound Poisson approximation; [48] propose to approximate the loss distribution by a normal power distribution.

[32] propose an approximation method based on power series expansions. These expansions express a CDO tranche price in a multifactor model as a series of prices computed within an independent default time model, which are easy to compute.

A new method based on Stein's approximation has been developed recently by [49] and seems to be more efficient than standard approximation methods. In practical implementation, the conditional loss distribution (conditional to the factor) can be approximated either by a Gaussian or a Poisson random variable. Then CDO tranche premiums can be computed in each case using an additional corrector term known in closed form.

When considering CDO tranches on standardized indices, it is sometimes convenient to consider a homogeneous credit portfolio. In that case, the computation of the loss distribution reduces to a simple numerical integration.

7.2.3 Factor Models in the Case of Homogeneous Credit Risk Portfolios

In the case of a homogeneous credit risk portfolio, all names have the same nominal E and the same recovery rate δ. Consequently, the aggregate loss is proportional to the number of defaults N_t, that is, $L_t = E(1 - \delta) N_t$. Let us, moreover, assume that default times $\tau_1, \ldots, \tau_n$ are exchangeable, that is, any permutation of default times leads to the same multivariate distribution function. Particularly, it means that all names have the same marginal distribution function, say F.

As a consequence of de Finetti's theorem,[5] default indicators $D_1, \ldots, D_n$ are Bernoulli mixtures[6] at any time horizon t. There exists a random mixture probability $\tilde{p}_t$ such that conditionally on $\tilde{p}_t$, $D_1, \ldots, D_n$ are independent. More formally, if we denote by v_t the distribution function of $\tilde{p}_t$, then for all $k = 0, \ldots, n$,

$$P(N_t = k) = \binom{n}{k} \int_0^1 p^k (1 - p)^{(n-k)} v_t(dp).$$

As a result, the aggregate loss distribution has a very simple form in the homogeneous case. Its computation only requires a numerical integration

---

[5] [1] gives a general account of de Finetti's theorem and some straightforward consequences.
[6] One needs that the default indicators are part of an infinite sequence of exchangeable default indicators.

over v_t which can be achieved using a Gaussian quadrature. Moreover, it can be seen that the factor assumption is not restrictive at all in the case of homogeneous portfolios. Homogeneity of credit risk portfolios can be viewed as a reasonable assumption for CDO tranches on large indices, although this is obviously an issue with equity tranches for which idiosyncratic risk is an important feature. A further step is to approximate the loss on large homogeneous portfolios with the mixture probability itself.

7.2.4 Large Portfolio Approximations

As CDO tranches are related to large credit portfolios, a standard assumption is to approximate the loss distribution with the one of an "infinitely granular portfolio."[7] This fictive portfolio can be viewed as the limit of a sequence of aggregate losses on homogeneous portfolios, where the maximum loss has been normalized to unity: $L_t^n = \frac{1}{n} \sum_{i=1}^n D_i$, $n \geq 1$.

Let us recall that when default indicators $D_1, \ldots, D_n, \ldots$ form a sequence of exchangeable Bernoulli random variables and thanks to de Finetti's theorem, the normalized loss L_t^n converges almost surely to the mixture probability $\tilde{p}_t$ as the number of names tends to infinity. $\tilde{p}_t$ is also called the large (homogeneous) portfolio approximation. In a factor framework where default times are conditionally independent given a factor V, it can be shown that the mixture probability $\tilde{p}_t$ coincides with the conditional default probability $P(\tau_i \leq t \,|\, V)$.[8] In the credit risk context this idea was firstly put in practice by [72]. This approximation has also been studied by [35], [38], and [67] for the pricing of CDO tranches. [11] compare the prices of CDO tranches based on the large portfolio approximation and on exact computations. The large portfolio approximation can also be used to compare CDO tranche premiums on finite portfolios.

7.2.5 Comparing Different Factor Models

Exchangeability of default times is a nice framework to study the impact of dependence on CDO tranche premiums. We have seen that the factor approach is legitimate in this context and we have exhibited a mixture probability $\tilde{p}_t$ such that, given $\tilde{p}_t$, default indicators $D_1, \ldots, D_n$ are conditionally independent. Thanks to the theory of stochastic orders, it is possible

---

[7] This terminology is taken from the Basel II agreement as it is the standard approach proposed by the Basel committee to determine the regulatory capital related to bank credit risk management.

[8] The proof relies on a generalization of the strong law of large numbers. See [72] for more details.

to compare CDO tranche premiums associated with portfolios with different mixture probabilities. Let us compare two portfolios with default indicators $D_1, \ldots, D_n$ and $D_1^*, \ldots, D_n^*$ and with (respectively) mixture probabilities $\tilde{p}_t$ and $\tilde{p}_t^*$. If $\tilde{p}_t$ is smaller than $\tilde{p}_t^*$ in the convex order,[9] then the aggregate loss associated with $\tilde{p}_t$, $L_t = \sum_{i=1}^{n} M_i D_i$ is smaller than the aggregate loss associated with $\tilde{p}_t^*$, $L_t^* = \sum_{i=1}^{n} M_i D_i^*$ in the convex order.[10] See [15] for more details about this comparison method. Then, it can be proved (see [11]) that when the mixture probabilities increase in the convex order, $[0, b]$ equity tranche premiums decrease and $[a, 100\%]$ senior tranche premiums increase.[11]

7.3 A REVIEW OF FACTOR APPROACHES TO THE PRICING OF CDOs

In the previous section, we stressed the key role played by the distribution of conditional probabilities of default when pricing CDO tranches. Loosely speaking, specifying a multivariate default time distribution amounts to specifying a mixture distribution on default probabilities. We thereafter review a wide range of popular default risk models—factor copulas models, structural, multivariate Poisson, and Cox process based models—through a meticulous analysis of their mixture distributions.

7.3.1 Factor Copula Models

In copula models, the joint distribution of default times is coupled to its one-dimensional marginal distributions through a copula function C:[12]

$$P\left(\tau_1 \leq t_1, \ldots, \tau_n \leq t_n\right) = C\left(F_1\left(t_1\right), \ldots, F_n\left(t_n\right)\right)$$

In such a framework, the dependence structure and the marginal distribution functions can be handled separately. Usually, the marginal default

---

[9] Let X and Y be two scalar integrable positive random variables. We say that X precedes Y in convex order if $E[X] = E[Y]$ and $E[(X - K)^+] \leq E[(Y - K)^+]$ for all $K \geq 0$.

[10] Losses given default $M_1, \ldots, M_n$ must be jointly independent from $D_1, \ldots, D_n$ and $D_1^*, \ldots, D_n^*$.

[11] As for the mezzanine tranche $[a, b]$ with $0 < a < b < 1$, it is not possible to infer such a comparison result. For example, it is well known that the present value of a mezzanine tranche may not be monotonic with respect to the compound correlation.

[12] For an introduction to copula functions with applications to finance, we refer to [14].

probabilities $F_i(t_i)$ are inferred from the credit default swap premiums on the different names. Thus, they appear as market inputs. The dependence structure does not interfere with the pricing of single name credit default swaps and is only involved in the pricing of correlation products such as CDO tranches. In the credit risk field, this approach has been introduced by [55] and further developed by [69].

Factor copula models are particular copula models for which the dependence structure of default times follows a factor framework. More specifically, the dependence structure is driven by some latent variables $V_1, \ldots, V_n$. Each variable V_i is expressed as a bivariate function of a common systemic risk factor V and an idiosyncratic risk factor $\bar{V}_i$:

$$V_i = f\left(V, \bar{V}_i\right), i = 1, \ldots, n$$

where V and $\bar{V}_i$, $i = 1, \ldots, n$ are assumed to be independent. In most applications, the specified function f, the factors V and $\bar{V}_i$, $i = 1, \ldots, n$ are selected such that latent variables V_i, $i = 1, \ldots, n$ form an exchangeable sequence of random variables. Consequently, $\bar{V}_i$, $i = 1, \ldots, n$ must follow the same distribution function, say $\bar{H}$. Eventually, default times are defined by $\tau_i = F_i^{-1}\left(H(V_i)\right)$[13] where F_i are the distribution functions of default times and H the marginal distribution of latent variables $V_i, i = 1, \ldots, n$. For simplicity, we will hereafter restrict to the case where the marginal distributions of default times do not depend on the name in the reference portfolio and denote the common distribution function by F.

In a general copula framework, computation of loss distributions requires n successive numerical integrations. The main interest of factor copula approach lies in its tractability as computational complexity is related to the factor dimension. Hence, factor copula models have been intensely used by market participants. In the following, we will review some popular factor copula approaches.

Additive Factor Copulas The family of additive factor copulas is the most widely used as far as the pricing of CDO tranches is concerned. In this class of models, the function f is additive and latent variables $V_1, \ldots, V_n$ are related through a dependence parameter ρ taking values in $[0, 1]$:

$$V_i = \rho V + \sqrt{1 - \rho^2}\,\bar{V}_i, \quad i = 1, \ldots, n$$

---

[13] Let us remark that default times in a factor copula model can be viewed as first passage times in a multivariate static structural model where V_i, $i = 1, \ldots, n$ correspond to some correlated asset values and where $F(t)$ drives the dynamics of the default threshold. In fact, default times can be expressed as $\tau_i = \inf\left\{t \geq 0 \,|\, V_i \leq H^{-1}\left(F_i(t)\right)\right\}$, $i = 1, \ldots, n$.

From what was stated in previous sections, the conditional default probability or mixture probability $\tilde{p}_t$ can be expressed as:

$$\tilde{p}_t = \bar{H}\left(\frac{-\rho V + H^{-1}\left(F(t)\right)}{\sqrt{1-\rho^2}}\right)$$

In most applications, V and $\bar{V}_i, i = 1, \ldots, n$ belong to the same class of probability distributions that is chosen to be closed under convolution.

The most popular form of the model is the so-called factor Gaussian copula that relies on some independent standard Gaussian random variables V and $\bar{V}_i, i = 1, \ldots, n$ and leads to Gaussian latent variables $V_1, \ldots, V_n$. It has been introduced by [72] in the credit risk field and is known as the multivariate probit model in statistics.[14] Thanks to its tractability, the one factor Gaussian copula has become the financial industry benchmark despite some well-known drawbacks. For example, it is not possible to fit all market quotes of standard CDO tranches of the same maturity. This deficiency is related to the so-called correlation skew.

An alternative approach is the Student-t copula which embeds the Gaussian copula as a limit case. It has been considered for credit risk issues by a number of authors, including [3], [29], [61], [39], [19], [67]. Nevertheless, the Student-t copula features the same deficiency as the Gaussian copula.

For this reason, a number of additive factor copulas such as the double-t copula ([46]), the NIG copula ([43]), the double-NIG copula ([51]), the double variance gamma copula ([62]) and the α-stable copula ([64]) have been investigated. Other heavy-tailed factor copula models are discussed in [73]. For a comparison of factor copula approaches in terms of pricing of CDO tranches, we refer to [11]. We plot in Figure 7.4 the mixture distributions associated with some of the previous additive factor copula approaches. Let us recall that mixture distributions correspond to the loss distribution of large homogeneous portfolios (see section 7.2.4).

Stochastic Correlation   Stochastic correlation models are other extensions of the factor Gaussian copula model. In this approach, the dependence parameter is stochastic. The latent variables are then expressed as:

$$V_i = \tilde{\rho}_i V + \sqrt{1 - \tilde{\rho}_i^2}\,\bar{V}_i, \quad i = 1, \ldots, n$$

---

[14] The multivariate probit model is a popular extension of the linear regression model in statistics. For a description of the model with applications to econometrics, we refer the reader to [37].

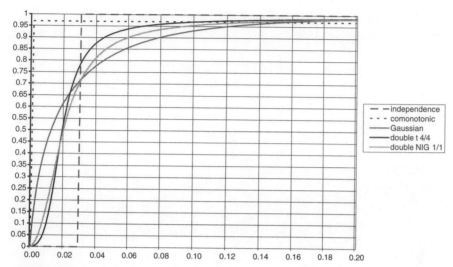

FIGURE 7.4 Graph showing the cumulative density functions of the mixture probability $\tilde{p}_t$ for the Gaussian, the double-t(4/4) and the double NIG (1/1) factor copula approaches. The marginal default probability is $F(t) = 2.96\%$ and we choose $\rho^2 = 30\%$ as the correlation between defaults. Eventually, we also plot the mixture distributions associated with the independence case ($\rho^2 = 0$) and the comonotonic case ($\rho^2 = 1$).

where V and $\bar{V}_i$, $i = 1, \ldots, n$ are independent standard Gaussian random variables and $\tilde{\rho}_i$, $i = 1, \ldots, n$ are identically distributed random variables taking values in $[0, 1]$ and independent from V, $\bar{V}_i$, $i = 1, \ldots, n$. A suitable feature of this approach is that the latent variables V_i, $i = 1, \ldots, n$ follow a multivariate Gaussian distribution.[15] This eases calibration and implementation of the model.

Let us remark that in this framework, default times are exchangeable. Then, the conditional default probability $\tilde{p}_t$ can be expressed as:

$$\tilde{p}_t = \int_0^1 \Phi\left(\frac{-\rho V + \Phi^{-1}(F(t))}{\sqrt{1 - \rho^2}}\right) G(d\rho)$$

where G denotes the distribution function of $\tilde{\rho}_i$, $i = 1, \ldots, n$ and Φ is the Gaussian cumulative density function.

---

[15] Thanks to the independence between $\tilde{\rho}_i$, V, $\bar{V}_i$, $i = 1, \ldots, n$, given $\tilde{\rho}_i$, V_i follows a standard Gaussian distribution. Thus, after an integration over the distribution of $\tilde{\rho}_i$, the marginal distribution of V_i is also standard Gaussian.

[11] investigated a two states stochastic correlation parameter. [70] also investigate a model with different states including a possibly catastrophic one. It has been shown by [12] that a three-state stochastic correlation model is enough to fit market quotes of CDO tranches for a given maturity. In their framework, the stochastic correlation parameters ρ_i, $i = 1, \ldots, n$ have also a factor representation:

$$\tilde{\rho}_i = (1 - B_s)(1 - B_i)\rho + B_s$$

where B_s, $B_1, \ldots, B_n$ are independent Bernoulli random variables independent from V, $\bar{V}_i$, $i = 1, \ldots, n$. Consequently, if we denote by $p_s = P(B_s = 1)$ and $p = P(B_i = 1)$, $i = 1, \ldots, n$, default times are comonotonic ($V_i = V$) with probability p_s, independent ($V_i = \bar{V}_i$) with probability $(1 - p_s)p$ and have a standard Gaussian factor representation with probability $(1 - p_s)(1 - p)$.

Mean-Variance Gaussian Mixtures In this class of factor models, latent variables are simply expressed as mean-variance Gaussian mixtures:

$$V_i = m(V) + \sigma(V)\bar{V}_i, \quad i = 1, \ldots, n$$

where V and $\bar{V}_i$, $i = 1, \ldots, n$ are independent standard Gaussian random variables. Two popular CDO pricing models have been derived from this class, namely the random factor loading and the local correlation model.

The random factor loading model has been introduced by [5]. In this approach, latent variables are modeled by:

$$V_i = m + \left(l1_{\{V < e\}} + h1_{\{V \geq e\}}\right)V + \nu\bar{V}_i, \quad i = 1, \ldots, n$$

where l, h, e are some input parameters such that $l, h > 0$. m and ν are chosen such that $E[V_i] = 0$ and $E[V_i^2] = 1$. This can be seen as a random factor loading model, since the risk exposure $l1_{\{V < e\}} + h1_{\{V \geq e\}}$ is state dependent. It is consistent with empirical researches showing that default correlation changes with respect to some macroeconomic random variables (see [18] and references therein). The conditional default probability can be written as:

$$\tilde{p}_t = \Phi\left(\frac{1}{\nu}\left(H^{-1}(F(t)) - m - \left(l1_{\{V < e\}} + h1_{\{V \geq e\}}\right)V\right)\right)$$

where H is the marginal distribution function of latent variables V_i, $i = 1, \ldots, n$. Let us remark that contrary to the previous approaches, latent

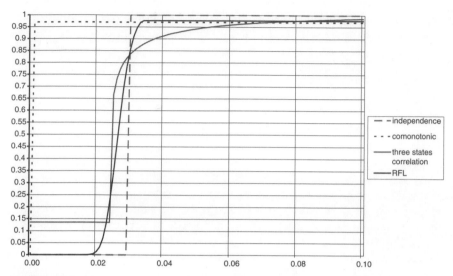

FIGURE 7.5 Graph showing the mixture distribution functions associated with the three-state stochastic correlation model of Burtschell *et al.* (2007) and the random factor loading model of Andersen and Sidenius (2005b). The marginal default probability, $F(t) = 2.96\%$ holds to be the same for both approaches. As for the stochastic correlation model, the parameters are respectively $p_s = 0.14$, $p = 0.81$, $\rho^2 = 58\%$. As for the random factor loading model, we took $l = 85\%$, $h = 5\%$ and $e = -2$. The graph also shows the mixture distribution functions associated with the independence and the comonotonic case.

variables here are not Gaussian and the distribution function H depends on the model parameters.

We compare in Figure 7.5 the mixture distribution functions obtained under a random factor loading model and a three states stochastic correlation model.

Like the three-state version of the stochastic correlation model, this approach has the ability to fit perfectly market quotes of standardized CDO tranche spreads for a given maturity.

The local correlation model proposed by [71] is associated with the following parametric modeling of latent variables:

$$V_i = -\rho(V) V + \sqrt{1 - \rho^2(V)}\bar{V}_i, \quad i = 1, \ldots, n$$

where V and $\bar{V}_i$, $i = 1, \ldots, n$ are independent standard Gaussian random variables and $\rho(.)$ is some function of V taking values in $[0, 1]$. $\rho(.)$ is known as the local correlation function. The conditional default probabilities can be written as:

$$\tilde{p}_t = \Phi\left(\frac{\rho(V)\,V + H^{-1}\left(F(t)\right)}{\sqrt{1 - \rho^2(V)}}\right)$$

where H is the marginal distribution function of latent variables V_i, $i = 1, \ldots, n$.

The local correlation can be used in a way which parallels the local volatility modeling in the equity derivatives market. This consists in a non-parametric calibration of $\rho(.)$ on market CDO tranche premiums. The local correlation function has the advantage to be a model based implied correlation when compared to some standard market practice such as the compound and the base correlation. Moreover, there is a simple relationship between $\rho(.)$ and market compound correlations implied from CDO tranchlets[16] (marginal compound correlation) as explained in [71] or [12]. But the trouble with this approach is that the existence and uniqueness of a local correlation function is not guaranteed given an admissible loss distribution function possibly inferred from market quotes.

Archimedean Copulas Archimedean copulas have been widely used in credit risk modeling as they represent a direct alternative to the Gaussian copula approach. In most cases, there exists an effective and tractable way of generating random vectors with this dependence structure. Moreover, Archimedean copulas are inherently exchangeable and thus admit a factor representation. [60] first exhibit this factor representation in their famous simulation algorithm. More precisely, each Archimedean copula can be associated with a positive random factor V with inverse Laplace transform $\varphi(.)$ (and Laplace transform $\varphi^{-1}(.)$). In this framework, the latent variables can be expressed as:

$$V_i = \varphi^{-1}\left(\frac{-\ln \bar{V}_i}{V}\right), \quad i = 1, \ldots, n$$

where $\bar{V}_i, i = 1, \ldots, n$ are independent uniform random variables. Then, the joint distribution of the random vector $(V_1, \ldots, V_n)$ is the φ-Archimedean

---

[16] CDO tranches $[a, a + 1\%]$ with $0 \leq a < 1$.

TABLE 7.1 Some Examples of Archimedean Copulas with Their Generators

Copula	Generator φ	Parameter
Clayton	$t^{-\theta} - 1$	$\theta \geq 0$
Gumbel	$(-\ln(t))^{\theta}$	$\theta \geq 1$
Frank	$-\ln[(1 - e^{-\theta t})/(1 - e^{-\theta})]$	$\mathbb{R}^*$

copula.[17] In particular, each latent variable is a uniform random variable. Then the conditional default probability can be written as:

$$\tilde{p}_t = \exp\left(-\varphi\left(F\left(t\right)\right) V\right)$$

Let us remark that the previous framework corresponds to frailty models in the reliability theory or survival data analysis.[18] In these models, V is called a frailty since low levels of V are associated with shorter survival default times. The most popular Archimedean copula is probably the Clayton copula (see Table 7.1). In a credit risk context, it has been considered by, among others, [69], [40], [54], [58], [30]. In addition, [66], and [67] have investigated other Archimedean copulas such as the Gumbel or the Frank copula.

In Figure 7.6, we compare the mixture distribution functions associated with a Clayton copula and a Gaussian factor copula. The dependence parameter θ of the Clayton copula has been chosen to get the same equity tranche premiums as with the one-factor Gaussian copula model.

It can be seen that the distribution functions are very similar. Unsurprisingly, the resulting premiums for the mezzanine and senior tranches are also very similar in both approaches.[19]

Perfect Copula Approach As we saw in previous sections, much of the effort has focused on the research of a factor copula that best fits CDO tranche premiums. Let us recall that specifying a factor copula dependence

---

[17] A random vector $(V_1, \ldots, V_n)$ follows a φ-Archimedean copula if for all $v_1, \ldots, v_n$ in $[0, 1]^n$:

$$P\left(V_1 \leq v_1, \ldots, V_n \leq v_n\right) = \varphi^{-1}\left(\varphi\left(v_1\right) + \cdots + \varphi\left(v_n\right)\right)$$

[18] We refer the reader to [44] for an introduction to multivariate survival data analysis and a detailed description of frailty models.

[19] See [11], Table 8, for more details about correspondence between parameters and assumptions on the underlying credit risk portfolio.

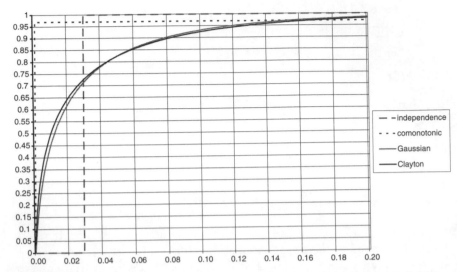

FIGURE 7.6 Graph showing the mixture distribution functions associated with a Clayton copula and a factor Gaussian copula $F(t) = 2.96\%$, $\rho^2 = 30\%$, $\theta = 0.18$.

structure is equivalent to specifying a mixture probability $\tilde{p}_t$. [47] exploit this remark and propose a direct estimation of the mixture probability distribution from market quotes. In their approach, for the sake of intuition on spread dynamics, the mixture probability is expressed through a hazard rate random variable $\tilde{\lambda}$ with a discrete distribution:

$$P\left(\tau_i \leq t \mid \tilde{\lambda} = \lambda_k\right) = 1 - \exp\left(-\lambda_k t\right), k = 1, \ldots, L$$

Then, defaults occur according to a mixture Poisson process (or a Cox process) with hazard rate $\tilde{\lambda}$. Once a grid has been chosen for $\tilde{\lambda}$, the probability $\pi_k = P\left(\tilde{\lambda} = \lambda_k\right)$ can be calibrated in order to match market quotes of CDO tranches. [47] have shown that this last step is not possible in general. Consequently, they allow recovery rate to be a decreasing function of default rates, as suggested in some empirical researches such as [2].

7.3.2 Multivariate Structural Models

Multivariate structural or firm value models are multiname extensions of the so-called Black and Cox model where the firm default time corresponds to the first passage time of its asset dynamics below a certain threshold. This approach has first been proposed by [6] (Chapter 5) in a general multivariate

Gaussian setting for the pricing of basket credit derivatives. More recently, [45] investigate the pricing of CDO tranche within a factor version of the Gaussian multivariate structural model. In the following, we follow the latter framework. We are concerned with n firms that may default in a time interval $[0, T]$. Their asset dynamics $V_1, \ldots, V_n$ are simply expressed as n correlated Brownian motions:

$$V_{i,t} = \rho V_t + \sqrt{1 - \rho^2} \, \bar{V}_{i,t}, i = 1, \ldots, n$$

where $V, V_i, i = 1, \ldots, n$ are independent standard Wiener processes. Default of firm i is triggered whenever the process V_i falls below a constant threshold a, which is here assumed to be the same for all names. The corresponding default dates are then expressed as:

$$\tau_i = \inf \left\{ t \geq 0 | \, V_{i,t} \leq a \right\}, i = 1, \ldots, n$$

Clearly, default dates are independent conditionally on the process V. Let us remark that as the default indicators are exchangeable, the existence of a mixture probability is guaranteed, thanks to the de Finetti's theorem. We are thus in a one factor framework, though the factor depends on the time horizon contrary to the factor copula case. No mixture distribution can be expressed in closed form in the multivariate structural model. But it is still possible to simulate losses on a large homogeneous portfolio (and then approximate the mixture probability $\tilde{p}_t$) in order to estimate the mixture distribution. Figure 7.7 shows that the latter happens to be very similar to the one generated within a factor Gaussian copula model. This is not surprising given the result of [45] where CDO tranche premiums are very close in both frameworks. Moreover, the factor Gaussian copula can be seen as the static counterpart of the structural model developed above.

The trouble with the first passage time models is that computation of CDO tranche premiums relies exclusively on Monte Carlo simulations and can be very time consuming. [52] propose an efficient Monte Carlo estimation of CDO tranche spreads in a multivariate jump-diffusion setting. Other contributions such as [57], [7], and [75] investigate the classical Merton model, where default at a particular time t occurs if the value of assets is below the barrier at that particular point in time. In this framework, default indicators at time t are independent given the systemic asset value V_t and semianalytical techniques as explained in Part I can be used to compute CDO tranche premiums. Moreover, several empirical researches claim that the Merton structural model is a reasonable approximation of the more general Black-Cox structural model when considering the pricing of CDO tranches. [57] consider a multivariate variance gamma model and show that

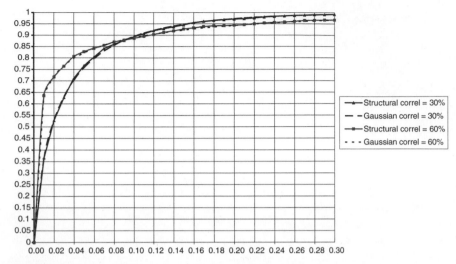

FIGURE 7.7   Graph showing empirical estimation of one-year mixture distributions corresponding to structural models with correlation parameters $\rho^2 = 30\%$ and $\rho^2 = 60\%$. The barrier level is set at $a = -2$ such that the marginal default probability (before $t = 1$ year) is the same in both approaches and is equal to $F(t) = 3.94\%$. We then make a comparison with the mixture distribution associated with factor Gaussian copula models with the same correlation parameters and the same default probability.

it can be easily calibrated from market quotes. [7] proposes to model the dynamics of assets with multivariate Lévy processes based on the gamma process, and [75] investigates a multivariate structural model as in [45] and adds a common jump component in the dynamic of assets.

7.3.3 Multivariate Poisson Models

These models originate from the theory of reliability where they are also called shock models. In multivariate Poisson models, default times correspond to the first jump instants of a multivariate Poisson process $(N_t^1, \ldots, N_t^m)$. For example, when the Poisson process N_t^i jumps for the first time, it triggers the default of name i. The dependence between default events derives from the arrival of some independent systemic events or common shocks leading to the default of a group of names with a given probability. For the sake of simplicity, we limit ourselves to the case where only two independent shocks can affect the economy. In this framework, each default can be triggered either by an idiosyncratic fatal shock or by a systemic but not necessarily fatal shock. The Poisson process, which drives default of name i, can be expressed as:

$$N_t^i = \bar{N}_t^i + \sum_{j=1}^{N_t} B_j^i$$

where N_t and $\bar{N}_t^i$ are independent Poisson processes with respectively parameter λ and $\bar{\lambda}$.[20] We further assume that B_j^i, $i = 1, \ldots, n$, and $j \geq 1$ are independent Bernoulli random variables with mean p independent of N_t and $\bar{N}_t^i$, $i = 1, \ldots, n$. Eventually, default times are described by:

$$\tau_i = \inf \left\{ t \geq 0 | N_t^i > 0 \right\}, i = 1, \ldots, n$$

The background event (new jump of N_t) affects each name (independently) with probability p. A specificity of the multivariate Poisson framework is to allow for more than one default occurring in small time intervals. It also includes the possibility of some Armageddon phenomenon where all names may default at the same time, then leading to fatten the tail of the aggregate loss distribution as required by market quotes. Let us stress that default dates are independent conditionally on the process N, while default indicators $D_1, \ldots, D_n$ are independent given N_t.

By the independence of all sources of randomness, N_t^i, $i = 1, \ldots, n$ are Poisson processes with parameter $\bar{\lambda} + p\lambda$. As a result, default times are exponentially distributed with the same parameter. It can be shown that the dependence structure of default times is the one of the Marshall-Olkin copula (see [56] or [25] for more details about this copula function). The Marshall-Olkin multivariate exponential distribution ([59]) has been introduced to the credit domain by [22] and also discussed by [55] and [78]. More recently, analytical results on the aggregate loss distribution have been derived by [56] within a multivariate Poisson model. Some extensions are presented by [31], [25], [9], and [10].

In this multivariate Poisson model, default times and thus default indicators are exchangeable. The corresponding mixture probability can be expressed as:

$$\tilde{p}_t = 1 - (1 - p)^N \exp\left(-\bar{\lambda}t\right)$$

As in the case of multivariate structural models, we are still in a one-factor framework, where the factor depends on the time horizon. We plot in Figure 7.8, the distribution function associated to a multivariate Poisson model. As the mixture probability is a discrete random variable, its distribution function is stepwise constant.

---

[20] $\sum_{j=1}^{N_t} B_j^i$ is assumed to be equal to zero when $N_t = 0$.

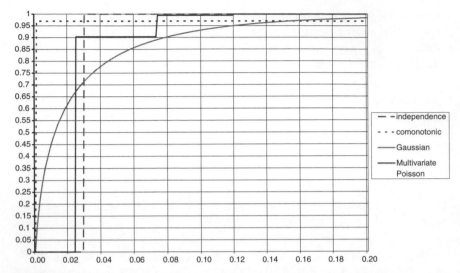

FIGURE 7.8 Graph showing the mixture distribution functions associated with a Multivariate Poisson model with $\bar{\lambda} = 0.5\%$, $\lambda = 2\%$ and $p = 5\%$. These parameters have been chosen such the marginal default probability before $t = 5$ years is $F(t) = 2.96\%$. For the sake of comparison, we also plot the mixture distribution function of the factor Gaussian copula with $\rho = 30\%$.

7.3.4 Affine Intensity Models

In affine intensity models, the default date of a given name, say i, corresponds to the first jump time of a doubly stochastic Poisson process (also known as a Cox process) with intensity λ_t^i. The latter follows an affine jump diffusion stochastic process that is assumed to be independent of the history of default times: there are no contagion effects of default events on the survival name intensities. Let us remark that, given the history of the process λ^i, survival distribution functions of default dates can be expressed as:

$$P\left(\tau_i \geq t \mid \lambda_s^i, 0 \leq s \leq t\right) = \exp\left(-\int\limits_0^t \lambda_s^i ds\right), i = 1, \dots, n^{21}$$

---

[21]Conditionally, on the history of default intensity λ_t^i, the default date τ_i is the first jump time of a nonhomogeneous Poisson process with intensity λ_t^i. Moreover, as far as simulations are concerned, default times are often expressed using some independent uniformly distributed random variables $U_1, \dots, U_n$ independent of default intensities: $\tau_i = \inf\{t \geq 0 \mid \exp(-\int_0^t \lambda_s^i ds) \leq U_i\}, i = 1, \dots, n$.

In affine models, dependence among default dates is concentrated upon dependence among default intensities. In the following, we follow the approach of [21], where the dependence among default intensities is driven by a factor representation:

$$\lambda_t^i = a x_t + x_t^i, i = 1, \ldots, n$$

a is a nonnegative parameter accounting for the importance of the common factor and governing the dependence. The processes x, x^i, $i = 1, \ldots, n$ are assumed to be independent copies of an affine jump diffusion (AJD) process. The choice of AJD processes is not innocuous. First, the intensities λ_t^i, $i = 1, \ldots, n$ remain in the class of AJD processes, which allow to derive marginal default probabilities in closed form.[22] It results into a flexible dynamics of default intensities while letting the prospect for numerical implementations. Unlike copula models, this approach does not guarantee a perfect fit to CDS quotes for all maturities. Moreover, the same parameters drive the marginal distributions and the dependence structure of default times, which makes the calibration process more complicated.

Let us remark that default times are exchangeable in this framework. Moreover, conditionally on $V_t = \int_0^t x_s \, ds$, the default indicators $D_i = 1_{\{\tau_i \leq t\}}$, $i = 1, \ldots, n$ are independent. It is then possible to express the mixture probability $\tilde{p}_t$ associated with this exchangeable Bernoulli sequence:

$$\tilde{p}_t = P\left(\tau_i \leq t \mid x_s, 0 \leq s \leq t\right) = 1 - E\left[\exp\left(-\int_0^t x_s^i \, ds\right)\right] \exp\left(-a \int_0^t x_s \, ds\right)$$

As in the two previous examples, multivariate structural and Poisson models, we are in a one factor framework though a different factor is required to compute the loss distribution for each time horizon. [40] first exhibited the form of the mixture probability stressing the factor representation in affine models. Thanks to what is stated above, it is possible to compute the characteristic function of $\tilde{p}_t$ and derive its density function using some inversion techniques. [63] and subsequently [24] gradually extended the approach, providing more flexibility in the choice of parameters, and developed efficient numerical methods for the calibration and the pricing of CDO tranches. [13] provided a slightly different specification that

---

[22] There exists some complex valued function $\alpha(.\,,.)$ and $\beta(.\,,.)$ depending on the process parameters such that $E[\exp(iu \int_0^t x_s \, ds)] = \exp(\alpha(u,t) + \beta(u,t)x_0)$. See [53] for more details.

guarantees a perfect calibration onto CDS quotes, but have to deal with positivity constraints on default intensities. [26] performed an empirical analysis of the model using a large data set of CDS and CDO tranche spreads. He shows that when calibrated to daily CDS spreads, the model has a good ability to match marked-to-market of risky CDO tranche spreads over time while it does not capture properly the variability of senior tranches spreads.

7.4 CONCLUSION

The factor representation leads to efficient computational methods for the pricing of CDO tranches. It encompasses a wide range of CDO pricing models and also provides a suitable framework for portfolio risk analysis thanks to the theory of stochastic orders. Besides, when considering homogeneous credit risk portfolios, the factor approach is not restrictive, thanks to de Finetti's theorem. We stressed the key role played by the mixture probability or the conditional default probability in factor models in terms of pricing CDO tranches and in deriving large portfolio approximations.

However, there are still a number of open questions to be dealt with among which we can mention:

- The calibration to CDO tranche quotes with different maturities and the same set of parameters is usually difficult.
- Whether one should choose a nonparametric approach such as an implied copula or a properly specified parametric model is still unclear.
- Dealing with heterogeneity between names or linking factors related to different geographical regions or sectors, which is especially important for the pricing of bespoke CDOs.

Hopefully, there is still room for further improvements of the factor approach both on theoretical and practical grounds.

REFERENCES

1. Aldous, D. J. (1985). *Exchangeability and Related Topics*, Lecture Notes in Mathematics 1117, New York: Springer.
2. Altman, E., B. Brady, A. Resti, and A. Sironi. (2005). The link between default and recovery rates: Theory, empirical evidence and implications. *Journal of Business* 78: 2203–2228.
3. Andersen, L., J. Sidenius, and S. Basu. (2003). All your hedges in one basket. *Risk* (November): 67–72.

4. Andersen, L., and J. Sidenius. (2005a). CDO pricing with factor models: Survey and comments. *Journal of Credit Risk* 1(3): 71–88.
5. Andersen, L., and J. Sidenius.(2005b). Extensions to the Gaussian copula: Random recovery and random factor loadings. *Journal of Credit Risk* 1(1): 29–70.
6. Arvanitis, A., and J. Gregory. *Credit: The Complete Guide to Pricing, Hedging and Risk Management.* London: Risk Books.
7. Baxter, M. (2007). Gamma process dynamic modelling of credit. *Risk* (October): 98–101.
8. Bielecki, T. R., and M. Rutkowski. (2004). *Credit Risk: Modeling, Valuation and Hedging.* New York: Springer.
9. Brigo, D., A. Pallavicini, and R. Torresetti. (2007a). CDO calibration with the dynamical generalized Poisson loss model. *Risk* (May): 70–75.
10. Brigo, D., A. Pallavicini, and R. Torresetti. (2007b). Cluster-based extension of the generalized Poisson loss dynamics and consistency with single names. *International Journal of Theoretical and Applied Finance* 10(4): 607–631.
11. Burtschell, X., J. Gregory, and J.-P. Laurent. (2008). A comparative analysis of CDO pricing models. Working paper, ISFA Actuarial School, University of Lyon and BNP Paribas.
12. Burtschell, X., J. Gregory, and J.-P. Laurent. (2007). Beyond the Gaussian copula: stochastic and local correlation. *Journal of Credit Risk* 3(1): 31–62.
13. Chapovsky, A., A. Rennie, and P. Tavares. (2007). Stochastic intensity modeling for structured credit exotics. *International Journal of Theoretical and Applied Finance* 10(4): 633–652.
14. Cherubini, U., E. Luciano, and W. Vecchiato. (2004). *Copula Methods in Finance.* Hoboken, NJ: John Wiley & Sons.
15. Cousin, A., and J.-P. Laurent. (2007). Comparison results for credit risk portfolios. Working paper, ISFA Actuarial School, University of Lyon.
16. Crouhy, M., D. Galai, and R. Mark. (2000). A comparative analysis of current credit risk models. *Journal of Banking and Finance* 24: 59–117.
17. Das, S. (2005). *Credit Derivatives: CDOs and Structured Credit Products.* Hoboken, NJ: John Wiley & Sons.
18. Das, S., L. Freed, G. Geng, and N. Kapadia. (2006). Correlated default risk. *Journal of Fixed Income* 16(2): 7–32.
19. Demarta, S., and A. McNeil. (2005). The *t* Copula and Related Copulas. *International Statistical Review* 73(1): 111–129.
20. De Prisco, B., I. Iscoe and A. Kreinin. (2005). Loss in translation, *Risk* (June): 77–82.
21. Duffie, D., and N. Gârleanu. (2001). Risk and the valuation of collateralized debt obligations. *Financial Analysts Journal* 57: 41–59.
22. Duffie, D., and K. J. Singleton. (1998). Simulating correlated defaults. Working paper, Stanford University.
23. Duffie, D., and K. J. Singleton. (2003). *Credit Risk: Pricing, Measurement and Management.* Princeton Series in Finance.
24. Eckner, A. (2007). Computational techniques for basic affine models of portfolio credit risk. Working paper, Stanford University.

25. Elouerkhaoui, Y. (2006). Étude des problèmes de corrélation et d'incomplétude dans les marchés de crédit. PhD Thesis, University Paris Dauphine.
26. Feldhütter, P. (2007). An empirical investigation of an intensity-based model for pricing CDO tranches. Working paper, Copenhagen Business School.
27. Finger, C. C. (2001). The one-factor CreditMetrics model in the New Basel Capital Accord. *RiskMetrics Journal* 2(1): 9–18.
28. Finger, C. C. (2005). Issues in the pricing of synthetic CDOs. *Journal of Credit Risk* 1(1): 113–124.
29. Frey, R., and A. McNeil. (2003). Dependent defaults in models of portfolio credit risk. *Journal of Risk* 6(1): 59–92.
30. Friend, A., and E. Rogge. (2005). Correlation at first sight. *Economic Notes* 34(2): 155–183.
31. Giesecke, K. (2003). A simple exponential model for dependent defaults. *Journal of Fixed Income* (December): 74–83.
32. Glasserman, P., and S. Suchintabandid. (2007). Correlation expansions for CDO pricing, *Journal of Banking and Finance* 31(5): 1375–1398.
33. Gordy, M. (2000). A comparative anatomy of credit risk models. *Journal of Banking and Finance* 24: 119–149.
34. Gordy, M. (2003). A risk-factor model foundation for ratings-based bank capital rules. *Journal of Financial Intermediation* 12: 199–232.
35. Gordy, M., and D. Jones. (2003). Random tranches. *Risk* (March): 78–83.
36. Gössl, G. (2007). The core factor—a fast and accurate factor reduction technique. Working paper, Unicredit Markets and Investment Banking.
37. Gourieroux, C. (2000). *Econometrics of Qualitative Dependent Variables.* Cambridge: Cambridge University Press.
38. Greenberg, A., D. O'Kane, and L. Schloegl. (2004a): *LH+: A* Fast analytical model for CDO hedging and risk management. Lehman Brothers, *Quantitative Credit Research Quarterly.*
39. Greenberg, A., R. Mashal, M. Naldi, and L. Schloegl. (2004b). Tuning correlation and tail risk to the market prices of liquid tranches. Lehman Brothers, *Quantitative Research Quarterly.*
40. Gregory, J., and J.-P. Laurent. (2003). I will survive. *Risk* (June): 103–107.
41. Gregory, J., and J.-P. Laurent. (2004). In the core of correlation. *Risk* (October): 87–91.
42. Gregory, J., and J.-P. Laurent. (2008): Practical pricing of synthetic CDOs. Working paper, Barclays Capital.
43. Guegan, D., and J. Houdain. (2005). Collateralized debt obligations pricing and factor models: A new methodology using normal inverse Gaussian distributions. Working paper, ENS Cachan.
44. Hougaard, P. (2000). *Analysis of Multivariate Survival Data.* New York: Springer.
45. Hull, J., M. Predescu, and A. White. (2005). The valuation of correlation-dependent credit derivatives using a structural model. Working paper, University of Toronto.
46. Hull, J., and A. White. (2004). Valuation of a CDO and an nth to default CDS without Monte Carlo simulation. *Journal of Derivatives* 12(2): 8–23.

47. Hull, J., and A. White. (2006). Valuing credit derivatives using an implied copula approach. *Journal of Derivatives* 14(2): 8–28.
48. Jackson, K., A. Kreinin, and X. Ma. (2007). Loss distribution evaluation for synthetic CDOs. Working paper, University of Toronto.
49. Jiao, Y. (2007). Le risque de crédit: modélisation et simulation numérique. PhD thesis, École Polytechnique.
50. Kakodkar, A., S. Galiani, J. G. Jónsson, and A. Gallo. (2006). *Credit Derivatives Handbook 2006*, vols. 1 and 2, Merrill Lynch.
51. Kalemanova, A., B. Schmid, and R. Werner. (2007). The normal inverse Gaussian distribution for synthetic CDO pricing. (Spring): 80–93.
52. Kiesel, R., and M. Scherer. (2007). Dynamic credit portfolio modelling in structural models with jumps. Working paper, Ulm University and London School of Economics.
53. Lando, D. (2004). *Credit Risk Modeling and Applications*. Princeton, NJ: Princeton University Press.
54. Laurent, J.-P., and J. Gregory. (2005). Basket default swaps, CDOs and factor copulas. *Journal of Risk* 7(4): 103–122.
55. Li, D. (2000). On default correlation: A copula approach. *Journal of Fixed Income* 9: 43–54.
56. Lindskog, F., and A. McNeil. (2003). Common Poisson shock models: Applications to insurance and credit risk modelling. *ASTIN Bulletin* 33(2): 209–238.
57. Luciano, E., and W. Schoutens. (2006). A multivariate jump-driven financial asset model. *Quantitative Finance* 6(5): 385–402.
58. Madan, D. B., M. Konikov, and M. Marinescu. (2004). Credit and basket default swaps. Working paper, Bloomberg LP.
59. Marshall, A., and I. Olkin. (1967). A multivariate exponential distribution. *Journal of the American Statistical Association* 62: 30–44.
60. Marshall, A., and I. Olkin. (1988). Families of multivariate distributions. *Journal of the American Statistical Association* 83: 834–841.
61. Mashal, R., M. Naldi, and A. Zeevi. (2003). Extreme events and multiname credit derivatives. In J. Gregory (ed.), *Credit Derivatives: The Definitive Guide*. London: Risk Books, pp. 313–338.
62. Moosbrucker, T. (2006). Pricing CDOs with correlated variance gamma distributions. Working paper, Centre for Financial Research, University of Cologne.
63. Mortensen, A. (2006). Semi-analytical valuation of basket credit derivatives in intensity-based models. *Journal of Derivatives* 13(4): 8–26.
64. Prange, D., and W. Scherer. (2006). Correlation smile matching with alpha-stable distributions and fitted Archimedean copula models. Working paper, Risk Methodology Trading, Model Validation Credit Derivatives, Dresdner Kleinwort Wasserstein.
65. Pykhtin, M., and A. Dev. (2002). Credit risk in asset securitizations: Analytical model. *Risk* (May): S16–S20.
66. Rogge, E., and P. Schönbucher. (2003). Modelling dynamic portfolio credit risk. Working paper, Imperial College.

67. Schloegl, L., and D. O'Kane. (2005). A note on the large homogeneous portfolio approximation with the Student t copula. *Finance and Stochastics* 9(4): 577–584.
68. Schönbucher, P. (2003). *Credit Derivatives Pricing Models*. Hoboken, NJ: John Wiley & Sons.
69. Schönbucher, P., and D. Schubert. (2001). Copula dependent default risk in intensity models. Working paper, Bonn University.
70. Tavares, P. A. C., T.-U. Nguyen, A. Chapovsky, and I. Vaysburd. (2004). Composite basket model. Working paper, Merrill Lynch.
71. Turc, J., P. Very, and D. Benhamou. (2005). Pricing CDOs with a smile, working paper, SG Credit Research. See also Chapter 9 in this volume.
72. Vasicek, O. (2002). Loan portfolio value. *Risk* (December): 160–162.
73. Wang, D., S. T. Rachev, and F. J. Fabozzi. (2007). Pricing of credit default index swap tranches with one-factor heavy-tailed copula models. Working paper, University of California, Santa Barbara.
74. White, R. P., and T. N. E. Greville. (1959). On computing the probability that exactly k of n independent events will occur. *Transactions of Society of Actuaries* 11: 88–95.
75. Willeman, S. (2007). Fitting the CDO correlation skew: A tractable structural jump-diffusion model. *Journal of Credit Risk* 3(1): 63–90.
76. Wilson, T. (1997a). Portfolio credit risk I. *Risk*(September): 111–117.
77. Wilson, T. (1997b). Portfolio credit risk II. *Risk* (October): 56–61.
78. Wong, D. (2000). Copula from the limit of multivariate binary model. Working paper, Bank of America Corporation.

CHAPTER 8

Factor Distributions Implied by Quoted CDO Spreads

Erik Schlögl and Lutz Schlögl

The rapid pace of innovation in the market for credit risk has given rise to a large market in synthetic collateralized debt obligation (CDO) tranches on standardized portfolios. To the extent that tranche spreads depend on default dependence between different obligors in the reference portfolio, quoted spreads can be seen as aggregating the market views on this dependence. In a manner reminiscent of the volatility smiles found in liquid option markets, practitioners speak of implied correlation "smiles" and "skews." We explore how this analogy can be taken a step further to extract implied factor distributions from the market quotes for synthetic CDO tranches.

8.1 INTRODUCTION

Implied correlation has become a buzzword in portfolio credit risk modeling. In a development similar to implied volatility for vanilla options, a model parameter affecting derivative financial instruments, but not directly observable in the market, is backed out from derivatives prices as those derivatives become competitively quoted. The derivatives in question are synthetic CDO tranches and the parameter is correlation in a Gaussian single-factor model of default, essentially along the lines of [31] and [21]. This model has become the point of reference when pricing portfolio credit derivatives, in this sense much like the [5] model in option pricing. Even more so than in the case of Black/Scholes, however, the severe limitations of this model are recognized by practitioners. Given these limitations, it is unsurprising that it cannot consistently fit the market, that is, for different tranches on the same portfolio, different values of the correlation parameter are required in order to fit observed tranche spreads. This has led market practitioners to speak of implied correlation "smiles" and "skews," evoking an analogy to the volatility smiles found in vanilla option markets.

Several alternative approaches to modeling portfolio credit risk, as required for pricing CDO tranches, have been proposed. These include lifting the structural (asset-based) models pioneered by [5] and [23] to the portfolio level, for example as illustrated by [13]. The intensity-based modeling approach initially proposed by [15] can also be applied at the portfolio level, by modeling dependent default intensities as in [9] or using a more general copula-based framework as introduced by [28]. Most recently, a new methodology for the pricing of portfolio credit derivatives has been proposed by [30], who takes a "top-down" approach (as opposed to the "bottom-up" approach of the aforementioned papers) to directly model the stochastic dynamics of portfolio losses (and the associated loss transition rates) in an arbitrage-free manner.[1]

The choice of approach to construct a model fitting observed tranche quotes primarily depends on the application envisioned for the calibrated model. The point of view that we take in this chapter is that we wish to price related (but illiquid) instruments in a manner consistent with the market quotes for standard synthetic tranches on standard reference portfolios (such as CDX or ITRAXX). We want to be reasonably satisfied that the calibrated model subsumes all the market information relevant to the pricing of the illiquid instruments. In this, the problem is somewhat more complicated than calibrating, say, a single-name equity option model to observed standard option prices.

Since we are concerned with relative pricing of similar instruments, we abstract from the fundamental asset values and use credit spreads (for single names as well as for competitively quoted synthetic CDO tranches) directly as inputs. Furthermore, the results of [7] suggest that credit spread *dynamics* are of minor importance in pricing CDO tranches. Consequently, the simplest solution would be to modify the Vasicek/Li static factor model to fit observed tranche spreads.

The normal distribution of the common factor in the Vasicek model implies a Gaussian dependence structure (copula) between the latent variables driving the defaults of the various obligors. Numerous authors have

---

[1] [30] demonstrates how his model can be disaggregated from the portfolio level all the way down to the level of multivariate, intensity-driven dynamics of the defaults of individual obligors, thus providing a general framework for the modeling of credit derivatives. The aim of this chapter is far less ambitious.

suggested replacing this by a Student-t, a Marshall/Olkin, or various types of Archimedean copulae.[2] [7] compare a selection of these models; in their study, the best fit to market data seems to be achieved by the double t one-factor model of [12].

The basic model can be extended in various ways, thus introducing additional parameters, which facilitate an improved fit. One obvious way to introduce further degrees of freedom into the model is to allow the systematic factor loadings (corresponding to the constant correlation parameter in the reference Vasicek model) to vary across obligors. However, doing so without any structural assumptions results in more than 100 free parameters in the typical case of a CDX or ITRAXX portfolio, making any meaningful calibration impossible. [22] suggest bringing the number of free parameters back down to one taking historical correlations as an input and scaling all correlations by a constant chosen to fit the market as well as possible. Between these two extremes, intermediate solutions could be achieved by perturbing one or more eigenvectors of the historical variance/covariance matrix.[3]

[2] pursue two possible extensions, one that allows for random recovery rates and another, in which the factor loadings are random. They motivate this by the stylized empirical observations that recovery rates are correlated with the business cycle and that default correlation appears stronger in a bear market. In particular for the latter case, examples are given where the model produces implied correlation skews qualitatively similar to those observed in the market.

We pursue a third path, seeking to imply the underlying factor distribution (and thereby the distribution of conditional default probabilities) directly from the market quotes for synthetic CDO tranches. In this, we build on the well-known methods of implying risk-neutral distributions from option prices, a strand of the literature initiated by the seminal paper of [6].[4]

As the normal factor distribution used by [31] and [21] remains the benchmark for pricing CDO tranches, this seems a natural starting point for a factor distribution calibrated to market data. The Edgeworth and Gram/Charlier Type A series[5] expand a distribution around the normal in terms of higher order moments. In the case of risk-neutral distributions

---

[2] See [7] and references therein.

[3] [22] mention only scaling all correlations by a single constant because of the attraction of being able to quote a single number, the "implied correlation bump," as representing the default dependence implied from market quotes.

[4] See [4] for an overview.

[5] See, e.g., [19].

implied by standard option prices, this is an approach that is well known in the literature,[6] where typically the series is truncated after the fourth moment (representing kurtosis). [16] show how one can ensure that the truncated series yield a valid density. In the sections that follow, we derive the theoretical results required to implement CDO tranche pricing where the common factor follows a Gram/Charlier density, fit this density to market data and apply the model to the pricing of general tranches on standard portfolios.

8.2 MODELING

Assumption 1. *Along the lines of [31], assume that the latent variable* ζ_i *driving the default (or survival) of the i-th obligor can be written as*

$$\zeta_i = \beta_i Y + \sqrt{1 - \beta_i^2} \epsilon_i \qquad (8.2.1)$$

where $Y, \epsilon_1, \ldots, \epsilon_M$ *are independent,* $\epsilon_i \sim N(0, 1)$ *and (departing from Vasicek's normality assumption) the distribution of* Y *is given by a Gram/Charlier Type A series expansion in the standard measure, i.e. the density f of* Y *is given by*

$$f(x) = \sum_{j=0}^{\infty} c_j \text{He}_j(x)\phi(x) \qquad (8.2.2)$$

$$c_r = \frac{1}{r!} \int_{-\infty}^{\infty} f(x)\text{He}_r(x)dx$$

$$\phi(x) = \frac{1}{\sqrt{2\pi}} e^{-\frac{x^2}{2}}$$

where $\text{He}_j(x)$ *denotes the Hermite polynomial[7] of order j.*

Default of obligor i is considered to have occurred before time t if the latent variable ζ_i lies below the threshold $D_i(t)$.

Note that in this context, a large homogeneous portfolio (LHP) approximation is easy to derive. Follow [31] and consider an LHP of M issuers. Homogeneity of the the portfolio means that, in addition to the ζ_i being

---

[6] See, e.g., [14], [8] and [17].
[7] See Definition 8.2 in the Appendix.

identically distributed, the exposures to each obligor in the portfolio are the same, as are the recovery rates R and the correlation (β_i) with the common factor.[8] In this case, the randomness due to the idiosyncratic risk factors ϵ_i diversifies out as the size M of the portfolio grows large. In the limit, given the value of the systematic risk factor Y, the loss fraction L on the portfolio notional is[9]

$$L \approx (1 - R)\Phi\left(\frac{D - \beta Y}{\sqrt{1 - \beta^2}}\right) \tag{8.2.3}$$

where $\Phi(\cdot)$ is the cumulative distribution function (CDF) of the standard normal distribution. Setting

$$h(x) = (1 - R)\Phi\left(\frac{x}{\sqrt{1 - \beta^2}}\right) \tag{8.2.4}$$

the CDF of the portfolio loss fraction can be expressed as

$$P[L \leq \theta] = 1 - F\left(\frac{D - h^{-1}(\theta)}{\beta}\right) \tag{8.2.5}$$

where $F(\cdot)$ is the CDF corresponding to the density $f(\cdot)$ given by (8.2.2).

The key result needed in order to implement the factor model of Assumption 1 is an explicit relationship between the default thresholds $D_i(t)$ and the (risk-neutral) probability of default of obligor i:

Proposition 8.1. *Under Assumption 1,*

$$P[\zeta_i \leq D_i(t)] = \Phi(D_i(t)) - \sum_{j=1}^{\infty} \beta_i^j c_j \phi(D_i(t)) \mathrm{He}_{j-1}(D_i(t)) \tag{8.2.6}$$

where $\Phi(\cdot)$ and $\phi(\cdot)$ are the CDF and density, respectively, of the standard normal distribution.

---

[8] Note that some authors write (8.2.1) as $\zeta_i = \sqrt{\rho_i}Y + \sqrt{1 - \rho_i}\epsilon_i$, in which case $\sqrt{\rho_i}\sqrt{\rho_j}$ is the correlation between the latent variables for obligors i and j. Then in the homogeneous case $(\rho_i = \rho_j = \rho)$, this correlation between latent variables is simply ρ.
[9] Cf. [25]

Proof. We first derive the density $g(\cdot)$ of ζ_i.

$$g(x) = \frac{\partial}{\partial x} P[\zeta_i \le x]$$

$$= \frac{\partial}{\partial x} \int_{-\infty}^{\infty} \int_{-\infty}^{\frac{x - \beta_i y}{\sqrt{1 - \beta_i^2}}} \phi(t) dt f(y) dy$$

$$= \int_{-\infty}^{\infty} \frac{1}{\sqrt{2\pi}} \exp\left\{ -\frac{(x - \beta_i y)^2}{2(1 - \beta_i^2)} \right\} \frac{1}{\sqrt{1 - \beta_i^2}} \sum_{j=0}^{\infty} c_j \mathrm{He}_j(y) \frac{1}{\sqrt{2\pi}} e^{-\frac{y^2}{2}} dy$$

$$= \exp\left\{ -\frac{1}{2(1 - \beta_i^2)}(x^2 - x^2 \beta_i^2) \right\} \int_{-\infty}^{\infty} \frac{1}{2\pi\sqrt{1 - \beta_i^2}}$$

$$\times \exp\left\{ -\frac{1}{2(1 - \beta_i^2)}(y^2 - 2x\beta_i y + x^2 \beta_i^2) \right\} \sum_{j=0}^{\infty} c_j \mathrm{He}_j(y) dy$$

$$= e^{-\frac{x^2}{2}} \int_{-\infty}^{\infty} \frac{1}{2\pi\sqrt{1 - \beta_i^2}} \exp\left\{ -\frac{(y - \beta_i x)^2}{2(1 - \beta_i^2)} \right\} \sum_{j=0}^{\infty} c_j \mathrm{He}_j(y) dy$$

Setting $z := (y - x\beta_i)/\sqrt{1 - \beta_i^2}$, this is

$$= e^{-\frac{x^2}{2}} \int_{-\infty}^{\infty} \frac{1}{2\pi} e^{-\frac{z^2}{2}} \sum_{j=0}^{\infty} c_j \mathrm{He}_j\left(\sqrt{1 - \beta_i^2} z + x\beta_i\right) dz$$

and applying lemma 8.3,[10]

$$= \phi(x) \int_{-\infty}^{\infty} \phi(z) \sum_{k=0}^{\infty} c_k \sum_{j=0}^{k} \binom{k}{j} \left(\sqrt{1 - \beta_i^2}\right)^{k-j} \mathrm{He}_{k-j}(z) j!$$

$$\sum_{m=0}^{[\frac{j}{2}]} \frac{1}{m! 2^m (j - 2m)!} (1 - \beta_i^2)^m \mathrm{He}_{j-2m}(xB_i) dz$$

---

[10] Reproduced from [27] for the reader's convenience in the Appendix. Note that this lemma is a special case of scaling and translation results well known in white noise theory see, e.g., [20] or [11]. We thank John van der Hoek for pointing this out.

These results essentially afford densities given in terms of Edgeworth or Gram/Charlier expansions the same amount of tractability as the Gaussian. Calculations can be performed directly at the level of the infinite series expansion, without the need to truncate the series before deriving the desired results (as has been the practice in the option pricing literature using these expansions). See [27] for an application to traditional option pricing.

which by the orthogonality property of Hermite polynomials[11] simplifies to

$$= \phi(x) \sum_{k=0}^{\infty} c_k k! \sum_{m=0}^{[\frac{k}{2}]} \frac{1}{m! 2^m (k-2m)!} (1-\beta_i^2)^m \mathrm{He}_{k-2m}(xB_i)$$

Reordering terms, this becomes

$$= \phi(x) \sum_{j=0}^{\infty} \mathrm{He}_j(x\beta_i) \underbrace{\sum_{m=0}^{\infty} c_{j+2m}(j+2m)! \frac{1}{m! 2^m j!} (1-\beta_i^2)^m}_{=:d_j}$$

Applying Corollary 8.4 (see Appendix),

$$= \phi(x) \sum_{j=0}^{\infty} d_j j! \sum_{m=0}^{[\frac{j}{2}]} \beta_i^{j-2m} \mathrm{He}_{j-2m}(x) \frac{(\beta_i^2-1)^m}{(j-2m)! 2^m m!}$$

$$= \phi(x) \sum_{k=0}^{\infty} \mathrm{He}_k(x) \frac{\beta_i^k}{k!} \sum_{m=0}^{\infty} d_{k+2m}(k+2m)! \frac{(\beta_i^2-1)^m}{2^m m!} \qquad (8.2.7)$$

Consider the term

$$\sum_{m=0}^{\infty} d_{k+2m}(k+2m)! \frac{(\beta_i^2-1)^m}{2^m m!} = \sum_{m=0}^{\infty} (k+2m)! \frac{(\beta_i^2-1)^m}{2^m m!}$$

$$\times \sum_{n=0}^{\infty} c_{k+2m+2n}(k+2m+2n)! \frac{1}{n! 2^n (k+2m)!} (1-\beta_i^2)^n$$

and change indices to $j := m+n$, so that this

$$= \sum_{j=0}^{\infty} c_{k+2j}(k+2j)! (1-\beta_i^2)^j \frac{1}{2^j j!} \sum_{m=0}^{j} \binom{j}{m} (-1)^m$$

The inner sum is zero for all $j > 0$, so that we have

$$= c_k k!$$

---

[11] See, for example, [19]

Substituting this into (8.2.7) yields

$$g(x) = \phi(x) \sum_{k=0}^{\infty} \mathrm{He}_k(x) \beta_i^k c_k \qquad (8.2.8)$$

It follows from lemma 8.5 (see Appendix) that

$$P[\zeta_i \leq D_i(t)] = \int_{-\infty}^{D_i(t)} g(x) dx$$

$$= \Phi(D_i(t)) = \sum_{j=1}^{\infty} \beta_i^j c_j \phi(D_i(t)) \mathrm{He}_{j-1}(D_i(t))$$

Lemma 8.1 permits the term structures of default thresholds to be fitted to the risk–neutral probabilities of default backed out of the single-name credit default swap spreads.[12] CDO tranche spreads can then be calculated by semi-analytical methods—we use the method described by [3], the only modification required being that the calculation of the unconditional loss probabilities from the conditional loss probabilities by numerical integration is carried out with respect to a factor distribution given by a Gram/Charlier density.

8.3 EXAMPLES

8.3.1 Implied Factor Distributions

To extract implied factor distributions from competitively quoted tranche spreads, we assume a flat correlation structure (i.e., $\beta_i \equiv \beta$ for all i) and truncate the Gram/Charlier series expansion after some even-numbered moment,[13] thus essentially generalizing the Vasicek/Li factor model by allowing for nonzero skewness, excess kurtosis and possibly higher order terms.

---

[12] For the relationship between CDS spreads and risk-neutral probabilities of default/survival, see [29].

[13] Truncating the expansion after an odd-numbered moment would unavoidably result in an invalid density. For truncation after an arbitrary even-numbered moment, [27] describes an algorithm, which ensures that the coefficients of the truncated expansion are calibrated in a way that ensures that the density is positive everywhere.

TABLE 8.1 Calibration to CDX NA I Tranche Quotes on April 21, 2004

| | Market | | | | Vasicek Model | | Gram/Charlier | |
| | Upfront (pts) | | Spread (bp) | | | | | |
Subordination	Bid	Ask	Bid	Ask	Upfront	Spread	Upfront	Spread
0%	37	42	500	500	41.79	500.00	39.88	500.00
3%	0	0	280	330	0.00	365.93	0.00	306.55
7%	0	0	102	110	0.00	93.71	0.00	104.84
10%	0	0	39	59	0.00	24.27	0.00	53.82
15%	0	0	6	16	0.00	1.60	0.00	9.48
30%								

Latent variable correlation coefficient β^2:	16.98%	17.58%
Skewness:		−0.2825
Excess kurtosis:		1.8986

We implement a nonlinear optimisation[14] to find β, skewness and excess kurtosis and any desired higher moments such that the squared relative error in the model tranche spreads versus the mid-market quoted spreads is minimized.

Two market data examples are given in Tables 8.1 and 8.2. For the CDX NA I tranche quotes on April 21, 2004, the Gram/Charlier calibration produces very good results, with the model spreads very close to the mid-market quotes, especially when compared to the spreads representing the best fit of a Vasicek flat correlation model calibrated using the same objective function. This is also reflected in the shape of the calibrated density itself, which is nicely unimodal, as Figure 8.1 shows. For the ITRX.EUR 2 tranche quotes on March 21, 2005, the fit is not as good. In fact, an unconstrained calibration of skewness and kurtosis to the market quotes in this case would not result in a valid density—the density shown here is the result of a constrained optimisation as suggested by [27]. Difficulties are encountered in particular in fitting the senior tranche spread—this appears to be a problem common to most (possibly all) variations of the Vasicek factor

---

[14] E.g., Powell's method (see [26]) modified as in [27].

TABLE 8.2 Calibration to ITRX.EUR 2 Tranche Quotes on March 21, 2005

	Market		Gram/Charlier 4		Gram/Charlier 6	
	Upfront (pts)	Spread (bp)				
Subordination	Mid	Mid	Upfront	Spread	Upfront	Spread
0%	17.5	500.00	17.36	500.00	17.39	500.00
3%	0.0	112.50	0.00	112.38	0.00	112.63
6%	0.0	36.13	0.00	35.69	0.00	34.95
9%	0.0	18.00	0.00	19.28	0.00	20.03
12%	0.0	10.00	0.00	6.27	0.00	7.20
22%						
Latent variable correlation coefficient β^2:			18.19%		18.22%	
Skewness:			0.5438		0.3929	
Excess kurtosis:			2.3856		1.9772	
Fifth moment about the mean:					2.6704	
Excess[15] sixth moment about the mean:					29.8882	

approach.[16] Adding a fifth and sixth moment to the expansion improves the situation somewhat and also smoothes the resulting density more toward the unimodal, as can be seen in Figure 8.2 (the thick line represents the higher-order fit).

A similar result is obtained for more recent data, as reported for July 2, 2007 in Table 8.3. Again, the fit via an implied factor distribution is difficult in particular for the most senior tranche, where calibrated spreads are too low. Adding a fifth and sixth moment to the expansion allows us to increase the model spread for the most senior tranche, but at the cost of radically changing the factor distribution: As Figure 8.3 shows, the Gram/Charlier four-moment fit (the nonnormal density plotted with a thin line) is very similar in shape to the March 21, 2005 result, while the six-moment fit (the thick line) is substantially different.[17]

---

[15] "Excess" is to be interpreted in a manner analogous to excess kurtosis, that is, the number quoted is the excess of the sixth moment about the mean above the corresponding moment of the standard normal distribution, which in this case is 15.
[16] We obtained similar results using other distributional assumptions on the common factor, including the normal inverse Gaussian along similar lines as [10] and [18].
[17] One can argue that this might be due to overfitting, as can be avoided by changing the weighting of the individual tranches in the objective function for the minimisation. For the results reproduced here, the relative pricing error for each tranche was weighted equally.

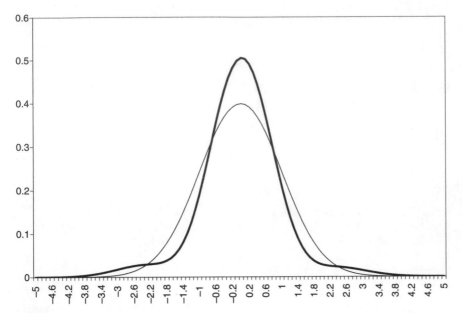

FIGURE 8.1 CDX data example. Fitted (thick line) versus normal densities.

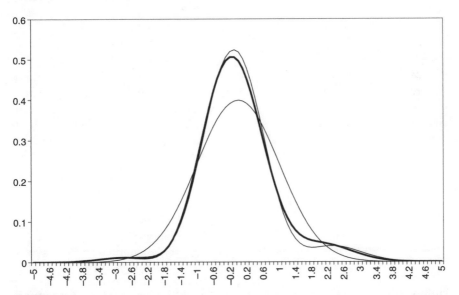

FIGURE 8.2 ITRAXX data example. Fitted (thick line) versus normal densities.

TABLE 8.3 Calibration to ITRX.EUR 2 Tranche Quotes on July 2, 2007

| | Market | | Gram/Charlier 4 | | Gram/Charlier 6 | |
| | Upfront (pts) | Spread (bp) | | | | |
Subordination	Mid	Mid	Upfront	Spread	Upfront	Spread
0%	13.01	500.00	12.74	500.00	12.89	500.00
3%	0.00	67.10	0.00	62.87	0.00	72.68
6%	0.00	17.93	0.00	16.86	0.00	15.17
9%	0.00	8.34	0.00	8.26	0.00	10.70
12%	0.00	3.28	0.00	0.99	0.00	1.33
22%						

Latent variable correlation coefficient β^2:	14.60%	14.49%
Skewness:	0.6886	−0.0047
Excess kurtosis:	2.3650	1.2638
Fifth moment about the mean:		−0.7185
Excess sixth moment about the mean:		30.5882

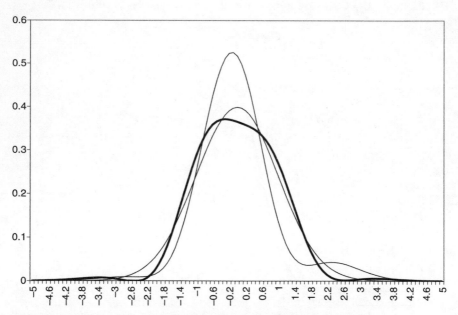

FIGURE 8.3 ITRAXX implied factor distribution for July 2, 2007.

One should also note that during the period of considerable turmoil in the credit markets (from August 2007) the quality of the fit deteriorated markedly (results not reported here), and it is a matter of further research whether this market situation can be accurately mirrored by any of the existing models, in particular those based on the one-factor approach.

8.3.2 Interpolation of Implied and Base Correlation

By fitting the factor distribution to the tranche spreads quoted in the market, we are essentially subsuming all departures from the flat correlation single-factor Gaussian model in the implied factor distribution. As such, the implied factor distribution is specific to the underlying portfolio, which limits the applicability—in the same way a risk-neutral distribution extracted from, say, S&P 500 index option prices is applicable only to that particular index. In practical terms, such implied distributions are useful for interpolating prices (or implied volatility/correlation) in a manner consistent with the absence of arbitrage. This is what is involved when pricing nonstandard tranches on the index portfolios.

The question that one might therefore ask is: Does the implied factor distribution also deal well with situations where the "implied correlation smile" is caused by influences *other* than nonnormality of the common factor? [22] identify heterogeneity in correlation and spreads as one of the potential causes of an "implied correlation smile." This motivates the following experiment: On a portfolio of 100 names, vary the CDS spreads between 30 and 300 basis points, and vary the β between 20 percent and 47.5 percent, (higher spread names have higher correlations). Calculate the "correct" spreads using a Gaussian model with the heterogeneous correlations, and then fit the (flat correlation) Gram/Charlier model to the standard tranches. The result of this calibration is given in Table 8.4. Then, calculate the spreads for nonstandard tranches using the previously fitted Gram/Charlier model and compare these with the correct spreads. As Table 8.5 shows, the spreads calculated using the fitted model agree very closely with those given by the postulated "correct" model, demonstrating that the portfolio heterogeneity has been absorbed well into the modified distribution of the common factor.[18]

---

[18] Incidentally, the numbers in Tables 8.4 and 8.5 also demonstrate a fact well-known to practitioners: The nonmonotonicity and relative instability of implied correlation for mezzanine tranches implies that if one does choose to interpolate the "correlation smile" directly, one should do this at the level of base correlation, rather than the

TABLE 8.4   Standard Tranches, Heterogeneous Portfolio

		Compound and base correlation as defined in [24]				
		Correlation		Gram/Charlier Fit		
Subordination	Actual Spread	Compound	Base	Spread	Compound Corr.	Base Corr.
0%	8170.34	13.72%	13.72%	8170.45	13.72%	13.72%
3%	2391.05	13.42%	13.54%	2390.92	13.42%	13.54%
7%	1172.06	12.67%	13.36%	1172.65	12.64%	13.37%
10%	568.41	17.72%	13.01%	567.6	17.26%	13.10%
15%	97.46	13.10%	11.71%	98.07	13.21%	12.41%
30%						

TABLE 8.5   Nonstandard Tranches, Heterogeneous Portfolio

		Correlation		Gram/Charlier Fit		
Subordination	Actual Spread	Compound	Base	Spread	Compound Corr.	Base Corr.
0%	5081.53	13.64%	13.64%	5082.33	13.64%	13.64%
5%	1428.59	13.00%	13.36%	1428.94	12.98%	13.37%
10%	739.64	7.27%	13.23%	739.58	7.30 %	13.26%
12%	463.83	15.08%	13.01%	462.59	14.81%	13.10%
15%	58.5	13.01%	10.56%	59.08	13.16%	—
40%						

When applied to market data, the model interpolates (and extrapolates) base correlation in a manner in line with the accuracy of the calibration. Compared to direct interpolation/extrapolation of the base correlation obtained from market quotes, base correlation calculated from a calibrated model has the advantage that it is guaranteed to be consistent with the absence of arbitrage.[19] Figure 8.4 shows the interpolation/extrapolation of base correlation the implied by the model fitted to ITRAXX market data on

---

correlation implied by tranche spreads. Base correlation for a subordination level of x percent is the implied correlation of an equity tranche covering losses from zero to x percent of the CDO notional.

[19] This is not guaranteed in the case of direct interpolation (see [24]).

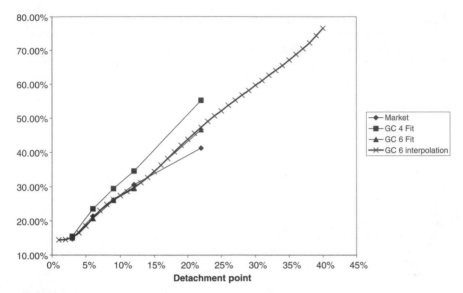

FIGURE 8.4   Interpolated base correlation for July 2, 2007.

July 2, 2007 (i.e., the calibration reported in Table 8.3). At the senior end, the model extrapolates based on the calibration of the most senior tranche (and thus departs substantially from what one would obtain by directly extrapolating the base correlations). At the equity end, directly extrapolating the market base correlations would result in much lower correlations (and thus much lower spreads or up-front payments) than the essentially flat extrapolation implied by the model.

8.4   CONCLUSION

In a way similar to volatility for standard options, (default) correlation is the key parameter for the pricing of CDO tranches, which is not directly observable in the market. As prices for these derivative financial instruments become competitively quoted in the market, values for these parameters can be implied. We have demonstrated how, in a way similar to how one can extract risk-neutral distributions from standard option prices, an implied factor distribution for a CDO pricing model can be constructed in a semiparametric way. Essentially, in the sense that the factor distribution determines the copula of the joint distribution of default times, a default dependence structure has thus been extracted from market quoted tranche spreads.

8.5 APPENDIX: SOME USEFUL RESULTS ON HERMITE POLYNOMIALS UNDER LINEAR COORDINATE TRANSFORMS

We use the definition of Hermite polynomials customary in statistics, as given for example in [19], where they are called "Chebyshev–Hermite polynomials." In the literature these polynomials are usually denoted $\mathrm{He}_i(\cdot)$, as opposed to a slightly different version of Hermite polynomials, which are usually denoted $H_i(x)$ (see e.g., [1]).

Definition 8.2. *The Hermite polynomials* $\mathrm{He}_i(\cdot)$ *are defined by the identity*

$$(-D)^i \phi(x) = \mathrm{He}_i(x)\phi(x) \tag{8.4.1}$$

where

$$D = \frac{d}{dx}$$

is the differential operator and

$$\phi(x) = \frac{1}{\sqrt{2\pi}} e^{-\frac{1}{2}x^2}$$

The following results are reproduced for the reader's convenience. See [27] for proofs.

Lemma 8.3. *The Hermite polynomials* $\mathrm{He}_i(\cdot)$ *satisfy*

$$\mathrm{He}_i(ax+b) = \sum_{j=0}^{i} \binom{i}{j} a^{i-j} \mathrm{He}_{i-j}(x) j! \sum_{m=0}^{\left[\frac{j}{2}\right]} \frac{1}{m! 2^m (j-2m)!} a^{2m} \mathrm{He}_{j-2m}(b)$$

$$\tag{8.4.2}$$

Corollary 8.4. *The Hermite polynomials* $\mathrm{He}_i(\cdot)$ *satisfy*

$$\mathrm{He}_i(y+a) = \sum_{j=0}^{i} \binom{i}{j} \mathrm{He}_{i-j}(y) a^j \tag{8.4.3}$$

$$\mathrm{He}_i(ax) = i! \sum_{m=0}^{\left[\frac{i}{2}\right]} a^{i-2m} \mathrm{He}_{i-2m}(x) \frac{(a^2-1)^m}{(i-2m)! 2^m m!} \tag{8.4.4}$$

Lemma 8.5. *We have for $i \geq 1$*

$$\int_a^b \text{He}_i(y) \frac{1}{\sqrt{2\pi}} e - \frac{(y-\mu)^2}{2} dy = \sum_{j=0}^{i-1} \binom{i}{j} \mu^j (\phi(a-\mu)\text{He}_{i-j-1}(a-\mu)$$

$$-\phi(b-\mu)\text{He}_{i-j-1}(b-\mu)) + \mu^i(\Phi(b-\mu) - \Phi(a-\mu)) \qquad (8.4.5)$$

where $\Phi(\cdot)$ is the cumulative distribution function of the standard normal disribution. If $\mu = 0$ and $i \geq 1$

$$\int_a^b \text{He}_i(y) \frac{1}{\sqrt{2\pi}} e^{-\frac{y^2}{2}} dy = \phi(a)\text{He}_{i-1}(a) - \phi(b)\text{He}_{i-1}(b) \qquad (8.4.6)$$

REFERENCES

1. Abramowitz, M., and I. A. Stegun (eds.). (1964). *Handbook of Mathematical Functions*. National Bureau of Standards.
2. Andersen, L., and J. Sidenius. (2005). Extensions to the Gaussian copula: Random recovery and random factor loadings. *Journal of Credit Risk* 1 (1): 29–70.
3. Andersen, L., J. Sidenius, and S. Basu. (2003). All your hedges in one basket. *Risk* (November): 67–72.
4. Bahra, B. (1997). Implied risk-neutral probability density functions from option prices: Theory and application. Working paper, Bank of England.
5. Black, F., and M. Scholes. (1973). The pricing of options and corporate liabilities. *Journal of Political Economy* 81 (3): 637–654.
6. Breeden, D. T., and R. H. Litzenberger. (1978). Prices of stage-contingent claims implicit in option prices. *Journal of Business* 51 (4): 621–651.
7. Burtschell, X., J. Gregory, and J.-P. Laurent. (2005). A comparative analysis of CDO pricing models. Working paper, BNP Paribas.
8. Corrado, C., and T. Su. (1996). Skewness and kurtosis in S&P 500 index returns implied by option prices. *Journal of Financial Research* 19 (2): 175–192.
9. Duffie, D., and N. Gârleanu. (2001). Risk and the valuation of collateralized debt obligations. *Financial Analysts Journal* 57: 51–59.
10. Guegan, D., and Houdain, J. (2005). Collateralized debt obligations pricing and factor models: A new methodology using normal inverse Gaussian distributions. Working paper 07-2005, IDHE-MORA.
11. Hida, T., H.-H. Kuo, J. Potthoff, and L. Streit. (1993). *White Noise: An Infinite Dimensional Calculus*, Vol. 253 of *Mathematics and Its Applications*. Norwell, MA: Kluwer Academic Publishers.
12. Hull, J., and A. White. (2004). Valuation of a CDO and an nth to default CDS without Monte Carlo simulation. *Journal of Derivatives* 2: 8–23.

13. Hull, J., M. Predescu, and A. White. (2005). The valuation of correlation-dependent credit derivatives using a structural model. Working paper, University of Toronto.
14. Jackwerth, J. C., and M. Rubinstein. (1996). Recovering probability distributions from option prices. *Journal of Finance* 51 (5): 1611–1631.
15. Jarrow, R. A., and S. M. Turnbull. (1995). Pricing derivatives on financial securities subject to credit risk. *Journal of Finance* 50: 53–85.
16. Jondeau, E., and M. Rockinger. (2001). Gram-Charlier densities. *Journal of Economic Dynamics and Control* 25: 1457–1483.
17. Jurczenko, E., B. Maillet, and B. Negrea. (2002). Multi-moment approximate option pricing models: A general comparison (Part 1). Working paper, CNRS—University of Paris I Panthéon-Sorbonne.
18. Kalemanova, A., B. Schmid, and R. Werner. (2007). The normal inverse Gaussian distribution for synthetic CDO pricing. *Journal of Derivatives* 14 (3): 80–93.
19. Kendall, M. G., and A. Stuart. (1969). *The Advanced Theory of Statistics*, 3rd ed., vol. 1. London: Charles Griffin & Company.
20. Kuo, H.-H. (1996). *White Noise Distribution Theory*. Boca Raton, FL: CRC Press.
21. Li, D. X. (2000). On default correlation: A copula function approach. *Journal of Fixed Income* 9 (4): 43–54.
22. Mashal, R., M. Naldi, and G. Tejwani. (2004). The implications of implied correlation. Working paper, Lehman Brothers Quantitative Credit Research.
23. Merton, R. C. (1974). On the pricing of corporate debt: The risk structure of interest rates. *Journal of Finance* 29: 449–470.
24. O'Kane, D., and M. Livesey. (2004). Base correlation explained. Working paper, Lehman Brothers Quantitative Credit Research.
25. O'Kane, D., and L. Schlögl. (2005). A note on the large homogeneous portfolio approximation with the Student-t copula. *Finance and Stochastics* 9 (4): 577–584.
26. Press, W. H., S. A. Teukolsky, W. T. Vetterling, and B. P. Flannery. (1992). *Numerical Recipes in C: The Art of Scientific Computing*, 2nd ed. Cambridge: Cambridge University Press.
27. Schlögl, E. (2008). Option pricing where the underlying asset follows a Gram-Charlier density of arbitrary order. Working paper, Quantitative Finance Research Centre, University of Technology, Sydney.
28. Schönbucher, P., and D. Schubert. (2001). Copula dependent default risk in intensity models. Working paper, University of Bonn.
29. Schönbucher, P. J. (2003). *Credit Derivatives Pricing Models: Models, Pricing and Implementation*. Hoboken, NJ: John Wiley & Sons.
30. Schönbucher, P. J. (2006). Portfolio losses and the term structure of loss transition rates: A new methodology for the pricing of portfiolio credit derivatives. Working paper, ETH Zürich.
31. Vasicek, O. (1987). Probability of loss on loan portfolio. Working paper, KMV Corporation.

CHAPTER 9

Pricing CDOs with a Smile: The Local Correlation Model

Julien Turc and Philippe Very

We introduce a new model for pricing collateralized debt obligations (CDOs) using ideas derived from the equity derivatives market. It introduces, in particular, a so-called local correlation function that fits to the correlation smile. This framework is well suited to the pricing of exotic CDOs and CDOs squared according to this smile. This chapter is based on joint work with David Benhamou, Benjamin Herzog, and Marc Teyssier, who are quantitative analysts in the Quantitative Credit Strategy team at Societe Generale Corporate and Investment Bank. Whereas the Gaussian copula model has become the established way to price correlation products, the market has felt the need to create a coherent framework in which both index tranches and nonstandard CDOs such as bespoke single tranches and CDOs squared could be valued. The Gaussian copula model does not provide an adequate solution for pricing simultaneously various tranches of an index, nor for adjusting correlation against the level of credit spreads. Recent research has explored some of the ways to account for the so-called correlation smile. Among these attempts, the most successful ones make correlation a function of the systemic factor (that we call the economy). Practitioners on their side have built rule-of-thumb techniques for pricing bespoke and exotic CDOs. In order to bridge the gap between quantitative research and practical CDO management, we suggest applying simple ideas that are already widely used on equity derivative markets.

In the first section, we introduce the local correlation model and compare it with local volatility models for equity derivatives.

In the second section, we present a technique for deducing the local correlation from the base correlation skew under the large pool assumption.

In the third section we present a process for fitting the local correlation curve directly to market data without the large pool assumption.

In the fourth section, we compare market practice for pricing and hedging CDOs to the local correlation model. We present the results of the fitting process and give first numerical results in terms of both marked-to-market and hedge ratios.

9.1 THE LOCAL CORRELATION MODEL

9.1.1 Correlation Becomes a Function of the Economy

Many ideas have been proposed to build correlation smile curves close to those observed in the index tranche market. The most promising approach, in our view, is to make correlation a random variable itself, by making it a function of the economy (the systemic factor). We suggest adopting a descriptive approach and starting from market observations to specify the correlation model.

In the one-factor model, the value A_j of each company in the index basket is the sum of two uncorrelated random normal variables: a systemic factor X representing the economy and an idiosyncratic factor Z_j. If the correlation is a function of the economy, the relationship between these three variables is:

$$A_j = -X\sqrt{\rho(X)} + Z_j\sqrt{1 - \rho(X)}$$

A default occurs when the value A_j of the firm goes below a given threshold s. Moreover, high values of X correspond to states of the economy with higher probabilities of default.

In the standard Gaussian copula framework (see [4] or [3]), ρ is constant and does not depend on X. We do not give any particular form to the local correlation function but we imply it directly from spreads of liquid index tranches.

The Individual Asset Value Law Is No Longer Gaussian If we consider a homogeneous portfolio, all the names have an identical default probability function p. All their asset values A_j have the same cumulative function G. This function is the Gaussian cumulative function in the Gaussian copula framework. It is not the case anymore in the local correlation framework and it is equal to:

$$G(s) = Q\{A_j \leq s\} = \int N\left(\frac{s + X\sqrt{\rho(X)}}{\sqrt{1 - \rho(X)}}\right)\varphi(X)dX \qquad (9.1.1)$$

where Q is the risk neutral probability, N the cumulative normal distribution, and φ the normal distribution.

This formula shows that G depends on ρ.

Pricing a CDO in the Local Correlation Framework The process of pricing a CDO with local correlation is very similar to the Gaussian copula framework. More precisely, it implies computing the expected loss at each coupon payment date and at maturity with the following three-step process:

1. Compute the individual default probability p_j of each name in the basket.
2. Invert these probabilities to deduce the threshold s_j such that $G(s_j) = p_j$.
3. Compute the expected loss EL by numerically integrating $EL(X,\rho)$, the expected loss given the state of the economy X, then:

$$EL = \int_X EL(X, \rho(X))\varphi(X)dX$$

The first step is exactly the same as in the Gaussian copula framework. The second is not as straightforward since we need to invert the G function which is no longer the normal distribution N. Nevertheless, in practice, G is very close to N and the two functions give almost the same thresholds. So we can use the value found for the Gaussian copula model as an approximation of the actual threshold. Based on this guess, we can use a root-finding algorithm to imply in few iterations the actual threshold in the local correlation framework. Finally, the integration done in the last step is the same as in the Gaussian copula framework: we discretize it using a numerical scheme, for instance a Gaussian quadrature (for more details, see [5]). The only difference lies in the fact that we need to use a different correlation at each step of the discretization, but this has no impact in terms of computation time.

Impact of a Correlation Shock on the Asset Density Now that we are able to price a basket tranche based on a local correlation function, let us look at the impact of a correlation shock on the asset density in order to better understand the influence of the correlation function.

We show in Figure 9.1 the impact of a 10 percent increase of the correlation function on a flat correlation smile at different states of the economy

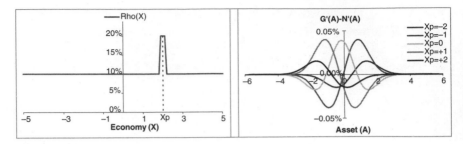

FIGURE 9.1 A correlation shock modifies the asset density.

X_p. The right-hand graph represents the difference between the actual asset density and the Gaussian density. Without any shock, this difference would be zero as the distribution G would be Gaussian. Increasing the correlation function at X_p increases the likelihood of the asset to be around $-X_p$ since for these states of the economy the asset is more correlated with the economy. For instance, when the correlation increases at $X_p = 2$, the probability of the asset to be around -2 is higher than for a normal distribution.

More generally, an increasing correlation function for extreme states of the economy generates an asset density with a fatter tail ($X_p > 1$ or $X_p < -1$). Conversely, if the correlation function is higher for a mid-level of the economy ($X_p = 0$), the probability of extreme events decreases.

Understanding the Sensitivity of Tranches to a Correlation Shock Figure 9.2 shows the impact of the same correlation shock as in the previous paragraph but on the model spread of 5y index tranches for different strikes. It represents the change in model spread for correlation shocks at different states X_p of the economy.

First of all, the sensitivity of tranches to a local increase in correlation is the same as in the base correlation framework: the equity tranche has a negative sensitivity to a correlation while the sensitivity of more senior tranches is positive. Furthermore, we see that shocks simulated for very healthy economies ($X_p < -3$) have no impact on the spread of all tranches since these types of scenarios correspond to an economy where defaults are very unlikely. Another effect one can observe on these graphs is the so-called toothpaste effect: because the expected loss of a 0 percent to 100 percent tranche does not depend on correlation, when the expected loss of one tranche increases or, equivalently, when its spread increases, the spread of other tranches decreases mechanically. That is why the sensitivity of the 5y equity tranche is the opposite of the sum of the sensitivities of all other tranches.

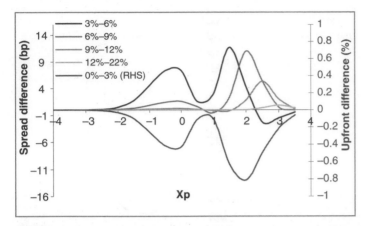

FIGURE 9.2 A correlation shock modifies the spread of each tranche.

Finally, the last noticeable phenomenon is a strong nonlinearity at $X_p \approx$ 0.75: the sensitivity of each tranche to a correlation shock seems to vanish in this area. This is explained by two contradictory effects:

1. *A correlation effect.* This is the usual effect of a correlation increase; the expected loss of senior tranches increases while it decreases for the equity tranche.
2. *A threshold effect.* A shock in local correlation modifies the asset density. Consequently, the threshold corresponding to a default is modified in order to keep the marginal probability of default of each issuer constant. For a shock at $X_p \approx 0$, the marginal distribution of the A_j has thinner tails and the default threshold decreases. For a shock at $X_p > 2$, the marginal distribution has a fatter tail and the default threshold increases.

Figure 9.3 shows the difference between the density of losses with a correlation shock and without it. For a shock at $X_p \approx 0$, the former effect dominates: the correlation in the most likely scenario, that is, when the economy is in a normal state, has increased and the likelihood of losses corresponding to senior tranches ($L > 3$ percent) has increased at the expense of more junior tranches ($L < 3$ percent). For a shock at $X_p \approx 2$, the distribution of the firm values A_j has a fatter tail on the default side ($A_j < 0$) and the threshold of default has therefore increased. For a normal economy ($X < 2$), since the correlation has not changed but the threshold of default increased, the likelihood of very few defaults ($L < 2$ percent) is higher, while

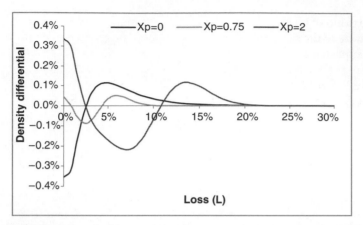

FIGURE 9.3 Impact of a correlation shock on the density of losses.

the probability of some defaults is smaller (2 percent $< L <$ 10 percent). For more extreme scenarios ($L >$ 10 percent), the increase in correlation for bad states of the economy makes extreme losses more likely and the correlation effect becomes preponderant. For a shock at $X_p \approx 0.75$, the two effects offset one another and the density of losses remains roughly stable. That is why spreads have a very small sensitivity to correlation in this area.

Local Volatility versus Local Correlation There is a striking similarity between our model and local volatility models used by equity derivatives traders to cope with the deficiencies of the Black-Scholes formula. The local volatility model (see [1]) manages to fit to the implied volatility smile by making volatility a function of the underlying stock. Here, our approach fits to the correlation smile by making correlation a function of the systemic factor.

9.2 SIMPLIFICATION UNDER THE LARGE POOL ASSUMPTION

In a limit case, on a very large and homogeneous portfolio, it is relatively simple to extract information on the level of correlation from the implied distribution of default losses.

The "large pool" approximation (see [6]) assumes that the underlying basket is large and homogeneous enough to be considered as a perfectly diversified portfolio of identical assets. This has a dramatic implication here: knowing the state of the economy, the loss suffered on the portfolio is simply given by the expected loss on a single company, handling the portfolio as such single issuer. This implies that, conditional to the state of the economy, the loss suffered on a large and homogeneous portfolio is given by the level of conditional default risk.

Under the large pool assumption, all the names have an identical default probability p. All their asset values A_j have the same cumulative function G. This function is the Gaussian cumulative function in the Gaussian copula framework. It is not the case anymore in the local correlation framework.

Using the law of large numbers, the cumulative loss function is given by:

$$L(K|X) = 1\left\{(1-\delta)Q\left(-X\sqrt{\rho(X)} + Z_j\sqrt{1-\rho(X)} \le G^{-1}(p)\right) \le K\right\}$$

where δ is the recovery rate and Q the risk neutral default.

Note $\varepsilon(x) = \frac{G^{-1}(p) + x\sqrt{\rho(x)}}{\sqrt{1-\rho(x)}}$ the individual default threshold conditional to the economy. We have: $L(K|X) = 1\left\{N(\varepsilon(X)) \le \frac{K}{1-\delta}\right\}$.

So, in a given state of the economy, the level of losses on the portfolio is deterministic and given by the level of individual default risk conditional to that economy. But this conditional risk depends only on the economy itself. Therefore, for each strike, there is only one state of the economy that triggers a level of losses just as high as the strike. We propose to associate to each strike this state of the economy, and reciprocally.

Mathematically, for each strike K, this state of the economy x_K is such that $N(\varepsilon(x_K)) = \frac{K}{1-\delta}$ or:

$$x_K = \varepsilon^{-1} \circ N^{-1}\left(\frac{K}{1-\delta}\right) \tag{9.2.1}$$

Furthermore, the cumulative loss is given by $L(K) = Q\{N(\varepsilon(X)) \le \frac{K}{1-\delta}\}$, so:

$$L(K) = N(x_K) \tag{9.2.2}$$

Local correlation can be interpreted as a marginal compound correlation under the large pool assumption.

Compound correlation is usually defined for traded CDO tranches as the correlation level that gives the right tranche spread when applied to both lower and higher attachment points of the tranche. We define the marginal compound correlation as the compound correlation of an infinitesimal piece centred on a given strike. For example, the marginal compound correlation at 6 percent would be the correlation of a mezzanine tranche with attachment points 6 percent and, say, 6.1 percent. Such a tiny CDO tranche can be viewed as a product that triggers a 100 percent loss should default losses exceed the strike, and involves no protection payment otherwise.

The expected loss of the infinitesimal $[K, K + dK]$ tranche is worth $L(K)dK$. Let's define ρ_K^M as the marginal compound correlation at strike K that is the compound correlation that gives the same expected loss as in the local correlation model, that is, such that: $L(K) = L(K, \rho_K^M)$.

But, using 9.2.1 and 9.2.2:

$$N^{-1}\left(\frac{K}{1-\delta}\right) = \varepsilon(x_K) = \frac{G^{-1}(p) + x_K\sqrt{\rho(x_K)}}{\sqrt{1-\rho(x_K)}} \text{ with } x_K = N^{-1}(L(K))$$

Whereas in the compound correlation framework and under the large pool assumption:

$$N^{-1}\left(\frac{K}{1-\delta}\right) = \varepsilon\left(x_K^M\right) = \frac{N^{-1}(p) + x_K^M\sqrt{\rho_K^M}}{\sqrt{1-\rho_K^M}} \text{ with } x_K^M = N^{-1}\left(L\left(K, \rho_K^M\right)\right) = x_K$$

If we assume that the asset value is Gaussian (that is $G = N$, which is almost true in practice), then the two expressions above are equal if and only if:

$$\rho(x_K) = \rho_K^M \tag{9.2.3}$$

The relationship between local and marginal compound correlation is of no practical use in itself, because tiny CDO tranches are not traded on the market. However, this relationship is extremely useful because it gives a concrete meaning to local correlation, as the correlation of a tiny CDO tranche. Moreover, it exhibits a mapping between strikes and the state of the economy, thereby making the model more concrete.

Furthermore, this gives a quick methodology for computing a local correlation function. Based on an interpolated base correlation smile, we can compute for each strike the loss function $L(K)$ and deduce the mapping between the universe of strikes and the economy (using 9.2.2). Then, we can directly imply the local correlation function according to this mapping. Indeed, if asset values are Gaussian, then the ε function depends only on

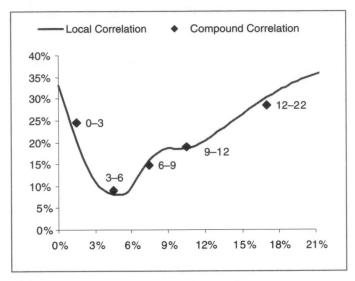

FIGURE 9.4 In the large pool framework, the local correlation curve is close to the compound correlation market data.

the local correlation at x_k so the correlation $\rho(x_k)$ can be deduced thanks to an equation (4) by solving a second degree polynomial equation. Following is an example of the local correlation curve obtained with this method. It shows that the local correlation curve is close to the compound correlation market data.

9.3 BUILDING THE LOCAL CORRELATION FUNCTION WITHOUT THE LARGE POOL ASSUMPTION

All the results in the last section have been deduced under the large pool assumption. It does not seem possible to build a simple one-to-one relationship between local and marginal compound correlation in the general case. Nevertheless, we think that the mapping of the economy into a strike helps design a parametric local correlation in a more natural and easy way. Moreover, our study gives a rough but good idea of the shape of local correlation and highlights its proximity with the compound correlations observed in the market. It seems to us that the finite size of the portfolio and the dispersion effect introduced by the heterogeneousness of the entities do not create a major change in the structure of the local correlation.

In practice, to use this model we need to define a parameterization of the local correlation function and fit its parameters so that the prices given by the model are in line with the prices of standard tranches in the market. This optimization problem is far from obvious: we need to have at least five degrees of freedom in the space of possible correlation function since we want the model to price the five standard tranches. Moreover, this 5D optimization problem is not separable. Indeed, for a finite portfolio, changing one point of the local correlation function affects the model price of all tranches and we cannot imply each parameter independently. Finally, as we saw in the first part of this chapter, tranche spreads are strongly nonlinear with respect to the correlation function. Consequently, the optimization will have to avoid local minima in order to fit the model to market spreads.

To avoid these obstacles we need to have a good guess of the local correlation function. Using the mapping between strike and economy, the compound correlation provides a good approximation of the local correlation function. With this estimate as an initial guess, fitting the local correlation function becomes tractable.

A Process for Estimating Local Correlation   The process for fitting the local correlation curve can be divided into two steps:

I: Finding a mapping from the economy into a strike $K(X)$
- Extrapolate and interpolate the base correlation smile using market base correlations.
- Compute the cumulative loss function $L(K)$ for each possible strike K.
- Imply the mapping of the economy into a strike $K(X)$ using the large pool assumption.

II: Implying the local correlation function $\rho(X)$
- Parameterize the local correlation curve $\rho(K)$ in the strike world.
- Deduce the local correlation curve $\rho(X)$ as a function of the economy.

Finding the Mapping of the Economy into a Strike (I)   The market for standard tranches provides with five different quotes and therefore five data points in the base correlation smile. The whole correlation smile for all strikes (ranging from 0 percent to 100 percent) is necessary to determine the mapping of the economy into a strike. It is therefore necessary to interpolate and extrapolate the existing data points.

In the large pool framework there is a simple formula that links the distribution of portfolio losses and the base correlation smile (see 9.2.2). It implies being able to compute the cumulative loss $L(K)$ for each strike K, taking the base correlation smile into account. Defining EL_k as the expected loss of the [0,K] equity tranche, the cumulative loss function satisfies:

$$EL_K = \int_0^K xdL(x) + K(1 - L(K)) = K - \int_0^K L(x)dx$$

and therefore, $\frac{\partial EL_K}{\partial K} = 1 - L(K)$.

Let's now define $L(K, \rho_K^B)$ the naive cumulative loss function in the base correlation methodology (ρ_K^B being the [0,K] base correlations). By definition, the expected loss can be expressed as:

$$EL_K = \int_0^K xdL\left(x, \rho_K^B\right) + K\left(1 - L\left(K, \rho_K^B\right)\right) = K - \int_0^K L\left(x, \rho_K^B\right) dx$$

and therefore:

$$\frac{\partial EL_K}{\partial K} = 1 - L\left(K, \rho_K^B\right) - \frac{\partial \rho_K^B}{\partial K} \int_0^K \frac{\partial L}{\partial \rho}\left(x, \rho_K^B\right) dx$$

$$= 1 - L\left(K, \rho_K^B\right) - \frac{\partial \rho_K^B}{\partial K} \frac{\partial EL_K}{\partial \rho_K^B}$$

If we call $Rho(K, \rho_K^B)$ the sensitivity of the [0,K] tranche expected loss to a change in correlation and $Skew(K, \rho_K^B)$ the slope of the correlation smile at strike K, we find the following expression for the cumulative loss adjusted by the correlation smile:

$$L(K) = L\left(K, \rho_K^B\right) - Skew\left(K, \rho_K^B\right) * Rho\left(K, \rho_K^B\right)$$

Based on this result, we can compute the mapping between strike and economy under the large pool assumption using 9.2.1. Not all base correlation smiles are consistent with this kind of mapping. Some of them give a mapping that is not strictly increasing, which is not acceptable. The two main characteristics that are required to give an appropriate mapping are sufficient regularity (at least continuous first derivatives so that a skew can be computed) and not too much concavity because concavity means a sharply decreasing base correlation skew and therefore a cumulative loss that can be negative.

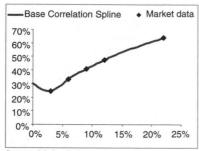

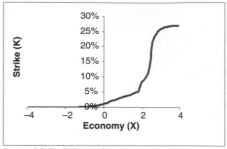

Source: SG Credit Research

Source: SG Credit Research

FIGURE 9.5 The whole base correlation smile is necessary to compute the mapping of the economy into a strike.

Figure 9.5 is an example of an extrapolated base correlation smile. In the right-hand graph we have plotted the corresponding mapping of the economy into a strike. We used a cubic-spline interpolation of the base correlation between two market strikes because it gave a sufficient amount of freedom to ensure the continuity of the first derivative of the base correlation smile. For the extrapolated part ($K < 3$ percent and $K > 22$ percent), we used the value of the correlation such that $L(K)$ remains a valid cumulative distribution (i.e. monotonically increasing).

Implying the Local Correlation Function (II) We chose to parameterize the local correlation curve as a function of the strike since it is much easier to interpret the curve and find fitting guesses for these parameters in this framework. This is the real added value of the mapping process. A natural guess for the initial parametrization of the correlation function is to use the corresponding compound correlation. Using a root-finding algorithm, we can then imply the local correlation which fits the model price to the market data for each standard tranche.

Pricing Bespoke CDO in the Local Correlation Framework Once the local correlation curve is determined as a function of the strike, it is easy to transform it into a function of the economy using the mapping $K(X)$. Figure 9.6 is an example of a local correlation curve resulting from this parameterization. The corresponding local correlation curve as a function of the economy is shown on the right-hand graph. These two graphs correspond to the local correlation curves as of May 5, 2005.

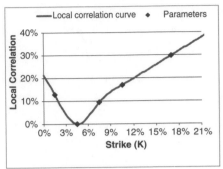

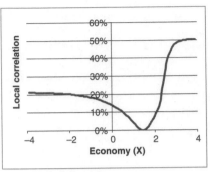

Source: SG Credit Research Source: SG Credit Research

FIGURE 9.6 The local correlation curve is parameterized as a function of the strike but can be seen as a function of the economy.

9.4 PRICING AND HEDGING WITH LOCAL CORRELATION

9.4.1 Local Correlation as a Constant across Different Portfolios

One of the main issues arising from the evolution of structured products is the pricing of nonstandard CDOs and CDOs squared. Such a valuation has to take into account the particular form of the correlation smile seen on the market. A few rules of thumb have emerged among practitioners for pricing nonstandard CDOs within the Gaussian copula framework (see [2]). By contrast, the local correlation model is well suited to pricing CDOs squared in a way that is consistent with the quoted prices in the correlation market.

Pricing nonstandard products with local correlation is indeed very simple. Local correlation may be viewed as a kind of universal constant that is not dependent on a particular portfolio. Once the local correlation function is estimated on index tranches, one can apply this structure to bespoke CDOs using the mapping of the state-of-the-economy factor into a strike.

Within the large pool framework and with the assumption that the asset value is Gaussian, the marginal compound correlation of a bespoke tranche of strike K is using 9.2.3:

$$\rho_{bespoke}(K) = \rho\left(x_K^M\right) = \rho \circ N^{-1} \circ L_{bespoke}(K) \qquad (9.4.1)$$

Although this relationship is only true under restrictive assumptions, it helps to understand the way the local correlation model adjusts for the change in the underlying portfolio.

A New Definition of Equivalent Tranches   There has been some debate on how base correlation should be adjusted from an index into a portfolio with a higher spread. In the base correlation framework, the most basic approach is to choose the correlation of the index tranche with the same strike as the bespoke CDO. This technique is called the *moneyness approach*.

The local correlation model directly characterizes equivalent tranches thanks to the cumulative loss function (L). From 9.4.1, identical correlations are given to strikes that have the same probability to be exceeded by the global loss of the portfolio. In more mathematical terms, the marginal correlation used when pricing a bespoke of strike K^B is the same as the index tranche of strike K^I such that $L_{Index}(K^I) = L_{bespoke}(K^B)$. We think that this specification is more coherent as it captures the nonlinearity of losses in a credit portfolio.

Implementing a probability-matching approach in the base correlation framework is quite complicated because this means being able to imply an equivalent strike using a root-finding algorithm. In the local correlation framework, once the correlation function is fitted to the index tranches, the model will naturally price any bespoke CDO according to the probability matching rule under the large pool assumption.

In Table 9.1 we give a list of the prices of different baskets with different portfolios using the base and the local correlation method. All the spreads from the index (with an average premium of 40 bp) have been shifted to give the portfolios more or less risk.

Results are significantly different, which is not surprising as methods have different definitions of subordination. The dynamics of subordination

TABLE 9.1   Comparison of Both Methods for Different Portfolios

Portfolio Premium	Base Correlation Approach	Local Correlation Approach
20 bp	40 bp	54 bp
30 bp	82 bp	91 bp
40 bp	149 bp	149 bp
50 bp	260 bp	230 bp

Source: SG Credit Research.

are less pronounced with the local correlation curve as it takes into account the convexity of the loss function.

The Correlation Roll-Down The correlation smile should have an impact on hedge ratios. A rise in spread is to some extent akin to a loss in subordination, so that a mezzanine tranche "rolls down" on the smile when spreads increase. If the CDO is senior enough, this roll-down effect leads to a decrease in compound correlation, and therefore an appreciation in the marked-to-market of the product. This mitigates the negative effect of the spread increase, and decreases the amount of CDS required to delta hedge the trade.

Deltas computed by the local correlation model take into account this roll-down effect. Table 9.2 compares leverages computed with the compound, base, and local correlation approaches.

We see that the results are substantially different. The gap between the compound and the local correlation approach is due to the roll-down effect. This effect depends directly on the sensitivity to the compound correlation but also on the slope of the marginal compound correlation curve and the sensitivity of the strike to changes in individual spreads. We obtain:

$$\Delta = \Delta_{Implied} + Rho * slope * \frac{\partial K}{\partial Spreads}$$

This adjustment is very similar to the adjustments made on equity derivative products. Equity traders usually adjust the Black-Scholes delta by the product of the vega of the option and the slope of the volatility smile. This usually leads to lower hedge ratios compared to the standard Black-Scholes formula. In these markets, the local volatility model manages to capture this roll-down effect on the volatility curve.

TABLE 9.2 Leverage Computations for Different Models

Leverage	0–3%	3–6%	6–9%	9–12%	12–22%
Compound correlations	18.4	10.1	3.4	2.0	0.9
Base correlations	18.4	6.3	2.5	1.6	0.7
Local correlations	20.6	6.9	1.3	0.8	0.5

Leverage is the nominal of the CDS index required to hedge CDO tranches against spread changes on the index level.
Source: SG Credit Research.

REFERENCES

1. Dupire, B. (1994). Pricing with a smile. *Risk* (January).
2. Jeffery, C. (2006). Credit model meltdown. *Risk* (November).
3. Laurent, J.-P., and J. Gregory. (2002). Basket default swaps, CDOs and factor copulas. (October).
4. Li, D. X. (2000). On default correlation: a copula approach. *Journal of Fixed Income* (March).
5. Andersen, L., and J. Sidenius. (2004). Extensions to the Gaussian copula: random recovery and random factor loadings. *Journal of Credit Risk*.
6. Vasicek, O. (1987). Probability of loss on a loan portfolio. *Moody's KMV* (February).

CHAPTER 10

Portfolio Credit Risk: Top-Down versus Bottom-Up Approaches

Kay Giesecke

Dynamic reduced-form models of portfolio credit risk can be distinguished by the way in which the intensity of the default process is specified. In a bottom-up model, the portfolio intensity is an aggregate of the constituent intensities. In a top-down model, the portfolio intensity is specified without reference to the constituents. This expository chapter contrasts these modeling approaches. It emphasizes the role of the information filtration as a modeling tool.

10.1 INTRODUCTION

A model of portfolio credit risk has three elements: a filtration that represents the observable information, a default process that counts events in the portfolio and a distribution for the financial loss at an event. Reduced-form models of portfolio credit risk can be distinguished by the way in which the intensity of the default process is specified. In a *bottom-up* model, the portfolio intensity is an aggregate of the constituent intensities. In a *top-down* model, the portfolio intensity is specified without reference to the constituents. The constituent intensities are recovered by random thinning. This expository chapter contrasts the two modeling approaches.

10.2 PORTFOLIO CREDIT MODELS

Consider a portfolio of credit sensitive securities such as loans, bonds or credit swaps. The ordered portfolio default times are represented by a sequence of stopping times $T^n > 0$ that is strictly increasing to infinity and defined on a complete probability space $(\Omega, \mathcal{F}, P)$ with a right-continuous and complete filtration $\mathbb{F} = (\mathcal{F}_t)_{t\geq 0}$ that represents the information flow. The random variable T^n represents the nth default time in the portfolio. Depending on the context, P can be the actual probability or a risk-neutral measure. Let N be the process that counts default events, given by

$$N_t = \sum_{n\geq 1} 1_{\{T^n \leq t\}}. \tag{10.2.1}$$

A portfolio credit model is a specification of the filtration $\mathbb{F}$, default process N, and distribution for the loss at an event. For a given filtration, the default process N is specified in terms of its compensator, which is the nondecreasing predictable process A such that $N - A$ is a local martingale. The compensator embodies the expected upward tendency of the default process. [39] shows that in the limit,

$$A_t = \lim_{\epsilon \downarrow 0} \frac{1}{\epsilon} \int_0^t E\left[N_{s+\epsilon} - N_s | \mathcal{F}_s\right] ds \tag{10.2.2}$$

weakly in L^1. Formula (10.2.2) emphasizes the dependence of the compensator on the filtration. The filtration, the probabilistic properties of the default times, and the analytic properties of the compensator are closely related. If the times are predictable, that is, if an event is announced by a sequence of predefault times, then A is equal to N. As an example, consider the familiar first passage credit models that descend from [3]. Here, a firm defaults if its continuous firm value process falls below a constant barrier. This definition of the default event generates a predictable default time. If, as in [14] or [21], the available information is insufficient to determine the precise value of the firm's assets or default barrier, then the default times are totally inaccessible or unpredictable. In this case, defaults come without warning and the compensator A is continuous. Unpredictable default times can conveniently be specified in terms of a nonnegative, adapted *intensity* λ that satisfies

$$A_t = \int_0^t \lambda_s \, ds, \tag{10.2.3}$$

almost surely. Together, formulae (10.2.2) and (10.2.3) show that the intensity is the conditional portfolio default rate in the sense that $\lambda_t \Delta$ is approximately equal to $P[N_{t+\Delta} - N_t = 1 | \mathcal{F}_t]$ for small Δ. If the compensator is of the form (10.2.3), then portfolio credit model is intensity based. In a top-down model the process λ is specified directly. In a bottom-up model, λ is an aggregate of constituent intensity processes.

10.3 INFORMATION AND SPECIFICATION

The structure of the information filtration $\mathbb{F}$ determines the key properties of a portfolio credit model. The filtration must always be fine enough to distinguish the arrival of events. Therefore, the smallest filtration that supports a portfolio credit model is the filtration generated by the default process N itself. Bottom-up and top-down model specifications are based on distinct filtrations, which explains many of the structural differences between them.

10.3.1 Bottom-Up Models

A bottom-up model filtration usually contains much more information than the minimal filtration. It is always fine enough to distinguish the identity of each defaulter so that the constituent default times τ^k are stopping times. The filtration may contain additional information about the prices of single- and multiname derivatives, macroeconomic variables and other systematic and idiosyncratic risk factors.

A constituent default time τ^k generates a default process N^k that is zero before default and one afterward. If the portfolio default process $N = \sum_k N^k$ is intensity based, then so is each constituent default process. In this case, there is a strictly positive intensity process λ^k that represents firm k's conditional default rate in the sense that $N^k - \int_0^{\cdot}(1 - N_s^k)\lambda_s^k ds$ is a martingale.

The researcher specifies the model filtration $\mathbb{F}$ and the constituent intensity processes λ^k. The dependence structure of all firms must be built into each of the constituent intensity processes. Empirical observation suggests distinguishing two sources of firm dependence. First, firms are exposed to common or correlated economic factors such as interest rates or commodity prices. The variation of these factors generates correlated changes in firms' default rates, and the cyclical pattern in the time-series behavior of aggregate default rates. Second, due to the complex web of business, legal, and informational relationships in the economy, defaults have a direct impact on the default rates of the surviving firms. For example, the collapse of automotive manufacturer Delphi in 2005 severely affected General Motors, whose production critically depended on Delphi's timely supply of parts. In response to the event, investors immediately demanded a higher default insurance premium for General Motors, reflecting the sudden increase in GM's likelihood to fail. [6], [32] and [31] show that this episode is not an isolated case.

We illustrate several constituent intensity specifications. Each example specification incorporates different channels for default correlation.

Example 10.1. Let $\mathbb{F}$ be the filtration generated by the constituent default processes. For a deterministic function $c^k > 0$ that models the base intensity, set

$$\lambda^k = c^k + \sum_{j \neq k} \delta^{kj} N^j$$

see [28] and [34]. At each event, a term is added to the intensity that reflects the response of firm k's default rate to the event. The sensitivity of firm k to the default of firm j is modeled by the deterministic function $\delta^{kj} \geq 0$. If these sensitivities are zero, then the intensity varies only deterministically and the constituent default times are independent.

Example 10.2. Let $\mathbb{F}$ be the filtration generated by the constituent default processes, a systematic risk factor X and a collection of idiosyncratic risk factors X^k that are independent of one another and independent of X. For a deterministic function α^k that describes the exposure of firm k to the factor X,

$$\lambda^k = \alpha^k X + X^k \tag{10.3.1}$$

All firms are sensitive to the systematic factor X. Movements of X generate correlated changes in firms' intensities. If the risk factors evolve independently of the firm default processes as in [8], [13], [16], [17], [19] and [40], then the specification (10.3.1) generates a doubly stochastic model. Here, *conditional* on a path of the systematic factor, firms default independently of one another. The specification (10.3.1) can be extended to include multiple common factors that model sectoral, regional or other risks. [41] partition firms into homogeneous groups or sectors, and take (10.3.1) as the common intensity of firms in a given sector k. The factor X induces correlation between sectors. The factor X^k models sector-specific risk.

Example 10.3. Let $\mathbb{F}$ be the filtration generated by the constituent default processes, a systematic risk factor X and a collection of idiosyncratic risk factors X^k that are independent of one another and independent of X. Let

$$\lambda^k = \alpha^k X + X^k + \sum_{j \neq k} \delta^{kj} N^j,$$

see [6], [20], [27], [30], [43] or [44]. This specification incorporates the sensitivity of firms to a common risk factor, and event feedback through the terms that reflect the default status of the firms in the portfolio. The factor sensitivity is ignored in Example 10.1. The doubly stochastic Example 10.2 ignores event feedback.

Example 10.4. Let $\mathbb{F}$ be the filtration generated by the constituent default processes, a systematic risk factor X and a collection of idiosyncratic risk factors X^k that are independent of one another and independent of X. Let U be another systematic risk factor that is not observable (i.e., not adapted to $\mathbb{F}$). This frailty factor must be projected onto $\mathbb{F}$ to obtain an observable process $\hat{U}$ given by $\hat{U}_t = E[U_t|\mathcal{F}_t]$. For a deterministic function δ^k that specifies the exposure of firm k to U,

$$\lambda^k = \alpha^k X + X^k + \delta^k \hat{U}$$

see [5], [12], [10], [23] and [42]. The projection $\hat{U}$ is updated with observable information. In particular, $\hat{U}$ is revised at events since the filtration contains information about firms' default status. Since events are unpredictable, the projection jumps at an event time. A jump corresponds to Bayesian updating of investors' beliefs about the distribution of the frailty factor U. This updating leads to intensity dynamics that are qualitatively similar to those in Example 10.3.

The constituent intensities λ^k determine the portfolio intensity λ. Since the portfolio default process N is the sum over k of the constituent default processes N^k and defaults occur at distinct dates almost surely, the portfolio intensity is given by

$$\lambda = \sum_k (1 - N^k)\lambda^k \tag{10.3.2}$$

see [24, Proposition 5.1]. At each event, a term drops out of the sum. The portfolio intensity λ is zero after all firms have defaulted.

10.3.2 Top-Down Models

In a top-down model, the researcher specifies the portfolio intensity λ without reference to the constituents. The name dependence structure is implicit in this specification. The goal is an intensity model that is more parsimonious than the bottom up portfolio intensity (10.3.2), which follows a complicated process that is driven by the constituent processes and depends on all single-name parameters. This is achieved by choosing a model filtration $\mathbb{F}$ that is coarser than the bottom-up model filtration. Typically, the top-down model filtration is not fine enough to distinguish the identity of a defaulter. This means that an event arrival can be observed, but not the identity of the defaulted name.

Example 10.5. Let $\mathbb{F}$ be the filtration generated by the portfolio default process N and a risk factor $X > 0$ that evolves independently of N. Set

$$\lambda = X(m - N) \qquad (10.3.3)$$

The risk factor X generates stochastic variation in the portfolio intensity between arrivals. It models the sensitivity of the portfolio constituents to a common economic factor. Conditional on a path of X, N is a time inhomogeneous death process. If X is a weighted sum of independent processes, then N is the generalized Poisson process of [4].

This example illustrates how a relatively coarse filtration supports a parsimonious portfolio intensity specification. Instead of describing the constituent intensities, we focus on the interarrival intensity. In other words, we change the perspective from the firm default times τ^k to the ordered default times T^n. The example also illustrates the connection between a top-down and bottom-up specification. The top-down portfolio intensity (10.3.3) coincides with the portfolio intensity (10.3.2) generated by an *exchangeable* bottom-up model for which $\lambda^k = X$ for all constituents k.

In Example 10.5, the response of the portfolio intensity to events does not represent feedback but merely an adjustment that accounts for the fact that the set of potential defaulters is reduced at an event. To incorporate event feedback, we need to allow for a more flexible interarrival intensity specification.

Example 10.6. Let $\mathbb{F}$ be the filtration generated by the portfolio default process and a collection of risk factors X^n that vanish for $n \geq m$,

$$\lambda = X^n 1_{\{N=n\}} \qquad (10.3.4)$$

The intensity is revised at an event. Between events, the stochastic evolution of the intensity is governed by the processes X^n. If $X^n = X(m - n)$ for an independent common risk factor X, we obtain the doubly stochastic death process of Example 10.5. If $X^n = X\beta^n(m - n)$ for a deterministic function β^n, then N is the bivariate spread loss process of [1]. If $X^n = X(c + \delta n)$ for constants c and δ, then N is the time-changed birth process of [11]. If $X^n = c + \delta n$ for deterministic functions c and δ, then N is the inhomogeneous birth process of [33]. If X^n is deterministic then N is a time-inhomogeneous

Markov jump process as in [7] and [36]. If for constants c, λ_0, κ and δ we set

$$X_t^n = c + (\lambda_0 - c)e^{-\kappa t} + \delta \sum_{j=1}^{n} e^{-\kappa(t-T^j)}$$

then N is the Hawkes process of [18], [9], [26], [37] and [38] propose further specifications of the model (10.3.4).

The change in perspective supports parsimonious specifications of the portfolio intensity λ, and as we illustrate below, it also leads to computational tractability of portfolio risk measurement and portfolio derivatives valuation. However, the top down approach calls for further steps if we require models for the constituent names. Constituent intensities are generated by *random thinning* (see [24]). Random thinning disintegrates the portfolio intensity process λ into its constituent intensity processes. It provides the inverse to the intensity aggregation formula (10.3.2).

We must be careful about the notion of default intensity of a constituent. If, as in Examples 10.5 and 10.6, the top-down model filtration $\mathbb{F}$ is not fine-enough to distinguish the identity of a defaulter, then the constituent default processes N^k are not observable (i.e., adapted to $\mathbb{F}$). Therefore, we consider the projections $\hat{N}^k$ onto $\mathbb{F}$. This is similar to the projection of the frailty factor onto the observation filtration in Example 10.4. Random thinning allocates the portfolio intensity λ to the intensities $\hat{\lambda}^k$ of the constituent default process projections $\hat{N}^k$. In [24], it is shown that for each portfolio intensity model, there exists a predictable thinning process Z^k such that

$$\hat{\lambda}^k = Z^k \lambda \tag{10.3.5}$$

The value Z_t^k is the conditional probability at time t that name k is the next defaulter given a default is imminent. Therefore, the sum of the Z_t^k over k must equal one unless all names in the portfolio are in default. If all constituents are in default, the thinning processes vanish. As the following examples illustrate, the constituent intensities $\hat{\lambda}^k$ inherit the properties of the portfolio intensity λ. In particular, they reflect the dependence structure of the ambient portfolio.

Example 10.7. Let $\mathbb{F}$ be the filtration generated by the portfolio default process N and an independent systematic risk factor $X > 0$. Let the portfolio intensity $\lambda = X(m - N)$ be as in Example 10.5. Consider the thinning process given by

$$Z_t^k = \frac{S^k}{\sum_{k=1}^{m} S^k} 1_{\{t \le T^m\}}$$

where the S^k are the credit swap spreads of the constituent names observed at time 0 for a short, fixed maturity. The portfolio intensity is distributed according to the relative spread of names. A name whose spread is relatively wide compared with other names in the portfolio is attributed a relatively large share of the portfolio intensity. We have

$$\hat{\lambda}_t^k = \frac{S^k}{\sum_{k=1}^m S^k} X_t(m - N_t) \tag{10.3.6}$$

so the exposure of firm k to the common factor is determined by the relative spread. However, the single name swap spreads implied by the constituent intensities (10.3.6) are not guaranteed to match observed spreads. Consider the alternative model

$$Z_t^k = s^k 1_{\{t \leq T^m\}},$$

where the s^k are nonnegative parameters such that $\sum_{k=1}^m s^k = 1$. Given a calibration of X from the tranche market, choose the parameters s^k such that the constituent intensities generate model credit swap spreads that are close to the market-observed credit swap spreads S^k. This calibration problem becomes well-posed if the constituent spreads are uniformly adjusted for the index basis, and the adjustment is calibrated along with the parameters s^k.

In the previous example, the thinning is static. Further, the portfolio and constituent intensities do not incorporate event feedback. The response of the intensities to an event merely represents an adjustment for the reduction in the set of potential defaulters.

Example 10.8. Let $\mathbb{F}$ be the filtration generated by the portfolio default process N and an independent systematic risk factor $X > 0$. For constants $c > 0$ and $\delta \geq 0$, let the portfolio intensity $\lambda = X(c + \delta N)1_{\{N < m\}}$, which generates the time-changed birth process of [11], see Example 10.6. This specification incorporates the feedback of events. Letting $T^0 = 0$, consider the thinning process

$$Z_t^k = \sum_{n=1}^m z^{kn} 1_{\{T^{n-1} < t \leq T^n\}}$$

where $(z^{kn})_{k,n=1,2,\dots,m}$ is a doubly stochastic matrix of nonnegative constants. The parameter z^{kn} represents the probability that firm k is the nth defaulter.

With each event arrival, the portfolio intensity, thinning processes and the constituent intensities

$$\hat{\lambda}^k = Z^k X(c + \delta N)$$

are revised. While the thinning is constant between events, the portfolio and constituent intensities fluctuate with the common factor X. The doubly stochastic thinning matrix is chosen so that the model-implied single-name swap spreads match observed spreads, see [11] and [29].

10.4 DEFAULT DISTRIBUTION

A portfolio credit derivative is a contingent claim on the portfolio loss due to defaults. To calculate derivative prices and portfolio risk measures such as value at risk, we require the distribution of portfolio loss at multiple future horizons. Below we contrast the calculation of this distribution in bottom-up and top-down model specifications. To simplify the exposition, we assume that the loss at an event is constant. Therefore, we can focus on the distribution of the default process N and its components N^k.

10.4.1 Bottom-Up Models

In a bottom-up model, the default process $N = \sum_k N^k$ is the aggregate of the constituent default processes N^k. It is natural to consider the constituent default processes first. Define $A_t^k = \int_0^t \lambda_s^k ds$, where λ^k is the intensity of firm k. If the variable $\exp(A_T^k)$ is square integrable for some horizon T, then for any time $t \le T$ before default we have the conditional survival probability formula

$$P[\tau^k > T \mid \mathcal{F}_t] = E^*[e^{-(A_T^k - A_t^k)} \mid \mathcal{F}_t^*] \qquad (10.4.1)$$

where the expectation on the right-hand side is taken under an absolutely continuous probability measure P^* defined by the density $\exp(A_T^k)(1 - N_T^k)$, see [6]. The probability P^* puts zero mass on paths for which default occurs before T. The conditional expectation is taken with respect to the filtration $(\mathcal{F}_t^*)$, which is the completion of the reference filtration $\mathbb{F}$ by the P^*-null sets. Formula (10.4.1) applies to all bottom-up constituent intensity specifications discussed in section 10.3.1. The measure and filtration changes are redundant for the doubly stochastic Example 10.2. In this case, formula (10.4.1) simplifies to the classic formula derived by [35].

The conditional expectation on the right-hand side of equation (10.4.1) is a familiar expression in ordinary term structure modeling. It is analogous to the price at t of a zero-coupon bond with unit face value and maturity

T, assuming the short-term rate of interest is λ. The calculation of this price is well understood for a wide range of parametric short rate specifications, including affine and quadratic models. Formula (10.4.1) thus extends the analytical tractability offered by existing term structure model specifications to the constituent default process N^k.

Example 10.9. Let $\mathbb{F}$ be the filtration generated by the constituent default processes N^k, a systematic risk factor X and a collection of idiosyncratic risk factors X^k that are independent of one another and independent of X. The risk factors are independent of the N^k. For a constant α^k, set $\lambda^k = \alpha^k X + X^k$. From formula (10.4.1) we get

$$P[\tau^k > T] = E[e^{-\alpha^k \int_0^T X_s ds}] E[e^{-\int_0^T X_s^k ds}]. \tag{10.4.2}$$

The two expectations on the right-hand side can be calculated explicitly if the risk factors follow affine jump diffusions or quadratic diffusions. In these cases, each expectation is an exponentially affine or quadratic function of the initial value of the risk factor.

It is challenging to calculate the distribution of the portfolio default process N in the general bottom-up setting. This is particularly true for intensity models with event feedback, where the calculations often rely on the special structure of the intensity parametrization. The calculations are most tractable in the doubly stochastic Example 10.2, which explains the popularity of this specification. Here, we exploit the fact that conditional on the common risk factor, the N^k are independent.

Example 10.10. Consider the doubly stochastic setting of Example 10.9. Define the integrated common factor $Z_t = \int_0^t X_s ds$ and let

$$p_k(T, z) = P[\tau^k > T \mid Z_T = z] = e^{-\alpha^k z} E[e^{-\int_0^T X_s^k ds}]$$

be the conditional survival probability of firm k given a realization of the integrated common factor. The conditional probability generating function of the constituent default process is given by

$$E[v^{N_T^k} \mid Z_T = z] = p_k(T, z)(1 - v) + v, \quad v \in \mathbb{R}.$$

By iterated expectations and conditional independence, the probability generating function of the portfolio default process N is

$$E[v^{N_T}] = \sum_{k=0}^n v^k P[N_T = k] = \int V(T, z, v) f_T(z) dz \tag{10.4.3}$$

where $f_T(z)$ is the density function of Z_T and

$$V(T,\ z,\ v) = \prod_{k=1}^{n} E[v^{N_T^k} \mid Z_T = z] = \prod_{k=1}^{n}(p_k(T,\ z)(1 - v) + v)$$

Expanding the polynomial $V(T,\ z,\ v) = V_0(T,\ z) + vV_1(T,\ z) + \cdots + v^n V_n(T,\ z)$, from formula 10.4.3 we get the distribution of the portfolio default process:

$$P[N_T = k] = \int V_k(T,\ z)\, f_T(z) dz$$

If the common risk factor follows an affine jump diffusion or quadratic diffusion, then the Laplace transform of Z_T is exponentially affine or quadratic in X_0, respectively, and the density $f_T(z)$ can be obtained by numerical transform inversion. Extensions of the single-factor model for λ^k to include multiple common factors that model sectoral, regional, or other risks are conceptually straightforward, but require multidimenional numerical transform inversion and integration which tend to be computationally very expensive.

10.4.2 Top-Down Models

In a top-down model the distribution of the portfolio default process N can be calculated directly in terms of the portfolio intensity λ. Let $A_t = \int_0^t \lambda_s ds$ be the compensator to N. If the variable $\exp(A_T)$ is square integrable for some horizon T and Y is an integrable random payoff at T, then for real z, v and $t \le T$ the default process transform

$$E[e^{izY+iv(N_T-N_t)} \mid \mathcal{F}_t] = E^v[e^{izY-(1-e^{iv})(A_T-A_t)} \mid \mathcal{F}_t] \tag{10.4.4}$$

where i is the imaginary unit and the expectation on the right hand side is taken under an equivalent complex measure P^v defined by the density $\exp(ivN_T + (1 - e^{iv})A_T)$, see [22]. The measure P^v neutralizes any feedback of events on the intensity λ. Formula (10.4.4) applies to all portfolio intensity specifications discussed in section 10.3.2.

The expectation on the right-hand side of equation (10.4.4) is a familiar expression in the defaultable term structure literature. It is analogous to the price at t of a security that pays $\exp(izY)$ at T if the issuer survives to T and 0 otherwise, assuming the issuer defaults at intensity $(1 - e^{iv})\lambda$. The calculation of this price is well understood for a wide range of parametric intensity specifications, including affine and quadratic models. The reason is that this price is analogous to the price of a security paying $\exp(izY)$ at T in a default-free economy, where the short rate is $(1 - e^{iv})\lambda$. Formula 10.4.4 thus extends the analytical tractability offered by existing term structure model specifications to the portfolio default process N.

To obtain the distribution of N we must invert the transform (10.4.4). To this end, for real a, b, and x consider the conditional expectation

$$G_t(x; a, b, T, Y) = E[(a + bY)1_{\{N_T \leq x\}}|\mathcal{F}_t] \tag{10.4.5}$$

which is almost surely an increasing function in x that is constant on the intervals $[n, n + 1)$ for n an integer, and vanishes for $x < 0$. The Fourier-Stieltjes transform of $G_t(x; a, b, T)$ can be obtained by integration by parts. For real v we get the formula

$$\mathcal{G}_t(v; a, b, T, Y) = \int_{-\infty}^{\infty} e^{ivx} dG_t(x; a, b, T, Y) = E\left[(a + bY)e^{ivN_T}|\mathcal{F}_t\right]$$

which can be expressed directly in terms of a partial derivative of the transform formula (10.4.4). For all nonnegative integers n we have

$$G_t(n; a, b, T, Y) = \frac{1}{2\pi} \int_{-\pi}^{\pi} \frac{e^{-ivn} - e^{iv}}{1 - e^{iv}} \mathcal{G}_t(v; a, b, T, Y) dv \tag{10.4.6}$$

The inversion formula (10.4.6) recovers the conditional distribution function of N_T for $a = 1$ and $b = 0$. The function 10.4.5 can also be used to calculate the conditional default probabilities of the portfolio constituents. As explained in section 10.3.2, in a top-down model the constituent intensities are obtained by random thinning of the portfolio intensity λ. For any thinning process Z^k for firm k such that for $t \leq T$,

$$P[t < \tau^k \leq T \mid \mathcal{F}_t] = \int_t^T E[Z_s^k \lambda_s | \mathcal{F}_t] ds \tag{10.4.7}$$

see [24]. The quantity $Z^k \lambda$ is the top-down counterpart to the constituent intensity λ^k in a bottom-up model, and formula 10.4.7 is the top-down counterpart to the bottom-up constituent probability formula (10.4.1).

Example 10.11. Let $\mathbb{F}$ be the filtration generated by the portfolio default process N. Suppose N is the Hawkes process considered in [18], which is calibrated to the tranche market by [25]. This model is a special case of

Example 10.6. The portfolio intensity λ satisfies

$$\lambda_t = c + \delta \int_0^t e^{-\kappa(t-s)} dN_s \qquad (10.4.8)$$

The parameter $c > 0$ describes the base intensity. The parameter $\delta \geq 0$ governs the sensitivity of the intensity to defaults, and $\kappa \geq 0$ is the rate at which the impact of an event decays exponentially. Writing $d\lambda_t = \kappa(c - \lambda_t)dt + \delta dN_t$ shows that N is an affine point process, that is, λ follows an affine jump diffusion process in the sense of [15] whose jump term is N. Further, a suitable version of the Girsanov-Meyer theorem implies that under the complex measure P^v, the point process N has intensity $e^{iv}\lambda$, see [22]. Together with the transform formula (10.4.4), these observations allow us to conclude that

$$E[e^{iz\lambda_T + iv(N_T - N_t)} \mid \mathcal{F}_t] = E^v\left[e^{iz\lambda_T - (1 - e^{iv})\int_t^T \lambda_s ds} \mid \mathcal{F}_t\right]$$

$$= e^{\alpha(t) + \beta(t)\lambda_t} \qquad (10.4.9)$$

where the coefficient functions $\beta(t) = \beta(z, v, t, T)$ and $\alpha(t) = \alpha(z, v, t, T)$ satisfy the ordinary differential equations

$$\partial_t \beta(t) = 1 + \kappa\beta(t) - e^{iv + \delta\beta(t)}$$
$$\partial_t \alpha(t) = -c\kappa\beta(t)$$

with boundary conditions $\beta(T) = iz$ and $\alpha(T) = 0$. By following the steps above, the transform (10.4.9) can be inverted to obtain the function $G_t(n; a, b, T, \lambda_T)$, which yields the distribution of the Hawkes process and is used to calculate the constituent default probabilities. To illustrate this, consider the thinning process of Example 10.8, given by

$$Z_t^k = \sum_{n=1}^m z^{kn} 1_{\{T^{n-1} < t \leq T^n\}}$$

where $(z^{kn})_{k,n=1,2,\dots,m}$ is a matrix of nonnegative constants for which all rows and all columns sum to 1, and m is the number of portfolio constituents. In view of the default probability formula (10.4.7), it remains to calculate

$$E[Z_s^k \lambda_s \mid \mathcal{F}_t] = \sum_{n=1}^m z^{kn}(G_t(n - 1; 0, 1, s, \lambda_s) - G_t(n - 2; 0, 1, s, \lambda_s))$$

The specification (10.4.8) does not guarantee that the portfolio intensity vanishes after the mth default in the portfolio. In other words, the process

N governed by the intensity (10.4.8) can have more than m events. This is innocuous for typical portfolios, for example, CDX index portfolios with more than 100 constituents. Here the distribution of the number of events is well approximated by the distribution of N. Nevertheless, it is straightforward to obtain the distribution of the stopped process $N^m = N \wedge m$ from that of N:

$$P[N_s^m - N_t^m = k \mid \mathcal{F}_t] = \begin{cases} P[N_s - N_t = k \mid \mathcal{F}_t] & \text{if } k < m - N_t^m \\ P[N_s - N_t \geq k \mid \mathcal{F}_t] & \text{if } k = m - N_t^m \\ 0 & \text{if } k > m - N_t^m \end{cases}$$

Note that the truncation is not required for the constituent models, since the thinning process vanishes at the mth default by construction.

10.5 CALIBRATION

Accurate and stable intensity parameter estimation is a prerequisite for many applications of a portfolio credit model. For measurement and management of portfolio credit risk, the model is formulated under actual probabilities and must fit to historical default experience. For trading and hedging of standard or exotic portfolio derivatives, the model is formulated under risk-neutral probabilities and must fit to index and tranche market prices.

A specification of the joint evolution of constituent intensities can be fitted jointly to single- and multiname market data. [17], [19], and [40] fit doubly stochastic models with jump diffusion risk factor dynamics to spreads of single name and tranche swaps observed on a given day. [41] fit models with stochastic volatility risk factors. These papers obtain accurate fits.

There are two distinct ways to fit a top-down model to market data. A specification of the portfolio intensity and the thinning processes can be calibrated jointly to single- and multiname market data. In a procedure that does not require single-name models or data, a stand-alone portfolio intensity specification can be fitted to index and tranche market data. Given the fit of the portfolio intensity, the constituent thinning processes can be calibrated to single-name market data in an *optional* second step.

Most available empirical analyses fit a stand-alone specification of the portfolio intensity. Using different models, [1], [4], [7], [11], [25], [36] and [38] obtain accurate fits to index and tranche spreads of several maturities, all observed on a fixed date. With time-dependent parameters, the data can be matched perfectly. [2] and [37] fit alternative portfolio intensity models with constant parameters to time series of index and tranche spreads for a fixed maturity. They find that the models replicate the time-series variation of market spreads for all tranche attachment points and maturities.

10.6 CONCLUSION

Dynamic reduced-form models of portfolio credit risk provide many advantages over the static copula models that are in widespread use in the financial industry. First, they have realistic features that are motivated by empirical observation. Second, they specify the time evolution of the portfolio default process, and generate the portfolio loss distribution for all future horizons. Third, they accurately fit index and tranche market prices for all attachment points and maturities.

Dynamic reduced form models can be specified in two ways. In a bottom-up model, the constituent default intensities are the primitives. Such a specification is appropriate for the analysis of portfolios of highly heterogeneous constituents. It brings the information of the single-name market to bear on the calibration of the model. In a top-down specification, the portfolio default intensity is the modeling primitive, and constituent intensities are generated by random thinning. Since constituent calibration is optional for such a specification, a stand-alone portfolio intensity model can be used in situations with little or unreliable single-name market information. An example is a reasonably granular portfolio of bonds or loans for which an index contract is traded. Even if single-name information is available in principle, the sheer size of a portfolio can motivate the use of a stand-alone portfolio intensity model. Another application area for such a model is the analysis of exotic portfolio derivatives such as index and tranche forwards and options. These products are driven by the volatility of portfolio loss, which is conveniently controlled by the portfolio intensity.

REFERENCES

1. Arnsdorf, M., and I. Halperin. (2007). BSLP: Markovian bivariate spread-loss model for portfolio credit derivatives. Working paper, Quantitative Research, J. P. Morgan.
2. Azizpour, S., and Giesecke, K. (2008). Premia for correlated default risk. Working paper, Stanford University.
3. Black, F., and J. C. Cox. (1976). Valuing corporate securities: Some effects of bond indenture provisions. *Journal of Finance* 31 (May): 351–367.
4. Brigo, D., A. Pallavicini, and R. Torresetti. (2006). Calibration of CDO tranches with the dynamical generalized-Poisson loss model. Working paper, Banca IMI.

5. Collin-Dufresne, P., R. Goldstein, and J. Helwege. (2003). Are jumps in corporate bond yields priced? Modeling contagion via the updating of beliefs. Working paper, Carnegie Mellon University.
6. Collin-Dufresne, P., R. Goldstein, and J. Hugonnier. (2004). A general formula for the valuation of defaultable securities. *Econometrica* 72: 1377–1407.
7. Cont, R., and A. Minca. (2008). Reconstructing portfolio default probabilities from CDO tranche spreads. Columbia University Financial Engineering Report 2008-1, http://ssrn.com/abstract=1104855.
8. Das, S., D. Duffie, N. Kapadia, and L. Saita. (2007). Common failings: How corporate defaults are correlated. *Journal of Finance* 62: 93–117.
9. Davis, M., and V. Lo. (2001). Modeling default correlation in bond portfolios. In C. Alexander (ed.), *Mastering Risk, vol. 2: Applications.* Upper Saddle River, NJ: Prentice Hall, pp. 141–151.
10. Delloye, M., J.-D. Fermanian, and M. Sbai. (2006). Estimation of a reduced-form credit portfolio model and extensions to dynamic frailties. Working paper, BNP Paribas.
11. Ding, X., K. Giesecke, and P. Tomecek. (2006). Time-changed birth processes and multi-name credit derivatives. Working paper, Stanford University.
12. Duffie, D., A. Eckner, G. Horel, and L. Saita. (2006). Frailty correlated default. Working paper, Stanford University.
13. Duffie, D., and N. Gârleanu. (2001). Risk and valuation of collateralized debt obligations. *Financial Analysts Journal* 57(1): 41–59.
14. Duffie, D., and Lando, D. (2001). Term structures of credit spreads with incomplete accounting information. *Econometrica* 69(3): 633–664.
15. Duffie, D., J. Pan, and K. Singleton. (2000). Transform analysis and asset pricing for affine jump-diffusions. *Econometrica* 68: 1343–1376.
16. Duffie, D., L. Saita, and K. Wang. (2006). Multi-period corporate default prediction with stochastic covariates. *Journal of Financial Economics* 83(3): 635–665.
17. Eckner, A. (2007). Computational techniques for basic affine models of portfolio credit risk. Working paper, Stanford University.
18. Errais, E., K. Giesecke, and L. Goldberg. (2006). Pricing credit from the top down with affine point processes. Working paper, Stanford University.
19. Feldhütter, P. (2007). An empirical investigation of an intensity based model for pricing CDO tranches. Working paper, Copenhagen Business School.
20. Frey, R., and J. Backhaus. (2004). Portfolio credit risk models with interacting default intensities: A Markovian approach. Working paper, Department of Mathematics, University of Leipzig.
21. Giesecke, K. (2006). Default and information. *Journal of Economic Dynamics and Control* 30(1): 2281–2303.
22. Giesecke, K. (2007). The correlation-neutral measure for portfolio credit. Working paper, Stanford University.
23. Giesecke, K., and L. Goldberg. (2004). Sequential defaults and incomplete information. *Journal of Risk* 7(1): 1–26.
24. Giesecke, K., and L. Goldberg. (2005). A top down approach to multi-name credit. Working paper, Stanford University.

25. Giesecke, K., and B. Kim. (2007). Estimating tranche spreads by loss process simulation. In S. G. Henderson, B. Biller, M.-H. Hsieh, et al. (eds.), *Proceedings of the 2007 Winter Simulation Conference*. IEEE Press.
26. Giesecke, K., and P. Tomecek. (2005). Dependent events and changes of time. Working paper, Stanford University.
27. Giesecke, K., and S. Weber. (2004). Cyclical correlations, credit contagion, and portfolio losses. *Journal of Banking and Finance* 28: 3009–3036.
28. Giesecke, K., and S. Weber. (2006). Credit contagion and aggregate loss. *Journal of Economic Dynamics and Control* 30: 741–761.
29. Halperin, I. (2007). Climbing down from the top: Single name hedging in top down credit models. Working paper, Quantitative Research, J. P. Morgan.
30. Jarrow, R. A., and F. Yu. (2001). Counterparty risk and the pricing of defaultable securities. *Journal of Finance* 56(5): 555–576.
31. Jorion, P., and G. Zhang. (2007). Credit correlations from counterparty risk. Working paper, University of California at Irvine.
32. Jorion, P., and G. Zhang. (2007). Good and bad credit contagion: Evidence from credit default swaps. *Journal of Financial Economics* 84(3): 860–883.
33. Kim, J. (2007). Time-inhomogeneous birth processes in credit modeling. Working paper, Stanford University.
34. Kusuoka, S. (1999). A remark on default risk models. *Advances in Mathematical Economics* 1: 69–82.
35. Lando, D. (1998). On Cox processes and credit risky securities. *Review of Derivatives Research* 2: 99–120.
36. Laurent, J.-P., A. Cousin, and J.-D. Fermanian. (2007). Hedging default risks of CDOs in Markovian contagion models. Working paper, BNP Paribas.
37. Longstaff, F., and A. Rajan. (2008). An empirical analysis of collateralized debt obligations. *Journal of Finance* 63(2): 529–563.
38. Lopatin, A., and Timur Misirpashaev. (2007). Two-dimensional Markovian model for dynamics of aggregate credit loss. Working paper, Numerix.
39. Meyer, P.-A. (1966). *Probability and Potentials*. London: Blaisdell.
40. Mortensen, A. (2006). Semi-analytical valuation of basket credit derivatives in intensity-based models. *Journal of Derivatives* 13: 8–26.
41. Papageorgiou, E., and R. Sircar. (2007). Multiscale intensity models and name grouping for valuation of multi-name credit derivatives. Working paper, Princeton University.
42. Schönbucher, P. (2004). Information-driven default contagion. Working paper, ETH Zürich.
43. Schönbucher, P., and D. Schubert. Copula-dependent default risk in intensity models. Working paper, Universität Bonn.
44. Yu, F. (2007). Correlated defaults in intensity based models. *Mathematical Finance* 17: 155–173.

CHAPTER 11

Forward Equations for Portfolio Credit Derivatives

Rama Cont and Ioana Savescu

The inadequacy of static, copula-based models for the pricing of collateralized debt obligations (CDOs) and other portfolio credit derivatives, as illustrated for instance during the credit crisis of 2007, has led to renewed interest in the development and study of dynamic pricing models for portfolio credit derivatives. While reduced-form models for portfolio credit derivatives have been present in the literature for a while, one of the issues has been the numerical obstacles that arise in the computation of quantities of interest such as CDO tranche spreads and sensitivities, for which the main approach has been quadrature methods and Monte Carlo simulation. These issues are further accentuated when it comes to the calibration of such models, which requires an inversion of the pricing procedure.

We introduce an alternative approach for computing the values of CDO tranche spreads in reduced-form models for portfolio credit derivatives ("top-down" models), which allows for efficient computations and can be used as an ingredient of an efficient calibration algorithm. Our approach is based on the solution of a system of ordinary differential equations, which is the analog for portfolio credit derivatives of well-known Dupire equation [11] for call option prices. It allows to efficiently price CDOs and other portfolio credit derivatives without Monte Carlo simulation.

The chapter is structured as follows. Section 11.1 defines the most common examples of portfolio credit derivatives: index default swaps and CDO tranches. Section 11.2 presents a general parametrization of the portfolio loss process in terms of a *portfolio default intensity* and introduces top-down pricing models. In section 11.3 we introduce the notion of *effective default intensity*, which is the analog for portfolio credit risk models of the notion of local volatility in diffusion models. Using the notion of effective default intensity, we derive in section 11.4 the main result: a forward differential equation for expected tranche notionals. This forward equation is used in section 11.5 to recover forward default intensities from a set of observations of CDO tranche spreads. Section 11.6 discusses various applications of our results.

11.1 PORTFOLIO CREDIT DERIVATIVES

Let $(\Omega, (\mathcal{F}_t)_{t \leq T})$ be the set of market scenarios endowed with a filtration $(\mathcal{F}_t)_{0 \leq t \leq T}$ representing the flow of information with time. Consider a reference portfolio on which the credit derivatives we consider will be indexed. The main object of interest are the number of defaults N_t and the (cumulative) *default loss* L_t in this reference portfolio during a period $[0, t]$. Although the discussion below can be generalized to account for correlation between interest rates and default rates, for simplicity we shall assume independence between default risk and interest rate risk. We denote by $B(t, T)$ the discount factor at date t for the maturity $T \geq t$.

A *portfolio credit derivative* can be modeled as a contingent claim whose payoff is a (possibly path-dependent) function of the portfolio loss process $(L_t)_{t \in [0, T]}$. The most important example of portfolio credit derivatives are *index default swaps* and *CDOs*, which we briefly describe now (see [4] for more details and examples).

11.1.1 Index Default Swaps

Index default swaps are now commonly traded on various credit indices such as ITRAXX and CDX series, which are equally weighted indices of credit default swaps on European and U.S. names [4]. In an index default swap transaction, a protection seller agrees to pay all default losses in the index (default leg) in return for a fixed periodic spread S paid on the total notional of obligors remaining in the index (premium leg). Denoting by t_j, $j = 1 \ldots J$ the payments dates,

- The default leg pays at t_j the losses $L(t_j) - L(t_{j-1})$ due to defaults in $[t_{j-1}, t_j]$
- The premium leg pays at t_j an interest (spread) S on the notional of the remaining obligors

$$(t_j - t_{j-1})S \left(1 - \frac{N_{t_j}}{n} \right) \tag{11.1.1}$$

In particular, the cash flows of the index default swap depend only on the portfolio characteristics via N_t and L_t. The value at $t = 0$ of the default leg is therefore

$$\sum_{j=1}^{J} E^{Q}[B(0, t_j)(L(t_j)) - L(t_{j-1})]$$

while the value at $t = 0$ of the premium leg is

$$S \sum_{j=1}^{J} E^{Q}\left[B(0, t_j)(t_j - t_{j-1})\left(1 - \frac{N_{t_j}}{n}\right)\right]$$

The index default swap spread at $t = 0$ is defined as the (fair) value of the spread which equalizes the two legs at inception:

$$S_{\text{index}} = \frac{E^{Q}\left[\sum_{j=1}^{J} B(0, t_j)(L(t_j) - L(t_{j-1}))\right]}{\sum_{j=1}^{J} E^{Q}\left[B(0, t_j)(t_j - t_{j-1})\left(1 - \frac{N_{t_j}}{n}\right)\right]} \tag{11.1.2}$$

11.1.2 Collateralized Debt Obligations (CDOs)

Consider a *tranche* defined by an interval $[a, b]$, $0 \leq a < b < 1$ for the loss process normalized by the total nominal. A CDO tranche swap (or simply CDO tranche) is a bilateral contract in which an investor sells protection on all portfolio losses within the interval $[a, b]$ over some time period $[0, t_J]$ in return for a periodic spread $S(a, b)$ paid on the nominal remaining in the tranche after losses have been accounted for.

The loss of an investor exposed to the tranche $[a, b]$ is

$$L_{a,b}(t) = (L_t - a)_+ - (L_t - b)_+ \tag{11.1.3}$$

The premium leg is represented by the cash flow payed by the protection buyer to the protection seller. In case of a premium S, its value at time $t = 0$ is

$$P(a, b, t_J) = \sum_{j=1}^{J} S(t_j - t_{j-1}) E^{Q}[B(0, t_j)((b - L(t_j))^+ - (a - L(t_j))^+)]$$

The default leg is represented by the cash payed by the protection seller to the protection buyer in case of default. Its value at time $t = 0$ is

$$D(a, b, t_J) = \sum_{j=1}^{J} E^{\mathbb{Q}}[B(0, t_j)(L_{a,b}(t_j) - L_{a,b}(t_{j-1}))]$$

The "fair spread" (or, simply, the tranche spread) is the premium value $S_0(a, b, t_J)$ that equates the values of the two legs:

$$S_0(a, b, t_J) = \frac{E^{\mathbb{Q}} \sum_{j=1}^{J} B(0, t_j)[L_{a,b}(t_j) - L_{a,b}(t_{j-1})]}{E^{\mathbb{Q}} \sum_{j=1}^{J} B(0, t_j)(t_j - t_{j-1})[(b - L(t_j))^+ - (a - L(t_j))^+]}$$

Table 11.1 gives an example of such a tranche structure and the corresponding spreads for a standardized portfolio, the ITRAXX index. Note

TABLE 11.1 CDO Tranche Spreads, in bp, for the ITRAXX Index on March 15, 2007. For the equity tranche the periodic spread is 500bp and figures represent up-front payments

Maturity	Low	High	Bid\Upfront	Mid\Upfront	Ask\Upfront
5Y	0%	3%	11.75%	11.88%	12.00%
	3%	6%	53.75	54.50	55.25
	6%	9%	14.00	14.75	15.50
	9%	12%	5.75	6.25	6.75
	12%	22%	2.13	2.50	2.88
	22%	100%	0.80	1.05	1.30
7Y	0%	3%	26.88%	27.00%	27.13%
	3%	6%	130	131.50	132
	6%	9%	36.75	37.00	38.25
	9%	12%	16.50	17.25	18.00
	12%	22%	5.50	6.00	6.50
	22%	100%	2.40	2.65	2.90
10Y	0%	3%	41.88%	42.00%	42.13%
	3%	6%	348	350.50	353
	6%	9%	93	94.00	95
	9%	12%	40	41.00	42
	12%	22%	13.25	13.75	14.25
	22%	100%	4.35	4.60	4.85

that these expressions for the tranche spreads depend on the portfolio loss process via the expected tranche notional

$$C(t_j, K) = E^{\mathbb{Q}}[(K - L_{t_j})^+] \tag{11.1.4}$$

11.2 TOP-DOWN MODELS FOR CDO PRICING

While many pricing models for such portfolio credit derivatives start from specifying, it is readily observed [18] that the above expressions for the spread of a CDO tranche depend on the portfolio characteristics only through the (risk-neutral) law of the loss process L_t. This allows to build parsimonious pricing models where, instead of manipulating 100-dimensional copulas, one directly models the aggregate loss process L_t [6], [1], [12], [14], [17] or the term structure of loss distributions [18]. An overview of such top-down models is given in [14].

11.2.1 The Aggregate Loss Process

The loss L_t is a piecewise constant process with upward jumps at each default event: its path is therefore completely characterized by the default times $(\tau_j)_{j \geq 1}$, representing default events and the jump sizes ΔL_j representing the loss given default. Here τ_j denotes the j-th default event observed in the portfolio: the index j is *not* associated with the default of a given obligor but with the ordering in time of the events. The idea of aggregate loss models is to represent the rate of occurrence of defaults in the portfolio via the *portfolio default intensity* λ_t: we model the number of defaults $(N_t)_{t \in [0,T^*]}$ as a point process with $\mathcal{F}_t$-intensity $(\lambda_t)_{t \in [0,T^*]}$ under $\mathbb{Q}$, that is,

$$N_t - \int_0^t \lambda_t dt$$

is an $\mathcal{F}_t$-local martingale under $\mathbb{Q}$ [2]. Intuitively, λ_t can be seen as probability per unit time of the next default conditional on current market information:

$$\lambda_t = \lim_{\Delta t \to 0} \frac{1}{\Delta t} \mathbb{Q}[N_{t+\Delta t} = N_t + 1 | \mathcal{F}_t]$$

Here $\mathcal{F}_t$ represents the coarse-grained information resulting from the observation of the aggregate loss process L_t of the portfolio and risk factors affecting it. In the simplest case, it corresponds to the information (filtration) generated by the variables τ_j, ΔL_j but it may also contain information on other market variables. This risk-neutral intensity λ_t can be interpreted as the short-term credit spread for protection against the first default in the portfolio [18].

Let us note that we do *assume* any conditional independence property here: the process N_t is not necessarily a Cox process and our setting includes the (realistic) situation where the default intensity depends on past default events (see, e.g., [13, 14] for examples), which is excluded by Cox process models.

11.2.2 Forward Loss Distributions

The value of European, nonpath dependent portfolio credit derivatives only depends on the loss process L_t through its (risk-neutral) transition probabilities, also called *forward loss distributions* [18].

In the following, we shall always assume a constant loss given default δ (also called the *loss increment* in the sequel) so that the cumulative loss process is given by $L_t = \delta N_t$. The forward loss distribution is given by

$$q_k(t, T) = \mathbb{Q}[N_T = k|\mathcal{F}_t] = \mathbb{Q}[L_T = k\delta|\mathcal{F}_t] \qquad (11.2.1)$$

The *loss surface* at date t is defined by the term structure $q_k(t, T)$ of forward loss distributions when the loss level k and the maturity T vary.

As observed above the valuation of CDO tranches at t_0 only depends on the expected tranche notionals $C_{t_0}(T, K)$ and it is clear that the expected tranche notionals

$$C_{t_0}(T, K) = E^{\mathbb{Q}}[(K - L_T)_+|\mathcal{F}_{t_0}] = \sum_{j=0}^{k-1} \delta(k - j)q_j(t_0, T) \qquad (11.2.2)$$

only depend on the portfolio properties through the loss surface $q(t_0, .)$. Therefore, one can represent the values of the CDO tranches by modeling the loss surface itself.

It is readily observed that the loss surface has the following properties [18]:

Property 11.1. (Properties of the loss surface). For any $T \geq t$, any $n = 0..N$,

- $q_j(t, T) \geq 0$ and $\sum_{j=1}^{N} q_j(t, T) = 1$
- $q_j(t, t) = 1_{L(t)=j}$
- $q_j(t, T) = 0$ for $j < N_t$
- $\sum_{k=0}^{n} q_k(t, T)$ is increasing in T

These conditions are necessary for a given family of distributions $q_j(t, T)$ to be conditional loss distributions of a certain portfolio. As shown by Schönbucher [18], these conditions, combined with a mild regularity condition in T, are also sufficient: any smooth term structure of distributions verifying the conditions above can be constructed as a term structure of loss distributions for some loss process and is therefore "arbitrage-free."

11.3 EFFECTIVE DEFAULT INTENSITY

We introduce in this section the notion of effective default intensity [6], which is the analogue for portfolio credit risk models of the notion of local volatility function introduced by Dupire [11] for models driven by Brownian motion.

11.3.1 A Mimicking Theorem

We first present a mimicking theorem in the spirit of Gyöngy [15] for point process. The following is a special case of a more general result presented in [6]:

Proposition 11.2. *Denote by* $(\lambda_t)_{t \in [0, T^*]}$ *the portfolio default intensity with respect to* $\mathcal{F}_t$. *Define* $(\tilde{N}_t)_{t \in [0, T^*]}$ *as the Markovian point process with intensity*

$$a_k(t) = E^{\mathbb{Q}}[\lambda_t | N_{t-} = k, \mathcal{F}_0] \qquad (11.3.1)$$

Then, for any $t \in [0, T^*]$, N_t *and* $\tilde{N}_t$ *have the same distribution conditional on* $\mathcal{F}_0$. *In particular, the marginal distributions of* $(N_t)_{t \in [0, T^*]}$

$$q_k(0, t) = \mathbb{Q}(N_t = k | \mathcal{F}_0)$$

only depend on the intensity $(\lambda_t)_{t \in [0, T^*]}$ *through the effective intensity* $(a_k(t))_{k \geq 0}$.

Proof. Consider any bounded measurable function $f(.)$. Using the pathwise decomposition of N_T into the sum of its jumps we can write

$$f(N_T) = f(N_0) + \sum_{0 < s \leq T} (f(N_{s-} + \Delta N_s) - f(N_{s-})) \qquad (11.3.2)$$

so

$$E[f(N_T)|\mathcal{F}_0] = f(L_0) + E\left[\sum_{0<s\leq T}(f(N_{s-}+\Delta N_s) - f(N_{s-}))|\mathcal{F}_0\right]$$

$$= f(L_0) + \int_0^T dt \quad E[(f(N_{t-}+1) - f(N_{t-}))\lambda_t|\mathcal{F}_0]$$

Denote

$$\mathcal{G}_t = \sigma(\mathcal{F}_0 \vee N_{t-})$$

the information set obtained by adding the knowledge of N_{t-} to the current information set $\mathcal{F}_0$. Define the *effective intensity*

$$a_k(T) = E^{\mathbb{Q}}[\lambda_t|\mathcal{F}_0, N_{t-} = k]. \tag{11.3.3}$$

Noting that $\mathcal{F}_0 \subset \mathcal{G}_t$ we have

$$E[(f(N_{t-}+1) - f(N_{t-}))\lambda_t|\mathcal{F}_0]$$

$$= E[E[(f(N_{t-}+1) - f(N_{t-}))\lambda_t|\mathcal{G}_t]|\mathcal{F}_0]$$

$$= E[(f(N_{t-}+1) - f(N_{t-}))E[\lambda_t|\mathcal{G}_t]|\mathcal{F}_0]$$

$$= E[a_{N_{t-}}(t)(f(N_{t-}+1) - f(N_{t-}))|\mathcal{F}_0] \quad \text{so } E[f(N_T)|\mathcal{F}_0]$$

$$= f(N_t) + E\left[\int_0^T dt\, a_{N_{t-}}(t)(f(N_{t-}+1) - f(N_{t-}))|\mathcal{F}_0\right]$$

The above equality shows that $E[f(N_T)|\mathcal{F}_0] = E[f(\tilde{N}_T)|\mathcal{F}_0]$ where $(\tilde{N}_t)_{0\leq t\leq T}$ is the Markovian point process with intensity $\gamma_t = a_{\tilde{N}_{t-}}(t)$ hence $\tilde{N}_t \overset{d}{=} N_t$.

The construction above is analogous to the construction of a local volatility model compatible with a flow of (conditional) marginal distributions [11], [9]. Just as in the local volatility case, the Markovian loss model $\tilde{N}_t$ is not the unique loss dynamics compatible with a given flow of conditional densities but it is somehow the 'simplest' one. More importantly, the effective intensity $a_k(T)$ summarizes all that needs to be known to price CDO tranches with various maturities and attachment levels.

Note that the construction above, done at $t = 0$, can be repeated at any time t: the result is then that the flow of conditional distributions $q_k(t, T)$, $T \geq t$ can be matched by a Markovian point process with intensity function

$$a_k(t, T) = E^{\mathbb{Q}}[\lambda_t | \mathcal{F}_t, N_{T-} = k]$$

This representation of the loss surface in terms of effective intensities also allows to verify more easily the absence of static arbitrage: in this case, it is simply equivalent to the positivity of $a_k(t, T)$ for all $k \geq N_t, T \geq t$. This situation is unlike the representation of loss distributions in terms of base correlations or implied correlation: there is no clear criterion for telling whether a given base correlation skew is arbitrage-free and, conversely, it is not clear whether any configuration of market tranche spreads can be represented in terms of a "base correlation." In fact, in late 2007–early 2008 it has become increasingly difficult to represent market index CDO quotes in terms of base correlations and such attempts often lead to implied correlations very close to 100 percent.

11.3.2 Computing the Loss Distributions from the Effective Intensity

From proposition 1, the term structure of loss distributions for the stochastic intensity loss model (L_t) is equivalent to computing the same loss distributions for the Markovian loss process with transition intensity $a_k(t)$. Therefore, the loss surface at t can be simply obtained by solving the Fokker-Planck (or forward Kolmogorov) equations for the Markov process with intensity $a_k(t, T) = E^{\mathbb{Q}}[\lambda_t | \mathcal{F}_t, N_{T-} = k]$:

$$\frac{\partial q_j(t, T)}{\partial T} = -a_0(t, T)q_0(t, T) \tag{11.3.4}$$

$$\frac{\partial q_j(t, T)}{\partial T} = a_{j-1}(t, T)q_{j-1}(t, T) - a_j(t, T)q_j(t, T) \quad 1 \leq j \leq n-1 \tag{11.3.5}$$

$$\frac{\partial q_n(t, T)}{\partial T} = a_{n-1}(t, T)q_{n-1}(t, T) \tag{11.3.6}$$

These equations can be also rewritten in the following form:

$$\frac{\partial q_j(t, T)}{\partial T} = - (a_{j+1}(T, t)q_{j+1}(t, T) - a_j(T, t)q_j(t, T)) \tag{11.3.7}$$

$$+ (a_{j+1}(T, t)p_{j+1}(t, T) - 2a_j(T, t)q_j(t, T) + a_{j-1}(t, T)q_{j-1}(t, T))$$

which shows the analogy with the Fokker-Planck equations in the diffusion case. This is a system of linear ODEs that can be easily solved to yield the term structure of loss distributions.

11.4 A FORWARD EQUATION FOR CDO PRICING

Since the term structure of loss distributions only depends on the effective intensity, one can integrate the Fokker-Planck equations (11.3.6) and compute expectations by quadrature: this operations requires a numerical solution of (11.3.6) plus as many quadratures as payment dates in the CDO, which can be quite intensive. But, as we show below, this procedure can be greatly simplified by computing the *expected tranche notionals*, which are then used to compute all quantities of interest by linear combination. In particular, we show that these expected tranche notionals solve a forward equation, analogous to the Dupire equation.

11.4.1 Expected Tranche Notionals

For the equity tranche $[0, K = k\delta]$ where $\delta = (1 - R)/N$ is the (normalized) loss given a single default, we define the expected tranche notional for maturity T as

$$C_{t_0}(T, K) = E[(K - L_T)_+|\mathcal{F}_{t_0}] \qquad (11.4.1)$$

We will fix the initial date t_0 and drop the t_0 subscript in the sequel when the context is clear. Using (11.2.2) one can easily derive the following properties:

Property 11.3. (Properties of expected tranche notionals).

$K \mapsto C_{t_0}(T, K)$ is increasing

$K \mapsto C_{t_0}(T, K)$ is convex

Slope formula: denoting by ∇^+ and ∇^- the forward and backward difference operators,

$$\nabla^+ C_{t_0}(T, K) = C_{t_0}(T, K + \delta) - C_{t_0}(T, K) = \delta \sum_{j=0}^{k} q_j(t_0, T) \qquad (11.4.2)$$

"Inversion" formula: for $k \geq 2$

$$\nabla^- \nabla^+ C_{t_0} = C_{t_0}(T, K + \delta) - 2C_{t_0}(T, K) + C_{t_0}(T, K - \delta) = \delta q_k(t_0, T)$$

$$(11.4.3)$$

Finally, we can observe that $C(T, 0) = 0$ and

$$C_1(T) = \delta q_0(T) = C_1(T) - C_0(T) \qquad (11.4.4)$$

11.4.2 Forward Equation

We now formulate the main result of this chapter, which is a Dupire-type forward equation for the expected tranche notional:

Proposition 11.4. *The expected tranche notional* $C_k(T) = C_{t_0}(T, k\delta)$ *solves the following forward equation, where* $a_k(T) = a_k(t_0, T)$:

$$\frac{\partial C_k(T)}{\partial T} = a_k(T)C_{k-1}(T) - a_{k-1}(T)C_k(T)$$

$$- \sum_{j=1}^{k-2} C_j(T)[a_{j+1}(T) - 2a_j(T) + a_{j-1}(T)]$$

$$= [a_k(T) - a_{k-1}(T)]C_{k-1}(T)$$

$$- \sum_{j=1}^{k-2} (\nabla^2 a)_j C_j(T) - a_{k-1}(T)[C_k(T) - C_{k-1}(T)] \quad (11.4.5)$$

for $T \geq t_0$, *with the initial condition*

$$C_k(t_0) = (K - L_{t_0})_+ \qquad (11.4.6)$$

Proof: Decomposing the payoff $(K - L_{T+h})^+$ along the path of the loss process ("Ito formula") we obtain

$$(K - L_{T+h})^+ = (K - L_T)^+ + \sum_{T < s \leq T+h} [(K - L_{s-} - \Delta L_s)^+ - (K - L_{s-})^+]$$

$$= (K - L_T)^+ + \sum_{T < \tau_i \leq T+h} [(K - L_{\tau_i-} - \delta)^+ - (K - L_{\tau_i-})^+] \qquad (11.4.7)$$

Taking conditional expectations with respect to $\mathcal{F}_0$ we obtain

$$E[(K - L_{T+h})^+ | \mathcal{F}_0] = C(T, K)$$
$$+ E\left[\int_T^{T+h} dt\lambda_t((K - L_{t-} - \delta)^+ - (K - L_{t-})^+) | \mathcal{F}_0\right]$$

So finally we obtain

$$C(T + h, K) - C(T, K)$$
$$= E\left[\int_T^{T+h} dt\lambda_t((K - L_{t-} - \delta)^+ - (K - L_{t-})^+) | \mathcal{F}_0\right]$$
$$= -E\left[\int_T^{T+h} dt\lambda_t 1_{K-\delta \geq L_{t-}} | \mathcal{F}_0\right] \text{ since } (K - j\delta - \delta)^+ - (K - j\delta)^+$$
$$= -\delta 1_{j \leq k-1}$$

Dividing by h and taking $h \to 0$ we obtain

$$\frac{\partial C(T, K)}{\partial T} = -E[\lambda_T 1_{L_{T-} \leq K-\delta} | \mathcal{F}_0] \tag{11.4.8}$$

Define the effective intensity by

$$a_k(t_0, T, L) = E[\lambda_T | L_{T-} = L \vee \mathcal{F}_{t_0}] \quad a_k(T) = a(t_0, T, k\delta) \tag{11.4.9}$$

Using the law of iterated expectations we obtain

$$\frac{\partial C(T, K)}{\partial T} = -\delta E[E[\lambda_T 1_{L_{T-} \leq K-\delta} | L_{T-}] | \mathcal{F}_0]$$

$$= -\delta E[a_{N_{T-}}(T) 1_{L_{T-} \leq K-\delta} | \mathcal{F}_0] = -\delta \sum_{j=0}^{n} q_j(T) a_j(T) 1_{j \leq k-1}$$

$$= -\delta \sum_{j=0}^{k-1} q_j(T) a_j(T) = -\sum_{j=1}^{k-1} [\nabla^+ C_j(T) - \nabla^+ C_{j-1}(T)] a_j(T) - C_1(T) a_0(T)$$

$$= -\sum_{j=1}^{k-1} a_j(T) \nabla^+ C_j(T) + \sum_{j=0}^{k-2} a_{j+1}(T) \nabla^+ C_j(T) - C_1(T) a_0(T)]$$

$$= \sum_{j=1}^{k-2} \underbrace{(a_{j+1}(T) - a_j(T))}_{u_j} \nabla^+ C_j(T) + C_1(T)[a_1(T) - a_0(T)]$$

$$- a_{k-1}(T)[C_k(T) - C_{k-1}(T)]$$

$$= \sum_{j=1}^{k-2} u_j C_{j+1}(T) - \sum_{j=1}^{k-2} u_j C_j(T) + C_1(T)[a_1(T) - a_0(T)]$$

$$- a_{k-1}(T)[C_k(T) - C_{k-1}(T)]$$

$$= \sum_{j=2}^{k-1} u_{j-1} C_j(T) - \sum_{j=1}^{k-2} u_j C_j(T) + C_1(T)[a_1(T) - a_0(T)]$$

$$- a_{k-1}(T)[C_k(T) - C_{k-1}(T)]$$

$$= -(a_2(T) - a_1(T))C_1(T) + [a_k(T) - a_{k-1}(T)]C_{k-1}(T)$$

$$- \sum_{j=2}^{k-2} (u_j - u_{j-1})C_j(T)$$

$$+ C_1(T)[a_1(T) - a_0(T)] - a_{k-1}(T)[C_k(T) - C_{k-1}(T)]$$

$$= [a_k(T) - a_{k-1}(T)]C_{k-1}(T) - a_{k-1}(T)[C_k(T) - C_{k-1}(T)]$$

$$- \sum_{j=1}^{k-2} [a_{j+1}(T) - 2a_j(T) + a_{j-1}(T)]C_j(T)$$

Since $a_{j+1}(T) - 2a_j(T) + a_{j-1}(T) = (\nabla^2 a)_j$ is the discrete Laplacian applied to a, we can rewrite the last equation as

$$\frac{\partial C_k(T)}{\partial T} = [a_k(T) - a_{k-1}(T)]C_{k-1}(T)$$

$$- \sum_{j=1}^{k-2} (\nabla^2 a)_j C_j(T) - a_{k-1}(T)[C_k(T) - C_{k-1}(T)]$$

$$= a_k(T)C_{k-1}(T) - a_{k-1}(T)C_k(T) - \sum_{j=1}^{k-2} (\nabla^2 a)_j C_j(T)$$

which is the desired result.

The forward equation (11.4.5) may be seen as the analog of the Dupire equation [11], [9], [5] for portfolio credit derivatives. In fact the proof given above is the analog of the probabilistic proof of the Dupire equation using the Tanaka formula. However, given the discrete nature of losses the "Tanaka" formula in this case is simply reduced to the identity (11.4.7). Finally, the integration by parts step which intervenes in the derivation of the Dupire equation is done here using an Abel transformation for the partial sums involved in 11.2.2.

The forward equation (11.4.5) is a (bidiagonal) system of ODEs which can be efficiently solved using high-order time stepping schemes. This yields an efficient method to price portfolio credit derivatives such as CDO tranches, forward starting tranches, and so on, without recourse to Monte Carlo simulation.

11.5 RECOVERING FORWARD DEFAULT INTENSITIES FROM TRANCHE SPREADS

In this section we will present some simple algorithms that can be used to compute portfolio default intensities from tranche spreads. We will first address the case where the loss increment is such that the number of loss levels matches the number of observed strikes, then address the realistic case where we only have a sparse set of market data. We apply these methods to two data sets, consisting of ITRAXX tranche quotes on March 15, 2007, and August 13, 2007, and compare the results.

11.5.1 Dimension Reduction by Default Clustering

If we consider a loss increment of 3 percent, then the number of loss levels matches the number of observed strikes market data for ITRAXX tranches (up to 12 percent). We therefore need no extra assumptions for retrieving the forward default intensities.

> **Step 1:** Deduce from market quotes for ITRAXX tranche spreads the values for $C_t(T, K) = E^{\mathbb{Q}}[(K - L_T)_+ | \mathcal{F}_t]$. We now have $C_{3\%}$, $C_{6\%}$, $C_{9\%}$, $C_{12\%}$.
>
> **Step 2:** Consider a loss increment of 3 percent (we are in possession of the values of C for consecutive strikes up to 12 percent).
>
> **Step 3:** Use the forward equation (11.4.5) to back out values for forward default intensities for each interval of 3 percent up to 12 percent.

The results obtained are presented in Table 11.2 and Figure 11.1 shows the forward default intensities as functions of the loss level and the maturity.

TABLE 11.2 Results of Model Calibration for a Loss Increment of 3 percent and Where Forward Default Intensities are Considered Piece-wise Constant Functions in T

	Attachment		Market	Forward	Computed
	Low	High	Quotes—mid	Default Intensities	Spreads
5Y	0%	3%	11.88%	0.075240	11.88%
	3%	6%	54.5 bp	0.034292	54.49 bp
	6%	9%	14.75 bp	0.200097	14.75 bp
	9%	12%	6.25 bp	0.493477	6.24 bp
7Y	0%	3%	27%	0.143920	27%
	3%	6%	131.5 bp	0.087866	131.49 bp
	6%	9%	37 bp	0.223637	37 bp
	9%	12%	17.25 bp	0.547950	17.253 bp
10Y	0%	3%	42%	0.126520	42%
	3%	6%	350.5 bp	0.183037	350.49 bp
	6%	9%	94 bp	0.151411	94 bp
	9%	12%	41 bp	0.323830	41 bp

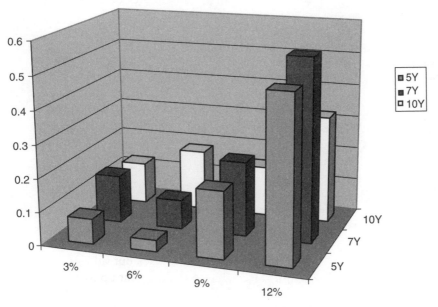

FIGURE 11.1 Values for forward transition rates for a loss increment of 3 percent.

TABLE 11.3 Results of Model Calibration for ITRAXX—March 15, 2007

| | | | | Computed Spreads | | |
| | Attachment | | Market Quotes | Equal Values for Forward Rates Between Strikes | | Interpolation for C |
	Low	High		Loss Increment = 1%	Loss Increment = 3%	Loss Increment = 1%
	0%	3%	11.88%	11.87%	11.88%	11.87%
	3%	6%	54.5 bp	54.5 bp	54.49 bp	54.52 bp
5Y	6%	9%	14.75 bp	14.753 bp	14.75 bp	14.75 bp
	9%	12%	6.25 bp	6.249 bp	6.24 bp	6.01 bp
	12%	22%	2.5 bp	2.498 bp	2.77 bp	2.57 bp
	0%	3%	27%	27%	27%	27%
	3%	6%	131.5 bp	131.49	131.49 bp	131.49 bp
7Y	6%	9%	37 bp	37	37 bp	37 bp
	9%	12%	17.25 bp	17.24	17.25 bp	17.02 bp
	12%	22%	6 bp	5.99	6.67 bp	6.06 bp
	0%	3%	42%	41.99%	42%	42%
	3%	6%	350.5 bp	350.5 bp	350.49 bp	350.47 bp
10Y	6%	9%	94 bp	94 bp	94 bp	94 bp
	9%	12%	41 bp	40.99 bp	41 bp	40.99 bp
	12%	22%	13.75 bp	13.75 bp	15.28 bp	13.75 bp

We observe that the values for tranche spreads computed with the model are very close to the market data to witch the model was calibrated. However, two problems arise when using this approach. First of all, we can't back out values for forward rates for the tranche 12–22 percent for example, as we are not in the possession of $C_{15\%}$, $C_{18\%}$. The second problem would be that we might need to consider a smaller loss increment in order to avoid the implicit assumption of default clustering, made when taking a loss step of 3 percent. Two possible solutions for these problems will be discussed.

11.5.2 Calibration to a Sparse Set of Strikes

We can avoid the implicit assumption of default clustering made when considering a (rather large) loss increment of 3 percent, by considering different methods. We propose here two other methods.

TABLE 11.4 Results of Model Calibration for ITRAXX—August 13, 2007

				Computed Spreads		
				Equal Values for Forward Rates between Strikes		Interpolation for C
	Attachment					
	Low	High	Market Quotes	Loss Increment = 1%	Loss Increment = 3%	Loss Increment = 1%
	0%	3%	26.25%	26.249%	26.25%	26.249%
	3%	6%	147 bp	147 bp	146.99 bp	147 bp
5Y	6%	9%	72 bp	72 bp	72 bp	72 bp
	9%	12%	45.5 bp	45.49 bp	45.5 bp	45.5 bp
	12%	22%	30.5 bp	30.49 bp	33.91 bp	30.475 bp
	0%	3%	35.75%	35.75%	35.749%	35.746%
	3%	6%	217.5 bp	217.498	217.5 bp	217.54 bp
7Y	6%	9%	123 bp	123.01	123 bp	123 bp
	9%	12%	85 bp	85	85 bp	85 bp
	12%	22%	48.5 bp	48.498	53.99 bp	48.5 bp
	0%	3%	45%	44.99%	45%	45%
	3%	6%	390 bp	390 bp	390.01 bp	389.97 bp
10Y	6%	9%	195 bp	195 bp	194.98 bp	195 bp
	9%	12%	130 bp	129.99 bp	130 bp	129.99 bp
	12%	22%	85 bp	85 bp	94.9 bp	85 bp

Equal Values for Forward Default Intensities between Strikes One option would be to consider constant forward transition rates between strikes. For example, for a loss increment of 1 percent, we have a common value for forward default intensities up to 3 percent, another from 3 percent to 6 percent and so on. This allows us take a loss step smaller than 3 percent without needing other values of C besides those retrieved from market quotes.

Tables 11.3 and 11.4 contain the spreads computed using forward transition rates that are considered piecewise constant functions in T and in the strike dimension for the two different sets of dates we have considered.

Interpolation of Expected Tranche Notionals An alternative approach would be to interpolate the values of the expected tranche notional C in the strike variable on a grid of given resolution (e.g., given a loss increment of 1 percent, we would have to interpolate in order to obtain values for $C_{1\%}$, $C_{2\%}$, $C_{4\%}$, $C_{5\%}$, ... etc.). According to the property mentioned

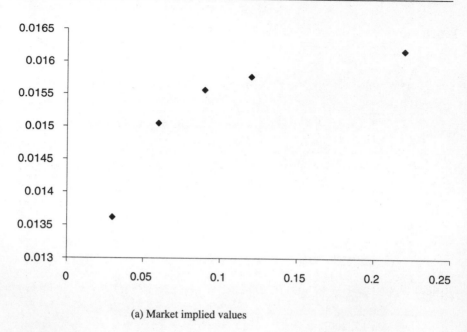

(a) Market implied values

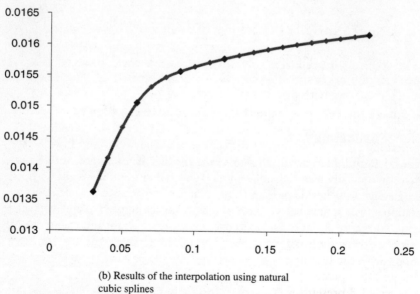

(b) Results of the interpolation using natural
cubic splines

FIGURE 11.2 X axis—strikes; Y axis—$C(0, x) - C(5Y, x)$

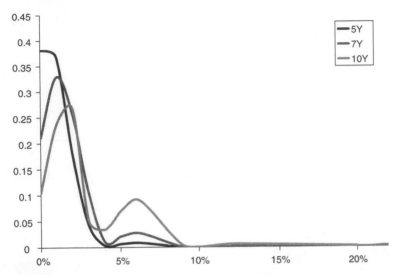

FIGURE 11.3 Expected loss distribution for a loss increment of 1 percent with forward rates obtained after the interpolation of $C_t(T, K)$ between strikes using splines—March 15, 2007.

above (section 11.4), $C(T, K)$ is an increasing and convex function. As $C(0, K) = E[(K - L_0)_+] = K$, we can deduce that $C(0, K) - C(T, K)$ has to be a concave function. Figure 11.2a shows the values for $C(0, K) - C(5Y, K)$ deduced from market spreads and Figure 11.2b shows the results obtained when interpolating with natural cubic splines.

11.5.3 Application to ITRAXX Tranches

Tables 11.3 and 11.4 contain the results of the calibration using the two approaches described earlier. In order to be able to use the solution with the interpolation of C, besides the interpolation assumption that has to be made to complete the sparse set of data, we also need to extrapolate to values of $C(T, K)$ where $K < 3$ percent. In the calibration results presented here we have used for the forward default intensities below 3 percent the ones obtained with the first approach (constant default intensities for 1 percent, 2 percent and 3 percent) (see also Table 11.5).

Figure 11.3 presents the expected loss distribution for different maturities obtained when calibrating the model using the interpolation for C with natural cubic splines.

Figure 11.4 presents the expected loss distribution for different maturities obtained when calibrating the model under the assumptions that

TABLE 11.5   Results of Model Calibration for ITRAXX—March 28, 2008

				Computed Spreads		
	Attachment			Equal Values for Forward Rates between Strikes		Interpolation for C
	Low	High	Market Quotes	Loss Increment = 1%	Loss Increment = 3%	Loss Increment = 1%
5Y	0%	3%	37.625%	37.626%	37.624%	37.626%
	3%	6%	440 bp	440 bp	440 bp	439.96 bp
	6%	9%	282 bp	282 bp	282 bp	282 bp
	9%	12%	197 bp	197 bp	197 bp	197 bp
	12%	22%	95 bp	95 bp	105.83 bp	95 bp
7Y	0%	3%	43.75%	43.75%	43.75%	43.75%
	3%	6%	531 bp	531.01	531 bp	530.98 bp
	6%	9%	328 bp	327.98	328 bp	328 bp
	9%	12%	218 bp	218	218 bp	218 bp
	12%	22%	111.5 bp	111.5	124.44 bp	111.5 bp
10Y	0%	3%	49.125%	49.122%	49.124%	49.122%
	3%	6%	651 bp	594.86 bp	651 bp	594.25 bp
	6%	9%	377 bp	421.88 bp	377 bp	422.44 bp
	9%	12%	248 bp	248 bp	248 bp	248 bp
	12%	22%	129 bp	129 bp	144.41 bp	129 bp

forward rates have equal values between strikes. These examples illustrate that, unlike the representation in terms of base correlations whose computation leads to instabilities since the 2007 credit crisis, the representation in terms of forward default intensities (or effective intensities) can be readily obtained across this period and leads to quantitative insights into market-implied forward looking default rates which have a direct interpretation (see also Figures 11.5 and 11.6 then comparisons in Figures 11.7 and 11.8).

11.6   CONCLUSION

We have shown, in a fairly general setting where the portfolio loss is parameterized by an arbitrary stochastic default intensity, common examples of portfolio credit derivatives can be priced by solving a set of *forward equations* for expected tranche notionals. These equations form a system of linear ordinary differential equations which can be readily solved with

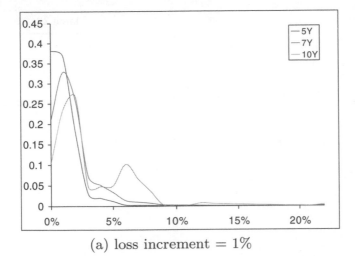

(a) loss increment = 1%

(b) loss increment = 3%

FIGURE 11.4 Expected loss distribution for different maturities under the assumption that the forward rates are constant between tranche levels—March 15, 2007.

high-order numerical methods, thus avoiding the need to use Monte Carlo simulation for the pricing of such portfolio credit derivatives and are derived in a similar way to the Dupire equation in diffusion models [11].

These forward equations also provide an insight into the inverse problem of extracting (forward) default intensities from CDO tranche quotes: they

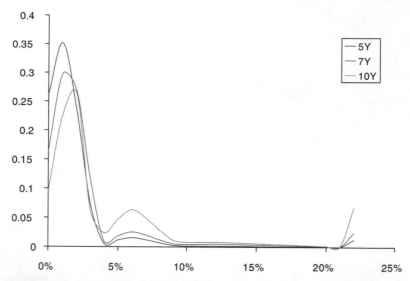

FIGURE 11.5 Expected loss distribution for a loss increment of 1 percent with forward rates obtained after the interpolation of $C_t(T, K)$ between strikes using natural cubic splines—August 13, 2007.

indicate what type of information can be extracted from observations and can serve as a guide in model parameterization ad the design of calibration methods for CDO pricing models.

We have given simple examples showing how the forward equations can be used to extract forward default intensities from CDO tranche spreads.

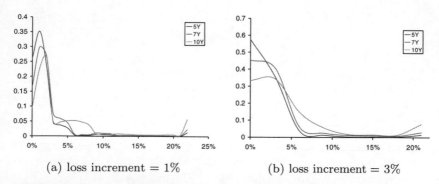

(a) loss increment = 1%   (b) loss increment = 3%

FIGURE 11.6 Expected loss distribution for different maturities under the hypothesis that the forward rates are constant between strikes—August 13, 2007.

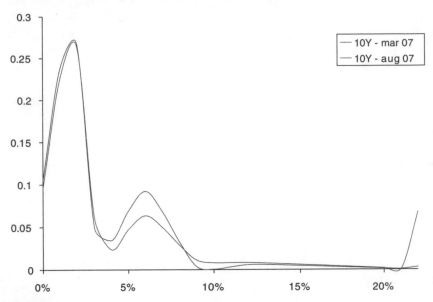

FIGURE 11.7 Comparison between the implied loss distribution for ITRAXX 10Y on March 15, 2007, and August 13, 2007.

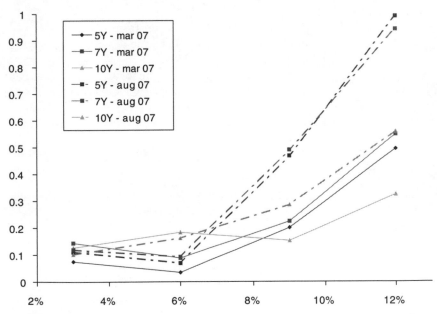

FIGURE 11.8 Comparison between the forward default intensities for ITRAXX on March 15, 2007, and August 13, 2007.

These procedures can also be used as a first step in implementing forward loss models proposed in [18], [19].

As noted above, the sparse nature of the observed data makes the calibration of forward default intensities to CDO data inherently ill-posed. The ideas exposed above can be combined with regularization methods to overcome the ill-posed nature of the calibration problem: we refer to [6] for an example of such calibration methods.

ACKNOWLEDGEMENTS

This project was conducted during I. Savescu's internship at Finance Concepts. We thank Igor Halperin, David Li, and Philipp Schönbücher for helpful comments.

REFERENCES

1. Arnsdorff, M., and I. Halperin. (2007). BSLP: Markovian bivariate spread-loss model for portfolio credit derivatives. S&P Credit Risk Summit, London.
2. Brémaud, P. (1981). *Point Processes and Queues*. New York: Springer.
3. Brigo, D., A. Pallavicini, and R. Torresetti. (2007). Calibration of CDO tranches with the dynamic generalized Poisson loss model. Working paper.
4. Bruyère, R., R. Cont, R. Copinot, et al. (2005). *Credit Derivatives and Structured Credit*. Chichester: John Wiley & Sons.
5. Carr, P., and A. Hirsa. (2003). Why be backward? Forward equations for American options. *Risk* (January): 103–107.
6. Cont, R., and A. Minca. (2008). Recovering portfolio default intensities implied by CDO tranches. Columbia University Financial Engineering Report No. 2008-01, http://ssrn.com/abstract=1104855.
7. Cousin, A., and J. P. Laurent. (2008). An overview of factor models for pricing CDO tranches. In R. Cont (ed.), *Frontiers in Quantitative Finance: Credit Risk and Volatility Modeling*. Hoboken, NJ: John Wiley & Sons.
8. Das, S., D. Duffie, and N. Kapadia. (2007). Common failings: How corporate defaults are correlated. *Journal of Finance* 62(1) (February): 93–117.
9. Derman, E., I. Kani, and J. Z. Zou. (1996). The local volatility surface: Unlocking the information in index options pricing. *Financial Analysts Journal* (July–August): 25–36.
10. Duffie, D., and N. Gârleanu. (2001). Risk and valuation of collateralized debt obligations. *Financial Analysts Journal* 57(1) (January/February): 41–59.
11. Dupire, B. (1994). Pricing with a smile. *Risk* 7: 18–20.
12. Errais, E., K. Giesecke, and L. Goldberg. (2006). Pricing credit from the top down with affine point processes. Working paper.

13. Giesecke, K., and B. Kim. (2007). Estimating tranche spreads by loss process simulation. In S. G. Hendersen, B. Biller, M.-H. Hsieh, et al. (eds.): *Proceedings of the 2007 Winter Simulation Conference*. IEEE Press.

14. Giesecke, K. (2008). Portfolio credit risk: Top-down vs bottom-up. In R. Cont (ed.), *Frontiers in Quantitative Finance: Credit Risk and Volatility Modeling*. Hoboken, NJ: John Wiley & Sons.

15. Gyöngy, I. (1986). Mimicking the one dimensional distributions of processes having an Ito differential. *Probability Theory and Related Fields* 71(4): 501–516.

16. Lipton, A., and A. Rennie (eds.). (2007). *Credit Correlation: Life after Copulas*. River Edge, NJ: World Scientific Publishing.

17. Longstaff, F., and A. Rajan. (2007). An empirical analysis of the pricing of collateralized debt obligations. *Journal of Finance*.

18. Schönbucher, P. (2005). A new methodology for pricing portfolio credit derivatives. Working paper.

19. Sidenius, J., V. Piterbarg, and L. Andersen. (2008). A new framework for dynamic credit portfolio loss modeling. *International Journal of Theoretical and Applied Finance* 11(2): 163–197.

Index